The Political Economy of
Public Service Employment

The Political Economy of Public Service Employment

Edited by

Harold L. Sheppard
W. E. Upjohn Institute
for Employment Research

Bennett Harrison
University of Maryland

William J. Spring
U. S. Senate Subcommittee on
Employment, Manpower, and Poverty

Preface by Senator Gaylord Nelson

Afterword by Congressman William Steiger

Lexington Books
D. C. Heath and Company
Lexington, Massachusetts
Toronto   London

213323

Table of Contents

Appendixes

Part V   **Public Sector Manpower Planning and the
                    Financing of Public Service Jobs**

Part VI   **Public Service Employment and the
                    Rural Sector**

List of Figures

List of Tables

Preface

The Seminars on Public Service Employment conducted by the W.E. Upjohn Institute for Employment Research during the spring of 1971 represent one of the most effective efforts to bring the knowledge of the academic community to bear on a pressing domestic problem that has come to my attention.

By spring of 1971 the issue of public service employment, long advocated as crucial to any successful effort to eliminate poverty and achieve full employment, had become a major concern of the entire Congress. The previous December the president had vetoed a public service employment program as part of a larger comprehensive manpower bill. Then in January 1971 a bipartisan group of 33 senators, including the minority leader, Senator Scott of Pennsylvania, introduced an Emergency Employment Act. With unemployment edging above 6 percent, the bill became law in July, providing $1 billion and about 120,000 jobs for the unemployed.

The seminars, which ran from April 21 to June 23, provided a rare opportunity for congressmen and their aides from both parties and both Houses of Congress to meet with academic experts and with one another for evenings of detailed and free-wheeling discussion of the policy issues raised by the consideration of public service employment. Many issues were clarified that will be discussed for years to come as the Congress and the nation continue to attempt to meet the challenge of devising policies to achieve full employment at decent wages.

Franklin Roosevelt included the right to work at decent wages in his Economic Bill of Rights during those hopeful days at the end of the Second World War. But in 1946 legislation that would have committed the government to a full employment policy was gutted in conference after passing the Senate. The results of our failure to take full employment seriously during the post-war decades while other industrialized western nations have maintained themselves at full employment are plain to see. Poverty, and its companions, crime, despair, and social disintengration are the chief domestic concerns of the richest nation in the world.

With the Kennedy administration in 1961 the nation began to use modern economic policies to stimulate the economy. Even an incumbent Republican president now describes himself as a Keynesian. However, the necessity for achieving and maintaining full employment is no more recognized now than it has been in the past. The same president who describes himself as a Keynesian based his economic policy during his first two years in office on fighting inflation by deliberately increasing the number of people who are unemployed. In 1969, as chairman of the Employment, Manpower and Poverty Subcommittee, I began a series of hearings across the nation looking into the effectiveness of the training programs that had been enacted during the course of the 1960s. The committee went to Los Angeles; Corpus Christi, Texas; Milwaukee; Cleveland, Ohio; and San Francisco. Remember that in 1969 national unemployment stood at only 3.5 percent; so we were studying the effectiveness of employment programs for the poor and the unemployed during times of relatively low unemployment. The results were essentially the same from city to city. Training programs were ineffectual because jobs at decent pay were simply not there for program graduates.

Aggregate demand efforts to eliminate unemployment and poverty had proved inadequate. For even during the height of the Vietnam war boom, unemployment and underemployment in the inner cities remained disastrously high. A study of ten ghetto labor markets released by Secretary of Labor Willard Wirtz in November 1966 — a study that grouped discouraged workers, part-time workers seeking full-time jobs, those working at below the minimum wage along with those who were unemployed by conventional measures, into a "subemployment" index — found that in New Orleans 45 percent of the inner-city work force was subemployed. In Harlem, Wirtz found 33 percent subemployed. For all the ghetto labor markets studied the average was nearly 35 percent subemployed.

The Labor Department study demonstrated that the problem of poverty is not merely one of unemployment itself — although rates of unemployment of over 30 percent for black teenagers are truly frightening — but of discouraged men and women no longer seeking work, and of people working at very low wage jobs.

In his 1945 State of the Union message, Franklin Roosevelt said: "Full employment means not only jobs — but productive jobs. Americans do not regard jobs that pay substandard wages as productive jobs."

In a memo to President Johnson based on the 1966 study, Wirtz said: "If a third of the people in the nation couldn't make a living . . . there would be a revolution. This is the situation — and the prospect unless action is taken — in the nation-within-the-nation, the slums and ghettos."

An effective national commitment to full employment will require a whole range of policies including regional and inner-city economic development policies, a national commitment to rebuilding inner-city housing, the development of new towns, and the designing of jobs in the economy with the specific purpose in mind of providing jobs at decent wages for all citizens. All these policies are essential if we are to achieve full employment. One step in that direction would be the enactment of a major public service employment program.

In the late 1960s much emphasis was put upon the responsibilities of the private sector in providing jobs for the disadvantaged and the unemployed. But the programs were only moderately successful, even when operated by the most dedicated businessmen. The fact of the matter is that the greatest employment growth sector is government. Between 1960 and 1970, state and local government payrolls grew 63 percent while the private sector grew only 20 percent. Here is proof of the public demand for expanded services.

More important, here is the most promising sector for new jobs. Government at all levels must accept its responsibilities to hire the unemployed and the disadvantaged. One of the most interesting findings reported in the Upjohn seminars was Jack Rutstein's report on the potential number of unskilled jobs as services expand in Chicago and in Connecticut. Rutstein found that 54 percent of the jobs in Chicago and 40 percent of the new jobs in Connecticut could be filled by the unskilled.

Since 1964, when I introduced the Human Resources Conservation Act to spend $1 billion in creating jobs in conservation and recreation development, I have been on record in favor of a major public service employment program. The hearings in 1969 and 1970 made it clear that our meager manpower training programs could not function effectively unless something was done about job supply for the poor and disadvantaged. However, broad support in Congress for public service employment began to grow only as unemployment for the work force as a whole rose toward 6 percent, with special problems for veterans and aerospace workers.

The questions discussed in the seminars are still very much with us — and will be during the coming years: how best to pay for expanded public services at the state and local level, how to improve civil service procedures so that the disadvantaged are not automatically excluded for lack of paper credentials. On this last point, it was most valuable to learn that most local civil service laws do not require rigid paper qualifications or tests, but simply that tests be fair and objective. The real problem lies in the administrative practices of local personnel systems. The National Civil Service League deserves a great deal of credit for the efforts it has made over the past few years to improve the performance of local civil service systems.

Perhaps the greatest difficulty surrounds the question of whether jobs created under public service employment programs are "real" or "unreal." There is a great deal of confusion on that point. To me it is essential that we recognize the place to begin is with a job that needs to be done. We must never consider providing make-work projects as a cover for the dole or for welfare payments. There is an enormous backlog of public work to be done. We must get about that business.

These sessions proved enormously helpful for congressmen and congressional staff. This present volume will, I hope, bring to a larger audience the very useful papers presented at those seminars and a summary of the discussion of these issues.

Senator Gaylord Nelson

Introduction

This book owes its unusually broad coverage of the multiple facets of public service employment in the context of national manpower policy to the novel circumstances of its origins. It comprises the record — the papers, the readings, and the background materials — developed for a unique educational experiment, a Congressional Seminar, conceived in the early months of 1971 by Senator Gaylord Nelson, Chairman of the Senate Subcommittee on Employment, Manpower and Poverty, and Representative William A. Steiger, Member of the House Committee on Labor and Education, as a way of dealing with a legislative impasse in Congress over conflicting approaches to the issue of public service employment.

Notwithstanding their own divergent views, the scope of the Congressional Seminar was broadly defined by Senator Nelson and Representative Steiger in a joint, bipartisan proposal to the W.E. Upjohn Institute for Employment Research on March 15, 1971, suggesting that "it would be of great assistance if the Upjohn Institute could conduct a series of seminars . . . exploring the issues involved in unemployment and public service jobs." In their communications to the Institute, both Senator Nelson and Representative Steiger noted that the possible role of public service employment in national manpower policy was at that juncture poorly understood, that the subject apparently had not enjoyed a high priority among manpower and labor economics researchers, and that the relatively little ongoing research had been reflected in a dearth of experts capable of testifying at congressional hearings to assist the Congress in this area of manpower policy. They expressed the need for further exploration of a range of issues that might clarify the role of public service employment in manpower policy, including "the question of the relationship between unemployment, underemployment and job supply, the demand for public services, the experience with public service employment programs in the past, current civil service practices and the potential for job creation at the state and local levels." Both legislators also agreed that a seminar format was a more preferable forum than were further congressional hearings, "for the purpose of bringing together . . . within a diverse group . . . of academic and other experts, and Congressmen and their staffs, for informed and informal discussions of these complex issues." Thus, two congressmen with long experience in manpower matters, and known for having led their respective branches of the Congress in sponsoring widely different approaches to public service employment, joined in proposing a novel educational forum for a broadly probing exploration of the subject's many facets. It was the breadth in perspective of their proposal, encompassing their interests as legislators in practical results, administration, and finance as these might be related to policy, research, and theory, which accounts for the comprehensive scope of this book.

The legislative impasse in Congress that evoked the seminar proposal developed during the latter half of 1970, as both the Senate and the House of Representatives were drafting new comprehensive manpower legislation. The issue of public service employment became a major subject of debate when the Senate, after extensive hearings between November 1969 and June 1970, in Washington and in other cities across the country, revised an administration manpower bill that had been introduced by Senator Jacob Javits in August of 1969, and added a new provision on public service employment not contained in the original administration bill. The new provision proposed an allocation of federal funds to state and local agencies of government and to certain private nonprofit groups, to provide public service employment for unemployed or underemployed members of the nation's labor force. The House of Representatives, on the other hand, adopted a public service employment provision in its comprehensive manpower bill that differed substantially from the Senate version. Also, after extensive hearings in and outside of Washington on several bills, and after a bill dealing exclusively with public service employment was reported in June of 1970 by the Select Subcommittee on Labor, the House adopted a provision for a "transitional" program of public service employment closely linked to manpower training programs.

The House and Senate manpower bills, which differed in other respects as well as in their public service employment provisions, were referred to a joint House-Senate Conference Committee on December 9, 1970. One of the few major differences the Conference Committee could not reconcile proved to be the intractable public service employment provisions. After intense but fruitless negotiations, the Senate's version was adopted. The Conference Committee's compromise manpower bill, the "Employment and Manpower Act of 1970," was adopted in both the Senate and the House on December 10, 1970; in the Senate by a vote of 68-13, and in the House by a vote of 177-159. President Nixon vetoed the Act on December 16, however, and the Senate failed to override the veto on December 21. The president's veto message directed its strongest language to the Act's public service employment provisions, in part as follows:

... The House-passed bill provided for transitional public employment that would be linked to training and other efforts to expand job opportunities in the labor market at large. Despite reservations about some of the House bill's provisions, this administration endorsed it, and I would have signed it.

The Senate adopted a bill which we found completely unacceptable because it ignored the lessons of the last decade and would create a national manpower program that would relegate large numbers of workers to permanent, subsidized employment . . .

The Conference bill provides that as much as 44 percent of the total funding in the bill go for dead-end jobs in the public sector. Moreover, there is no requirement that these public sector jobs be linked to training or the prospect of other employment opportunities. WPA-type jobs are not the answer for the men and women who have them, for Government which is less efficient as a result, or for the taxpayers who must foot the bill. Such a program represents a reversion to the remedies that were tried 35 years ago. Surely it is an inappropriate and ineffective response to the problems of the seventies.

Even as the president was vetoing the Employment and Manpower Act of 1970, it was virtually certain in view of steadily rising unemployment – the December 1970 jobless rate reached a nine year high of 6 percent – that public service employment legislation would again be introduced in the next session of Congress. Indeed, on the opening day of the new session of Congress, January 21, 1971, Representative Carl Perkins introduced a bill in the House designed "to provide authority for a public service employment and training program," and in the Senate, Senators Nelson and Javits jointly sponsored a $2 billion public service employment bill for the creation of an estimated 200,000 jobs.

These bills, in preserving the essential differences of the last session's House and Senate bills, raised the prospects of a second House-Senate impasse and of a second presidential veto. It thus became evident that if Congress was to enact viable legislation on public service employment, the persistent differences on the issue between the House and the Senate required deeper exploration, taking into account the reservations that were expressed in the president's veto message on the Act that the Congress had adopted in its previous session. It was against this background of the frustrated legislative efforts of 1970, of the new efforts begun in 1971, and of the need for further study nearer to the roots of the divergent approaches to public service employment, that the suggestion of conducting a Congressional Seminar was proposed to the Upjohn Instiitute.

The Congressional Seminar met over a two month period between April 21 and June 23, 1971, in seven, three hour sessions. The sessions were regularly attended by 25-30 congressmen and congressional aides of five Senate and House Committees: the Joint Economic Committee; the Senate Subcommittee on Employment, Manpower, and Poverty; the Senate Labor and Public Welfare Committee; the House Education and Labor Committee; and the House Select Subcommittee on Labor. A group of "resource persons" – expert practitioners in the manpower field – from some ten private nonprofit organizations and government agencies attended each session and provided a source of experience, technical expertise, and technical data upon which the congressional participants were able to draw in the course of their discussions. Finally, with the aid of a grant from the Ford Foundation, a group of specially invited panelists, in groups of three or four, launched each seminar session with a formal presentation. A complete, verbatim transcript was taken of each seminar session.

It was understood at the outset by all who attended the seminar – and indeed it was urged by the congressional participants – that some kind of document, hopefully a book, would be edited as a permanent record of the papers and discussions of the seminar. The Ford Foundation generously agreed that its grant could support a publication, the editors were selected at the outset, and the seminar was structured with this purpose in mind.[a] Thus, the seven parts of this book correspond faithfully in subject matter and in sequence to the seven sessions of the seminar as they took place. Sixteen of the panelists' papers were edited for publication and appear in the parts of the book corresponding to the seminar sessions at which they were presented. These were in each case original essays prepared for the seminar. The discussions that took place at each seminar session among the panelists, congressmen and their aides, and the resource persons, are summarized in the editors' introduction to each of the book's parts. Part 7 of the book includes the editors' summary of one of the seminar's most fruitful disucssions, dealing with the agenda of policy and research issues for the 1970s on public service employment.

Thus, owing to the unique circumstances of its origins, this volume that emerged from the Congressional Seminar constitutes a very complete analytical and critical commentary on a major contemporary issue: the role of public service employment in national manpower policy. Out of the rigors of a search for some of the answers, or at least to define the dimensions of the problems, the volume addresses itself to what at this juncture at least appear to be most of the key questions surrounding this important issue of national policy: the nation's historical experience with public service employment; the contemporary diagnoses of persistent unemployment; the deficiencies of statistical measurements of the unemployed and the underemployed; the "failure" of economic theory; unemployment and inflation; the structure of the "dual" economy and its meaning for the unemployed and for the working poor; the ability for the private sector to provide "full employment"; the needs of our impoverished public services at national, state, and local levels; the measurement of efficiency and productivity in the public sector; the barriers to public service employment for the "hard core" unemployed — "credentialism," education and civil service regulation barriers; training; the financing of public service employment — revenue sharing or direct federal financing; and — although the list of key questions is not here exhausted — public service employment as a "transitory" or as a "permanent" instrument of national manpower policy.

In its treatment of these and other key questions, this volume provides a timely source of analysis for the most recent "breakthrough" in public service employment; the Emergency Employment Act adopted by Congress and signed by the president in July 1971. The powerful pressure of continued high unemployment, hovering at 6 percent during the first half of 1971, was the major factor in the "breakthrough," although Congressman Steiger, in a

---

[a]Arrangements for the seminar, and the participation of speakers and "students" alike, would not have been possible without the enthusiastic assistance of Nancy Caine, a Manpower Intern of the Manpower Assistance Project in Washington.

communication to the Upjohn Insitute, credited the Congressional Seminar with facilitating the process in having "played an important role in examining the issues and impact of legislation such as the Emergency Employment Act and of proposals for comprehensive manpower reform." The Emergency Employment Act, at least temporarily, reconciled the earlier differences between the Senate and the House positions on public service employment. The Senate's concession was the acceptance of the measure as providing "transitional" jobs, for a two year period, and relating these jobs to training; the House concession was the acceptance of a larger financial outlay – $2.4 billion – and of accepting in principle, at least, that the new "transitional" jobs could become permanent jobs.

The operation of the Emergency Employment Act at this writing – six months after its adoption – is encouraging. A study of the first 17,000 hirees employed since the program began in mid-August of 1971 indicated that 91 percent had been unemployed and 9 percent underemployed. Nearly 40 percent of the 17,000 had been jobless fifteen weeks or longer. A total of 42 percent were veterans, 30 percent of the Vietnam era; 35 percent were disadvantaged and 31 percent members of minority groups. Only 14 percent of the 17,000 had been previously employed by the agency hiring them, indicating that governmental units were creating new jobs and not merely hiring laid-off workers. As to local impact, a city government was the employer in 42 percent of the jobs, a county government in 33 percent, a state government in 11 percent, and other kinds of local government agencies for the balance of the jobs. Average earnings for the 17,000 were $3.03 per hour. As of January 1972, $870 million of the first year's $1.4 billion appropriation had been to 650 governmental units and other agenices designated as program agents. Of a total of 135,000 jobs created, about 100,000 persons had been hired. Finally, about 94 percent of the funds made available to state and local governments were directly spent on wages and employment benefits, 2 percent for training and supportive services, and only 4 percent for local and federal administration.

If this initial study is borne out as the national experience comes into view, many reservations and anxieties about the effectiveness of public service employment will be allayed, although suspicions concerning "make work" may linger until it is demonstrated that needed public services are being performed. What lies ahead, however, is the answer to a fundamental question that the Emergency Employment Act has not resolved: Will the Act indeed be transitional, or does it constitute the first step in the evolution of a permanent instrument of public service employment in our national manpower policy? No doubt, the rate and the degree of recovery from the present levels of unemployment will be decisive factors in answering this question. For those who will be wrestling with this basic question on our nation's agenda – as well as for those to whom it is important to understand and to judge the choices in policy to be made – we present this volume as offering some useful guidance along the way.

Ben S. Stephansky
The W.E. Upjohn Institute

**Part I
Employment, Unemployment, and Public
Service Jobs**

Introduction to Part I

What are the major justifications for an expansion of public service employment in our country? When should such an expansion be put into effect? And for *whom* should such employment be planned? These issues, plus many others, occupied the attention and debate of the first 1971 Upjohn Institute Seminar on Public Service Employment.

The topic is furthermore surrounded by a number of misleading assumptions, images, and clichés, which in part provide the reason for seven evenings of discussion. Harold Sheppard listed some of these assumptions, including the following:

1. There is a clear-cut distinction between "private" and "public" sectors in our economy. The meaning of public services is simple and self-evident.
2. "Real" jobs are to be found primarily, or only, in the "private" sector.
3. A public service employment program is essentially based on the theory of "government as employer of last resort."
4. The prime target population to be employed under such a program consists of the poor, the disadvantaged, men and women on welfare — those outside the "mainstream" of the labor force.

The questions or issues cited, however, are not easy to answer. The seminar discussions themselves served only to highlight them, and to illustrate their importance. And the assumptions listed are not accepted by every man or woman who has taken an intensive look at them.

In the opinion of Sheppard, the major justification for a program of service employment must be based on the *services* provided, or more properly, the services that any society or economy requires to function effectively. In his view, government does not exist primarily in order to provide jobs. Its own *raison d'être* lies in the services it provides to the citizens living and working within any given administrative jurisdiction. The obvious examples include education, health protection, national defense, highway construction, water services, police and fire protection, etc. The argument can be made that even where some of these functions actually are carried out under private auspices, they nevertheless constitute public services.[1]

Both the private nonprofit and public service sectors of the working population have grown in the recent past at a rate much higher than the rest of

3

that population. To put it another way, job growth within the private nonagriculture industry sector has not been very promising over the past several years. Taking the period of 1960-70, for example, employment outside of all government agencies (including federal, state and local) grew by only 20 percent. But within the single category of state and local government employment — the classification with which most discussions about public services are concerned — jobs grew by 63 percent!

Equally important, employment in the *private* sector attributable to purchases by state and local governments grew — from 1962 to 1970 (the longest period for which data have become available) — by 50 percent. Job growth in the private sector *not* attributable to such state and local government activities during the same period was extremely low, below 20 percent. For all jobs in the total economy, the increase during 1962-70 was only 22 percent (see table I.1).

Table I.1

Employment in Private Industry Resulting from State and Local Government Purchase of Goods and Services, Compared with Non-Agriculture Employment in Total United States (1962 and 1970)

	1962	1970	Percentage Change
Private Industry Employment Attributable to Gov't purchases (Millions of Employees)	2.4	3.6	50
Non-agriculture Employment in Total United States	61.8	75.2	22

Source: *Manpower Report of the President,* 1971, Tables A-11 and G-11

Such facts do not necessarily make an iron-clad case for expanded public service employment, although many advocates of this expansion tend to think so. Furthermore, the past growth of state and local government employment does not mean that *enough* jobs are currently being created — either in terms of meeting the need to solve unemployment or in terms of supplying adequate public services. For one thing, many local jurisdictions are actually cutting *back* on their payrolls, because of financial crises. Even without such crises, local governments might be unable to *expand,* or create *new* public services.[a]

But one major implication of the above statistics is that the growth of state and local public services can lead to the growth of jobs in the private sector. Harold Sheppard felt that too few economists and politicians recognize this

---

[a]See Harold L. Sheppard, "The Nature of the Job Problem and The Role of New Public Service Employment," chapter 1 in this volume.

growth function of the public sector. Health and sanitation activities require the construction (through private firms) of facilities and the purchase of equipment (from private firms). Similarly, education means the construction of schools and the purchase of classroom equipment, textbooks, etc. — all from the private sector. Purchases of goods and services by state and local governments grew from $58.2 billion to $120.8 billion from 1962 to 1970. And by 1970, education alone accounted for nearly 43 percent of this total.

Obviously, the financing of public services is based in large part on the ability and the willingness of the general society and economy to pay (i.e., through taxes) for those services. But Sheppard's additional point is that there is a corollary to this: the ability of the private sector side of the general economy to maintain itself and to thrive depends to a considerable extent on the quantity and quality of a wide range of public services and facilities.

Furthermore, a country's standard of living is not measured merely by the dollar and cent value of the activities of those private enterprises providing manufactured private goods and private services. In other words, we are not dealing with a question of either-or. Perhaps the critical issue is the *balance* in the interrelationship of activities in the public and private sectors, the mix of "private" and "public" goods and services. But that issue cannot be faced, Sheppard argued, until we accept the proposition that public services are among the *contributors* to total economic progress, and not among the *detractors*.

As the Council of Economic Advisors stated in its 1971 Report, there is a need to raise total production and employment to the level of the "Nation's capacity to produce," but at the same time there are certain measures that will promote such growth, "and bring about its utilization for the most important purposes. Our success in achieving these goals will significantly affect the quality of American life for years to come."

The Council goes on to raise the question that has come to the fore in recent years, concerning the issue of the *value* placed on certain goods and services: " . . . economic growth means increasing capacity to *produce what is wanted* — as indicated by the term 'goods and services', meaning goods for or service to someone." (Italics added)

The product is not measured in tons or miles or calories. It is measured by the value that someone puts on it. The key question is whose value counts.

The aggregate measure of Gross National Product by itself can thus be misleading. If clean water is a primary valued product, it can be argued that "there has been no economic growth since the time of Hiawatha." Thus the argument for a particular quantitative measure of production such as the GNP, "and the case for economic growth is not necessarily a case for increasing the gross national product." This measure, the GNP, has many limitations, chief among them its inability to differentiate between deteriorations and improvements in the environment resulting from the processes of production and the provision of services. The development costs of a new park or health facility go into the GNP, but these may add economic value to other properties.

The "market system" is presumably ideally suited to the provision of goods and services for private use. But Sheppard's question is, can the same thing be said when it comes to a number of social needs and wants which cannot be obtained merely through individual decisions operating within that market system? An individual by himself cannot opt to reject the polluted atmosphere in which he and millions of other individuals live and work, in favor of a cleaner atmosphere. Here the market system concept is irrelevant. Reliance on the market mechanism may actually be counter-productive (in the apt phrase of Francis Bator, the economy suffers "market failure"). The individual can choose non-leaded gasoline (if available in his community) for use in his automobile as over against leaded fuel. But can he effectively act within a market system to create a significant decrease in polluted waters and air? Short of hiring his own individual private police for security and the apprehension of persons committing crime against his person and property (which may be possible for persons of great wealth), the individual by his own market system decisions cannot provide for this type of public service need.

Sheppard would agree that these types of examples supporting the argument for a greater emphasis on public service needs through legislative and executive action do not, of course, detract from any argument concerning the need for productivity gains in the production of private goods and services. But, such gains do not have to be achieved at the cost of sacrificing an expansion of public services.

As the Council of Economic Advisers puts it, "the way the national output is used is decided by millions of decisions of private households." But the nation as a whole has increasingly been raising the issue of national priorities – the issue of *how* this output shall be used. Decisions by the federal government itself influence that issue: "the degree and pattern of Federal influences that are desirable is itself an open question." And the wisdom of private individual decisions concerning how resources are used is increasingly being challenged.

At the same time, we are witnessing increased recognition of the need to devote more of those resources to the improvement of public service functions. As discussed by Sheppard in his Chapter, the Joint Economic Committee of Congress, in its 1966 study of *State and Local Public Facility Needs and Financing,* cited six major types of public services which it felt were not being adequately provided under current levels of commitment:

1. *Basic community needs.* For example, provision of water, electricity, gas and sanitary services, as well as anti-pollution and environmental protection measures.
2. *Transportation services.* These include urban transit systems, parking fa-

cilities, airports, train and bus stations, and port facilities – not merely the construction and maintenance of highways, roads, streets, and bridges.

3. *Educational services.* Public as well as private schools at all levels, including vocational institutions; and the ancillary services relating to these, such as food services, publications, educational TV, etc.

4. *Health services.* For example, hospitals, clinics, nursing homes, medical research projects, services and facilities for the mentally retarded; family planning services. etc.

5. *Recreational and cultural activities.* These include outdoor and indoor play centers, parks and marinas, neighborhood athletic centers; theaters, museums, libraries, etc.

6. *Other services.* Child care centers, jails and prisons; fire and police protection, etc.

The critical points about these and many other types and examples of public services are: (1) they cannot be provided or expanded effectively through reliance on individual decisions or preferences; (2) state and local governments, at least under current financing approaches (and current revenue levels determined by those approaches), cannot support any substantial increase in them; and (3) once the commitment is made to expand and/or to improve these services, and a way out is found for the financing dilemma – created through overreliance on property and sales taxes, for the most part, and/or inadequate state income tax rates – a major consequence would be an increase in *jobs*.

Public service expansion, therefore, should be looked upon also as a major *job-creation* source. But its key justification is in the provision of much-needed services. Sheppard referred to a number of other implications which can raise some controversy, two of which are: (a) this does not mean that public service jobs are *temporary* ones, lasting only as long as the private sector of economy is sluggish; and (b) it does not mean that such jobs are only, or primarily, for the poor, the disadvantaged, or minority groups.

On the first point, it may be good strategy to introduce legislation for public service employment during periods of high unemployment, but if we look upon such employment as available only when private sector jobs are scarce, how will we assure any continuity of services? Sheppard asked the seminar participants, do we pull back on a program to combat pollution, or to reduce crime, when manufacturers begin to demand, once again, more workers for the factories? Must "progress" in the public services sphere depend upon recession in the private sector?

On the second point, increased employment through the public service route is not, or should not be, an either-or proposition. It should not imply the creation of jobs for one class of occupations vs. another; or one age group vs. another; or one race against another; or one income group against other income groups. Sheppard reminds us that every enterprise has a *heterogeneous* mix of occupational levels, a division of labor. It is difficult to envision a comprehensive public service program that is required to use only the services of people with little income, little educational or vocational training. A full-blown continuing campaign against air pollution would require personnel at professional and technical levels, as well as nonprofessional and previously untrained men and women.[2]

But as long as public service is treated only as a countercyclical measure to combat high unemployment, or as a source of employment by government only as a "last resort," of the otherwise marginally employed, including the "welfare" population, these types of controversies will continue. Indeed, during the autumn and winter of 1971, it seemed as though the poor and the not-so-poor unemployed (including returning veterans and scientists and engineers from the aerospace industry) were being pitted against each other in the scramble for the small number of jobs made possible through the Emergency Employment Act of 1971.

Be that as it may, there is no question that public service employment can be a valuable program in any real war against poverty, especially in any effort to assimilate the working poor, the marginally employed, into the "mainstream" of our general economy. This is the major thrust of Bennett Harrison's presentation to the first seminar session (see chapter 2). Professor Harrison (an economist at the University of Maryland) painted a portrait of the labor market which calls attention to the transitory character of the employment status of a major segment of our population — a segment which moves into and out of training programs, onto and off of welfare assistance rolls, in large part as a result of the nature of the jobs they can obtain — especially in our inner cities. In addition, we have the phenomenon of millions of families whose heads *do* work — and on a year-round, full-time basis — and still do not earn enough to move them or keep them over the poverty line. Again, this is partly due to the nature of the jobs they perform. It is also related to region of the country.[b]

But Harrison's major factual finding, as detailed and documented at length in the concluding section of his chapter, is that there are relatively few "poverty jobs" in public service employment, compared with the private sector. For persons living in our central cities and working in government jobs (even when "teaching" is eliminated from the analysis), the lower risk of being in poverty is a result not only of the higher wage rates or salaries offered in such employment, but also a result of the greater *stability* in such jobs. Harrison's analysis demonstrates the value of public service employment for individuals who otherwise would be in low-paying and/or unstable occupations and indus-

---

[b]For example, in the mid-60s, slightly more than one-half of *poor* family heads working year-round, full-time were living in the South, while for all family heads with such jobs, only 29 percent were in the same region.

tries – especially for individuals from the "new" urban groups seeking a firmer stake in the mainstream of our labor force. In passing, it should be noted that only about 58 percent of *all* employed persons (in nonagriculture) work on a year-round, full-time basis. But for all persons employed in "public administration," the proportion working on a year-round, full-time basis is about 77 percent. Indeed, while the number of persons employed *outside* of public administration positions in nonagriculture increased by only 27 percent from 1959-69, the rate of increase within public administration employment for the same period was 44 percent. Thus, not only have the total number of jobs in the private sector increased at a much lower rate than in the public sector: the same lack of growth characterizes the private sector when it comes to the *quality* of the jobs (as measured by degree of year-round, full-time employment).

Harrison's case for increased public service employment as an antipoverty measure is based on at least five arguments:

1. Public service is a "growth industry" – even during all four post-war recessions;
2. Employment in that sector pays better wages, even when we concentrate only on persons employed year-round, full time – for blacks as well as for whites;
3. *Non*-wage benefits also tend to be better in public service employment jobs;
4. Such jobs provide greater stability; a prime condition for moving and keeping people employed within the "mainstream."
5. Sites of public service employment are more likely to be within the central cities of our metropolitan areas, where the employable poor persons are concentrated.

Many of us seem to forget, but Harrison reminds us, that public service employment historically has been the "port of entry" for an underclass into the general American society. Moreover, the establishment through such a route of secure employment with adequate income (and frequently with improved social status) for one generation affects the life and career chances of the offspring of that generation. Furthermore, the stability of a legitimate job (as an alternative to "hustling" and intermittent employment in the secondary labor market) is among the indispensable prerequisites for the development of work attachment attitudes and behavior patterns conducive to successful entry into the mainstream labor force. And public service employment clearly belongs in the core of the economy. To treat it as otherwise can only lead to failure in the attempt to administer an effective public service program. If one of the functions of a good manpower and economic development policy is to move more people from the secondary labor market to the core economy, then public service employment must be a vital element in such a policy.

The importance of this type of discussion lies partly in how persuasive it is in convincing the poor (and their appointed and self-appointed representatives) about the potential value of employment in the public sector. Unfortunately, much of the popular rhetoric – and even much of the discussions among administrators, legislators, and their staffs – could discourage the poor who seek better income through employment. This rhetoric often conveys to the poor the impression that public service employment programs were enacted only because "real" jobs were not available in the private sector; that the "unreal" jobs offered to them are part of the ritual required to transfer income to them – the "real" purpose of such public service jobs (which are not socially useful in the first place); and that even these undesirable jobs are temporary.

This is an image of public service jobs that exists among the poor, as a result of the kinds of discussions and logic engaged in by many public leaders. There are many "experts" on employment problems who similarly have contributed to this impression. The very term, "government as employer of last resort," itself connotes such negative feelings. But the data provided by Harrison should help to dispel unfavorable attitudes toward the employment potentials of an effective public service program expansion. Such jobs need not be temporary. They need not be of a "make-work" nature, since there are many socially useful jobs to be performed. Their wage and salary levels can be respectable and adequate. And they need not be low-level, "dead-end," and demeaning jobs. In many areas, they are among the best jobs to be had.

There is another nuance to the impact of an expanded public service employment program that must be taken into consideration. From a labor point of view, an increase in the availability of jobs resulting from increased public services is beneficial in that it reduces the excess supply of labor – the "labor reserve." This not only obviously decreases unemployment, but increases the probability of better wages and working conditions throughout the general economy, since employers will more likely have to compete with each other to attract or to maintain employees.[c] This notion is implied in Harrison's reference to "expanding the core at the expense of the periphery."

The discussion that followed Harrison's presentation at the first seminar provoked almost the entire gamut of issues scheduled for fuller examination during the subsequent evenings. Such issues included the problems of the measurement and definition of unemployment, for example. On the substantive, policy side, they involved the need to cope with the problems of rural areas and with the problems of minority groups other than blacks; the lack of more precise information on "real" unemployment in the rural and urban areas (often obscured by the phenomenon of discouragement in the job-seeking process); the challenge of who pays (and how) for an expansion of much-needed public

---

[c]Many types of employers, of course, will continue to offer relatively low wages in order deliberately to encourage high turnover which in certain industries proves to be more "efficient" from the enterprise standpoint.

services – and how priorities could be set on even these services. The issues ranged also from the cause of low wages (is it the skill or educational level of the workers? the technology of particular industries? the nature of their markets?); why tenure should necessarily be less secure in the private sector; the total cost to the economy and society if we do not find solutions to the problems of income and employment for the "secondary" or peripheral" labor market. Isn't aggregate purchasing power increased (with the multiplier effect in the private sector) by the employment of otherwise unemployed or underemployed persons in the public sector?

Another sobering issue was introduced into the free-for-all discussion: if all the employable poor (a term which itself defies definition) were to be employed through an expanded public service employment program financed in the most ideal way, would we thereby eliminate all the problems of poverty? And apart from the remaining problems among the poor, what would be the impact of such a policy or program on the numbers and quality of the many jobs in occupations and industries which currently pay subsistence wages?

Suppose it is true that secretaries, for example, earn more in public agencies than in private industry, as revealed in the statistics described by Harrison. Does this automatically mean that there is a *need* for more secretaries at the state and local levels of government? In other words, shouldn't a program of expanded public services be geared, above all, to the need for those services, and not merely to the need for solving the problem of unemployment? This issue seemed to be lost in much of the seminar discussions, throughout the seven evenings of formal presentations and informal conversations.

As a counterbalance to Sheppard's emphasis on the need for improved public services as the basis for an expanded program of employment, Howard Wachtel and Charles Betsey – along with Harrison – stress the value of such a program to the solution of the problem of the "working poor." Their brief and succinct paper on "The Determinants of 'Working Poverty'" (see chapter 3 in this volume) forces us to look beyond the personal characteristics of this part of the labor force to the *industries* in which they are employed. For them, merely providing jobs in the Keynesian sense of "full employment" is not enough; we need also to be concerned with the "decency-level" of jobs, i.e., the adequacy of wages. Their argument provide one more basis for the expansion of the public service sector, on the assumption that employment in that sector will lift significant segments of our working population out of poverty.

Inevitably the first evening also raised the fundamental question of national priorities. If we argue, for example, that the Boeing Corporation and its workers could be employed to meet the challenges of mass *ground* transportation (instead of "elite" SST travel), are there not – even if we won the argument – the problems of transferability and convertibility of human and material resources to meet those challenges? Are those problems completely unsolvable?

Finally, the first seminar's discussion brought forward the obstacles that might be encountered in making any public service employment program a success. For example, the barriers of "credentialism" imposed by custom and administrative regulations, for men and women otherwise capable of performing a variety of job tasks, or capable of being trained on the job for such tasks. This wall exists in private as well as in public organizations. Another obstacle might be residence requirements; for example, inner-city job seekers might not be allowed to take jobs in suburban governments which nevertheless might be experiencing a shortage of applicants from their own resident populations.

Regardless of the administrative machinery created to realize an expanded public service employment program, such a program ultimately depends on the nature of *local* public service needs which in turn requires some know-how and expertise in public service manpower planning. Whether this program is administered directly by federal, state, or local agencies (public or private nonprofit), the services to be rendered must have a relevance to local public service needs. The mechanism or method for ascertaining these needs is frequently lacking — all of which points also to the poverty of competence at all levels of government.

Notes

1. Eli Ginzberg and his associates at Columbia University have written extensively on the emergence of organizations in the private, not-for-profit service sector in the United States over the past few decades — organizations that also provide public services. See Eli Ginzberg, Dale Hiestand, and Beatrice Reubens, *The Pluralistic Economy* (New York: McGraw-Hill, 1965). The entire seven weeks seminar series, however, did not deal with this sector at all, and the facts and controversies surrounding the job implications of meeting public service needs concentrated exclusively on different levels of government in the United States.

2. In one study, it was found that estimates of the percentage of new public service jobs requiring professional personnel to perform them varied, depending on the type of function or program involved, from 24 to 72 percent. See Harold L. Sheppard, "Job Redesign, New Careers and Public Service Employment — Their Potentials and Limits," *Good Government,* Fall 1970, p. 3.

1

The Nature of the Job Problem
and the Role of New Public
Service Employment

HAROLD L. SHEPPARD

Introduction

This brief report is intended to provide a springboard for discussion about the nature and size of the job problem in America, especially the question of who among the poor do and do not work and why; the characteristics of the working poor (including their occupations, industries in which they work, and their location); the variety of estimates as to how many more jobs could be filled or created; and the role of private and public employment in meeting the employment needs of the poor and the underemployed.

Estimates of the number of people in need of jobs or better jobs range from 4.6 million family heads and unrelated individuals to 7.3 million, as discussed in this paper. These should be compared with 2.4 million (as of March 1968) who were working part time but wanting full-time jobs, or unemployed for fifteen or more weeks. As for the *sources* of new jobs for such persons, there is no one simple estimate as to what the potential might be in the private sector of the economy. In the public sector, one estimate has been as high as 5.3 million for a given number of public service functions. If we take the maximum estimate of 7.3 million family heads and unrelated individuals in need of jobs or better jobs, and assume that the 5.3 million public service jobs could be filled by them, we would then have a gap of about 2 million persons in need of jobs. To date, efforts to create that many new jobs in the private sector have not succeeded, partly because of a lack of an intrinsic demand for private industry employees at the job levels they now might qualify for.

The Poor Who Do Not Work

Before discussing in detail the estimates of unemployment and underemployment, we should first lay to rest the issue of the poor who do not work.

Reprinted with permission of the W.E. Upjohn Institute; originally published as an Upjohn Institute Staff Paper, January, 1969.

Heads of Families

In 1966, there were 2.3 million nonworking heads of poor families, of all ages. But nearly one-half of these family heads were 65 years old or more. Of the remaining 1.2 million poor nonworkers *under* 65, more than three-fifths (63 percent) were female heads of families. The vast majority of them did not work because of family responsibilities and health problems.

We are left then with about 450,000 male heads of poor families under the age of 65, and of these:

64% were ill or disabled
10% were unable to find work
 8% were in school
18% gave a variety of other reasons
100%

According to these figures, then, there were in 1966 about 45,000 male heads of poor families under the age of 65 who did not work because of inability to find a job. This number is not much to get excited about in any discussion of the poor who don't work. Approximately one-fourth of this group were between the ages of 55 and 65.

Unrelated Individuals

In the same year there were nearly 3.2 million nonworking poor persons who were unrelated individuals, but more than 70 percent of these persons were 65 years old and more! And among the remaining 900,000 or so, 70 percent were women, again with illness and home duties as the major reasons for not working. There were thus only about 275,000 poor unrelated males under the age of 65 who did not work that year, of whom

44% were ill or disabled
15% were unable to find work
20% were in school
21% gave a variety of other reasons
100%

According to these percentages, then, about 41,000 male unrelated individuals under the age of 65 did not work at all because of inability to find employment.

The Working Poor

The working poor can be divided into two groups: (1) those who worked but not on a year-round, full-time basis; (2) those who did work on such a basis (at least forty weeks a year, full time).

The first group contained, in 1966, about 1.7 million heads of poor families and about 1.2 million poor unrelated individuals. Among the family heads, 15 percent were 65 or older, and 39 percent were females under the age of 65. In other words, 45 percent were under-65 male heads of families.

A. In actual numbers this means that in 1966 there were more than 750,000 under-65 male heads of poor families not working on a full-time basis at least forty weeks in the previous year. The number would be even higher if we had information on how many working male heads of poor families did not work full time at least *fifty* weeks a year, a more meaningful definition of decent employment. Nevertheless, this figure of 750,000 under-65 working male heads of poor families provides us with the first step toward a *minimum* estimate of the underemployment problem in the United States.

B. We must add another group of persons not working full time at least 40 weeks a year and who are poor — the 1.2 million unrelated individuals. Only 28 percent of these persons were males under the age of 65, or about 337,000. Another 563,000 were females under that age.

If these two figures are added to the 750,000 under-65 male heads of poor families who worked on less than a full-time basis 40 weeks or more, we arrive at a minimum figure of approximately 1.65 million persons (under-65 male family heads *and* under-65 unrelated individuals) who might be deemed as underemployed.

C. But we cannot stop there. In 1966 there were also about 2.4 million family heads and about 540,000 unrelated individuals who worked 40 or more weeks in the previous year on a full-time basis, and were nevertheless poor. Approximately three-fourths of these persons were white, incidentally.

The total *minimum* or conservative estimate, therefore, of underemployment among poor persons in the nation's labor force is roughly 4.6 million persons:

1.65 million under-65 male family heads and under-65 unrelated individuals working *less* than year round on a full-time basis
2.40 million family heads working year round, full time
 .54 million unrelated individuals working year round, full time
_____
4.59 million, minimum estimate of underemployed

This estimate omits (1) most of the aged who might be working and yet are poor; (2) a sizable number of female heads of families with the same work-and-poverty characteristics; (3) working wives and children of the male heads of families included in the 4.6 million; and (4) the 86,000 under-65 males (family heads and unrelated individuals) unable to find any employment.

Nearly 1.5 million poor families had *more* than one earner in the labor force during 1966. In other words, 45 percent of all the poor families with labor force participants depended on two or more family members for income (see table 1.1).

Table 1.1

Number of Poor Families in Labor Force and Percentage Having Two or More Wage Earners by Color and Sex of Family Head, 1966

Item	All	Family heads			
		White		Nonwhite	
		Male	Female	Male	Female
Number of families, in thousands	3,268	1,827	391	729	318
Percent with 2 or more earners	45	39	38	63	55

Source: Derived by H. L. Sheppard from Social Security table based on Mollie Orshansky's analysis of Bureau of the Census tabulations from the *Current Population Survey* for March 1967, Social Security Administration, *Research and Statistics Note,* December 6, 1967. Numbers in first row do not add to 3,268 because of rounding.

D. Another way of estimating the size of the problem is to start with data on number of earners in poor families, compiled by the Census for the Office of Economic Opportunity (OEO). If we tally all the members of poor families who earned and thus worked in 1966, the number adds to at least 6 million.

This number does not include unrelated individuals who were in the labor force as of the same survey, which counted more than 1.3 million.

Therefore, using this approach to estimate the magnitude of the job problem, we arrive at a figure of more than 7.3 million men and women who are labor force participants and yet are poor. At least 6 million are members of families and 1.3 million are unrelated individuals. Most of them are employed, but still do not earn enough to raise their families or themselves out of poverty.

Occupations and Poverty

In March 1967, there were nearly 3.3 million heads of poor families who were in the labor force, of all ages and in all sections of the country. This figure does not include persons who were not members of families or other family members also in the labor force. Nearly 8 percent of these 3.3 million were unemployed at the time of the March 1967 survey, with the greatest percentage of them male heads of white families.

Table 1.2 reveals how these poor family heads were distributed in terms of occupation, color, and sex.

Table 1.2

Distribution of Poor Family Heads in the Labor Force by Occupation, Color, and Sex, March 1967 (in percent)

Occupation	All	Family heads			
		White		Nonwhite	
		Male	Female	Male	Female
All labor force members	100.0	55.9	12.0	22.2	9.8
Employed	92.4	52.3	11.0	20.4	8.7
Professional, technical, and kindred workers	3.9	2.9	0.5	0.4	0.1
Farmers and farm managers	9.6	7.9	0.1	1.6	—
Managers, officials, and proprietors, excluding farm	7.1	6.2	0.5	0.4	—
Clerical and sales workers	6.9	3.1	2.6	0.7	0.4
Craftsmen, foremen, and kindred workers	10.8	8.3	—	2.4	—
Operatives and kindred workers	19.8	11.1	1.9	5.5	1.2
Service workers	17.9	4.3	4.9	2.2	6.5
Private household workers	4.7	—	1.1	—	3.5
Laborers	16.3	8.6	0.3	7.2	0.2
Unemployed	7.6	3.6	1.0	1.9	1.1

Source: Derived by H. L. Sheppard from Social Security table based on Mollie Orshansky's analysis of Bureau of the Census tabulations from the *Current Population Survey* for March 1967, Social Security Administration, *Research and Statistics Note,* December 6, 1967.

Note: Based on 3,268,000 heads of poor families who were members of the labor force in March 1967. Rows and columns may not add to 100.0 percent because of rounding.

Eleven percent of all the poor family heads at that time were white males employed as operatives; 7 percent were nonwhite males working as laborers. Approximately 3.5 percent were nonwhite female heads employed as private household workers (about 36 percent of *all* poor nonwhite female heads in the labor force were in this occupation).

Taking the total group "dissected" in that table, the three largest occupational categories of the employed poor family heads were operatives (nearly 20 percent); service workers (nearly 18 percent); and laborers (slightly more than 16 percent) — totaling 54 percent of all the poor family heads in the labor force.

When we add the unemployed to this list, the percentage adds up to 62 percent — that is, more than three-fifths (about 2 million) of all the labor force members who are heads of poor families are either operatives, service workers, laborers, or unemployed.

But these low-level occupations (and unemployment situations) are not distributed evenly among the labor force poor. While more than three-fifths of the total group are in these categories, less than one-half of the male white family heads (they are still the biggest single group as far as size goes — about 900,000) are in these low-level jobs or are unemployed. Nearly 70 percent of *female* heads of white families (265,000), 75 percent of male nonwhites (549,000), and more than 80 percent of female nonwhites (258,000) are either operatives, service workers, laborers, or unemployed.

Industries of the Working Poor

Poverty is not strictly a matter of occupation, region, or family status; it is also related to the *type of industry* in which a breadwinner is employed. Unfortunately, the official government data pertaining to the characteristics of those below the accepted pvoerty line (based on income, location, and family size) do not report the industry distribution of the poor. However, in a recent article by Barry Bluestone[1] some of the industries having at least 40 percent of their employees earning below a relatively low wage for all nonsupervisory employees — stipulated at $2.25 per hour or less by Bluestone — are listed (see table 1.3).

It should be kept in mind, when assessing these several million workers employed at less than $2.25 per hour, that:

1. The list is not exhaustive; it refers only to selected industries, and within them, just the ones in which at least 40 percent of the employees earned less than the cited hourly wage.
2. There is no indication in the data as to number of weeks worked full time per year; in other words, it would be misleading to assume that we are talking in every instance about an annual wage income of $4,500 ($2.25 x 2,000 hours).

Table 1.3
Industries in Which 40 Percent or More of Workers Earned Less Than $2.25 per Hour, 1962-1966

Item	Year	Percent of workers below $2.25 per hour	Estimated number of workers below $2.25 per hour
Industry			
Southern sawmills and planing mills	1962	88.2	97,600
Nursing homes and related facilities	1965	86.3	148,986
Work Clothing	1964	72.8	41,983
Children's hosiery mills	1964	67.3	11,686
Men's and boy's shirts	1964	70.4	68,242
Laundries and cleaning services	1966	72.5	288,343
Men's hosiery mills	1964	65.2	13,837
Synthetic textiles	1963	55.5	46,739
Cigar manufacturing	1964	50.7	10,989
Wood household furniture	1965	48.1	57,720
Footwear	1965	50.6	87,945
Women's hosiery mills	1964	45.0	19,946
Hospitals (excluding federal)	1966	41.2	733,896
Retail trade			
Limited price variety stores	1965	87.9	243,571
Eating and drinking places	1963	79.4	1,021,646
Hotels and motels	1963	76.1	316,796
Drug and proprietary stores	1965	71.3	265,093
Gasoline service stations	1965	66.7	317,559
Apparel and accessory stores	1965	59.7	347,514
Department stores	1965	59.6	607,503
Miscellaneous retail stores	1965	58.0	561,556
Retail food stores	1965	47.6	650,597

Source: Industry Wage Surveys, Bureau of Labor Statistics, Department of Labor, 1962-66.

3. On the other hand, the data in the table do not tell us whether or not other members of the workers' families are also employed, and thus the extent to which total family income (relative to region and size of family) is above or below the poverty line.

Nevertheless, it is clear that certain industries have substantial numbers of men and women whose earned incomes keep them below the level of a decent income, and who may therefore be considered as underemployed. In hospitals, nursing homes, laundries, and restaurants alone we can be sure that most of their 2 million or so workers earning less than $2.25 are in this category.

Location of Poor Workers

In 1964, among all production workers in manufacturing industries (numbering 12.6 million), 47 percent earned less than $2.20 per hour. But in the South 71 percent were below this figure; 49 percent in the Northeast; 36 percent in the North Central region; and only 26 percent in the West.

Thirty-five percent of all production workers earning less than $2.20 lived in the South. However, if we concentrate only on workers earning less than $1.60 per hour in 1964, we find that the South had 47 percent of them (Keep in mind also that 63 percent of the nation's poor rural families are in the South.)

Of these lower wage production workers earning under $1.60 per hour in 1964, the Northeast region contained 30 percent; the North Central region, 19 percent; and the West, only 4 percent.[2]

Among poor families with a head working even year round on a full-time basis, more than one-half of all of them are in the South (although that region has less than 30 percent of all families whose heads have year-round full-time jobs). Among unrelated individuals working year round full time, the South has 31 percent of the poverty-income jobs, but less than one-fourth of all of the country's year-round full-time jobs occupied by unrelated individuals. The Northeast region also is overrepresented among poor unrelated individuals (table 1.4 gives regional comparisons).

Table 1.4
Regional Distribution of Family Heads and Unrelated Individuals With Year-Round Full-Time Jobs, 1964 (in percent)

Region	Family heads		Unrelated Individuals	
	All	Poor	All	Poor
Total	99	100	99	100
Northeast	26	13	31	37
North Central	29	25	27	24
South	29	53	23	31
West	15	9	18	8
Number, in thousands	30,705	2,104	4,215	573

Source: Derived from Tables 2 and 5 in "More About the Poor in 1964," by Mollie Orshansky, Social Security Bulletin, May 1966.

As might be expected, the small towns and rural areas of America have a disproportionate number of workers who are heads of poor families (see table 1.5). This is indicated by the fact, for example, that more than one-half of the *poor* families with working heads are in areas with less than 50,000 population (areas outside SMSAs), while for *all* families with working heads, only one-third are in such areas.

Table 1.5

Location of Families With Working Heads and With Two or More Wage Earners by Size of Area, 1966 (in percent)

Size of Area	Families with working heads		Families with 2 or more earners	
	All	Poor	All	Poor
Total	100	100	100	100
SMSAs 250,000+	56	39	55	32
SMSAs under 250,000	10	9	10	8
Areas outside SMSAs	34	52	35	60
Number of families, in thousands	44,416	4,654	23,710	1,575

Source: Bureau of the Census, unpublished data from 1966 survey, prepared by H. L. Sheppard.

Furthermore, three-fifths of all poor families with two or more workers in them are in these smaller and rural areas of the country.

Central Cities

According to some recent OEO preliminary estimates, the central cities of our country contain nearly 1.3 million jobseeking or underemployed poor persons of all ages (half of whom are white) who are in *one* of the following categories:

> aged 16-21;
> member of an ethnic minority;
> physically handicapped; or
> a school dropout before completing high school.

The distribution of these persons by age group is as follows:

Age group	Percentage
16-21	33
22-54	43
55-64	14
65+	10
	100

Contrary to some expectations, 56 percent of this group of central city unemployed and underemployed poor are females, amounting to more than 700,000.

How Many Jobs for the Poor?

There is no "one best way" for estimating how many job vacancies could be filled now by the jobseeking and underemployed poor or how many *more* new jobs could be created for such persons. The experts have a variety of methods for coming up with "intelligent guesstimates," and this is what we will do in this report, too. But it is nevertheless safe to say that most, if not all, of these experts would agree that: (1) there are vacancies going unfilled in the private and public sectors; (2) many of these vacancies could be filled by the jobseeking and underemployed poor — with and without further training.

They would also argue that some things *are* quite certain and predictable; for example, the *size* of the labor force in the future. It does not take any great computer or complicated mathematical formula to state that if the population today is of a certain size in each age group of males and females, and if the percentage of each age-sex group that is in the labor force remains constant (or continues to change under current trends), the picture, say, for 1975 is as table 1.6 shows.

These figures show rather forcefully that (1) the greatest increases in the labor force will occur among the young adult segments of the population, from 20 to 34 — persons who in 1965 were only 10-24 years old; and (2) we will have to create or find, by 1975, at least 15 million more jobs than there were in 1965.*

Regional Change

The same sources estimate that the greatest rates of increase in the labor force will take place in the following regions.

South Atlantic	Mountain States
West South Central	Pacific[a]

---

*In the six years already transpired since 1965, 8 million additional jobs were created, which means that between 1971 and 1975 — only four years — 7 million more jobs will have to be created. At the 1965-71 rate we will be short by 1.7 million jobs. This does not include the already unemployed. – EDS.

[a]*South Atlantic* — especially Delaware, Maryland, Virginia, South Carolina, Georgia, and Florida. *West South Central* — especially Arkansas, Louisiana, and Texas. *Mountain* — especially Idaho, Colorado, New Mexico, Arizona, Utah, and Nevada. *Pacific* — especially California and Hawaii.

Table 1.6
Projected Labor Force, 1975 and Percentage Change, 1965-1975 by Sex and Age

Sex and Age	Labor force, 1975 (millions)	Percentage change 1965-1975
Both sexes		
14 and over	93.6	19.5
Male		
14 and over	60.3	16.6
14 to 19	5.6	21.7
20 to 24	8.3	40.6
25 to 34	15.0	40.5
35 to 44	10.7	−7.0
45 to 54	10.8	6.7
55 to 64	7.8	15.2
65 and older	2.1	−2.1
Female		
14 and over	33.4	25.1
14 to 19	3.7	27.2
20 to 24	4.9	44.1
25 to 34	6.1	44.2
35 to 44	5.6	−2.5
45 to 54	7.0	22.9
55 to 64	4.8	34.5
65 and older	1.2	23.5

Source: Based on Table E-2, *Manpower Report of the President, 1967.*

These four growth regions in the near future will have about 42 percent of the national labor force (as compared to only 39 percent in 1960).

Regions with sharp declines in the size of the labor force are expected to be:

New England   East North Central
Middle Atlantic   West North Central[b]

In the near future, these four regions are expected to have 52 percent of the total national labor force (as compared to 55 percent in 1960). To be sure, each of these regions will experience an increase in the *number* of persons in the labor force, but such an increase will be at a slower pace than for the country as a whole.

[b]*New England* — especially Maine, Massachusetts, and Rhode Island. *Middle Atlantic* — especially New York and Pennsylvania. *East North Central* — especially Illinois, Michigan, and Wisconsin. *West North Central* — especially Iowa, Missouri, North Dakota, Nebraska, and Kansas.

Occupational Change

In terms of *occupations,* the Department of Labor estimates that between 1965 and 1975 changes in the number of employed persons in each major occupation group, as shown in table 1.7, may be expected.

Table 1.7
Projected Employment Change by Major Occupation Group, 1965-1975

Major occupation group	Change, 1965-1975	
	Number (millions)	Percent
Total employment	16.5	22.8
Professional, technical, and kindred workers	4.0	45.2
Managers, officials, and proprietors, except farm	1.9	25.3
Clerical and kindred workers	3.4	30.8
Sales workers	1.1	23.0
Craftsmen, foremen, and kindred workers	2.2	23.6
Operatives and kindred workers	1.6	12.0
Service workers, including private household	3.2	34.5
Laborers, except farm and mine	−0.1	−3.0
Farmers and farm managers, laborers, and foremen	−0.8	−18.9

Source: Table E-8, *Manpower Report of the President, 1967.*

Incidentally, these estimates are based on the assumption of a 3 percent rate of unemployment for 1975, and are based also on the assumption that employment at that time will be determined by the level of employment over the past decade — i.e., that government policies will *not* lower unemployment below 3 percent of the labor force, and that *no* significant changes in technology, job design, etc., will take place. Some students of manpower and economic development might be skeptical about using *factual* trends of the past, based on one particular set of public policies and programs, as a source of decision making as to what to do about the future. This skepticism is derived partly from the belief that we should concentrate more on creative policies leading to new job ideas for the future, and not just on statistics of the past.

Industry Changes

The same qualification also applies to Department of Labor employment projections by *industry* division, cited in table 1.8.

Several features of these projections should be noted. *One,* the fantastic drop in the number of people that will be working in agriculture, 840,000. We are all familiar with the magnitude of the shift that has *already* taken place. For example, in just the five years after 1960, 1.1 million jobs in agriculture simply disappeared, a percentage decline of 20 percent.

Table 1.8

Projected Change in Employment, by Major Industry Division, 1965-1975

Industry division	Change, 1965-1975	
	Number (thousands)	Percent
Agriculture	−840	−18.3
All nonagricultural wage and salary workers	15,105	24.9
Goods-producing industries	2,685	12.3
Mining	−12	−1.9
Contract construction	1,009	31.7
Manufacturing	1,688	9.4
Durable goods	1,094	10.5
Nondurable goods	595	7.8
Service-producing industries	12,421	31.9
Transportation and public utilities	487	12.1
Wholesale and retail trade	3,432	27.1
Retail only	2,614	27.9
Finance, insurance, and real estate	706	23.4
Service and miscellaneous	3,852	42.3
Government	3,944	39.1
Federal	257	10.8

Source: Table E-9, *Manpower Report of the President, 1967.*

As the National Industrial Conference Board's Desk Sheet of Business Trends (April 1968) tells us:

. . . fast-growing productivity in agriculture reduces the size of the work force needed on the farm — even as output increases. The drop in farm population is concentrated among families with young children, especially among non-whites . . . Between 1960 and 1967, output per man-hour on farms jumped 45%; man-hours of labor required on farms dropped 27%, and total farmland acreage shrank 3% . . .

It appears that consolidation of small farms into larger ones or retirement of small marginal farms has affected nonwhites particularly, and especially so in the South. Between 1960 and 1967 the nonwhite population on farms fell 50% − 1.28 million.

Incidentally, we must also keep in mind that *income from farming only* is actually a small source of total income to the farm population: the fact is that 60 percent of the income of farm operators and 75 percent of the income of their other family members are derived from *work off the farm.* And these percentages continue to rise.

Furthermore, between 1959 and 1966, the number of *poor* persons living on farms fell from 6.8 to 2.4 million men, women, and children – a percentage decline of 65 percent! *For the most part, they moved to the urban areas, seeking work for themselves and their families* but woefully unprepared by their previous environment, experience, and education to cope with the labor market of the urban world.

The *second* feature about the previous two tables is that the bulk of the employment increase (63 percent) will probably occur in the professional, technical, and white-collar kinds of occupations, which traditionally call for males with higher education or for females. This becomes significant when we consider that by 1975 we will still have nearly a third of young males (under 35) without a high school diploma. And this age group will rise more sharply than all others, as noted earlier. Just among males 25-34 years old, the estimate is that 4.2 million of them will be without a high school diploma but nevertheless in the labor force. If these projections are correct, we will continue to need training programs and even pressures to redesign job requirements to fit the individual.

Third, despite some contrary beliefs, the number of *craftsmen and foremen* will increase by 2.2 million between 1965 and 1975. This estimate should be coupled with the one relating to *industry* changes, in which it is expected that in contract construction the projected increase of one million jobs will constitute a proportional rise in that 10 year period of nearly one-third – *the highest proportional rise of all goods-producing industries.* In other words, apprentice-ships, middle-echelon jobs, upgrading, and housing and office-building construc-tion – in a word, urban reconstruction activities – do offer a promising source of employment opportunities *if the proper manpower and economic policies and programs are started on now.*

Fourth, there is the rather vague and miscellaneous job category un-fortunately labeled in the aggregate as "service occupations," but which could contain a great potential for increased job opportunities. For the record, we ought to make clear what is included in this grab-bag. It includes the following types of jobs: barbers, firemen, waiters, bartenders, protective service workers, policemen and detectives, private household workers, hairdressers, and janitors.

We should not confuse this *occupational* category with the *industry* category of the same name. The *"service industries"* include: advertising, private households, barber and beauty shops, auto repairing, hotels and motels, hospitals, theaters and movie houses, schools, and governments.

To pinpoint the matter further, in the last full Census count (1960), 59 percent of all male service *workers* were in service *industries* (professional and related services, government, and "other" industries); and 74 percent of female service *workers* were in the same types of service *industries.*[c]

Fifth, and the main point, service *jobs* and service *industries* are going to increase tremendously by 1975. If we concentrate only on the service industries, regardless of occupation, the projection is that in government alone nearly 4 million *additional* jobs will be available – an increase of 39 percent. More than 93 percent of such jobs will be with state and local government agencies, *not* with the federal government – and even the latter excludes military service jobs. This increase raises the question of public service employment as a major policy issue – discussed below.

An almost equal number of additional jobs in other service industries (such as advertising, maintenance, tourism, health, etc.) is expected – about 3.8 million; and another 3.4 million additional ones in trade activities – and more than three-fourths of this increase in retail trade alone.

The basic conclusion from all of this analysis of projections is that, given the right economic policies and conditions for sound economic growth (and excluding the risks of a resource-wasting war), *and from the standpoint of numbers only,* there can be enough jobs to employ all persons who need and want to work. But this simple statement raises some further questions:

1. Will the society, through government and private industry, pursue the "right" policies and establish the "right" conditions?
2. To what extent will the underemployed, the working poor, and other jobseekers be qualified to fill the jobs ostensibly available as a result of effective policies in the public and private spheres; will they also be in the right places, i.e., where the jobs are?

These two questions have to do with the outcome of current proposals and ongoing programs in the field of economic and manpower development.

Private and Public Employment

At the current time, a great deal of government energy and resources is being put into appeals to the private sector (especially the giants of private industry) to hire, train, and keep employed large numbers of unemployed and underemployed youths and adult men and women. In addition to the government's relying on basic motive of sheer community civic service – and perhaps even of

---

[c]But more than one-half of all these female service workers were employed in private households as domestics. And nearly one-half of all such female service workers in private households were nonwhite, with mean earnings in 1959 of $864. Even if nonwhite females in this job and industry worked fifty or more weeks in that year, the mean earnings were only $1,157 (as compared to $2,055 mean earnings for all year-round employed nonwhite females, and $1,809 for year-round employed white females in the same job and industry).

pure and simple survival, in the light of the recent "civil disorders" (on the assumption that lack of jobs or low-level jobs are the root cause of the rioting and looting) — the government has also sought to use "incentives" with private industry in the form of subsidies to offset the costs of recruiting, training, supervising, and maintaining on the job residents of our cities' slum areas.

It may be too soon to judge such effects as CEP, MA-1 through MA-3, etc., but it appears that to date the efforts have not produced large numbers of successful placements. Perhaps the incentives have not been enough for potential employers. Perhaps too few potential employers have been reached (the techniques and/or the target employers may have been limited). Possibly there may be problems not anticipated by the administrators and employers in these various programs and projects around the country — problems caused by handicaps of the hard-core unemployed and underemployed such as illiteracy, poor health, fears and misconceptions about the nature of work and supervision; by lack of preparation of trainers and supervisors on the job for coping with the handicaps of such persons, etc. Discrimination based on racism continues to plague the job market also.

At any rate, it may well be that even with the best of motives, the best of recruiting, training, on-the-job techniques, etc., the actual *numbers* of jobs now available for the hard-core unemployed and underemployed in private industry are limited, or not readily accessible to such persons (in terms of location of jobs versus location of people). In general, it may well be that at the present time the demand within private industry for entry jobs (even with needs for meeting normal turnover, retirements, etc.) is too low to absorb all jobseekers in the areas where the jobs are.

A preliminary report by the National Committee on Employment of Youth regarding the accomplishments of job-creation and job-placement programs by the government and by the National Alliance of Businessmen (NAB) — a private-sector approach backed up by government incentives — stated that "employers in the public sector seem to be achieving the hiring goals more readily than those in the private sector."[3] The survey's data on eighteen of the fifty largest cities in which NAB projects were initiated revealed that as of mid-July only 31,184 jobs were filled — in contrast to 131,000 originally planned as the summer job goal in those cities.

This is not necessarily a criticism of the sincerity and intent of the many dedicated employers and their representatives involved in the campaign of the National Alliance of Businessmen. Samuel M. Burt and Herbert E. Striner, in a recent staff paper published by the W.E. Upjohn Institute, pointed out in great detail what the limitations are of a job-creation program relying heavily on the private sector. For one thing, it may be too much for middle-sized and small companies to provide the total gamut of services (including recruiting, remedial reading, health services, redesigning of jobs, counseling, financial assistance in crises of new workers, and reorientation of regular workers and supervisors) required to make such campaigns a success.

Burt and Striner also raise the question as to whether there is a real and effective demand in the private sector sufficient to employ the majority of the hard-core unemployed and underemployed – adults as well as youths – in addition to those jobseekers already qualified to fill entry-level jobs. Furthermore, they point out:

> The lesson is really simple . . . don't ask the employer to turn his plant and office into a social service agency or an educational institution. He is paying taxes to the government and is contributing huge sums to educational and charitable institutions to provide [the supportive and remedial services necessary for training and/or hiring the disadvantaged] . . . If he can be persuaded that any particular new program or programs will do the job more effectively, he will support them either by paying the additional taxes or by increasing his contributions.[4]

The most telling comment these two authors have to make is that many observers are beginning to ask if government itself has done enough to create and provide job opportunities in the *public* sector. They suggest very strongly that employers in private industry have the right to ask government at all levels to "take the initiative . . . in attempting to remedy its own past and present failure before throwing the major remedial burden on private industry."

To repeat, it is highly probable that the private sector – even with the best of intentions – cannot find enough jobs in its various production and commercial service activities to employ all the youths, men, and women with whom we are all concerned.

At the same time, there is a need for more workers in what has been called "public service employment." Unfortunately, this need has been obscured by the use of such terms as "government as employer of *last* resort," which implies that such employment should be advocated and provided only *after* private enterprise has failed to employ everyone; that these jobs with government agencies are only temporary, pending the rise in demand for workers in private enterprise; and that such jobs are not very desirable for the individual or useful and worthwhile to the community.

But government is more than an employer: more accurately, its function is to provide services to citizens – such as education, health protection, national defense, park and recreation facilities, waste disposal, water services, construction and maintenance of highways and other transportation facilities, police and fire protection, etc.

In living up to these and other obligations, the government obviously employs persons in jobs which are vital to the functioning of the society and the economy. The main point here is that *the need for the services to be provided is the underlying justification for public service employment.*

There are several categories of public service functions which are not being adequately served under existing levels of expenditure and administrative-legislative commitment. The Joint Economic Committee of the United States Congress, in its 1966 report on public facility needs, cites six major types of public services:[5]

1. *Basic community services.* Such as provision of water, electricity, gas, and sanitary services, and including a wide variety of antipollution needs. Some of these services may be provided by private profit-making organizations, but this does not detract from the fact that they are public services.
2. *Transportation services.* These cover not only construction and maintenance of highways, roads, streets, and bridges, but urban transit systems, parking facilities, airports, train and bus stations, and port facilities. Again, some of these are privately run, but they are nevertheless public in their function, and are ultimately subject to public jurisdiction.
3. *Educational services.* These include not only public elementary and secondary schools, but private ones as well; vocational schools and institutes; community and junior colleges; and universities – plus college housing and ancillary services such as food services, publications, and educational TV.
4. *Health services.* Hospitals, clinics, medical research projects, nursing home and chronic disease centers, community health clinics, services and facilities for the mentally retarded, family planning centers, etc.
5. *Recreational and cultural activities.* Embracing outdoor play centers, parks and marinas, neighborhood athletic centers, theaters, museums, auditoriums, libraries, etc.
6. *Miscellaneous.* Child care centers, jails and prisons, fire protection facilities, etc.

The present level of services in all these categories is inadequate to meet public needs; an expansion of services would provide more jobs. Furthermore, it can be argued that these public services facilitate growth in the private sector, and that if the latter is to prosper, it requires an "infrastructure" of the public service facilities, provided by public service employees.

The emergence of new needs in the public service sector of urban America will in turn generate certain manpower needs that will require: (1) the design of new occupations for residents of the inner city; (2) the effective recruitment and training of these residents; (3) their placement in appropriate public agencies once trained (or perhaps after being trained on the job in those agencies); and (4) the development of "job maintenance" techniques in order to keep inner-city residents interested in the new positions (including career ladder opportunities, decent wages, trained supervisors, etc.)

The actual number of new jobs that could be created through implementation of commitments to the public sector (not counting the new jobs in the *private* sector that would result from increased purchasing power in the pockets of new public service employees) can only be estimated at this point, but all such estimates conclude with sizable numbers of increased jobs. The "backlog" or "shelf" of public service needs contains a huge potential for jobs, regardless of what method of estimating the numbers is used.

One source of estimates is the Commission on Technology, Automation, and Economic Progress (1966) which – without citing the source or method – claimed that 5.3 million new jobs through public service employment in the following fields could be created:

Field	Number of jobs (millions)
Medical institutions and health services	1.2
Educational institutions	1.1
National beautification	1.3
Welfare and home care	0.7
Public protection	0.35
Urban renewal and sanitation	0.65
	5.3

A much more documented study is the one carried out in 1965 by Greenleigh Associates for OEO, entitled *A Public Employment Program for the Unemployed Poor.* This report cites a minimum, first of all, of 3.5 million unemployed and underemployed poor Americans capable of productive work. But more important, the study estimates that at least 4.3 million jobs could be filled in public service activities if the nation were to fulfill its obligation in these activities through government and private nonprofit agencies.

These 4.3 million estimated job opportunities were distributed as follows:

Public service group	Number of jobs (millions)
Health, including hospitals and mental health	1.355
Education	2.017
Day care	0.014
Recreation and beautification	0.136
Libraries	0.063
Public welfare	0.065
Probation and parole	0.016
Institutions for dependent and delinquent children	0.039
Public works	0.150
Police and fire	0.050
Prisons	0.024
Defense	0.350[d]
	4.3

These 4.3 million jobs, of course, could not be made available all at once. In the first year, the Greenleigh report states, about 470,000 jobs might be possible under a well-planned public employment program, with more than 70 percent of them in the fields of health and education alone.

The critical features about these first-year estimates are: *First,* such jobs would be socially useful with a "legitimate place in the economy." They would not be "made-work" jobs. *Second,* they could be filled by persons with low-entry skills and training. *Third,* the employing organizations would be prepared to absorb the extra employees and provide necessary training and supervision on the job without any costly capital expenditures.

The same features apply to the types of jobs considered in a third and more recent study in the spring of 1968, by the present author, at the request of the National Urban Coalition. In an effort to determine as quickly as possible, and within the bounds of realistic estimates, the job possibilities through an expansion of existing local public services, the U.S. Conference of Mayors asked the mayors of 50 cities with a population of 100,000 or more (exclusive of suburban populations) to answer a brief inquiry, the preface to which stated:

The purpose of this inquiry is to estimate the degree to which local governments in the United States could be expanding their delivery of services to their community and citizens, if the usually cited obstacles to such expansion did not exist (such as budgets).

We would appreciate your answer to the following questions after consulting with the heads and personnel chiefs in the types of agencies listed below, if such a survey has not already been conducted.

The mayors were then asked to indicate which public service functions among the following thirteen had a need for at least a 10 percent increase in services and/or personnel:

> Antipollution enforcement
> Education
> General administration
> Health and hospitals
> Highway and/or traffic
> Housing codes and inspection
> Library

---

[d]This includes "an estimated theoretical potential of 350,000 jobs that could be established for civilians on military bases if, as a matter of policy, it were decided to convert many jobs now performed by armed forces personnel to civilian employment."

Police
Fire
Recreation and parks
Urban renewal (or rehabilitation),
   including Model Cities
Sanitation
Welfare

Following that question, they were requested to answer the following:

... could you provide *estimates* of how many additional personnel would be needed to implement these increased services? Plausible, reasonable estimates are perfectly satisfactory here. We are not insisting on precise to-the-last-man figures.

On the basis of the answers to this question supplied by the thirty-four cities returning the forms, it is possible to estimate that among the 130 or so cities of over 100,000 population there are approximately 280,000 job possibilities among the thirteen municipal public service functions cited in the questionnaire (including some functions which may be under county or state jurisdiction, such as education and welfare). (See table 1.9.) The figures exclude estimates based on replies *volunteered* regarding "other" unlisted public service functions. These possibilities, of course, are at the present time only theoretical in that funds are not currently available to make them into real job openings.

It should be emphasized also that the 280,000 potential positions include occupations and professions which require some degree of technical proficiency, and which could not be filled by the typical hard-core unemployed or underemployed resident of the central city. But a major purpose of this inquiry was to arrive at some intelligent estimate of the total number of the *less* technical positions deemed needed to provide the increased services in the thirteen functions cited. Accordingly, the mayors were presented with the following statement and request for information:

In many of these potentially expanded departments and functions, there is always the strong probability that new professional personnel may not be available in the numbers desired. Partly as a means of solving this type of personnel shortage, some agencies around the country have recently begun to recruit and train (A) men and women without the regularly required advanced preparation to perform those aspects of "professional" jobs which actually could be performed by such men and women. In other departments and functions needing more personnel, the only major reason for not hiring them is simply the problem of inadequate funds, and (B) men and women could be employed in a variety of jobs that are not rigidly professional in nature (for example, playground aides, urban beautification personnel, certain kinds of hospital employees, etc.).

Table 1.9
Projection of Additional Public Service Job Possibilities in 130 Cities With Population of 100,000 or More by Population Size, 1968

Function or program	Total (130 cities)	Population size		
		100,000- 250,000 (80 cities)	250,000- 750,000 (40 cities)	750,000 or more (10 cities)
Total	279,415	100,144	74,316	104,955
Antipollution enforcement	1,748	1,072	368	308
Education	84,598	33,944	27,896	22,758
General administration	13,940	5,952	3,064	4,924
Health and hospitals	34,534	12,368	11,920	10,246
Highway and/or traffic	9,786	4,512	3,456	1,818
Housing codes and inspection	5,199	968	1,544	2,687
Library	5,619	2,232	1,804	1,583
Police	37,408	10,016	8,992	18,400
Fire	14,994	7,664	3,348	3,982
Recreation and parks	18,896	7,296	3,800	7,800
Urban renewal (or rehabilitation), including Model Cities	12,198	7,440	1,944	2,814
Sanitation	13,586	4,160	2,416	7,010
Welfare	26,909	2,520	3,764	20,625

Note: Based on replies of 34 cities. Excludes answers to "other" categories.

In column 3, would you indicate what percent of the numbers cited in column 2 might consist of these two types, A and B, of new employees? In answering this question, please do not feel constrained by any *existing* budgetary or entrance-requirement limitations. Again, no iron-clad precise percentage is requested here — only your best estimate as to what proportion of these jobs could conceivably be filled by nonprofessional personnel.

The results of analysis of this information revealed that more than one-half of all the job possibilities cited previously could be filled, according to the mayors and their agency heads, by persons without technical or professional training. In other words, *at least* 140,000 job possibilities for inner-city residents may be said to be present in the 13 public service functions in cities of over 100,000 population (see table 1.10).

Table 1.10

Projection of Additional Nonprofessional Public Service Job Possibilities in 130 Cities With Population of 100,000 or More, by Population Size, 1968

Function or program	Total (130 cities)	Population size 100,000-250,000 (80 cities)	250,000-750,000 (40 cities)	750,000 or more (10 cities)
Total	141,144	44,920	40,580	55,644
Antipollution enforcement	900	568	232	100
Education	39,134	10,704	15,000	13,430
General administration	5,313	2,864	1,236	1,213
Health and hospitals	18,790	6,120	6,596	6,074
Highway and/or traffic	7,179	3,608	2,168	1,403
Housing codes and inspection	1,473	440	576	457
Library	3,159	1,176	908	1,075
Police	11,616	2,360	3,916	5,340
Fire	5,390	2,720	1,648	1,022
Recreation and parks	14,359	5,696	2,900	5,763
Urban renewal (or rehabilitation), including Model Cities	7,800	5,304	1,104	1,392
Sanitation	7,534	2,816	1,868	2,850
Welfare	18,497	544	2,428	15,525

Note: Based on replies of 34 cities. Excludes answers to "other" categories.

Most of these public service jobs are apparently needed in schools, health centers, recreation, welfare, and protective service agencies (see table 1.11). Their distribution by size of city is shown in table 1.12.

This survey of local governments concentrated on a limited approach to the need to estimate on an intelligent basis essentially those manpower needs just for the expansion of *existing* local urban government programs; it was limited further to a small number of such functions in cities with a population of 100,000 or more. The implications of this survey include the following:

A. The fact that the estimates pertain primarily to existing programs suggests that the additional jobs could be filled without too much delay if funds could be made available.

B. For a number of reasons, the figure of 140,000 is a *minimum* estimate of the overall potential of public service employment.

Table 1.11

Projected Additional Public Service Job Possibilities in 130 Cities With Population of 100,000 or More by Type of Function, 1968 (in percent)

Function	New public service positions	
	All	Nonprofessional
Total	100.0	100.0
Antipollution enforcement	0.6	0.6
Education	30.3	27.7
General administration	5.0	3.8
Health and hospitals	12.4	13.3
Highway and/or traffic	3.5	5.1
Housing codes and inspection	1.9	1.0
Library	2.0	2.2
Police	13.4	8.2
Fire	5.4	3.8
Recreation and parks	6.8	10.2
Urban renewal (or rehabilitation), including Model Cities	4.4	5.5
Sanitation	4.9	5.3
Welfare	9.6	13.1
Percentages based on	279,415	141,144

Note: Based on replies of 34 cities. Excludes answers to "other" categories.

Columns may not add to 100 because of rounding.

Table 1.12

Projected Additional Public Service Job Possibilities in 130 Cities With Population of 100,000 or More by Size of City, 1968 (in percent)

Size of city	New public service positions	
	All	Nonprofessional
Total	100.0	100.0
100,000-250,000	35.8	31.8
250,000-750,000	26.6	28.8
750,000 or more	37.6	39.4
Percentages based on	279,415	141,144

Note: Based on replies of 34 cities. Excludes answers to "other" categories.

First, the data on which the number is based exclude many other municipal functions not asked about in the survey. *Second,* the estimates apply only to urban places of over 100,000 population – which encompass about one-third of the total population in the United States. *Third,* they do not include any estimates from nonprofit private organizations in equal, if not greater, need of expansion of their services in urban and rural areas. *Fourth,* the 140,000 figure does not include the estimates by the mayors of some cities volunteering responses to the "other" category in the questionnaire. (If the "other" category is used in the estimate, it is safe to add an additional 10,000 job possibilities in public service employment for inner-city residents, raising the minimum estimate to 150,000 for cities of over 100,000.) *Fifth,* it must be remembered that the 150,000 figure *excludes* an identical estimate for professional and technical personnel needed in these few public service categories. We are talking here only about *non*professional – or "subprofessional" jobs.

C. There is another significant reason for considering the estimate of 140,000 to 150,000 to be a conservative figure. It has to do with the possibility that too little thought has been given by city administrators to the actual extent of need for expanded and new public services. Antipollution enforcement is one example. This is a new and growing area of public concern, and in the next few years the manpower and personnel aspects of the enforcement and implementation of antipollution and other environmental health measures can be expected to become a major administrative challenge to urban areas. It is extremely doubtful that among the 130 cities with over 100,000 population only 1,700 additional positions – as determined by the estimates of the 34 cities providing information – will be required to carry out such measures.

Not only do we have a *backlog* of unmet public service needs: there is also a vast amount of *unanticipated and unplanned* needs for which little preparation has been made. In strong contrast to those students of manpower projections who foresee fewer and fewer jobs, there are other persons (including this writer) who fear that we have not begun to prepare for the wide and expanding range of human and public service functions that will be necessary to make life viable in our urban areas – that we will have a need for more and more employees.

D. In this connection, it may also be pertinent to mention that the need for such *public* service may be accelerated by growth in the *private* sector of our economy and society. This need, in other words, is not *sui generis,* i.e., something that develops by itself in isolation from other conditions and trends. For example, in the use of automobiles and trucks by the private sector of the urban economy, certain public-function needs must be met such as driver education, vehicle inspection, traffic and parking control, highway construction and maintenance, and air pollution control.

E. It may be pushing the point too far, but a further effect of the employment of an additional 150,000 professionals and another 150,000 non-professionals in the public sector at the local level alone would be to place new purchasing power into the total economy of the country, which in turn could provide a more realistic demand for increased employment in the private sector. In this indirect way (rather than via direct employment *at first* of the so-called "unemployables" through exhortation and goodwill) an intrinsic demand among private employers for more workers would result. At the present time, however, the demand is not enough to absorb all (or a substantial majority of) these jobseekers. Despite all the moral and practical reasons for the contemporary involvement of the private sector in the urban job crisis, if there is no such intrinsic employer demand for thousands of more workers, that crisis will not be effectively overcome.

F. New needs in the public service sector of urban America are emerging. These along with older unmet needs, will require, first of all, the design of new occupations for residents of the inner city; second, the effective recruitment and training of these residents; third, their placement in appropriate agencies in the city after training (or perhaps after being trained on the job in those agencies); and finally, the development of techniques of what might be called "job maintenance" in order to keep such inner-city residents attracted to these new positions.

Summary

The solution to our problems of "hard-core" unemployment and underemployment must combine (a) the current efforts of the private sector to train and hire; with (b) the expansion and provision of public services at various levels of government and in nonprofit organizations. Neither approach by itself will go very far in meeting the urgent needs of the unemployed and the general community.

The overall picture is of an economy and society with many unmet needs — unfilled jobs — and with the *potential means* to meet the needs and fill the jobs — *potential* only because we have not placed a high enough priority on the goal of providing the services to meet the needs, and thus to create the jobs involved. It is rather ironic that by 1975, according to an estimate by the National Planning Association in a report for the Manpower Administration, *Manpower Requirements for National Objectives in the 1970's,* we shall need 10 million more individuals to fill the optimum manpower requirements of the nation than we are likely to have in the total labor force. Compared to 1962, we shall need, in 1975, nearly twice as many workers in education and health services; nearly twice as many in social welfare; about 60 percent more in housing programs; and 60 percent more in urban development. The percentage increases in the various other public service categories are almost as high, if not higher. If the 1-to-1 ratio in the Sheppard study for the Urban Coalition is any basis for estimating what portion of the *extra* jobs in these categories might be filled by underemployed and nonprofessional persons, the estimate would be about 8.5 million in just health and education, housing, social welfare, and urban development.

At any rate, there is an urgent need to start now to take the necessary first steps toward providing the much needed public services — and thus the accompanying new jobs for the unemployed and underemployed if we are to realize to any degree the national aspiration goals for 1975. These first steps include the passage of legislation to create the public service employment jobs at local, county, state, and national levels of government; a more rational and improved program — with realistic recognition of the intrinsic demand problem — of private industry training and hiring of the hard-core unemployed and underemployed; and, of course, the maintenance of those fiscal and monetary policies conducive to a "full-employment" economy.

Notes

1. Barry Bluestone, "Low-Wage Industries and the Working Poor," *Poverty and Human Resources Abstracts* 3,2 (March-April 1968).

2. U.S. Department of Commerce, *Statistical Abstract of the United States,* 1967, Table 336, p. 238.

3. *Summer Jobs for Youth,* 1968, National Committee on Employment of Youth, July 29, 1968, mimeographed, p.8.

4. Samuel M. Burt and Herbert E. Striner, *Toward Greater Industry and Government Involvement in Manpower Development* (Kalamazoo: The W.E. Upjohn Institute, September 1968), p. 11.

5. *State and Local Public Facility Needs and Financing,* Volume I: *Public Facility Needs,* December 1966.

2

Public Employment and the Theory of the Dual Economy

BENNETT HARRISON

In response to the proliferation of manpower programs during the 1960s, a number of young economists have investigated the extent to which such "human capital"—oriented policies "impact" the interrelated problems of unemployment, poverty, and job discrimination. Out of these deeply critical studies has gradually emerged the outline of a new theory about the structure of American labor markets. This new theory of economic "dualism" leads its proponents to advocacy of a number of rather unconventional policy prescriptions, including significantly expanded public service employment.

This paper describes the origins of the new theory, its principal hypotheses, and its relationship to the subject of federally subsidized public sector employment.

Poverty, Discrimination, and Unemployment

Neoclassical explanations of unemployment and underemployment have, until very recently, been oriented almost entirely toward analysis of labor supply. During the 1950s, discussions of "structural unemployment" turned on the premise that certain kinds of labor (distinguished by ethnic origin, education, or location) were unable to respond "normally" when effective demand for goods and services is translated into derived demand for labor. Then,

... as aggregate demand lowered unemployment and the structural hypothesis became less tenable as an explanation of high unemployment, the manpower training programs gradually shifted character and became anti-poverty programs ... They readily harmonized with the early puritan ethic of the war on poverty. Poverty was to be eliminated by raising everyone's marginal product to the level where [they] would be able to earn an acceptable income. Education and training programs were to be the principal means for raising marginal products ... increasing workers' human capital could eliminate poverty ... [1]

The author of the previous statement, Lester Thurow, is one of the most prominent members of the "human capital" school. His assessment is shared by Thomas Ribich, whose analysis of the relationship between education and poverty begins with the proposition that "a major presumption of the war on poverty is that education and training are especially effective ways to bring people out of poverty."[2]

But investments in the human capital of ghetto workers have not eliminated poverty. The results of recent quantitative studies demonstrate a fundamental flaw in the conventional wisdom, and call for a revision of the current orthodoxy which asserts that poverty is a function of inadequate human capital.[3]

A few neoclassical economists have attempted a modest revision, according to which minority underemployment is explained by the "market imperfection" of racial discrimination.[4] These theorists have been criticized for attributing unrealistically calculated, marginalist decision-making behavior to discriminating employers, and for their inability or unwillingness to recognize that discrimination by employers takes place within the larger context of institutional racism throughout the economy.[5] Limited though they may be, however, the neoclassical studies are at least addressed to the "demand side" of the problem.

Gary Becker's analysis of discrimination is founded on the notion that every employer has his price for hiring blacks. "For each employer, for each job, there is a crucial wage differential which would make the hiring of a white and an equally qualified Negro a matter of indifference to him. This crucial wage differential, expressed as a ratio of the white wage, Becker calls the 'discrimination coefficient.'"[6] The market acts so as to cause the available supply of blacks to be hired by employers with relatively low discrimination coefficients. The observed differential between black and white pay is the discrimination coefficient of the employer on the margin, the employer of blacks who is most prejudiced against them. For Becker, in other words, discrimination takes place at the point of job entry. Thurow's approach is similar in placing the focus of discrimination within the firm which pays Negroes a wage discounted to take into account the employer's "psychic cost" of integrating his workforce.

For Barbara Bergmann, on the other hand, the focus is on those employers who will not hire blacks at any wage. This is the "crowding hypothesis:

The most important feature of an economy in which discrimination is practiced is the simple fact that some jobs are open to Negroes and some are not. The jobs open to Negroes are not a random selection, even allowing for Negroes' relatively lower education. They tend to be predominantly low in status, and to be concentrated very heavily in a few occupations. Following Donald Dewey, we might call this a "racial division of labor . . . " Another major difference with the view of this paper is the identification of the villain of the piece. For Thurow, he is the man who hires Negroes and pays them low wages. Under the crowdedness hypothesis . . . the villain is the entrepreneur who will not hire Negroes, perhaps on behalf of or under pressure from his white workers. The entrepreneur who does hire Negroes acts towards them the way he is presumed to act towards any other factor of production: he pays them the price for which he can get them. The fact that the price for Negro labor is a lower price than he need pay white workers is attributable not to the entrepreneur who hires Negroes, but to the entrepreneur who refuses to do so, and so crowds them into the janitorships at low pay.[7]

Arrow's analysis is similar to Bergmann's in emphasizing the significance of "corner" (i.e., either-or) solutions to the intrafirm (or intrashop) labor allocation decision.

The emphasis in this paper will also be on minority workers, especially blacks, and we, too, will often speak of racial discrimination. But this study will also show that lower-class whites — those who still live in the central city poverty areas and "ghettos" — receive returns to their human capital which are substantially lower than the returns received by whites who have "escaped" the ghetto. Our analysis, in other words, leads us to hypothesize the existence of *class* as well as *race* discrimination.

Bradley Schiller has succeeded in making a quantitative distinction between the effects of class discrimination (with "class" defined by income stratum) and racial discrimination, as these are manifested through restricted access to educational and occupational opportunities.[8] Schiller estimates that, if working sons in black families enrolled in the Aid to Families with Dependent Children program could convert their inherited status (defined by parental occupation and education) and their own years of schooling into occupational status at the same "rate" that poor (i.e., AFDC-enrolled) *white* sons do, they would gain 3.32 occupational status points (on an ordinal scale of 0-100). This is, therefore, a kind of measure of the extent of racial discrimination, holding "class" constant.

If poor white sons could convert *their* inherited status and their own education into occupational status at the same "rate" that *non-poor* white sons do, they would gain 2.74 status points. This is Schiller's measure of class discrimination, holding race constant.

Finally, if poor black sons could convert their inherited status and their own schooling into occupational status at the same "rate" that non-poor white sons do, they would gain 5.66 status points. This is a measure of the *joint* effects of racial and class discrimination.

These findings require us to ask whether common structural characteristics of the economic system underlie both white and black poverty. If such is the case, then neither appeals to racial justice nor coercive antidiscrimination policies will be sufficient to eliminate poverty. As Barry Bluestone observes:

"While particular individuals now denied high-wage jobs may benefit from a removal of market barriers, low-wage jobs will still exist. At best, increased mobility will distribute workers more "fairly" over the existing sets of jobs . . . Some black workers will exchange places with some white workers in the occupational hierarchy and some women will replace men, but increased mobility will *not*, in general, increase the number of high-wage jobs or reduce the number of jobs at poverty wages.[9]

This important proposition has received some support from Ms. Bergmann's study of the income effects of occupational "crowding." Without any compensating increase in the stock of jobs in the economy, the elimination of occupational discrimination by race would (according to the Bergmann equations) cause a 6-9 percent reduction in the incomes of white men lacking an eighth grade diploma – a group which constitutes 14 percent of all adult white men in the United States. The displacement of white women would be even greater. For both sexes, the conflict becomes greater the less substitutable we assume whites and nonwhites to be in production.[10] These calculations imply that the ofttimes vocal opposition of lower-class white ethnic groups to government programs designed to expand job opportunities for blacks is – in an economy such as ours – not without some reason.

Confronting the facts of class conflict and continued poverty in the United States, even after a decade in which "the federal government directed between $140 and $170 billion in aid to the poor,"[11] a small, but growing, number of young economists have begun to develop an alternative theory – what David Gordon (after Thomas Kuhn) calls a new "paradigm"[12] – to explain these phenomena.

Some of this new research to which I have alluded has grown out of what began as fairly pedestrian evaluations of various training and education programs connected with the federal "war on poverty." These studies frequently showed that training programs had little positive effect on the work situation of the poor. Enrollees in such programs typically earned no higher wages after graduation than before undertaking training. Many refused to take the programs seriously at all, remaining in them for short periods of time, earning small training stipends, and then dropping out. In fact, many enrollees told evaluators frankly that they thought of the manpower training system in the same way they thought of any other form of low-wage, marginal activity: as a temporary source of income, a place to go for short periods of time to supplement family income. They entertained little hope or expectation of actually acquiring decent permanent employment as a result of their participation in the program.

At about the same time, other researchers discovered an important flaw in the conventional wisdom about welfare recipients. It was popularly held that there exists in the economy a large, permanent "welfare class," consisting of individuals and families who themselves remain on the relief rolls for long periods of time and who not infrequently raise their children to become similarly dependent on public assistance. The researchers found, instead, that people tended to move on and off the welfare rolls, over and over again, in a fashion reminiscent of the behavior of the manpower trainees. The analogy was reinforced by the publication in 1967 of the Bureau of Labor Statistics' Minimum Urban Family Budgets, which showed clearly that families in even the richest states whose incomes derived entirely from welfare would be "enjoying" a seriously deficient standard of living. High turnover and low rates of income seemed to characterize both of our major antipoverty programs.

Anecdotal accounts of the extent to which the urban poor are forced to depend for part of their livelihood on illegal or other "irregular" activities have been available at least since the publication of the autobiographies of Claude Brown, Eldridge Cleaver, and Malcolm X.[13] Gradually, economists and sociologists began to realize that these activities were themselves organized into "markets," and that — given the unalterable constraints of the twenty-four hour day — ghetto workers might logically be assumed to allocate part of their labor time to "work" in the irregular market at the expense of time spent in other forms of income-bearing activity. When the structure of this "market" was explored, it was quickly found to be characterized by high turnover, unstable participation, and (after accounting for the high risks involved) relatively low average "wages." The similarity to the training and welfare "markets" was unmistakable — and quite dramatic.

Even before these discoveries were made, a few scholars had documented the existence and magnitude of "working poverty." In 1966, more than 7.3 million men and women in America were labor force participants and yet were poor.[14] In 1968, 1.3 million family heads worked thirty-five hours per week, fifty weeks a year, but still earned less than $3,500, the official poverty line then; 1.6 million part-time working family heads were also poor.[15] In terms of the much higher (but hardly luxurious) BLS Minimum Urban Family Budget, the incidence of working poverty was considerably greater: perhaps a third of all American families and 40 percent of the labor force had incomes in 1967 which fell below the BLS' "minimum" budget standard.[a] And in 1970, 4.7 million full-time male and 6.6 million full-time female workers earned less than the $1.60 per hour "minimum" wage.[16] These workers occupied a class of jobs which bore precisely the characteristics found to be associated with the above-mentioned non-labor market activities: low pay and high turnover. Moreover, evaluations of government institutions designed to place low-income workers into "good" jobs concluded that these placement programs were succeeding only in recirculating the poor among the very low-paying, unstable jobs which they already held.

Thus, a substantial number of seemingly disparate work activities and public programs were found to share certain important commonalities. Could these interrelationships be systematic? And if so, how did these various poverty income level activities relate to the conventional American mode of family support: non-poverty wage labor? These are some of the questions that have led to the development of the germ of a new labor market theory, often referred to as the "theory of the dual economy" or the "theory of labor market segmentation."[17]

---

[a]In 1967, one-third of all families earned less than the $6,000 BLS family standard. The median number of earners per family was 1.2. The equivalent BLS standard for individuals is therefore $5,000. In 1967, two-fifths of all persons earned less than $5,000.

The "Core" of the Economy

Dual market analysts believe the economy to be stratified into what Barry Bluestone calls a "core" and a "periphery" (see figure 2.1). The division is functional and not simply semantic; workers, employers, and even the underlying technologies in the two strata behave very differently in important

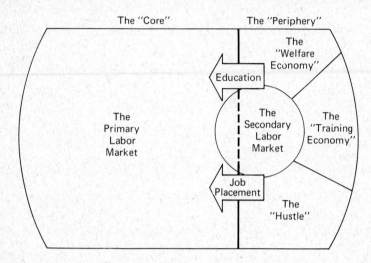

The "Core"   The "Periphery"

Figure 2-1. The Dual Economy.

qualitative ways. The central institution of the "core" has been called the "primary labor market," and this is the part of the core which we shall study here.[18] In the primary labor market, the attributes of jobs and the behavioral traits of workers interact (e.g., by mutual reinforcement) to produce a structure characterized by high productivity, non-poverty wages, and employment stability.

The high productivity of primary labor is a function not only of the knowledge and skills (i.e., the "human capital") of the workers, but also (and perhaps more fundamentally) of the capital equipment with which they generally work. The market power of the typical primary firm, and the relatively high degree of profitability which is the usual corollary of such power, enable the employer to invest in modern capital equipment (frequently embodying "leading edge" technologies), to maintain that equipment, and to replace it when necessary. The same factors make it possible for such firms to invest in the "human capital" of their employees, so that the equipment will be used efficiently. While this is, of course, an ideal construct, it does seem to be broadly descriptive of the technical conditions of production in the leading, highly concentrated industries in the American economy, and provides a plausible, albeit partial, explanation of the relatively high average productivity of the core of the American labor force.[19]

Primary employers typically pay non-poverty wages. This may be partly explained by the aforementioned high average and marginal productivity of core labor, but most dual market theorists prefer a more institutional explanation. The very economic power which underlies the profits which enable primary employers to make productivity-enhancing investments also permits them to pass along a share of wage (and other cost) increases to their customers. In other words, their oligopoly position *permits* them to maintain non-poverty wage levels without seriously eroding their profit margins. At the same time, the economic power of concentrated primary industries has induced the organization of what Galbraith calls "countervailing power" by labor unions. The evidence on how unions have affected the American wage structure is surprisingly ambiguous; there is, however, no question about the ability of unions to prevent employers from paying poverty-level wages.

There is an important feedback mechanism at work here. In conventional ("neoclassical") price theory, profit-maximizing employers are assumed to pay a wage rate for all workers equal to the value of the marginal product of labor: the contribution of the last worker hired to the firm's revenue. Some economists believe that the relationship between wages and productivity is more complex, that, in particular, work effort (and therefore measured productivity) may well be an increasing function of wages.[20] If this view is correct, then the relatively high wages which primary employers are able to pay (and which primary unions "encourage" them to pay) in turn induce the productivity increases by labor which (coming full circle) generate the profits out of which those non-poverty wages are paid.

Workers in the primary labor market tend to be relatively stable.[21] There are at least three plausible explanations of why primary employers value workforce stability. First, their investments in the "specific training" of their workers—training highly specific to the particular conditions of this particular firm (or plant) and not easily transferred to other work environments—represents a "sunk cost" which they naturally wish to recoup. Workers who quit before repaying this investment in the form of contributions to output must be replaced, and the replacements must then be trained anew. In the primary labor market, turnover is *obviously* expensive and therefore undesirable from the point of view of the employer.

A second and somewhat more controversial explanation has to do with the development within large firms of what Doeringer and Piore call the "internal labor market."[22] During the 1950s, economists discovered that large corporations had developed internal capital "markets" in the form of large pools of retained earnings, the existence of which helped to insulate them from the periodic increases in the external cost of capital (and as it turns out, from government anti-inflationary monetary policy as well).[23] With large stocks of internal capital, firms could engage in long-run capacity expansion plans without having to concern themselves with changes in interest rates. During normal times, investment capital could be borrowed as usual. When interest rates rose, perhaps through government policy designed to slow down corporate investment in new plant and equipment, the firm could turn to its internal capital "market," thereby enabling the "plan" to continue. Doeringer and Piore believe that a similar process has now developed within large corporations with respect to labor as well as capital. Firms can go into the external labor market at times when conditions, such as excess supply, favor the firm in the wage-bargaining process: an obvious example is the extent to which corporations flood college campuses at graduation time each year. Since the employer-employee relation in the core of the economy is often characterized by the use of fairly long-term contracts, firms can then retain (or "hoard") this relatively cheaply-bought labor against those times when external labor is more expensive. Such internal labor markets are, therefore, institutional manifestations of the employers' desire for workforce stability.

A third explanation of firms' demand for stability is derived from the work of Kenneth Arrow, who observed that most of what workers learn about the equipment and systems with which they work is probably really learned "on-the job"; it is "learning by doing."[24] The more complex the job, i.e., the more intricate or subtle the technology and the equipment, the longer it takes the average worker to "learn" the job and to reach the point where—for all practical purposes—he has obtained his peak of efficiency. The concept is illustrated by figure 2.2, where the typical "learning curve" is represented by a logistic. However "productivity" is measured, the question is: for any given job, how

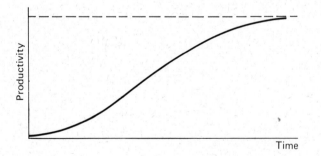

Figure 2-2. Hypothetical Learning Curves in the Primary Labor Market.

long does it take the average worker to reach his or her maximum efficiency? Is the concept of an asymptotic maximum (a limit to individual) efficiency meaningful for that job? If so, is the average learning period three weeks, three months, or three years? Consider the contrast between keypunch operators and computer operators. Both are very nearly unskilled or at best semi-skilled jobs; student computer operators are often trained by their colleges in a week. Any upper limit to the potential productivity of a computer operator is undoubtedly quite "high," so varied are the technical possibilities for performing the highly discretionary tasks associated with this job, e.g., filing, classifying, and retrieving tapes, learning to take advantage of the capabilities of a system with respect to the batching of "jobs," discovering and accommodating oneself to the idiosyncracies of one's fellow operators. Contrast this with keypunch operators who—like clerk-typists—tend increasingly to be organized into large work pools and whose maximum efficiency is essentially determined by their physical dexterity and the capacity of their machines. Once such workers reach their maximum punching, or typing, speed, continued tenure is unlikely to lead to significant improvements (and may very well lead to the opposite, as the job becomes "routine"). An even more dramatic contrast exists between the clerk-typist and the executive secretary. The latter may literally never "peak out"; he or she has to learn not only the mechanics of the job, but is also continually in the process of acquiring such subtle skills as the ability to locate his or her boss' business (and perhaps even extra-business) associates at any hour of the day at any of their favorite haunts. Clearly, it is to the employer's advantage to retain an employee whose capacity for improvement has not been exhausted.

At the same time, workers in most primary jobs seem to *want* to remain in those jobs, at least for a noticeably longer period than is the case for what we will later call "secondary workers." This is admittedly somewhat vague; while the threshhold between "primary" and "secondary" wages seems to have been quantitatively identified – at from $2.25 to $3.50 per hour – very little quantitative work has yet to be perfomred on the tenure variable. The jobs pay relatively well, and employers, as we have seen, encourage the workers to stay. This stability of the workforce feeds back into the wage-bargaining process. Stable workers are more easily organized, and unions generally prefer to organize stable rather than unstable workers, perhaps because of the obvious consequences for strike funds, etc. To the extent that this unionization is successful, it reinforces the maintenance of non-poverty wages (as described earlier), which, in turn, induces the continued stability which, in turn, supports unionization, ad infinitum.

Efficient operation of the primary labor market requires the development of certain behavioral attitudes on the part of workers and employers, attitudes which it is the purpose of such social institutions as the educational system to inculcate. Herbert Gintis writes that:

Economists have long noted the relationship between the level of schooling in workers and their earnings . . . Almost no attempt has been made, however, to determine the mechanism by which education affects earnings or productivity. In the absence of any direct evidence, it is commonly assumed that the main effect of schooling is to raise the level of cognitive development of students and that it is this increase which explains the relationship between schooling and earnings. This view of the schooling-earnings linkage has provided the conceptual framework for studies which seek to "control" for the quality of schooling through the use of variables such as scores on achievement tests and I.Q.

The objective of this paper is to demonstrate that this interpretation is fundamentally incorrect.[25]

Instead, Gintis believes that "schools affect earnings" by creating an internal "social structure" whose "authority, motivational, and interpersonal relations" are designed to replicate "those of the factory and office." One of the most important instruments of this social development process is the grading system which, quite apart from (and beyond) its ostensible function of measuring cognitive ability, affords "independent reward to the development of traits necessary to adequate job performance."[26] Samuel Bowles has uncovered evidence that eighteenth and nineteenth century manufacturers consciously supported public education as a means of teaching young people, at public expense, discipline, punctuality, acceptance of outside authority, and individual accountability — behavioural traits crucial for the efficient operation of the factory system.[27]

Taken alone, there is nothing either novel or obviously pathological about these observations. Schools prepare students — behaviorally as well as technically — for the "world of work"; every manpower training agent and antipoverty warrior takes this for granted. The problem, according to Gintis, is that society and its individual members pay a very high price for the "pre-vocational training" which schools provide for primary employers. "The economic productivity of schooling is due primarily to the inculcation of personality characteristics which may be generally agreed to be inhibiting of personal development." Gintis analyzes a rich body of data on "649 upper-ability senior high school males (National Merit Scholarship Finalists)" who were scored on five achievement variables (e.g., scientific performance, humanities comprehension) and sixty-five personality variables, and a second group of 114 high school seniors "of varying ability." The measures of achievement were then correlated with the measures of personality. Gintis found that "schooling is conducive to the development of [those] traits . . . requisite for adequate job functioning in production characterized by bureaucratic order and hierarchical control." Personality traits such as perseverance, self-control, suppression of aggression, and deferred gratification were positively correlated with achievement scores. But the data also showed that "students are uniformly penalized for creativity, autonomy, initiative, tolerance for ambiguity, and independence, even after correcting for achievement."[28] From these results, and from the inference that "successful" students and workers even in the core of the economy must have learned to suppress their most creative and deeply human personality traits in order to *be* successful, Gintis concludes that "The economic productivity of schooling must be measured against an opportunity cost reflected in the development of an alienated and repressed labor force."[29]

The "Periphery" of the Economy

The so-called "periphery" of the American economy is assumed to consist of at least four "segments," the manpower characteristics of which are remarkably similar to one another (figure 2.1). Mobility among these segments seems to take place regularly, while, by contrast, workers in the peripheral stratum are able to move into the core of the economy only very infrequently.

The "Secondary Labor Market"

Research — much of it concerned with the study of ghetto labor markets[30] — has indicated the existence of a class of jobs which contrast sharply with the primary labor market along each of the three dimensions we have discussed.

Secondary workers tend to display relatively low average and marginal productivity. Until recently, one explanation for this was the dearth of "human capital," particularly formal education of at least average quality, possessed by these workers. While this continues to provide a partial explanation, it is becoming increasingly less convincing as even ghetto blacks gradually close the education gap between themselves and the average American. By 1970, the gap between the median schooling of young whites and blacks had fallen to less than half a year, as the figures in table 2.1 show.

In any case, the importance of formal education in determining worker productivity is itself now in some doubt, as we have seen. Probably more

Table 2.1
Median Years of Schooling, for Blacks and Whites, by Age

Age	Median Years of School Completed	
	Blacks	Whites
20-21 years	12.4	12.8
22-24	12.3	12.7
25-29	12.2	12.6
30-34	12.0	12.5

Source: U.S. Department of Commerce, Bureau of the Census, *Current Population Reports,* Series P-23, No. 38 (BLS Report No. 394), "The Social and Economic Status of Negroes in the United States, 1970," Washington, D.C., July, 1971, Table 65.

important is the absence of economic power in this segment of the periphery of the economy. With little or no oligopolistic market control, and with small profit margins, secondary firms tend to use more antiquated capital, which, of course, tends to diminish productivity. Finally, the jobs themselves often do not *require* skills of any great consequence, involving instead the kind of routine unskilled tasks which attract (and at the same time reinforce the life styles of) casual laborers.

Workers in the secondary labor market receive, and firms in this stratum of the economy pay, very low wages. During the period July 1968 to June 1969, 37 percent of the black and 51 percent of the Puerto Rican male household heads living in Harlem and working at least thirty-five hours a week, fifty weeks a year averaged less than $100 per week in earnings. Nationally, in 1966, 36.3 percent of all employees working in nursing homes and related facilities earned less than $1.60 per hour, the legal minimum wage. For employees of laundry and cleaning services, fertilizer manufacturers, eating and drinking places, gasoline service stations, and retail food stores, the 1966 percentages were 75.4 percent, 41.7 percent, 79.4 percent, 66.7 percent, and 47.6 percent (table 1.3).[31] Annual wage income is the product of an average wage *rate* and the number of hours, days or weeks during the year in which a person works. The instability of secondary labor (discussed shortly) drives down the duration of work, while the economic structure of the peripheral firm causes it to pay a low wage rate. Taken together, these factors guarantee that workers will be forced to subsist on a poverty-level income — to the extent that they rely for income entirely on what they can earn in the secondary labor market. Low productivity contributes to the explanation of these low wages, but so does the lack of market power among peripheral employers. Moreover (as indicated earlier), dual labor market theorists believe that these factors are interdependent; the marginal firm, by paying low wages and by not providing its workers with adequate complementary capital, discourages its labor force from taking those actions or developing those attitudes which would lead to increased productivity which, if capitalized, could increase the firm's capacity to pay higher wages. The lack of economic power which characterizes peripheral firms (as reflected, for example, in the relatively high elasticity of their output demand curves) also makes it impossible for them to raise wages and other input costs without eroding profit margins, perhaps to the shut-down point. Finally, the low wages found in the secondary labor market are partly the result of the relative simplicity of the technologies in secondary industries; since skill requirements are minimal, the opportunity cost of secondary labor is low, given the large pool of readily available substitutable workers out "on the street."

While the primary labor market is characterized by a mutual employer-employee "taste" for stability, both firms and workers in the secondary labor market seem to benefit from unstable workforce behavior. That secondary labor is significantly more unstable than primary labor is incontestable. Hall, for example, writes:

Some groups exhibit what seems to be pathological instability in holding jobs. Changing from one low-paying, unpleasant job to another, often several times a year, is the typical pattern of some workers. The resulting unemployment can hardly be said to be the outcome of a normal process of career advancement. The true problem of hard-core unemployment is that a certain fraction of the labor force accounts for a disproportionate share of unemployment because they drift from one unsatisfactory job to another, spending the time between jobs either unemployed or out of the labor force [where they go when they drop out of the labor force will be discussed later]. The most compact evidence in favor of the hypothesis that such a group exists is provided by the data on the number of spells of unemployment experienced by the labor force. Among those who were unemployed at some time in 1968, 69 percent had only one spell of unemployment, 15 percent had two spells and 16 percent had three or more. Now the overall unemployment rate in 1968 was 3.6 percent. Suppose that the average person changing jobs required one month to find a satisfactory new job. Then the average duration between spells of unemployment would be about twenty-seven months. In order to have two, much less three, spells of unemployment in the same twelve months, an individual could hardly be making normal changes in jobs, even if it is true that the normal person changes jobs every twenty-eight months. Yet almost a third of those unemployed at all in 1968, more than three million individuals, had two or more spells. The existence of this group is surely a matter of social concern.[32]

In their studies of the hard-core unemployed in St. Louis, Edward Kalachek and his colleagues concluded that "the relatively high rates of unemployment experienced by St. Louis Negroes appear to be more the result of frequent job changes than of the inability to find employment . . . Job stability develops and unemployment experiences diminish among older workers with dependents . . . For our sample, however, the stabilizing influence of age was not discernible until respondents were in their early 30's."[33] The researchers tested for differential work attitudes and values between the young blacks who were their principal object of study and control groups of other workers.

A number of respondents, particularly young men in the fifteen to eighteen years of age category, admitted to engaging in nonlegitimate "hustles" . . . Still like other younger members of the study population, [such individuals] clearly see the value of jobs and education . . . The high quit rates of young Negroes appear due not to a deviant value system, but to the frustration of low-wage-paying jobs . . . Younger workers appear less willing or able to accept poverty level wages when they perceive the value system of the "American Dream" to be promising more.[34]

Secondary employers have several reasons for placing a low value on turnover, in sharp contrast to their fellows in the primary labor market. They can, as a rule, neither afford nor do their technologies require them to invest heavily in "specific training." Instead, they tend to rely on the "general training" (e.g., literacy, basic arithmetic) provided socially. With minimal investment in their current labor force, and given the ready availability of substitute labor outside the firm, such employers are at the very least indifferent to the rate of turnover. Moreover, these firms lack the size and wealth necessary for the development of internal labor markets. Nor have they any reason to want to develop such institutions; since their skill requirements are minimal, they are unlikely to encounter periods where the labor they need is scarce and therefore expensive to recruit through conventional ("external") labor markets. Finally, everything we have hypothesized about the technology of secondary industries implies that the typical job is easily and quickly learned, so that learning curves probably look more like that depicted in figure 2.3 than that shown in figure 2.2. We have

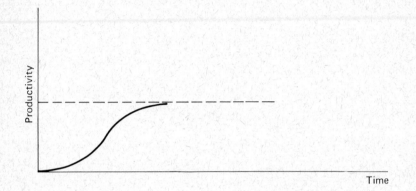

Figure 2-3. Hypothetical Learning Curves in the Secondary Labor Market.

already discussed some of the implications of the shape of this function. It may be added at this point that to keep a worker employed for an extended period usually requires the granting of raises in pay and various employee benefits. Moreover, there is a definite correlation between labor force stability and the probability of that force being organized. It follows that employers who already have little to lose (in terms of foregone output) by discouraging long tenure of specific workers will have still other rational reasons for discounting stability.

Workers, for their part, seem similarly to have a rational preference for instability in the secondary labor market. The jobs are boring, and do not pay well. Employers seem not to mind — and perhaps even to encourage — casual attitudes toward work. The penalities for poor industrial discipline are generally not severe. Doeringer's studies of antipoverty programs in Boston led him to conclude about the job placement system for ghetto workers that it was seldom able to refer its clients to jobs paying more than they were earning before — "only $2.00 an hour or less." This lack of upward mobility in the placement system contributes to the poor work habits and weak job attachment of the "hard-to-employ": "The availability of alternative low-wage job opportunities and the unattractiveness of such low-wage work interact to discourage the formation of strong ties to particular employers." That low wages are the principal motivating factor seems to be confirmed by the finding that, "for wage rates higher than the 'prevailing' ghetto wage, disadvantaged workers are more likely to be stable employees than other workers." These relationships between tenure and wage rates were found to be at best only weakly related to the educational attainment of the workers.[35] And, of course, this entirely rational instability frustrates union organization so that there is no pressure for change, e.g., improvement in wages and working conditions — pressure which has been institutionalized in the core of the economy.

Thus, where primary employers and employees interact in an institutional setting characterized by high productivity, non-poverty level wages and high workforce stability, the firms and work forces in the secondary labor market tend to organize themselves into production systems displaying low productivity, poverty level wages and low stability (high turnover). It is interesting to observe that what appears to be "subemployment" or "underemployment" from the conventional persepective of an essentially unified economy is now seen to be the *normal* mode of employment in a backwater of that economy, a sector cut off from the mainstream.

The "Welfare Economy"

The principal conclusion to be drawn from the previous description of the secondary labor market is that it is virtually impossible for an individual confined to that segment of the periphery to earn a living. This simple fact motivates the supply of part of the peripheral worker's time and effort to other income-bearing activities. The most obvious (or at least the most widely-publicized) of these alternative "activities" is to "go on welfare." According to the Manpower Administration of the U.S. Department of Labor:

Another possible alternative to low-wage, irregular jobs for some slum residents, especially women with children but no husbands to help in family support, is public assistance. The division of the poor between those with jobs and those depending on welfare is by no means stable or clear cut. Women may receive assistance in some months of the year and work in other months, or they may be on welfare and at the same time work openly or covertly.[36]

Recipients of (Aid to Families with Dependent Children) have been widely regarded as caught in a chronic, static condition of dependency, handed down from one generation to the next. Welfare has been viewed as an alternative to work, increasingly unrelated to such economic factors as the general level of unemployment or the participation of women in the labor force . . . But there are also many families whose members are on welfare rolls for very short periods of time and never sever their connection with the labor force, even when they are on welfare.[37]

There is substantial evidence that many people on welfare display much the same kind of turnover found in the secondary labor market. In 1966, about 12 percent of the AFDC cases closed in that year were closed because of the employment (or re-employment) of the individual. In the same year, one million AFDC cases were carried over from the previous year, but 584,000 new cases were authorized and 508,000 cases were closed. "Averaged over the year, about 45,000 new families were added to the rolls each month, while 41,000 left." Moreover, "of the cases added in 1966, about thirty-four percent had received assistance previously"; i.e., had been on welfare, dropped off, and were now enrolling again.

In the same edition of the *Manpower Report of the President* from which I have been quoting, the Labor Department recognized that, according to the conventional wisdom, "Welfare and employment are widely regarded as alternative rather than complementary or overlapping sources of income. The AFDC caseload is generally seen as made up of nonworking mothers."[38] In fact, however, large numbers of "welfare mothers" work – in the secondary labor market. Indeed, "Public assistance often serves as a form of wage supplementation for the low-paid, partially employed worker."[39]

In 1961, some 26 percent of the white and 41 percent of the black children on the AFDC rolls had mothers who worked at least part-time, half of them regularly. A study of the Philadelphia AFDC caseload in 1962 showed that only 13 percent of the mothers had no history of work. Most remarkable of all, of those who did have a work history, "forty percent had been employed in skilled or semi-skilled jobs."[40] In a study of the Harlem economy, Professor Thomas Vietorisz and I found that nearly 38 percent of the workers unemployed in November 1966 lived in families which received some form of welfare during that year. Of the full-time employed, 6.7 percent, and of the part-time employed, 11.8 percent of the workers had families who received welfare that year.[41]

Just as the "welfare economy" shares the peripheral characteristic of instability, so it is that the typical "rate" of welfare income in the U.S. is extremely low – the conventional wisdom about welfare and Cadillacs notwithstanding. In 1966, of the 3.1 million people who received public assistance, only 304,000 (less than 10 percent) were in families (cases) receiving more than $2,000 during the entire year; only 834,000 (a quarter of the total) received more than $1,000.[42] This little-known fact about the *magnitude* of the average welfare payment obtains in even the wealthiest urban areas. In New York, for example, the average weekly welfare allowance in 1967 for a family of four was only $63.22 (during the same year, manufacturing workers in the city averaged $106.60 per week). Even the poorest-paying industry in the city – rubber and miscellaneous plastics – paid an average wage of $87.20, almost $25 a week above the welfare "rate."[43]

It is also possible to get a fix on the combined work-welfare possibilities for New York City. A sample survey conducted in June 1964 revealed that "over twenty-five percent" of the city's welfare recipients "were earning hourly rates of less than $1.25" in the secondary labor market, "sixty percent [were] below $1.50, and all but a smattering [were] below $2.00." In 1966, 90 percent of all the jobs solicited by one Human Resources Administrator for welfare recipients paid between $1.25 and $1.75 per hour.[44] In the four principal ghettos of New York City, over the period July 1967 to June 1969, "families headed by women drawing welfare allowances at some time during the year preceding the interview had a median income of $2,713 . . . such a mother . . . would need to have grossed $74 in weekly wages in order to earn what she would receive in welfare allowances, and to pay for work-related expenses . . . for employed poverty-area women heading households and working full-time, weekly gross earnings [in fact] averaged $84 per week during the survey period [but] close to one-third of these women earned less than $75."[45]

Workers' willingness to accept jobs paying less than (say) $1.30 to $1.60 per hour appears to depend upon the availability of supplemental forms of income — such as welfare. If workers refused to take such low-paying jobs, many firms would — predicts Bluestone — go bankrupt and many services would — in Gans' view — go unproduced. It is in this sense that the welfare system may be said to constitute a public subsidy for low-wage "secondary" employers.

The Training Economy

The Johnson Administration officially recognized that "a man may enroll in one of the training programs which pay stipends, in order to get funds to tide him over a lean period."[46] More recently, *New York Times* reporter John Herbers wrote:

a good many of the manpower training programs are tending to become more of a holding action to keep people out of the unemployed columns than a means of putting them permanently into the work force. There are reports of men going out of one training program into another.[47]

In fact, at least one official program (STEP) is designed explicitly for the purpose of providing "further training" for those program graduates unable to find work.

The training programs of the federal government have thus taken on the basic attributes of the peripheral stratum of the economy: low "wages" and low stability. Cumulative figures from 1968 through January 1970 show that, of 84,703 actual hires in the National Alliance of Businessmen's Job Opportunities in the Business Sector program (initiated by President Johnson and Henry Ford II), 50,225 quit or were laid off. The high implicit quit rate is not surprising;

jobs in the NAB-JOBS program paid low wages, the core employers participating in the program often segregated their "hard-core" workers from the "mainstream" force, and layoffs were (as indicated) highly probable. In fact, one steel firm reported to an investigating congressional committee that, since layoffs are "an inherent part of the American economy," it used part of the Manpower Administration subsidies "in counseling for anticipated layoffs. Many of the trainees at this firm since have been laid off."[48]

Of the several components of the relatively new Public Service Careers Program, only the New Careerists receive a training stipend, which averaged $2,819 per trainee in 1968.[49] The Department of Labor recently reported that 40 percent of the New Careerists leave the program within the first six months of training.[50] Again, we see the combination of low earnings and high turnover which are the identification marks of the peripheral economy.

Sar Levitan and Robert Taggert III describe the government's principal program for young dropouts, the Neighborhood Youth Corps:

Almost all are entry level positions requiring few skills. Men are usually assigned to maintenance and custodial work, while women typically work in clerical or health positions. Most [jobs] pay near the minimum wage [$1.60 an hour], with extra stipends for household heads with dependents . . . Stripped of their titles, almost all the jobs were menial and unattractive . . . A comprehensive follow-up of enrollees leaving the program between January and September, 1966, found that forty weeks after termination, less than two-fifths were employed (and) more than a fourth were not in the labor force . . . [51]

The Work Incentive Program guarantees participants a minimum of $30 a month plus their normal welfare payment (which we have already seen to be extremely small). Together, these still constitute a poverty-level income. A major evaluation of the WIN program was completed recently, in which individual project performance was measured by an index consisting of six variables, including enrollee course completion rates and the proportion of WIN graduates who are successfully placed into jobs. This weighted index is then related to enrollee characteristics (race, age, sex, and educational attainment) and to program characteristics (fifty-six variables measuring project staff efforts and capabilities, interagency linkages, the attention given to new enrollees, training activities themselves, placement activities, and supportive services). The study found that completion rates are not significantly related to the activities of the project staff, to the quantity and quality of the training imparted, or to how well or how poorly the program is geared to place its graduates. Then, in trying to explain intercity variations both in the placement rate and in the composite six-variable index itself, the evaluators found that the only class of variables that "counted" were those entirely exogenous to the WIN system: the measures of the strength of the demand for labor in the local market (e.g., the unemployment rate, average hourly wages, job vacancies, etc.):

From the data available to this study it appears that systematic variation in WIN program inputs has no impact on overall WIN effectiveness. There is no suggestion whatsoever in the empirical record that better staff, interagency cooperation, supportive services, or other program components will enhance aggregate, or even particularized WIN outputs. Much the same degree of effectiveness has been achieved by local programs of widely divergent quality.

A very similar conclusion has been reached concerning the characteristics of WIN enrollees ... Programs with higher proportions of whites, males, high school graduates, or prime-aged enrollees [in other words, programs which engage in "creaming"] do not perform better than other programs ... Labor market conditions appear to be the only relevant determinant of local WIN effectiveness.[52]

These findings are easily explicable in terms of the dual labor market theory. If workers treat training programs as temporary sources of income, then we would expect their tenure to be more or less insensitive to changes in any program element other than the training wage. The finding on placement and overall program effectiveness can be explained with the same apparatus. Employers in the primary labor market will, for the most part, simply not hire the poor, regardless of the training acquired by the latter. Note the similarity between this premise and that employed by Ms. Bergmann in the "crowding hypothesis."

It has recently become possible to examine the attitudes of discriminating employers. Following the 1967 riots, the National Advisory Commission on Civil Disorders (the Kerner Commission) asked the Department of Social Relations at Johns Hopkins University to study "the interface between [city] institutions and urban ghettos" by interviewing samples of policemen, educators, social workers, merchants, and political party personnel, all of whom worked inside the ghetto. The Johns Hopkins sociologists also interviewed the personnel officers of 434 large firms in fifteen cities who might, by virtue of their size and location, be in a position to hire workers from the ghetto. The survey researchers concluded that

... the employers as a group tend to see Negroes as simply not qualified – by preparatory institutions or by past employment experiences – for good jobs. [Yet] forty-one percent of the employers had no Negro applicants or did not know the number of Negroes among the last twenty persons applying to their firms for white collar jobs. Forty-eight percent report no recent experiences with Negro applicants for skilled level openings. We can surmise then that the potential "Negro employee" is for a large number of our employers an applicant seeking laborer's work.[53]

These are the attitudes of primary employers. Secondary employers, who will (indeed must) hire these workers, do not require training, and so are indifferent to the "quality" of the training that, for example, WIN enrollees receive, i.e., to variations in program characteristics. Moreover, the same underlying conditions which explain this disinterest in training — the relative simplicity of secondary industry skill requirements and the ready availability of unskilled labor on the street — also account for the willingness of these employers to accept blacks, women, youths, and dropouts. It is thus altogether predictable that intercity variations in placement rates would be independent of enrollee characteristics.

The "Hustle:" Ferman's "Irregular Economy"

Our analysis thus far indicates that a labor supply model which ignores the welfare and training economies as possible objects of part of the attention (and time) of the urban poor is clearly incomplete. And there is still another source of unconventional income available to ghetto dwellers, the existence of which confounds the neoclassical analysis even further. This is the set of activities which Ferman and (then) Fusfeld have named the "irregular economy."[54] "A man may have his own type of hustle — an easy way to money, sometimes legitimate, sometimes partly not, that puts him in a quasi-entrepreneurial role."[55] While all irregular activity is not illegal, it is the latter type of "work" which is undoubtedly the most controversial — and the most lucrative (although the high risk associated with narcotics distribution, grand theft, and other serious criminal activities probably induces the same kind of discontinuous work patterns found elsewhere in the periphery of the economy, with the result that annual income is still relatively low for all but a very few professional criminals).

Stanley Friedlander's interviews in Harlem have led him to conclude that perhaps two-fifths of all adults in that ghetto had some illegal income in 1966, and that 20 percent appeared to exist entirely on money derived from illegal sources (it is, for obvious reasons, not possible to quantify this illegal income.)

The young people interviewed had little hope of significant increases in [legal] earnings, because they saw so little chance of an occupational breakthrough. At best, they expected marginal employment at wages which would allow them to "get by" . . .

Hustling was often regarded as a logical and rational option. The market for gambling, numbers, prostitution, and narcotics is large and highly profitable, and the possibility of "being on one's own" competes powerfully with the opportunities available in the regulated middle-class world.

Criminal activities and the possible handicap of an arrest record did not seem to present problems for these Harlem youth . . . No great social stigma accompanies arrest, so far as the immediate neighborhood is concerned. Job opportunities are already limited by other barriers, so that the effect of an arrest record is not considered important. The probability of being apprehended is considered relatively small. And the penalty for a particular offense, if one is caught, can be calculated with reasonable accuracy.[56]

Friedlander also found that the unemployment rates in sixteen cities in 1966 correlated negatively with the crime rates in these cities, suggesting that, "the larger the sources of illegal income, the fewer the people in the slums who persist in looking for legitimate jobs (or the greater the numbers who report themselves as employed when they are not, in order to explain their style of life to the enumerators)." This makes it clear why conventional labor-leisure constructs must be expanded in order more realistically to "model" the time-allocation decision process in the inner city.

Intersectoral Mobility

This chapter began with references to the elaborate mythology which has developed in America, according to which generations of immigrants were allegedly able to lift themselves out of poverty through education and training. During the "manpower decade" of the 1960s, moreover, billions of dollars were expended on the operation of public job placement institutions. It is therefore important to examine the extent to which "upward" mobility from the periphery to the core of the economy is facilitated (or hindered) by the school and job placement systems to which peripheral workers and their children have access.

We may begin with the school system; it is to this piece of the "puzzle" that the results of my own basic research are addressed. The purpose of my doctoral dissertation was to estimate the "payoff" to investments in the human capital of nonwhite urban workers, taking explicit account of whether they live in a core city ghetto (or Census poverty area), in the non-ghetto central city, or in the suburban ring. Three measures of "payoff" were specified: weekly earnings, average annual unemployment or the conditional probability of being unemployed, and occupational status (as measured by a scoring procedure which assigns an ordinal rank of 0-100 to each of 308 Census occupational titles). The policy variables of interest were years of school completed and participation in any of five formal training programs; all were given dummy variable specifications to permit tests for nonlinearity. Control variables specified both additively and interactively included age, sex, race, and industry group in which the person works (the latter serves also as a proxy for the complementary capital with which the person works).

The primary sample studied consisted of over 11,000 micro household interviews from the twelve largest SMSAs in the country, drawn from (even more extensive) interviews conducted in March 1966 and March 1967 by the Bureau of the Census for the Office of Economic Opportunity. These data files are referred to as the *Survey of Economic Opportunity.*

Additional samples studied (using somewhat different models) were drawn from the nearly 40,000 household interviews from the eight cities (ten ghettos) in the *1966 Urban Employment Survey.* These are Department of Labor materials.

Multivariate regression analysis showed (1) that ghetto nonwhites lag significantly behind even ghetto whites in terms of economic welfare; (2) that the economic welfare of urban nonwhites is relatively insensitive to variations in intrametropolitan residential location, although the economic welfare of whites increases substantially with the "move" from ghetto to non-ghetto central city to suburbs; and (3) that the returns to education for ghetto nonwhites are significant in terms of improved occupational status, nominal in terms of higher wages, and statistically insignificant in terms of reduced probabilities of unemployment (the number of trainees in the samples was insufficient to permit confident inference about the impact of training programs on the welfare of ghetto residents). Taken together, this third set of findings assigns a quantitative dimension to the concept of underemployment which has heretofore been unavailable in studies of poverty, discrimination, urban, and labor economics.

That the white-nonwhite welfare differentials (i.e., the differences in earnings, unemployment and occupational status) remain – even among samples of similarly-educated individuals living in the same urban neighborhoods – suggests the need for a major reorientation in both our intellectual and policy approaches to poverty. Specifically, we must shift our emphasis away from exclusive concentration on the alleged "defects" of the poor themselves toward the investigation of defects in the market system which constrains the poor from realizing their potential.

These studies compel us to conclude that the public education system does not – by itself, at any rate – promote the kind of intersectoral mobility for the peripheral worker which he or she has been led to expect. What effect *does* education have, then, particularly on ghetto blacks? For a small number, it probably does provide access to primary jobs. But the expectation certainly is otherwise. It follows that, with blacks crowded disporportionately into the secondary labor market, increasing educational investments *ceteris paribus* may only increase the effective supply of secondary labor, which might then drive black wages down even further.

Two different explanations of this insufficiency of education may be proposed. From the point of view of conventional liberal theory (i.e., a racially discriminating, but structurally integrated economy), a "market imperfection" (discrimination) is preventing the education system from functioning in its "normal capacity." In a nondiscriminating economy, those ghetto workers who made the effort to "lift themselves up" by investments in their own "human capital" *would* be rewarded with higher incomes, fewer unemployment "spells", and higher status jobs.[5,7]

Bowles and Gintis, on the other hand, would argue that the "normal capacity" or true social function of the education system is not so much to develop job skills as to socialize young people to the roles they are most likely to play as adult workers, given their (and their parents') place in the class structure.

By this interpretation, the low returns to education received by the urban poor of both races and particularly by blacks are not the result of improper or inadequate functioning of the ghetto schools. Quite the contrary; those schools are performing precisely the function they are "intended" to perform. Their indulgence of irregular behavior (within the classroom and in terms of class attendance) prepares their students for the peripheral lifestyle which the majority of them will probably be forced to adopt. The stifling of creativity and imagination reported so often by such educational critics as Edgar Friedenberg, Ivan Illich, Jonathan Kozol, and Christopher Jencks conditions ghetto children to accept the uncreative, routine kind of unskilled work which most of them will be required to perform after they "graduate." Most important of all, the failure of ghetto schoolteachers and education programs to acquaint their students with primary lifestyles, and the tendency of teachers and guidance counsellors to "steer" their students into secondary jobs,[58] have the latent function of frustrating the development among lower-class youth of aspirations which might become socially destabilizing. That such aspirations are often formed anyway, and that the kind of schooling we are analyzing has not succeeded completely in preventing social tension, is due not so much to the inability of the schoools to train productive workers because of discrimination as to the fact that the educational system does not operate in a vacuum. Other forces, over which the schools have little or no control (e.g., mass communication, the emergence of black pride and, in some places, volatile black nationalism) have – by this theory – interfered with the "normal function" of the schools. That function, to repeat, is to prepare lower-class students for secondary social and economic roles.

Another institution whose ostensible function is to promote "upward" mobility is the elaborate placement system developed over the last forty years. Students of the operation of these systems – some of which were developed explicit for the purpose of "helping the poor" in the periphery of the economy – have concluded that placement programs have not made significant contributions to intersectoral mobility. Earl Main studied the institutional training programs financed under the Manpower Development and Training Act. He concludes that the placement function has succeeded in helping the disadvantaged to find new jobs, but not in increasing their wage incomes.[59] Doeringer's study of the poverty program in Boston came to a similar conclusion.[60] Together, these results imply that government placement programs simply *recirculate* the poor among a class of employers who tend to pay low wages. In other words, public programs designed to promote mobility in fact serve as a recruiting instrument for employers in the secondary labor market.

This interpretation is argued most forcefully by Stephan Michelson, who addresses himself to the U.S. Training and Employment Service, the government's principal placement institution:

With local budgets often being a function of placements, local offices are discouraged from sending Negroes for jobs from which they will be automatically excluded. Thus, [U.S.T.] ES tacitly aids the job discrimination which, with a different administrative procedure, it could confront.[61]

Recently, the Urban Coalition cosponsored a penetrating evaluation of U.S.T.E.S., which supports the hypotheses presented previously about the de facto role of government job placement programs.

The Employment Service today is an inflexible bureaucracy, absorbed in its own paper work, with a staff that is either incapable of or disinterested in committing the resources necessary to make the chronically unemployed self-supporting. The inability of the ES to provide meaningful assistance results in more individuals dropping out of the labor force, thereby contributing to the very problems the manpower programs were designed to solve. In 1970, despite a growing national work force and increased unemployment, only 11.5 percent of the work force sought out the service of the ES' 2,200 local offices. Those who actually received job placements as a result of ES assistance represented 5.3 percent of the work force.

The jobs listed with the Service have decreased over the past five years and, for the most part, represent only the lowest levels of the economy. Almost half are considered unfillable by ES administrators because of low salaries, excessive job requirements or untenable working conditions. For their part, employers view the ES as the placement agency of last resort. Major employers, including state and local governments, conduct their own recruiting or rely on public advertising.[62]

More explicitly,

The chief weakness of the ES with regard to minorities is that it mirrors the attitudes of employers in the community. The ES could provide a model of vigilance and aggressiveness toward affirmative action for equal employment opportunity. Instead, it is frequently a passive accessory to discriminatory employment practices; it is widely viewed in that light by the minority community.[63]

That U.S.T.E.S. placements are concentrated in what we have been calling the secondary labor market is illustrated by the fact that "over sixty percent of [non-agricultural U.S.T.E.S.] placements are in positions receiving less than $1.60 per hour."[64] Only 5 percent of U.S. placements in fiscal 1969 were in the professional, technical, or managerial categories.[65] That nonwhites are placed in the least desirable of this class of generally undesirable jobs is exemplified by the fact that (again) in fiscal 1969, between 80 and 100 percent of all domestic service placements among the largest states were assigned to nonwhites.[66]

Public Employment and the Dual Labor Market

Having presented an outline of the emerging theory of economic dualism in the United States, it is now possible to turn to one theme of these Upjohn Seminars: is there a special role in antipoverty and manpower development policy for public service employment? How does the public as an employer fit into the segmented market model?

Locked out of existing primary jobs by discrimination, class bias, and the institutionalized perogatives of primary labor, and segregated into the peripheral economy with its secondary jobs and "irregular" means of supporting a family, the urban poor (and indeed the working poor everywhere) need *new jobs*. These jobs must offer adequate pay, promotional opportunities, and attractive benefits. They must be *stable* jobs, and this stability may be exactly what is needed to motivate the development among the disadvantaged of new attitudes toward the "world of work." Finally, the new jobs must be accessible to the poor, in terms of both location and skill requirements. In other words, we desperately need in the United States an explicit economic development policy. As Bluestone notes: "Funds for economic development — the creation of new jobs and new and expanded industries — were limited to a total of $508 million in 1969, less than a quarter of the budget for manpower programs,"[67] and less than three-tenths of 1 percent of the $185 billion federal budget in that year.

By each of the criteria of primary labor market activity — relatively high wages and job stability, for example — public service employment may be shown to fall squarely within the core of the economy.[68]

Public Sector Wages. Among all full-time, year-round workers in 1968, over 12 percent of those who were employed in the private sector of the economy earned less than $3,000 in wages. Among full-time *public* sector employees, however, only 5 percent earned less than that amount. For black men, the two figures were 16.3 percent and 7 percent respectively. For black women, they were 49.3 percent and 15.5 percent. These private sector-public sector comparisons hold up with thresholds at least as high at $6,000. For example, nearly 28 percent of all full-time, year-round male private sector workers in 1968 earned less than $6,000; among public employees, the figure was only 15.9 percent. For both sexes and races, there are apparently fewer poverty-level jobs in the public than in the private sector, even after education workers have been removed from the public sector totals. This is confirmed by a recent National Planning Association study of a 1966 sample of poor persons, using unpublished Census data. For individuals aged 16-64 and living in poverty, NPA found that only 1.6 percent of those who were employed full-time in 1966 — the "working poor" — worked in the public sector, contrasted with 20.5 percent in manufacturing and 23.5 percent in other (private) services. My own studies of low income workers living in central city ghettos, non-ghetto central city neighborhoods, and suburban communities show that, for whites and nonwhites of both sexes (and regardless of where in the metropolitan area they happen to live), public sector jobs pay significantly higher weekly wages and salaries than do private sector jobs.

The Middle Atlantic Bureau of Labor Statistics Office conducted a comparative analysis of public and private sector wages in New York for the year 1970. Among the conclusions of this study was the finding that "the pay rates for 1,350 maintenance workers employed by the city — carpenters, electricians, automotive mechanics, painters and plumbers — were 51 percent above the private industry average." Moreover, "city employees here received better holiday, vacation, health insurance and pension benefits than those in similar occupations in private industry." The study noted that all municipal workers in New York City receive four weeks' paid vacation after only one year of service. After 15 years, only one-fourth of the plant and one-third of the office workers in New York's private industries are eligible for such a long vacation.[69]

Public Sector Job Stability. With wages and benefits as high as they are, relative to the private sector, it is not surprising that turnover rates in government employment are considerably smaller than the rates in the private sector. In 1970, for example, state and local turnover averaged 18.9 percent, compared with a rate of 60 percent in private manufacturing.

"The great majority (89 percent) of state and local government personnel systems follow the federal practice of requiring employees to serve a one-year probationary period," which is followed in 90 percent of the jurisdictions by the granting of tenure.[70] While precise figures on this variable are not available for private industry, there is no question that this enormously attractive and stabilizing benefit is not so readily available to most private employees, particularly those who do not belong to unions (as is the case for most workers in the secondary labor market).

Indeed, the civil service system which operates in 85 percent of the state and local governments in the United States acts as a kind of "internal labor market" institution itself. The best example of this is the finding that, in jurisdictions covered by civil service, two-thirds of all skilled, unskilled and administrative-professional-technical workers, and seven-tenths of all office-clerical workers, are eligible for upgrading under well-defined internal promotion procedures, and enjoy hiring preference over workers trying to enter the system from outside. This is one of the principal distinguishing characteristics of the "manorial" industry with an internal labor market — the dominant institution in the core of the economy.[71]

Finally, public employment is characteristically more stable than private employment *within* the year. Between 1960 and 1970, the proportion of year-round workers among all nonagricultural employees with some work experience during the year ranged between 54.9 percent and 59.4 percent. For public sector employees, the ratio of year-round workers averaged 74.4-79.8 percent.[72]

Physical and "Technical Accessibility. In 1966, within the largest metropolitan areas, an average of two-thirds of the public service jobs (federal, state and local) were physically located within the central city, where most of the urban poor live.[73] Moreover, according to the 1960 Census, at least 60 percent of the public sector jobs in that year were nonskilled (office and clerical and blue collar), and one recent study of Chicago municipal employment expansion plans indicates that perhaps as many as 70 percent of the new jobs planned for the next three years in that jurisdiction will be "nonskilled" (aide, subprofessional, clerical, unskilled blue collar and custodial).[74] Recent studies by the National Civil Service League indicate that between one-half and two-thirds of the new positions in a sample of other state and municipal governments are of the "nonskilled" category.

Public service employment may be able to provide a major share of the new jobs that are needed. This is already the fastest growing sector of the economy.[75] Federal subsidization in order to assure the continued expansion of this sector (as in the new Emergency Employment Act of 1971, which will fund $2.25 billion in public sector wages and benefits over the next two years), and federal efforts to "broker" a share of these public service jobs for the poor (as in the Office of Economic Opportunity's Project PACE MAKER),[76] constitute an essential part of what ought to be a concerted national effort to reduce the degree of segmentation in American labor markets.

By providing non-poverty jobs for workers now employed in the secondary labor market, a public service employment program will unquestionably compete with secondary private employers for the services of the secondary labor force. Those workers who actually move from secondary private to primary public employment will benefit directly.[77] Moreover, there is every reason to expect that those who are left behind will benefit from the upward pressure exerted on secondary labor market wages and benefits by the competition.[78] And in the process – as Harold L. Sheppard has tirelessly argued for many years[79] – the production and delivery of public services which are now in critically short supply will be expanded.

Notes

1. Lester Thurow, "Raising Incomes Through Manpower Training Programs," in Anthony H. Pascal (ed.), *Contributions to the Analysis of Urban Problems* (Santa Monica, Calif.: The RAND Corporation, August, 1968), Document No. P-3868, pp. 91-92.

68

2. Thomas I. Ribich, *Education and Poverty* (Washington, D.C.: The Brookings Institution, 1968) p. 1.

3. Cf. Bennett Harrison, *Education, Training, and the Urban Ghetto* (Baltimore: Johns Hopkins Press, 1972), and Randall Weiss, "The Effect of Education on the Earnings of Blacks and Whites," *Review of Economics and Statistics,* May 1970.

4. Cf. Kenneth J. Arrow, *Some Models of Racila Discrimination in the Labor Market* (Santa Monica, Calif.: The RAND Corporation, February 1971), Document No. RM-6253-RC; Gary S. Becker, *The Economics of Discrimination* (Chicago: University of Chicago Press, 1957); Barbara R. Bergmann, "The Effect on White Incomes of Discrimination in Employment," *Journal of Political Economy,* March/April 1971; Anne O. Krueger, "The Economics of Discrimination," *Journal of Political Economy,* October 1963; and Lester C. Thurow, *Poverty and Discrimination* (Washington, D.C.: The Brookings Institution, 1969).

5. Cf. Raymond Franklin and Michael Tanzer, "Traditional Microeconomic Analysis of Racial Discrimination: A Critical View and Alternative Approach," in David Mermelstein (ed.), *Economics: Mainstream Readings and Radical Critiques* (New York: Random House, 1970); Michael Reich, "Economic Theories of Racism," in David M. Gordon (ed.), *Problems in Political Economy: An Urban Perspective* (Lexington, Mass.: D.C. Heath, 1971); and David P. Taylor, "Discrimination and Occupational Wage Differences in the Market for Unskilled Labor," *Industrial and Labor Relations Review,* April, 1968.

6. Bergmann, "The Effect on White Incomes," p. 308

7. Ibid., pp. 295, 310.

8. Bradley R. Schiller, "Class Discrimination vs. Racial Discrimination," *The Review of Economics and Statistics,* August 1971.

9. Barry Bluestone, "The Tripartite Economy: Labor Markets and the Working Poor," *Poverty and Human Resources,* July/August 1970, pp. 23-24.

10. Bergman, "The Effect on White Incomes," pp. 303-304.

11. Bluestone, "The Tripartite Economy," p. 15.

12. David M. Gordon, *Theories of Poverty and Underemployment* (Lexington, Mass.: Heath-Lexington Books, 1972). Gordon builds upon an excellent history of science by Thomas S. Kuhn, *The Structure of Scientific Revolutions* (Chicago: University of Chicago Press, 1962).

13. Claude Brown, *Manchild in the Promised Land* (New York: Signet, 1965); Eldridge Cleaver, *Post-Prison Writings and Speeches* (New York: A Ramparts Book, Random House, 1969); *The Autobiography of Malcolm X* (New York: The Grove Press, 1966).

14. Harold L. Sheppard, *The Nature of the Job Problem and The Role of*

New Public Service Employment (Kalamazoo, Mich.: The W.E. Upjohn Institute, January 1969), p. 4.

15. U.S. Department of Labor, *1970 Manpower Report of the President* (Washington, D.C.: U.S. Government Printing Office, 1970), pp. 121-22. Barry Bluestone notes that the Census Bureau's sexist designation of families with working wives and unemployed husbands as "families with an unemployed head of household" tends to understate the number of working poor household heads.

16. Estimated from distributions in U.S. Bureau of the Census, *Current Population Reports,* Series P-60, No. 80, "Income in 1970 of Families and Persons in the U.S.," Government Printing Office, Washington, D.C.: Oct. 4, 1971.

17. For a good working bibliography on economic dualism in the American context, see the references cited in Gordon, *Theories of Poverty and Underemployment;* and in Bennett Harrison, "Human Capital, Black Poverty, and 'Radical' Economics," *Industrial Relations,* October 1971.

18. Some of the other interlocking institutions in the core include the schools that prepare people to work in the primary labor market, the financial intermediaries which fund the activities of primary employers, and the federal government which serves as a Keynesian "regulator," of aggregate demand and − more recently − as guarantor of demand through direct contracts. See Robert Averitt, *The Dual Economy* (New York: W.W. Norton, 1968); John Kenneth Galbraith, *The New Industrial State* (New York: Houghton-Mifflin, 1967); and Herbert Gintis, "Repressive Schooling as Productive Schooling," in Gordon, *Problems in Political Economy.* We shall have more to say about the role of the education system at the end of this section.

19. According to Michael Tanzer, "the degree of discrimination against Negroes of either sex is highly correlated with the job structure of the industry. Specifically, the greater the proportion of total jobs in an industry which are laborer jobs, the greater the proportion of Negroes found in the industry as a whole and in each occupational job category separately." Franklin and Tanzer, "Traditional Microeconomic Analysis of Racial Discrimination," p. 120n. In other words, labor-intensive industries tend to employ nonwhites both aggregatively and in many different positions, while capital-intensive industries are less likely to do either.

20. Cf. Harvey Leibenstein, *Economic Backwardness and Economic Growth* (New York: Wiley-Science Editions, 1963), pp. 62-69. This is one of the earliest discussions of "the interesting possibility that the energy level of a tenant or worker rises as his income rises." At a more aggregative level, a recent United Nations study developed "social profiles" for developing countries, composed of indicators of nutrition, education, health, housing, and leisure. The researchers found that "those developing countries which had a favorable social profile in

the early 1950's also tended to show more rapid economic growth in the following ten years." Salvatore Schiavo-Campo and Hans W. Singer, *Perspectives of Economic Development* (New York: Houghton-Mifflin, 1970), pp. 76-78. It is not at all uncharacteristic of the dual labor market theory that some of its roots are to be found in studies of the "Third World."

21. "The most important characteristic distinguishing jobs in the primary sector from those in the secondary sector appears to be the behavioral requirements which they impose upon the work force, particularly that of employment stability." Michael J. Piore, "The Dual Labor Market: Theory and Implications," in Gordon, *Problems in Political Economy*, p. 91.

22. Peter B. Doeringer and Michael J. Piore, *Internal Labor Markets and Manpower Analysis* (Lexington, Mass.: D.C. Heath, 1971).

23. John R. Meyer and Edwin Kuh, *The Investment Decision* (Cambridge, Mass.: Harvard University Press, 1957). See also Galbraith, *The New Industrial State,* and Robin Marris, *The Economic Theory of Managerial Capitalism* (Glencoe, New York: The Free Press, 1964).

24. Kenneth Arrow, "The Economic Implications of Learning-by-Doing," *Review of Economic Studies,* June 1962.

25. Herbert Gintis, "Education, Technology, and the Characteristics of Worker Productivity," *American Economic Review/Proceedings,* May 1971, p. 266.

26. Ibid., p. 267.

27. Samuel Bowles, "Unequal Education and the Reproduction of the Social Division of Labor," in Richard Edwards, Michael Reich, and Thomas Weisskopf (eds.), *The Capitalist System* (Englewood Cliffs, New Jersey: Prentice-Hall, 1972).

28. Gintis, "Education, Technology, and the Characteristics of Worker Productivity," pp. 273-74.

29. Ibid., p. 267. Bowles has posited a theory which integrates Gintis' conception of the function of schooling with the model of labor market segmentation and the findings on class discrimination. According to this theory, schools "reproduce" (i.e., preserve) class cultures from generation to generation. Labor markets then "translate" these differences in class culture into income inequalities and occupational hierarchies which in turn determine which schools the children of workers will be able to attend. See Bowles, "Unequal Education." We shall make use of this theory later, in the discussion of the role of public education as an instrument of mobility between the core and the periphery of the economy.

30. Cf. Peter B. Doeringer, with Penny Feldman, David M. Gordon, Michael J. Piore, and Michael Reich, *Low-Income Labor Markets and Urban Manpower Programs,* Department of Economics, Harvard University, January, 1969,

mimeographed; Thomas Vietorisz and Bennett Harrison, *The Economic Development of Harlem* (New York: Praeger, 1970); and other references cited in Gordon and Harrison (see note 17).

31. Bluestone, "The Tripartite Economy," p. 25.

32. Robert E. Hall, "Why is Unemployment So High at Full Employment?" *Brookings Papers on Economic Activity* No. 3 (Washington, D.C.: The Brookings Institution, 1970), pp. 389-90.

33. Edward D. Kalachek and John M. Goering (eds.), *Transportation and Central City Unemployment,* Institute for Urban and Regional Studies, Washington University, Working Paper INS 5, March 1970, p. 8.

34. Ibid., pp. 8-9.

35. Peter B. Doeringer, "Ghetto Labor Markets – Problems and Programs," Program on Regional and Urban Economics, Discussion Paper No. 35, Harvard University, May 1968, mimeographed, pp. 10-11.

36. U.S. Department of Labor, *1971 Manpower Report of the President* (Washington, D.C.: U.S. Government Printing Office, 1971), p. 97.

37. U.S. Department of Labor, *1968 Manpower Report of the President* (Washington, D.C.: U.S. Government Printing Office, 1968), p. 96.

38. Ibid., p. 97.

39. Ibid., p. 98. Some analysts believe that "welfare" has also served as an instrument of social control. In the South, it has traditionally been used to keep "field hands alive at federal expense during the winter, then forcing them into the fields at low wages in the spring and summer. When civil rights activism disturbed the calm of Southern rural life, the welfare system was available for, and easily adapted to, discouraging 'troublemakers'. County officials systematically suspended commodity distributions and warned that benefits would be restored only when local blacks surrendered their 'uppity' ideas about changing the local balance of power." Lester M. Salamon, "Family Assistance: The Stakes in the Rural South," *The New Republic* February 20, 1971, p. 18. Piven and Cloward have published a major work which argues that these two functions go hand in hand. Welfare serves both to buy off the poor so they will not rebel, and to provide workers who will take the worst jobs at the lowest possible pay. The former is the primary purpose; welfare aids the rest of society by keeping the poor in what the affluent have determined is their proper place. Relief actually means social control, not social welfare. Frances Fox Piven and Richard Cloward, *Regulating the Poor* (New York: Pantheon, 1971). See also Herbert Gans, "Income Grants and Dirty Work," in Mermelstein (ed.), *Economics: Mainstream Readings and Radical Critiques.*

40. *1968 Manpower Report,* p. 98.

41. Thomas Vietorisz and Bennett Harrison, *The Economic Development of Harlem,* pp. 234-35.

42. U.S. Office of Economic Opportunity, *1966 Survey of Economic Opportunity: Unweighted Counts,* 1969, mimeographed, pp. 2, 48.

43. Elizabeth Durbin, *Welfare Income and Employment* (New York: Praeger, 1969), p. 34.

44. Ibid., p. 78.

45. U.S. Department of Labor, Bureau of Labor Statistics, Middle Atlantic Regional Office, *Poverty Area Profiles: Working Age Nonparticipants,* Regional Report No. 22, June 1971, p. 3.

46. *1968 Manpower Report,* p. 94.

47. Quoted in Bennett Harrison, "National Manpower Policy and Public Service Employment," *New Generation,* Winter 1971, p. 4.

48. U.S. Senate Committee on Labor and Public Welfare, *The JOBS Program* (Washington, D.C.: U.S. Government Printing Office, May 1970). For a more extended discussion of the JOBS Program, see Harrison, *Education, Training, and the Urban Ghetto,* Ch. 6.

49. Bennett Harrison, "Public Service Jobs for Urban Ghetto Residents," *Good Government,* Fall 1969, p. 14; reprinted in U.S. Senate Subcommittee on Employment, Manpower and Poverty, *Hearings,* 91st Congress, 2nd Session (April 1, 1970), p. 1437.

50. *1971 Manpower Report,* p. 43.

51. Sar Levitan and Robert Taggart III, *Employment of Black Youth in Urban Ghettos* (New York: Twentieth Century Fund, 1971), p. 101.

52. Pacific Training and Technical Assistance Corporation, *Effectiveness of Urban WIN Programs, Phase I: Final Report,* Office of Research and Development, Manpower Administration, U.S. Department of Labor, Contract No. 51-09-70-10, June 7, 1971, pp. 39-40.

53. Peter H. Rossi et al, "Between White and Black: The Faces of American Institutions in the Ghetto," in *Supplemental Studies for the National Advisory Commission on Civil Disorders* (Washington, D.C.: U.S. Government Printing Office, July 1968), pp. 122-23. It has also been hypothesized that, where typically secondary workers (such as urban blacks) *are* employed by primary firms — as, for example, in the NAB-JOBS program — they tend to be confined to jobs and promotion ladders not involving positions of status or authority (this is why the secondary labor market has been depicted in figure 2.1 as overlapping part of the core of the economy). Evidence for this has been presented by the Equal Employment Opportunity Commission and by David P. Taylor (op. cit). In fact, it has recently been shown that such *internal segmentation* within core firms is greatest in precisely those industries which pay the highest wages — the "leading edge" of the core. In other words, in those core firms where average black earnings are at a maximum, the black share of high-paying, high-status jobs is at a minimum. See A.A. Alexander, *Structure, Income and Race: A Study in*

Internal Labor Markets (Santa Monica: The RAND Corporation, October 1970), R-577-OEO.

54. Cf. Barry Bluestone, "The Tripartite Economy"; Louis A. Ferman, "The Irregular Economy: Informal Work Patterns in the Ghetto," Dept. of Economics, University of Michigan, 1967, mimeographed; Daniel Fusfeld, "The Basic Economics of the Urban and Racial Crisis," *Conference Papers of the Union for Radical Political Economics,* December 1968; David M. Gordon, "Class and the Economics of Crime," *the Review of Radical Political Economics,* Summer 1971.

55. *1968 Manpower Report* p. 94.

56. *1971 Manpower Report,* p. 98-99.

57. For example, Glazer and Moynihan assume that public education would help to improve the employment status of blacks if only the "serious obstacles to the ability to make use of a free educational system to advance into higher occupations" could be removed. Moreover, "there is little question where [these obstacles] must be found: in the home and family and community." Nathan Glazer and Daniel P. Moynihan, *Beyond the Melting Pot* (Cambridge, Mass.: Harvard University Press, 1963), pp. 49-50. Herman Miller, Chief Economist of the Census Bureau, has written that "it is entirely possible and indeed likely that productivity potentials of nonwhites have been raised, as suggested by the theory that correlates increases in years of schooling with additions to human capital, but [that] these potentials may not have materialized, owing to discrimination." Herman P. Miller, "Does Education Pay Off?", in Selma J. Mushkin (ed.), *Economics of Higher Education,* (Washington, D.C.: U.S. Department of Health, Education, and Welfare, 1962), p. 132.

58. I refer here to the common practice of advising lower-class students that they will be unable to obtain work in certain occupations and should therefore concentrate on other "traditional" positions. When such advice is taken, it amounts to self-fulfilling prophecy. It is important to note that not all the students in a predominantly lower-class school are treated this way. Many schools use an internal "tracking" system, in which students with "promise" are placed in substantially separate curriculums from those with less or no "promise." "Placement in these curriculums may determine the student's entire future life [and] it is known . . . that even very able boys from working-class homes who fail to make really good grades in the seventh and eighth grades are seldom advised to take a college preparatory course. This is not equally true of boys from white-collar homes." Patricia Cayo Sexton, "Education and Income: Senior High Schools," in Gordon, *Problems in Political Economy,* pp. 201-202. Lee Webb is currently attempting to explore the relationship between this fascinating internal segmentation of education "markets" and the labor market segmentation described in the text.

59. Earl Main, "A Nationwide Evaluation of MDTA Institutional Job Training," *Journal of Human Resources,* Spring 1968.

74

60. Doeringer et al, *Low-Income Labor Markets.*

61. Stephan Michelson, *Income of Racial Minorities* (Washington, D.C.: The Brookings Institution, 1968), unpublished manuscript, p. 8-23. In remarks to the Faculty Study Group on the State and the Poor at the Kennedy Institute of Politics in October 1969, Michael Piore suggested that "the best operational definition of a secondary job is one which the Employment Service has in its files and is able to fill."

62. The Lawyers' Committee for Civil Rights Under Law and the National Urban Coalition, *Falling Down on the Job: The United States Employment Service and the Disadvantaged* (Washington, D.C.: The National Urban Coalition, April 1971), p. III.

63. Ibid., p. 60.

64. Ibid., p. 45.

65. Ibid., p. 39.

66. Ibid., p. 67.

67. Bluestone, "The Tripartite Economy," p. 18.

68. For a more complete exposition of the following materials, with tabular documentation, see Bennett Harrison, *Public Employment and Urban Poverty* (Washington, D.C.: The Urban Institute, June 1971).

69. Damon Stetson, "Public Employees Top Private in Pay," *New York Times,* June 28, 1971.

70. Jacob Rutstein, "Survey of Current Personnel Systems in State and Local Governments," *Good Government,* Spring 1971, p. 6. For a brief summary of this extensive study, see Bennett Harrison, "State and Local Government Manpower Policies," *Industrial Relations,* February 1971. It may also be observed that public employment displays a secular stability which the private sector has lacked in postwar America. "Since 1948, there have been at least three major downturns in the percentage rate of growth of private employment: 1948-49, 1953-54, and 1957-58. The civilian public sector has, by contrast, experienced no downturns; the trend of percentage growth of public sector employment has been uniformly positive throughout the period. Current estimates by the Bureau of Labor Statistics indicate that these patterns have held through the current recession . . . The percentage rate of growth of private employment between 1969 and 1970 was only barely positive; for the public sector it remained substantial." Harrison, *Public Employment and Urban Poverty,* p. 32.

71. Cf. Doeringer and Piore, *Internal Labor Markets.*

72. U.S. Department of Labor, *1972 Manpower Report of the President* (Washington, D.C.: U.S. Government Printing Office, 1972), p. 212.

73. Harrison, *Public Employment and Urban Poverty*, p. 35.

74. Ibid., p. 19.

75. "A fifth of all wage and salary employees in America already work in federal, state and local government, and . . . one out of every four new jobs in the economy is in the public sector . . . in the nation's cities . . . one out of every *three* new workers is engaged in the delivery of such crucial services as education, health protection, recreation, waste disposal, police and fire protection". Ibid., p. 2.

76. For a discussion of PACE MAKER and other federal experiments in opening up public employment for the poor, see the *1971 Manpower Report of the President* (Washington, D.C.: Government Printing Office, 1971), pp. 171-176.

77. Comparison of the existing wages of a sample of 15,000 ghetto workers with the entry-level salaries obtaining in municipal government indicates that "those ghetto residents who can be moved into the public service agencies in their respective cities might expect to increase their wage incomes by a factor of between one and three times". Harrison, *Public Employment and Urban Poverty,* p. 23.

78. For an elaboration of this argument, see Barry F. Bluestone, "Economic Theory, Economic Reality, and the Fate of the Poor," Chapter 5 in this volume.

79. Cf. Harold L. Sheppard, "The Nature of the Job Problem and the Role of New Public Service Employment," Chapter 1 in this volume.

3

The Determinants of "Working Poverty"

Howard M. Wachtel

Charles Betsey

"People are poor because the rate of wages paid by the industries of the United States will not permit them to be anything but poor."

[Scott Nearing, *Poverty and Riches. A Study of the Industrial Regime,* (1916) p. 190.]

In our society work is invariably prescribed as the path out of poverty. However, for a significant proportion of the poor this remedy falls on deaf ears, since they *work* but are *poor.* The working poor earn their poverty! Perhaps this segment of the poor has been neglected precisely because its existence belies our belief that work is the panacea for all societal ills.[1]

The focus of this study is the individual full-time wage earner and the forces affecting his (her) wage income. In particular, we are interested in evaluating the relative importance of the individual characteristics of workers and the structure of the labor market in which they work.

Since the Second World War, two separate schools of thought pertaining to the labor market have developed. One dominated during the 1950s, followed by a competing view of labor markets during the 1960s, with little attention given to any possible synthesis of these differing analyses of the labor market.

In the 1950s, with public attention directed towards the economic power of trade unions and concentrated industries, labor market analysis was focused upon the demand side of the market. This became translated into operational terms via the specification of several characteristics of industries and labor markets as determinants of wages among fairly aggregrated categories of labor markets. For example, the studies of Levinson, Segal, Ross, and others specified variations in profits, industrial concentration, labor union membership, rates of change in productivity, and employment as determinants of wage differentials among industries.[2] The *structure* of an industry was analyzed for its impact upon the wages of workers in those industries.

In the 1960s, with public attention diverted from problems of the interaction

This chapter is an abbreviated version of a longer technical paper by the authors, entitled: "Employment at Low Wages," *Review of Economics and Statistics,* May 1972.

of unions and corporations toward low income concerns, labor market analysis became directed towards what can be construed as supply considerations. This was translated into operational terms with analyses of the "human capital" an individual brings to the labor market.[3] Of primary concern were the determinants of human capital, although some attention has also been directed toward the effect of human capital upon an individual's opportunity in the labor market. The focus was the individual's opportunity in the labor market as determined by his (her) supposedly inherent productivity.

In view of the fact that both supply and demand considerations are important, it would be wise to reconsider the two rather separate views of the labor market toward the objective of developing a synthesis. Bluestone (1970) has recently outlined such a synthesis in a model of *bilateral labor market segmentation,* according to which segmentation exists on both sides of the market, a condition in the labor market which is quite consistent with the dual labor market theories described elsewhere in this volume. Now the problem of wage determination for the individual assumes more complexity, but hopefully greater realism. Thus, for example, wages vary across industries for individuals with identical human capital, depending upon the structure of those industries. On the other hand, wages will vary within a given industry depending on the differing amounts of human capital of its employees. It follows that individuals with low amounts of human capital will, under certain circumstances, earn the same as (or more than) individuals with larger amounts of human capital. This occurs because of the balkanization of labor markets and the important barriers to mobility that can persist in labor markets over long periods of time. These barriers can arise because of direct discrimination in the labor market (by sex and race), trade union barriers to entry, high financial cost and risk involved in geographic mobility, insufficient labor market information, artificial educational barriers to job entry, and so on.

These hypotheses have been supported by us in a series of statistical analyses which have succeeded in decomposing the supply and demand determinants of variations in individual wages. Our experiments were conducted on data from the 1967 Survey of Consumer Finances conducted by the Institute for Social Research of the University of Michigan on a group of representative dwelling units for the continental United States. The empirical research was confined to full-time, full-year workers, defined as individuals working at least forty weeks during 1967 and working an average of at least thirty hours per week. The year 1967 was chosen because employment levels were high. The study was also confined to the following occupations: laborers, service workers, craftsmen, operatives and kindred workers, and foremen. This yielded 1,023 individuals, with mean annual wage earnings of $6,223. Some 14 percent of the sample are "working poor" – individuals employed full-time with earnings below the poverty level.

There are two basic results to report (for details, see the original, extended paper). First, the most important determinant of individual wages by far is the industry-occupation of the worker. Even after "removing" the explanatory effects of education, job tenure, race, sex, age, marital status, region, union status, and city size, the variable "industry-occupation" continues to "count" significantly. According to a standard statistical test of "relative importance," this variable dominates all others.

Secondly, there is a substantial variation in wage earnings across industry categories, after the effects of personal characteristics (including occupation) have been eliminated. For example, individuals employed as laborers, with the same personal characteristics (education, years on job, age, race, etc.), earn from $4,718 to $6,136 depending upon the industry in which they are employed, after adjusting for the effect of personal characteristics on the wage. This observation lends considerable support to the dual economy hypothesis, and challenges (for example) the hypothesis that wage discrimination results exclusively from the "crowding" of the lower class into certain occupations and their exclusion from others. Ultimately, the earnings of poorly educated big city black laborers (say) will depend on the structure of the industry which employs them.

These findings have some important policy implications. Two themes have dominated the ideology and attitudes towards the poor in western countries since the industrial revolution. First, being poor is usually considered to be the result of some individual failure; and second, the state of individual poverty is due to the absence of work, caused either by individual laziness or the absence of jobs (cf. Coll). Since the New Deal and the post-war Employment Act, public policy – where it has concerned itself at all with job development – has been concerned almost exclusively with the quantity but not with the quality or wage levels of jobs. George Shultz reflected this bias most cogently when he testified as Secretary of Labor on the Nixon Family Assistance Plan:

I hasten to add that the labor market itself must be recognized as a constraint . ,. It is a fact that our economy has a lot of jobs that pay low wages. We are not going to be remaking the economy in this program. We can only put people in the jobs that exist . . . we will have to thread our way between our goals of providing good jobs . . . and the realities of the kinds of jobs that are available [p. 16].

The human capital concerns of the 1960s, translated into programatic terms in training and education legislation, are based on the premise that workers have made inadequate investment in themselves. The cause of this investment failure has been traced either to simple irrationalities on the part of the investors or discrimination in educational markets. This approach is not too far removed from the nineteenth century view of poverty in which the poor were blamed for their own condition.[4]

Public policy and its supporting research has focused almost exclusively on the problem of the *acquisition of human capital* — the level and distribution of education and training and the way in which human capital is produced. But the problem of low income does not end there; along with the process of acquisition of human capital, there is a question of *how this human capital is used in the labor market.* A clue to the reason for the ambiguous results of training programs is to be found in this distinction. Perhaps human capital has been augmented somewhat by these programs, but is it put to different uses in the labor market? If not — if the individual is removed from one structural environment only to be placed back in the same structural environment — then we should not be surprised by the absence of any significant improvement in the worker's earning ability.

In this chapter a theory of the labor market was developed which integrated both supply and demand considerations into a model of bilateral labor market segmentation. The data and method used to test for the validity of the model supported the existence of bilateral labor market segmentation, in which the structure of labor demand exerted a dominant, though not exclusive, influence upon individual earnings.

The poverty research of the last decade has focused, almost entirely, upon the *characteristics* of the poor, not the *causes of* poverty. The *causes* of poverty are to be found in the functioning of our economic and social institutions. The research on the characteristics of the poor has merely identified the differential probabilities of becoming poor, given the existence of poverty in our society. Perhaps the most important of the economic institutions causing poverty is the *labor market,* both for people presently attached to the labor force and for individuals whose income derives primarily from previous attachment to the labor force — the retired, disabled, etc.

The evidence developed in this chapter raises several important issues for public policy. Recently, 2.9 million poor family heads worked full time. For these people the problem is not simply providing jobs in an aggregate Keynesian sense, but in providing decent jobs at adequate wage levels. Rather, structural conditions tend to exert a substantial influence upon wage levels. This study has identified the importance of these structural variables. A laborer in personal services, or in transportation, communication and public utilities will receive low earnings, independent of the personal characteristics of the worker. As long as public policy focuses on the characteristics of individuals, and not the structure of the economic environment in which the individual works, we can continue to anticipate the same disappointing results that public policy has produced in the last decade.

Notes

1. In contrast to the relatively abundant literature on other aspects of

poverty, the material on wage poverty is quite sparse. See: Bluestone (1968); Cummings; Perrella; Orshansky (1968); Dawn Day Wachtel; Delehanty and Evans; U.S. Department of Commerce; Sinfield and Twine; Doeringer; Harrison; and Lecht.

2. Levinson, pp. 1-22; Segal; and Ross-Goldner.

3. Thurow (1970); Thurow (1969), Ch. V; and Mincer.

4. Wachtel (1970).

Bibliography

Andrews, Frank et al. *Multiple Classification Analysis.* Ann Arbor, Mich.: Institute for Social Research, 1967.

Astin, Alexander. "Undergraduate Achievement and Institutional 'Excellence'." *Science* 161 (August 1968): 661-68.

Bluestone, Barry. "Low Wage Industries and the Working Poor." *Poverty and Human Resource Abstracts* 3 (March-April 1968): 1-14.

_____, "The Tripartite Economy: Labor Markets and the Working Poor." *Poverty and Human Resources*, July-August 1970, pp. 15-35.

Bremner, Robert H. *From the Depths: The Discovery of Poverty in the United States.* New York: The New York University Press, 1967.

Coll, Blanche D. *Perspectives in Public Welfare: A History.* Washington, D.C.: Government Printing Office, 1969.

Creager, John A. "Academic Achievement and Institutional Environments: Comparison of Two Research Strategies." (mimeographed, n.d.).

Cummings, Laurie D. "The Employed Poor: Their Characteristics and Occupations." *Monthly Labor Review* 88 (July 1965): 828-41.

Current Population Report, Series P-60, no. 78, U.S. Department of Commerce, Bureau of the Census.

Delehanty, George E. and Evans, Robert Jr. "Low-Wage Employment: An Inventory and an Assessment." (mimeographed, n.d.).

Doeringer, Peter B. "Manpower Programs for Ghetto Labor Markets." *Proceedings of the Industrial Relations Research Association* 1968.

Goldberger, Arthur S. *Econometric Theory.* New York: John Wiley, 1964.

Harrison, Bennett. Education and Underemployment in the Urban Ghetto." *American Economic Review,* September 1972.

Katona, George. et al. *1967 Survey of Consumer Finances* Ann Arbor, Mich.: Survey Research Center, 1968.

Lecht, Leonard. *Poor Persons in the Labor Force: A Universe of Need.* Washington: National Planning Association, 1970.

Leftwich, Richard H. "Personal Income and Marginal Productivity." In David M. Gordon (ed.) *Problems in Political Economy: An Urban Perspective.* Lexington: D.C. Heath and Company, 1971, pp. 79-85.

Levinson, Harold M. *Postwar Movement of Wages and Prices in Manufacturing Industries.* Study Paper No. 21, Joint Economic Committee Study of Employment, Growth, and Price Levels.

Mincer, Jacob. "The Distribution of Labor Incomes: A Survey with Special Reference to the Human Capital Approach." *Journal of Economic Literature* 8, 1 (March 1970): 1-26.

Orshansky, Mollie. "More about the Poor in 1964." *Social Security Bulletin* 29 (May 1966): 3-38.

_____,"The Shape of Poverty in 1966." *Social Security Bulletin* 31 (March 1968): 2-32.

Perrella, Vera C. "Low Earners and Their Incomes." *Monthly Labor Review* 90 (May 1967): 35-40.

Piore, Michael J. "On-the-Job Training in the Dual Labor Market." in Arnold Weber et al. *Public-Private Manpower Policies.* Madison: Industrial Relations Research Association, 1969.

Rees, Albert, and Shultz, George P. *Workers and Wages in an Urban Labor Market.* Chicago: University of Chicago Press, 1970.

Ross, Arthur M. and Goldner, William. "Forces Affecting the Interindustry Wage Structure." *Quarterly Journal of Economics,* May 1950, pp. 254-81.

Segal, Martin. "Unionism and Wage Movements." *Southern Economic Journal,* 28 (October 1961): 174-81.

Shultz, George. "Statement of George Shultz, Secretary of Labor, Before Committee on Ways and Means on the Family Assistance Act of 1969." (mimeographed, 1969)

Sinfield, Adrian, and Twine, Fred. "The Low-Paid: The Employment Market and Social Policy." (mimeographed, 1968)

Thurow, Lester. *Investment in Human Capital.* Belmont: Wadsworth Publishing Company, Inc., 1970.

_____,*Poverty and Discrimination.* Washington D.C.: The Brookings Institution, 1969.

U.S. Department of Commerce, Bureau of the Census. "Year-Round Workers with Low Earnings in 1966." *Current Population Reports,* No. 58 (April 4, 1969).

U.S. Department of Labor, Bureau of Labor Statistics, *Three Standards of Living for an Urban Family of Four Persons,* Bulletin No. 1570-5

Wachtel, Dawn Day. *The Working Poor.* Ann Arbor, Mich.: Institute of Labor and Industrial Relations, 1967.

Wachtel, Howard M. "Looking at Poverty from a Radical Perspective." in James Weaver (ed.) *Political Economy; Radical Versus Orthodox Approaches.* Boston: Allyn and Bacon, forthcoming.

The literature on the economics of the public sector is remarkably scant, considering that a fifth of all employees in the United States now work for government. One of the earliest — and still the best — treatments of the issues discussed in the Upjohn Seminar (e.g., "the private sector bias" in the United States; the inability of private markets to produce and distribute certain kinds of "public" goods and services; the relative inefficiency of the public versus the private sector) is Francis M. Bator, *The Question of Government Spending* (New York: Macmillan — Colliers, 1960). The "private sector bias" is also discussed in John Kenneth Galbraith, *The Affluent Society* (Boston: Houghton-Mifflin, 1958). A collection of statistical tables on the rapid growth of public sector employment, and a comparison of public and private sector wages, are contained in Bennett Harrison, *Public Employment and Urban Poverty* (Washington, D.C.: The Urban Institute, June 1971). Among the several text books on public sector economics, the one which is most closely grounded in the actual practices of federal agencies is Neil Singer, *Public Microeconomics* (Boston: Little, Brown and Company, 1972).

One of the earliest articles to set forth a model of segmented labor markets was Barry Bluestone, "The Tripartite Economy," *Poverty and Human Resources,* July-August 1970. In their policy statement issued during the summer of that year, the Committee for Economic Development referred for the first time to the new theory of the dual structure of labor markets; see *Training and Jobs for the Urban Poor* (New York: Committee for Economic Development, July 1970). For a more extensive treatment by two economists who were among the first to do research in this field, see Peter B. Doeringer and Michael J. Piore, *Internal Labor Markets and Manpower Analysis* (Lexington, Mass.: Heath-Lexington Books, 1971). By far the most complete treatment of the subject — one which places it in the larger context of conservative, liberal, and radical analyses of unemployment, poverty, and labor market structure — is David M. Gordon, *Economic Theories of Poverty and Underemployment* (Lexington, Mass.: Heath-Lexington Books, 1972).

Part II
National Manpower Policy — An
Historical Perspective

Introduction to Part II

The second seminar evening attempted to cover a number of topics, with major emphasis on the evolving role of government as an employer since the decade of the Great Depression.

Alden Briscoe's presentation, based on his recent study of the Works Progress Administration, dealt with the degree of success of that vast program in placing unemployed persons into publicly financed projects and in producing socially useful output of goods and services. While no one argues that WPA (which aimed primarily at reemploying people who had previously been employed before the Great Depression) should be the model for any contemporary policies, it is nevertheless important to review that experience, if only to dispel some of the stereotypes that persist even today. These stereotypes have frequently been deployed by opponents to any form of new governmental proposals for public service employment. Chief among these stereotypes is, of course, the charge of "leaf-raking," "make-work" — in other words, that the WPA did nothing but give unemployed men and women "something for nothing."

It is difficult to accept this allegation when we consider the kinds of facts garnered by Briscoe. For example:

651,000 miles of new roads constructed under WPA;
 24,000 bridges and viaducts;
120,000 public buildings.

The speaker concluded that over the six years of its existence, WPA employed approximately 8.5 million people (with an annual average enrollment of slightly over 1 million per year).

Unlike the recent proposals, and the new Emergency Employment Act of 1971, WPA was heavily involved in construction projects. It did not concern itself with training the unemployed for new skills (few of them were "hardcore"), and it was not created with any intention of upgrading its employees or integrating them into any regular employment within the existing state and local civil service systems. To be sure, it did have some anti-illiteracy projects (which helped to reduce the illiteracy rate substantially in several states). It did demonstrate that "if you want to get something going really fast, you can set up a separate agency and you can get it done." But, current proposals and actual programs do not call for separate agencies to carry out the various public service employment programs.

The manpower training programs developed in the 1960s reflected a new philosophy toward unemployment and poverty: the concept (taken from

The second seminar evening attempted to cover a number of topics, all for the modern economic theory) that these conditions are a direct result of low worker productivity, which in turn results from inadequate education and training. Professor Barry Bluestone of Boston College addressed the theoretical issues underlying recent manpower policy. One of Bluestone's criticisms of much of contemporary economic thinking and research on employment problems, especially the problems of lower-income populations, is that this thinking and research are based too frequently upon logically and mathematically correct "models" of the labor market which, unfortunately, do not have much to do with reality. Nor are they very useful to decision makers forced to confront reality. Bluestone's critique is addressed to the relevancy of traditional economics to an understanding of (and therefore, to the search for adequate solutions to) the employment and income problems of the working poor. Given the assumptions of what has come to be called "the theory of human capital," it is not surprising that relatively few academic economists have expressed their support for public service employment as an antipoverty strategy. Some of the assumptions concern the nature of competitive markets, labor mobility, and labor market opportunities and information. Too frequently, for example, one finds in traditional economics the outright declaration – or implication – that low wages are essentially the result of low-level skills, poor health, or inappropriate attitudes. "Nontraditional" economists (one does not have to be a "radical" economist to be nontraditional) would include in their conceptual approach as basic, major – not residual – such variables as:

a. the role of government
b. effects of minimum wages
c. unionization
d. institutional philosophies and practices
e. differences between industries, regions, and labor markets

Many of the differences between wage levels, according to Bluestone, are therefore the result of differences in the nature of the industries or firms involved, and not primarily (let alone entirely) the result of differences in the characteristics of the individual employees themselves (as Wachtel and Betsey have also stressed). A typical example would be the high wages paid in the auto industry, or the steel industry, to men who – if employed in textile or in agriculture – would otherwise be receiving much lower pay. Studies of shutdowns, or mass layoffs, in auto or steel are replete with cases of previously high-wage workers (with relatively low educational backgrounds) unable to find new jobs at the same high wages in other industries in their communities.

The "human capital" interpretation of poverty and unemployment is based on the well-known aggregate correlation between education and wages. But Bluestone would argue that it is not safe to extrapolate that finding to every segment of the labor force. His emphasis is on the many exceptions to this finding, the possibility of the confusion between cause and effect, and the omission by the "human capital" approach of many other possible causes of low wages, as suggested already.[1] Yet advocates of the theory of human capital continue to argue that low wages and high unemployment can best be ameliorated by investments in improved formal education, institutional and on-the-job skill training, improved health services, and programs to facilitate migration to areas of economic opportunity.

It is important to note that neither the findings of Bluestone nor of other critics of the human capital approach to manpower obviate the necessity for some degree of public investment in human capital formation. Policy makers must be concerned with *all* of the factors in the equation, and not merely those to which Bluestone would have us pay attention (the economic power of industries, their choice of technology, etc.).

All of this, of course, does not detract from such facts as the high proportion (about one-fourth) of all poor families having an employed head working year-round and full-time; the tremendously high proportion (40 percent) of black males with high school degrees earning less than $2.25 per hour in 1967; or the opposite type of finding that significant numbers of workers *without* a high school degree are earning high wages (due to the nature of the industries employing them).

Bluestone bears down on the need, when all is said and done, to tackle both the deficiencies attributable to inadequate skill training and those associated with low-wage industries; i.e., the "lack of good jobs." But how does one create good jobs?

Public service employment offers one avenue toward this goal. It has, Bluestone told the Seminar, a "brilliant, but normally ignored, potential." To begin with, the working poor population includes many individuals who have already acquired adequate skills. Much of our unemployment is due to the shortage of jobs in the private sector. Low wages are in part due to the absence of job opportunity *alternatives.* Our efforts to date to create employment growth through tax cuts for individuals and employers, and through general public expenditure, "have never been able to develop the right kinds of jobs for the right people." Such efforts have, of course, resulted frequently in an "overdemand" for skilled professionals and technicians, but not for persons who are the special concern of Bluestone's studies. "The result has been continued unemployment and low wages for the poor *and* employment bottlenecks which cause inflation for everyone." Thus it is possible to have what the Keynesian-oriented textbooks could never predict: "the co-existence of rising unemployment and rising prices."

On the other hand, a large-scale expansion of public service career opportunities would (1) provide desperately needed public services; (2) develop meaningful job opportunities for the unemployed and underemployed; and (3) bring pressure to bear on low-wage private employers to bid up wages, as the excess supply of labor is reduced. It would, of course, also inject an increase in aggregate purchasing power through the incomes of those employed directly in the new or expanded public service programs.

One of the more successful — and relevant — programs of the 1960s was "Operation Mainstream," conducted under the Manpower Development and Training Act (MDTA). This program was created as part of that Act to provide jobs for chronically unemployed adults.[a] Mainstream participants are employed by local public and nonprofit agencies, who apply the efforts of those workers to the expansion of local community services. Unlike WPA, Operation Mainstream was initiated at a time when unemployment in the nation was relatively low, and one of its chief purposes was to provide special groups such as unemployed, low-income older workers with supplemental income through employment in socially useful projects.

The experience under this program was presented to the Seminar by Mr. Richard Kirschner (of Kirschner Associates, a research firm based in Albuquerque, New Mexico). First of all, he noted, the program is small when considered in terms of the numbers of people enrolled — about 14,000 throughout various parts of the United States (primarily in rural areas). According to Kirschner, Operation Mainstream is clearly a program of "last resort." There are few jobs to be had in rural area private employment. The applicants are typically over 55 (indeed, often in their 70s and 80s), and are frequently unwanted by employers (private and public), because of age, even when the demand for labor is relatively tight. But of equal importance is the fact that local public and nonprofit agencies are unable financially to employ such persons, although the agencies might have a need for expanding their services to the community. It is precisely for that reason that federally financed programs for expansion of public services are indispensable at this time (and probably in the future as well). Typical employers are highway departments, hospitals, and welfare agencies. Employment in these agencies is unquestionably contingent upon the availability of federal funds.

The discussion following Kirschner's remarks led the seminar group into the issues surrounding the problems of rural, small-town employment; the need to specify, to stipulate to public employers that they must hire certain selected segments of the labor force who otherwise would be neglected; the relative importance of wage rates to persons receiving meager incomes through income-transfer payments; the value of the work done by such people, for themselves and for the community; and the role of public service employment as a stimulus to economic development in general (a theme discussed in the Introduction to Part 1).

---

[a]Not necessarily "hardcore" since most of the participants, by design, are supposed to be older men and women, especially in rural areas and small towns, many of whom had prior regular work experience.

Because the Upjohn Seminar Series concluded before the actual implementation of the Emergency Employment Act, none of the discussions could deal with actual experience under that legislation.[b] However, we have included in Part 5 in this volume a brief report by Dr. Earl Wright, of the Upjohn Institute's Kalamazoo staff, who has been intimately involved in the preparation of that community's public service employment program. It is too premature, perhaps, to make any solid judgments as to the actual success of EEA.

William Spring's paper, "Congress and Public Service Employment," updates the history of national and congressional discussions and action on the role of government in directly creating jobs, from the perspective of a Senate staff member who has participated in the legislative process through which these efforts passed. He moves into the 1965-71 years bringing the story of public service job legislation up through the 1970 presidential veto and the final passage, in mid-1971, of the Emergency Employment Act. His final point is that "there is not as yet evidence that Congress is willing to enact major public service employment for those unable to find adequate opportunities in the private sector."

Notes

1. For a review of this literature, cf. Bennett Harrison, *Education, Training and the Urban Ghetto* (Baltimore: The Johns Hopkins Press, 1972).

---

[b] A brief description of the provisions of the Act is included in Appendix A of Part 2.

4

Public Service Employment in the 1930s: The WPA

ALDEN F. BRISCOE

Introduction

In the present discussion on public service employment, the WPA is frequently referred to. In most cases the referrals are not flattering. For mention of this program generally evokes a vision of shovel-leaning and leaf-raking men and "dead-end jobs." However, despite the frequent references to this massive effort of the 1930s few people seem to have more than a sketchy knowledge of the program. The WPA appears to lie in that netherworld between current events and history.

The present chapter is meant to provide some knowledge of one of the largest programs of public service employment. However, beyond that it is an attempt to use some of the analytical tools and knowledge gained about manpower in the 1960s to re-examine the WPA as a manpower program. Manpower programs can have many goals and like other efforts they must be measured against these goals. We shall see that the WPA achieved some of the goals of manpower programs and did not achieve others.

As this session developed, two things became clear: First, there is a dearth of research on the WPA despite its size and unquestioned importance. The author was unable to find any analysis of the WPA in the light of present knowledge and experience with manpower programs. Second, the WPA has always been a highly controversial program, so much so that in 1939 when the Institute of Public Opinion polled a sample of people asking, among other things, for "the greatest accomplishment" of the Roosevelt administration and also the "worst thing" the Roosevelt administration had done, the WPA won – in both categories.[1]

This paper is a revised version of *The WPA: What Is to Be Learned?*, which was prepared under a contract with the Manpower Administration, U.S. Department of Labor. However, points of view or opinions stated in this document are those of the author, and do not necessarily represent the official position or policy of the Department of Labor or of the board of directors or other staff members of the Center for Governmental Studies.

A Backward Glance

History

There were 12-14 million unemployed when Franklin Roosevelt was inaugurated president in March 1933. The WPA was not the administration's first program designed to deliver jobs and relief. Within two months of the Inauguration the Federal Emergency Relief Act (FERA) – modeled on a New York State program which Franklin Roosevelt had instituted when he was governor of that state – permitted the federal government to make grants-in-aid to states to stimulate private employment if possible, to create public jobs if not, and to provide relief if necessary. FERA lasted until the end of 1935, when the relief responsibilities were returned to the states. Meanwhile, in November 1933, the Civil Works Administration (CWA) was hastily launched by executive order to provide work relief, especially during the winter months. Half of the employees were to be from the relief rolls and the other half from the ranks of the unemployed not on relief (for whom there was no means test). The program was expensive and not very successful and was terminated in July 1934.[2]

Two programs were developed especially for youth. The Civilian Conservation Corps (CCC) was organized in April 1933. It employed an annual average of 250,000 to 300,000 youths, who lived in work camps and built trails, roads, cabins, and firebreaks, and who did other conservation work. The National Youth Administration (NYA) was started in June 1935, and was administered more or less as part of the WPA. NYA employed on the average 150,000 to 190,000 in-school and out-of-school youth, mostly on part-time jobs.[3]

At the end of 1934 the administration developed proposals for a new program which were submitted to Congress in January 1935. After three months of debate, on April 8, 1935, Congress passed the Emergency Relief Appropriation Act of 1935. This act appropriated $4.88 billion "to provide relief, work relief, and to increase employment by providing useful projects." The money was divided up mostly among existing federal agencies with the idea that each would sponsor temporary projects for the employment of then unemployed workers, and a new agency, the Works Progress Administration (WPA), received $1.4 billion to finance "small useful projects."

However, most projects were soon run directly by the WPA, because of the difficulties other federal agencies had in developing projects and the dynamism of the WPA and its first director, Harry Hopkins. By February 1936, employment on WPA projects was over 3 million, and it averaged over 2 million per year until the program's termination in June 1943. During that period the program paid out an average of nearly $1.4 billion per year in wages to WPA workers. WPA workers during that period constructed roads, buildings, airports, and stadiums; painted murals and pictures; wrote books and poems; sewed garments; served meals; and did a hundred other things.[4]

The WPA was the biggest of the New Deal programs and the one referred to most today. In 1939 it was looked upon as both the worst and the best program of the New Deal. Now it is frequently scorned as a leaf-raking, shovel-leaning boondoggle. What, then, was the WPA? Let us look at several aspects of the program, keeping in mind that the WPA was constantly changing. Differences appeared yearly in its design and operation. The administration was pragmatic and retained things which worked and discarded those that did not. And since the WPA got annual authorization, each year Congress reviewed and made changes in program design and direction.

Goals

The purpose of the WPA was to provide temporary work-relief to needy unemployed people. Although as in any large program the goals did not always manifest themselves in each local administrative decision and the WPA had secondary goals and effects which many of its local administrators pursued strongly, the WPA was not only surprisingly single-purposed, but surprisingly open about its goals. Administrator Hopkins, a former social worker and previously administrator of Roosevelt's New York state program, explained the WPA's purpose to his staff in June 1935 in unequivocal terms:

What is more important, that the fellow who has been kicked around now for years and given a lot of relief, some of it pretty miserable and uncertain, be given a job, or that some great bridge be built and he not get a job? . . . Never forget that the objective of this whole program as laid down by the President . . . is the objective of taking 3,500,000 people off relief and putting them to work, and the secondary objective is to put them to work on the best possible projects we can, but don't ever forget that first objective, and don't let me hear any of you apologizing for it because it is nothing to be ashamed of.[5]

Yet this goal opened other questions which were never adequately answered, particularly the question of who was to be enrolled. The administration and Congress never specified how many people were to be given work, and there was never any attempt to employ all the needy unemployed. In January 1935 testimony before a Senate Committee, Hopkins justified the $4 billion request for relief work as the amount necessary to provide a job for one member of every needy family whose breadwinner was capable of work. But this was never expressed as the policy of the WPA, and the program never employed this many people. The final decision on the number of jobs to allocate was based on need as well as the financial condition of the government.[6]

As the program developed, other goals were expressed, including training and retention of skills, but these were not pushed as major goals, for the program was looked upon as temporary, and it was expected that once the economy expanded, people would be able to get the types of jobs most of them had previously held. Furthermore, there was a constant struggle between utility of the projects and the desire to employ workers. Part of this reflected an underlying struggle – fostered by Roosevelt – between Hopkins and Secretary of the Interior Harold Ickes who administered the Public Works Administration.[7] But the major part was the eternal struggle between utility and employment which always exists in public employment.

Administration

It has generally been accepted that the New Deal used a pragmatic approach to the administration of programs. Perhaps nowhere is that more clearly demonstrated than in the WPA, which never worked according to the original plan. The Federal Emergency Relief Act of 1935 had left the question of organization nearly open. A month later Executive Order 7034 designated three new administrative elements: a Division of Applications and Informations within the National Emergency Council, which was supposed to accept applciations for local projects and serve as a clearinghouse for information on the program; an Advisory Committee on Allotments, to advise the President on approval of projects and allocations of funds; and the WPA. It was expected that the Public Works Administration and the Bureau of Roads would provide most of the jobs. The WPA would provide coordination and employ the small residue of workers not employed by the other agencies. But the WPA, with Hopkins directing, soon became the major operating division, and the other divisions became practically vestigial.[8]

Until 1939 the Works Progress Administration was an independent agency. Thereafter, with its name changed to Works *Projects* Administration, it was part of the Federal Works Agency. The WPA had its central headquarters in Washington, with regional offices, state directors (who had to be approved by the Senate), and district offices presiding over several counties. It usually employed about 30,000 people, most of them in state and district offices. These people were hired – according to the original legislation – "without regard to the provisions of the civil-service laws." Requests by the Agency to institute civil service status were turned down by Congress in 1939 and 1940.[9]

Projects had to be initiated locally by a state or local government or a federal agency. The "sponsor" had to be legally empowered to carry out the work proposed. A project proposal had to give an estimated cost of the proposal and the amount and kind of labor required. Sponsors also had to guarantee necessary architectural and engineering plans and a part of the cost. This local share requirement was not formalized into a fixed percentage until 1940 when it was set at 25 percent for each state's average, although individual sponsors could be under this. Previously the local contribution – which could be in kind – averaged about 19 percent. In all construction projects the final product belonged to the local sponsor who had to guarantee upkeep.

The majority of projects were initiated locally by municipal, township, or county governments. A 1937 study showed the following percentage distribution of sponsoring agencies in terms of cost:

Table 4.1
WPA – 1937: Percentage Distribution of Sponsoring Agencies in Terms of Cost

Class of Sponsoring Agency	Percent
Municipal	39.3
Township	14.5
County	26.7
State	15.6
Federal	3.7
Other	0.2
Total	100.0

Actually a significant problem was often finding local units to sponsor projects, and in many cases the WPA district offices had to recruit project sponsors. Plans were then worked out between the district office and the sponsoring agency and forwarded to the state office and from there to the national office. After national approval the proposal was returned to the state office which had to decide how to allot its quota of jobs among approved projects.

When the project was in operation, the WPA district office (and not the local sponsor) was responsible for hiring and paying workers, securing necessary materials, supplies, and equipment, and supervising the work. Contractors were not used because, despite or because of their greater efficiency, they were generally unable to hire a large proportion of needy people on their projects.[10]

Eligibility

The two major criteria for employment on WPA were need and employability. Although these were the major criteria, other factors were considered, many of which were changed over the years by Congress. Furthermore, local administrators made their own decisions about who should be chosen, and not every charge of personal or political favoritism was without foundation.

No one under eighteen could qualify for WPA, since the National Youth Administration and the Civilian Conservation Corps were designed to serve youth. There was no upper age limit, and because of their inability to find other employment, older workers tended to be a high percentage of WPA enrollees. The official position of the WPA was that there would be no discrimination on account of sex, race, residence, or citizenship, although after 1939 Congress made it more difficult for noncitizens to get on WPA (and preference was given to veterans and their families). On the local level there is considerable evidence of individual acts of discrimination against potential WPA workers on account of sex, race, and lack of residence in the area of the project. Women usually made up between 12 and 20 percent of the workers. Between 10 and 20 percent were blacks. From inception to termination of the WPA the percentages of women, older workers, and blacks increased steadily.

As mentioned, the first criterion was need, because Congress did not create enough work for all unemployed. However, a small percentage of WPA enrollees (10 percent until 1937, when it was cut to 5 percent) who were not certified as needy could be hired on each project. This was done partly in an attempt to remove some of the stigma of work relief, but more in order to provide workers with needed skills for particular projects.

State and local relief agencies were usually approved by the WPA to certify need and in only a few cases did WPA do its own certification. The determination of when an individual was in need was difficult and not always uniform. Several factors were taken into consideration in the determination. The income of the "family group" — those living in one household — was the usual basis for computation.

At the time of the WPA's inception most relief agencies used a "budgetary deficiency" principle promulgated by the FERA. If the family income was 15 percent below an estimated minimum budget, the family was certified in need of relief. After the dissolution of the FERA, family income was often measured against the lowest WPA wage paid in the state. But this method often yielded to more flexible methods which took account of family size and special requirements in determing need. Thus people with dependents tended to qualify more often than single people; people with another income, such as a son enrolled in NYA or CCC, old age assistance, or aid to dependent children under the new Social Security Act, often did not qualify; and it was general policy not to certify more than one person from each family. The "need level" varied among certifying agencies, but it was usually set higher than the need level for welfare. People who had assets such as homes, automobiles, and property, were a special eligibility problem, and these cases were usually decided individually. The question of whether people eligible for special assistance under existing categorical programs should qualify was answered in different ways at different times.[11]

Once the question of need was settled, the question of employability arose. To follow the original aims completely — to get money to needy people — would have meant that employability was no criterion, but it would be difficult to have a work project in which people were unable to work. Therefore, in most local projects the factor of employability was taken into account and the most employable often were hired first — although in some cases they were hired last since local administrators felt that they would be most likely to get a private job if one became available. Many times the decision on employability only begged the question of employable for what. The WPA tried to utilize the skills of the enrollees. However, most of the WPA jobs involved manual labor and many people who had held white-collar jobs previously might not be considered employable for building roads. On the other hand, some local administrators felt that white-collar workers should get first opportunity at jobs since a lack of income was a greater hardship on them than on unemployed blue-collar workers.

When all was said and done, the WPA workers hired were for the most part people who had had previous work experience. A January 1936 study showed that only 13 percent of the workers were "inexperienced," and in 1939, 97 percent had been regularly employed in private jobs before enrollment in the WPA. The WPA did not employ large numbers of the type of people whom we would now call "hardcore."[12]

Nearly as important as the question of who should get the job in the first place was the question of how long an employee should stay on the job. All WPA workers had to register with the United States Employment Service, and it was accepted policy from the beginning that WPA workers should be cut from the rolls if they refused employment on private jobs providing that (a) the jobs were full time, (b) they paid standard wages, (c) they were not in conflict with union relationships, and (d) the workers were offered the opportunity to return to WPA if the job was temporary or if they lost it through no fault of their own. Hopkins was emphatic about the fact that the WPA would not force people to accept substandard employment.

In 1937 Congress tightened the private employment requirement by stipulating that WPA workers upon pain of discharge must accept private employment under reasonable conditions if the pay was the same or better than WPA. This change from "prevailing wages" led to some abuses, for although WPA wages were lower than prevailing wages, they were generally less liable to seasonal or climatic interruptions, which often depressed wages from private jobs.

As can be expected, there were complaints at various times that the WPA soaked up too much of the available labor supply in certain skills and certain areas so that there were allegations of a shortage of apple pickers in New York and New England in 1936 and 1937, shoe stitchers in Lynn, Massachusetts, in

1937, dairy farm help in Connecticut and Minnesota in 1937 and 1939, taxi cab drivers in New York City in 1935, and others in other locations. For the most part these complaints proved groundless.[13]

Some critics began to fear the creation of permanent WPA workers. They felt that since there was a limited amount of WPA work (Congress never seriously considered increasing the size of the WPA to provide work for all), this should be split up among all the needy people, and those who were "making a career" of WPA should be eliminated. Actually in 1939 estimates were that overall only 16.7 percent of workers on WPA had been on continuously for three years or more — although in New York City 42.1 percent had been on for three or more years.

In 1939 Congress required that anyone who had been on WPA more than eighteen months should be dismissed and remain off for at least thirty days. This effected 171,000 dismissals in July and 611,733 in August. This requirement was eased in 1941. Since there were simply not enough private employment opportunities available, removal of some from WPA rolls, or "rotation" as it was called, was no solution. As Mayor Reading of Detroit stated, "It is pretty hard to rotate your appetite."[14]

Wages and Hours

The rate of remuneration (or relief) was an issue which caused as much difficulty as the choice of clients for the WPA. The method of determining remuneration and the actual rates were changed several times. In 1935 President Roosevelt set the policy for wages by declaring that compensation would be in the form of "security payments, which should be larger than the amount now received as a relief dole, but . . . not so large as to encourage the rejection of opportunities for private employment." A schedule of monthly security wages was drawn up based on degree of skill, geographic region, and degree of urbanization. Four classes of work, four regions, and five degrees of urbanization determined the maximum wages paid. This schedule was revised with the result that the lowest wages, especially in southern states, were raised in 1936 and again in 1939. In 1941 and 1942 certain defense projects were exempted from wage and hour limits.

Upon the establishment of the policy of security wages, organized labor immediately pointed out that since working hours were established at from 120 to 140 hours per month, the actual hourly rates for skilled workers would be below prevailing rates. Therefore, in 1936 Congress required that WPA workers be paid at hourly rates not less than prevailing rates for similar work. However, since the policy of monthly security wages had not changed, this new policy meant simply that skilled workers worked fewer hours for the same monthly wages. In 1939 the policy of paying prevailing hourly rates was abandoned and 130 hours was set as the monthly requirement for all workers.

In any case the money that workers received was not munificent. In Mississippi, where wages were lowest, in May 1935 they ranged from a minimum of $19/month to a maximum of $55. In August 1939 they had risen to $31.20 and $75.40 respectively. In the District of Columbia, where wages were high, in 1935 they ranged from $45 to $79 and in 1939 from $52 to $94.90, the maximum paid anywhere for skilled work. The average WPA worker earned $52.14/month in 1936, which grew to $58.79 in 1941, but much of this apparent gain was eaten up by a rise in the cost of living in the intervening years.

Although these figures were above those given on relief, they must be considered in terms of the fact that it was generally WPA policy to accept no more than one person from any family and no one who had significant outside income. That such limits were extremely low is illustrated by the WPA regulations in effect in Mississippi in 1941. A family of four was regarded as in need if it had less than approximately $73 per month for food, shelter, clothing, fuel, electricity, medical care, household supplies, church, recreation, education, and personal incidentals. Still, monthly WPA wages for the higher grade of unskilled labor in this state ranged from $35.10 in rural areas to $48.10 in cities over 25,000. Only WPA skilled professional and technical workers in counties including cities having a population of 25,000 or more earned $74 per month in Mississippi — one dollar above the estimated need level for a family of four, while the average family size of WPA workers was 3.75.

Although the WPA usually attempted to permit workers who lost time because of sickness, bad weather, or other factors outside of their control to make it up, it was estimated that workers averaged a loss of 5 percent of their wages per year, such loss being concentrated in winter months and times of sickness. Although there were no fringe benefits, workers were generally guaranteed compensation for accidents as a result of work.[15]

Training and Education

As mentioned, the WPA was thought of primarily as a temporary work relief program for temporarily unemployed. As such, one of its goals was to preserve skills and work habits of the unemployed, and it was WPA policy to place workers as much as possible in jobs which would utilize their skills. There are no good statistics on the success in achieving this goal, but since approximately 55 percent of WPA workers in 1940 had been previously employed in unskilled occupations, it is obvious that many of these workers did not have significant skills to preserve. On the other hand defenders of the WPA pointed out that doing almost any job was better for retention of basic work habits than remaining idle.

There was, however, some training for WPA workers. For those who had never worked, the WPA was an introduction to the world of work. Many others learned some skills on the job, although often these skills were not salable in the job market. Some labor leaders argued that WPA laborers receiving security wages learned and were employed at skilled occupations. It is, however, doubtful if this was a major problem.

There were, however, some particular training programs. In 1937, the WPA instituted a voluntary training course for foremen which was completed by more than 46,000 WPA workers, many of whom had been promoted from WPA laborers. In 1936, a training program for household workers was established which was operated in thirty-five states and is estimated to have trained about 22,000 persons. The WPA worked in close cooperation with state departments of education and local school districts in order to coordinate with vocational training classes conducted under the adult education program.

In 1940, with the expansion of defense work, the WPA initiated a program for training WPA workers in manual occupations needed in defense industries. Nearly 330,000 WPA workers received training in these projects in the eighteen months from July 1, 1940 to December 15, 1942. Nearly half of them were trained in machine shop, while approximately another third were trained in sheet metal, welding, and aviation services. Most of these courses lasted four to twelve weeks. Trainees were selected by the WPA and paid a security wage.

There were other smaller training programs. However, especially before 1940 the WPA did little training. Between 1940 and 1943 it did considerable training in refresher courses and short courses for factory work designed to help the war effort.

The WPA did conduct other educational activities with its Division of Education. Over half of this education was for general adult education and literacy and naturalization education or leisure time activities, with only one-eighth spent for vocational education. Table 4.2 shows how the 1,641,000 educational enrollees of May 1937, a fairly typical period, were broken down[16]

Placement

Placement into outside jobs from the WPA was not very successful — for during most of the WPA's life there weren't many other jobs available. All WPA workers had to register with the United States Employment Service, and attempts were made to inform the Civil Service Commission and private employers of the available labor supply. However, only after the war production began to roll in the early 1940s was the WPA successful in placing its workers.[17]

Projects

Seven basic criteria were used in choosing projects although final decision on

Table 4.2
WPA Division of Education: Breakdown of Educational Activities of 1,641,000 Enrollees (May 1937)

Educational Activity	Percentage Enrolled
General adult education	25.4
Literacy and naturalization	15.5
Avocational and leisure time activities	13.3
Vocational education	12.6
Homemaking	7.4
Parental education	3.9
Workers education	3.5
Nursery schools	3.1
Public affairs education	2.2
Correspondence instruction	1.6
Other	11.5
Total	100.0

Source: See footnote 16.

putting a project into operation lay with the state director. Criteria included:

1. Utility
2. Labor intensiveness
3. Dollar return from the facility once it was built
4. Immediacy
5. Amount of employment provided for those on relief rolls
6. Proximity to domicile of unemployed
7. Speed with which unemployed could be put to work.

Using these basic criteria the WPA funded many and varied projects, ranging from small efforts costing a hundred dollars or so to New York's North Beach Airport (La Guardia), which cost $40 million. The WPA classified its projects under either the Division of Operations or the Division of Community Service Programs. Of total money spent the former used 78 percent and the latter 21.6 percent, with the remainder in other projects. Table 4.3 shows the distribution.

Over the eight years of its lifetime the WPA spend $8,990,600,000 on enrollee wages averaging close to $1.4 billion per year during the first six years. During that time there was an average of 2 million persons enrolled at all times. In 1938 the number enrolled was equal to three times the combined workforce of American Telephone and Telegraph, General Electric, Westinghouse, U.S.

Table 4.3

Distribution of WPA Projects Between Division of Operations and Division of Community Service Programs

Type of Project	Percentage Spent
Division of Operations	78.0
Highways and roads	38.9
Construction and repair of buildings	10.4
Recreational facilities	8.3
Sewage collection and disposal	6.7
Other (water supply, airports & airways, con- servation, sanitation & engineering surveys)	13.7
Division of Community Service	21.6
Sewing	6.4
Education	2.0
Recreation	2.0
Research and surveys	2.0
Public records	1.5
Library	1.0
Other	6.7
Miscellaneous (including national defense and vocational training)	0.4

Steel, Bethlehem Steel, Republic Steel, and the B & O, New York Central, Pennsylvania, and Union Pacific Railroads. However, this was only 5 percent of the total number of workers gainfully employed in the U.S., and at its highest point in October and November 1936 and 1938, the WPA enrolled no more than 31 percent of the unemployed. In February 1939, over 1,330,000 unemployed people certified eligible for the WPA were not employed on its rolls.

Over the life of the Agency 8-1/2 million people with 30 million dependents worked more than 12 million man-years for the WPA. This is more than six times the amount estimated utilized in building the pyramids in Egypt. Some of this work was wasted. WPA workers were under numerous constraints, not the least of which was their lack of tools and materials to compete with private employees. Estimates of efficiency of WPA workers range from 20 to 80 percent. Local WPA administrators have stated that the efficiency of WPA workers compared favorably with that of local road and telephone crews in spite of the constraints under which they operated. But the program did accomplish a vast amount.[18]

Accomplishments

And what did the WPA accomplish?

It built 617,000 miles of new roads, enough to go twenty-four times around the world. It built or reconstructed 124,000 bridges and viaducts, which, if placed end to end, would stretch over 800 miles. It built or reconstructed 120,000 public buildings, including enough new buildings (35,000) for ten in every county in the United States. Some of the other project areas shown in Table 4.4.

Table 4.4
Number of WPA Construction Projects (Other than Roads, Bridges, and Buildings)

Project Type	Number		
	New Construction	Additions	Reconstruction or improvement
Sidewalks and paths	23,607*	–	6,972
Curbs	25,073*	–	3,441
Stadiums, grandstands and bleachers	2,302	129	797
Parks	1,668	189	6,335
Playgrounds	3,085	107	9,581
Athletic fields	3,026	68	2,457
Swimming pools	805	–	339
Utility plants	2,877	123	1,172
Water mains and distribution lines	16,117*	–	3,658
Landing fields	353	131	469
Road and street lights	30,556	–	69,474
Traffic signs	937,282	–	–
Golf courses	254	–	378

* Miles

These figures include the construction of New York's Central Park Zoo, San Francisco's Aquatic Park, San Antonio's and Chicago's waterfronts, the Philadelphia Art Museum, and the restoration of Independence Hall in Philadelphia and Faneuil Hall in Boston. Furthermore WPA workers sewed 382,756,000 garments, served over 1.2 billion school lunches, preserved 84 million quarts of food, and repaired 94 million books. WPA orchestras played 5,974 live concerts before 2,423,217 listeners, as well as 112 radio concerts. WPA educational projects are estimated to have cut the illiteracy rate in Arkansas by 40 percent. The tangible monuments to the WPA abound furthermore in books, plays, hiking guides, and murals – some of them undistinguished, others real contributions to culture.[19]

However, the projects constructed and the services rendered are less important than the money paid out in salaries. Jackson Pollock, Conrad Aiken, Orson Welles, and William de Kooning were only a few of the creative men who worked on WPA. Richard Wright supported himself as a WPA manual laborer, and in 1936, on the basis of a sample of his writings, he was transferred to a writer's project for which he wrote *Uncle Tom's Children.* Four years later he published *Native Son,* a best-seller. Few people wrote *Native Sons,* but millions maintained their self-respect and fed themselves and their dependents as a result of the WPA.[20]

Another Look

On several grounds the WPA can be rated a success, but nearly thirty years have passed since the end of the program, and we have learned much about the art of manpower, particularly in the last decade. Therefore, it is worthwhile looking back at the WPA from 1971 and seeing what we can learn in terms of our present criteria.

Putting People to Work

The WPA averaged about 2 million people at work throughout its lifetime. It proved once and for all — if such proof was needed — that unemployed people can be put to work quickly if the society makes a commitment to that goal. Furthermore, judging from the results in terms of concrete (and esthetic) products, most of them can be put to work usefully. Naturally there will be waste, confusion, and occasional boondoggling. However, the wastage of having people who wish to work sit idle is immeasurably greater — not only in terms of goods and services not produced, but in terms of the individual frustrations and suffering.

Actually the time has arrived in this society when we cannot simply let people starve because the economy does not produce jobs. We must provide income to the unemployed and to those who depend on them for support. Most will agree with President Nixon that "workfare" is indeed better than welfare.

Clients

The WPA employed men and women above eighteen who were in need and able and willing to work. For various reasons, including the fact that preference was given to heads of families, about 80 percent of the workers were men and nearly the same percentage was white.

Statistics have shown that a majority of people on the WPA had a history of attachment to the workforce. Critics will point out that today's unemployed do not have such a history. However, with the unemployment rate presently near 6 percent, there are several million unemployed who do have a history of steady employment. The WPA has proved that those with some attachment to the workforce can rapidly and relatively efficiently be put to work. It has not proved that "hardcore" people can or cannot be put to work.

Types of Jobs

The WPA put most people to work on construction jobs at manual labor. The program had trouble creating and filling white-collar jobs. Nevertheless, "skilled workers" made up between 10 and 15 percent of WPA enrollees and professional and technical employees generally made up another 3 to 5 percent, while supervisory employees added about another 3 to 5 percent.[21] Thus approximately 20 percent of WPA workers were skilled or supervisory workers.

At present there is still a need for the construction of buildings and recreation facilities, as there was in the thirties. At the same time there is a great need for services and technological work in crime, pollution control, transportation, recreation, education, health, and a number of other fields. The WPA proved that the unemployed can be effectively employed on construction projects. Its limited evidence points toward the fact that though such projects are more difficult to administer, the unemployed can be put to work on education, research, health, and other service projects.

The WPA was made up of a series of short-term projects outside of the normal public administrative system. Although a few of the service projects were transferred directly to local governments as permanent programs, for the most part at the completion of the project, WPA workers were released, although they might be hired again for a similar project. This suggests the use of a project approach for future public service employment.

Training

The WPA was not primarily a training program, but rather a temporary job creation program. Only in the early 1940s, as the country developed a war economy, did the WPA do significant amounts of training. As mentioned, most of this training was for defense industries. Perhaps the most important lesson to be learned from the WPA experience is that training is only useful if there are jobs available.

There were, of course, other residual training benefits from the WPA. Some workers were able to retain skills through a period of idleness. Other workers were able to develop new skills on-the-job. However, many of the skills which

WPA workers developed, such as construction labor with a minimum of tools or sewing, were not salable on the open market and therefore were of little use except on a WPA job.

Overall, WPA did some training, but it was not a major component of the program, and it was not very successful in imparting skills which had value in the employment market. In the future if training is a goal of a public employment program, it must be planned as a part of the program, and it must impart skills which will enable the trainees to get regular public or private jobs. The WPA showed that both institutional and on-the-job training can impart the skills but that the acquiring of skills does not assure a job.

Placement

There was usually fairly close liaison between the employment services and the WPA local projects, but job placement as we know it today was not practiced. Many people left the WPA for private employment, but most of these people found their own jobs. Because the projects were independent of state and local government, there was no opportunity simply to move people off a "subsidized" payroll onto the "regular" payroll without changing his employment. Our sophistication about placement in the manpower field, learned in the last ten years, has outstripped anything that was known in the WPA. We now know that placement is an important component of any public employment program. In this area, too, the WPA's weakness stemmed from the fact that it conceived of itself as a temporary work program outside the regular system. If a program is to have effective links to the normal employment system — both public and private — then it must be planned with that in mind, and if permanent jobs are a goal, placement must be an important component of the program.

Wages

The question of wages was one of the most controversial in the WPA. As mentioned, the program usually attempted to pay "security wages" between welfare and prevailing wages, taking into account both skill involved and differences in prevailing wages around the country. No attempt was made to give supplements for workers with many dependents. Certainly, the WPA has proved that this question will be a controversial one no matter how it is handled.

There is very little evidence that the wages were too high. Thousands of people transferred off WPA when offered private jobs paying prevailing wages, and despite the numerous complaints there is little evidence that the WPA used up enough of the labor supply in any industry so as to create a shortage. On the other hand there is considerable evidence that the WPA wages were too low in many cases for WPA workers to support families. Certainly the examples given above for people in rural areas of Mississippi suggest wages which were too low.

Some critics presently argue that paying prevailing wages will give workers no incentive to get off a work program and into a regular job. In 1939 the congressional demand that anyone who had been more than eighteen months on a WPA job should be dropped stemmed from this worry that there was not enough incentive to leave a work program for a regular job. But the fact is — as proved in the WPA — that until there are enough regular jobs for the unemployed, incentives are useless. In any case, the WPA gives evidence that security wages are not large enough to adequately support a family. It gives no evidence that prevailing wages are too large to prove a disincentive to finding a private or "non-subsidized" public job.

Administration

The WPA was a separate federal agency. It was not part of any cabinet department or other agency (until the very end when it became part of the Federal Works Agency). Except for requiring local sponsorship, which meant the recommendation and planning of a project, the WPA bypassed state and local government in administering its projects. Furthermore, all projects were temporary and terminated upon completion, at which time whatever "product" existed belonged to the local jurisdiction which had sponsored the project. Direct federal administration was the quickest method of getting organized and putting people to work in a hurry.

At this point in time, it appears unlikely that a program would be directly administered by the federal government. Present rhetoric is to cut back on the federal administration of programs, and the latest thrust is to increase the role of the state and local governments, with more powers put into the hands of the elected chief executives. The WPA tells us little about the abilities of state and local government to administer programs and the effects of such local administration.

Impact upon Hiring and Personnel Structures

Because the WPA was a separate program for the most part without administrative connections or career ladders to federal, state, and local agencies, it had a negligible impact upon the hiring and personnel systems of these institutions. If, as many people are saying, one of the major goals of a public service employment program is to impact the hiring practices and personnel systems of public agencies in order to make them receptive to workers whom they previously rejected or held in dead-end jobs, then the WPA can teach us little. We can learn that if a public service employment program is to develop the opportunity for long-term employment and create an impact on the system which leads to upward mobility and the sensitive and efficient use of all employees, it must be designed as part of the structure of ongoing public personnel systems.

Labor Intensiveness

The WPA was extremely labor intensive. Of the over $10 million of WPA funds expended, more than $8.9 million (88.7 percent) went for wages. This was accomplished by allowing only $7 of materials per man per month — later reduced to $6. Any amount larger than this had to be paid for locally by the "sponsor." Even considering the higher value of the dollar in the 1930s, $7 was a very small materials expenditure, especially for construction work. Many localities provided larger amounts, although others could not afford more. But putting so much money into wages had a price, and most local supervisors complained about the inefficiency of work caused by the lack of materials and equipment which any contractor would use. Some estimates were that the project costs could have been decreased by one-third if more had been spent for materials.[22]

We can learn some things about labor-intensiveness of public employment projects from the WPA. First, if the goal is to employ the largest number of people, then the projects should be planned as labor-intensively as possible. However, in most projects there is a tradeoff between efficiency and labor intensiveness. The level of this tradeoff varies, but in construction the lack of tools and equipment seriously limits efficiency. There are other types of projects where the lack of tools is not as important. In planning future public service employment projects, projects with the smallest need for capital expenditures should be chosen.

Economic Impact

It is difficult to determine how much impact the WPA had on the economy. The author has found little research on the subject. Certainly the program must have had considerable impact. On the average 2 million families were receiving approximately $1.4 billion per year for six years. Almost all of this money was spent immediately for necessities, thereby creating a multiplier effect.[a] This

---

[a]It is interesting to contrast WPA type projects with the accelerated public works projects of the New Deal period. John Kenneth Galbraith has pointed out that public works expenditures are massed toward the beginning of a project but that at some point, since there is a limited amount of construction capacity, added public works expenditures simply begin to bid up the cost of available construction without creating any more employment or construction. (The Economic Effects of Federal Public Works Expenditures, 1933-1938, Study for the National Resources Planning Board, Washington, D.C., U.S. GPO, 1940).

money either came from taxes — in which case a higher percentage was spent than had it not been taxed — or it was deficit spending. In any case this was at a time when the Gross National Product ranged from $72.5 billion (1935) to $100.6 billion (1940) to $192.5 billion (1943), and federal expenditures went from $6.5 billion (1935) to $9.0 billion (1940) to $79.4 billion (1943). Thus through 1940 WPA wages were approximately 1.5 percent of the GNP and between 20 and 30 percent of annual federal expenditures.[23]

On the other hand, despite an expenditure of some $11 billion for the WPA and more on the other New Deal programs, the United States did not totally recover from the depression until the war economy began in the early forties. Thus, the WPA's counter-cyclical effect was not enough by itself to increase overall demand and thus stimulate private production sufficiently to decrease unemployment. We will, of course, never know how much worse the depression might have been without WPA.

Two factors must be kept in mind. First, if jobs are short term, as the WPA jobs were, something must be put in their place when they end. Otherwise, not only are people thrown out of work, but there is also a loss of a multiplier effect as wages are terminated. In the 1940s the U.S. involved itself in a world war. Today we do not want to use such an option. Secondly, public employment jobs have little counter-cyclical effect if they are simply paid for out of funds taken from some other program. If they are to have a counter-cyclical effect, they must be financed by additional money, over and above the expenditures previously budgeted for goods and services, and apparently they must be created on a massive scale. Most economists agree deficit spending must accompany such programs.

In short, the WPA experience suggests that it is not a good idea to bet on the counter-cyclical aspect of public service employment. Nor, incidentally, will public service employment totally solve the problem of unemployment, although it can give jobs to some of the unemployed. With the expenditure of some $1.4 billion per year in 1930s dollars for security wages, the WPA employed only 31 percent of the unemployed at its point of highest impact. In the 1970s, even with a lower unemployment rate, no one is considering a program to hire that percentage of the unemployed.

A present-day public service employment program can give jobs and income to some of the unemployed and produce a number of needed goods and services. This is no small achievement. But if we wish to achieve other goals — training, placement, and institutional change in the hiring and upgrading patterns of public and private employers — we must design programs different from the WPA. The WPA was a program of the New Deal, and it must be judged as part of the 1930s. For the 1970s we must look at the WPA as a program not to disparage, but to learn from and to improve upon.

114

Notes

1. Donald S. Howard, *The WPA and Federal Relief Policy* (New York: Russell Sage Foundation, 1943), p. 105.

2. Josephine C. Brown, *Public Relief, 1920-1939* (New York: Henry Holt & Co., 1940), pp. 149-59.

3. John Charnow, *Work Relief Experiences in the United States* (Washington, D.C.: Committee on Social Science, Social Science Research Council, 1943), pp. 1-10.

4. Howard, *WPA*, pp. 18, 35; Brown, *Public Relief*, pp. 165-68.

5. Lois Craig, "Beyond 'Leaf-Raking': WPA's Lasting Legacy," *City* 4, 3 (October/November 1970): 23.

6. Howard, *WPA*, pp. 561-66; Arthur W. Macmahon, John D. Millett, and Gladys Ogden, *The Administration of Federal Work Relief* (Chicago: The Public Administration Service, 1941), p. 41.

7. Howard, *WPA*, pp. 578-83; Macmahon, Millett, and Ogden, *Admin.*, pp. 67-69.

8. Macmahon, Millett, and Ogden, *Admin. Fed. Work Relief*, pp. 66-77.

9. Howard, *WPA*, pp. 106-121.

10. Ibid., pp. 144-53; U.S. Government, *Final Report on the WPA Program, 1935-1943*, Washington, D.C., 1943.

11. Howard, *WPA* pp. 267-447. *Final Report*, pp. 42-45.

12. Howard, *WPA*, pp. 448-66.

13. Ibid., pp. 473-87.

14. Ibid., pp. 498-527.

15. Ibid., pp. 33, 158-243; *Final Report*, pp. 23-26.

16. Doak S. Campbell, Frederick H. Blair, and Oswald L. Harvey, *Educational Activities of the Works Progress Administration*, A Staff Study, #14, prepared for the Advisory Committee on Education (Washington, D.C.: Government Printing Office, 1939), pp. 1-102; *Final Report*, pp. 90-93.

17. *Final Report*, p. 93.

18. Howard, *WPA*, pp. 34-35, 105-131, 531-57; *Final Report*, pp. 110-112, 124.

19. Garth L. Mangum, "New Deal Job Creation Programs," *Emergency Employment Act Background Information* (Washington, D.C.: Subcommittee on Employment Manpower and Poverty of the Committee on Labor and Public Welfare, 1967), p. 135; *Final Report*, pp. 131-33.

20. Charnow, *Work Relief*, p. 85. Craig, "Beyond 'Leaf-Raking' ", pp. 23-29.

21. *Final Report*, p. 102.

22. Ibid., p. 38.

23. Historical Statistics of the United States (Washington, D.C.: U.S. Department of Commerce, 1961), pp. 139, 771.

Bibliography

Adams, Grace. *Workers on Relief.* New Haven: Yale University Press, 1939.

Brown, Josephine C. *Public Relief, 1929-1939.* New York: Henry Holt & Co., 1940.

Campbell, Doak S.; Frederick H. Blair; and Oswald L. Harvey. *Educational Activities of the Works Progress Administration.* A Staff Study, #14, prepared for the Advisory Committee on Education. Washington, D.C.: Government Printing Office, 1939.

Charnow, John. *Work Relief Experience in the United States.* Committee on Social Science, Social Science Research Council. Washington, D.C.: U.S. Government Printing Office, 1943.

Craig, Lois. "Beyond 'Leaf-Raking': WPA's Lasting Legacy." *City* 4, 3 (October/November, 1970).

Howard, Donald S. *The WPA and Federal Relief Policy.* New York: Russell Sage Foundation, 1943.

Macmahon, Arthur W.; John D. Millett; and Gladys Ogden. *The Administration of Federal Work Relief.* Chicago: The Public Administration Service, 1941.

U.S. Senate, Subcommittee on Employment, Manpower, and Poverty of the Committee on Labor and Public Welfare, *Emergency Employment Act, Background Information.* Washington, D.C., U.S. Government Printing Office, 1967.

U.S. Government, *Final Report on the WPA Program, 1935-1943,* Washington, D.C., U.S. Government Printing Office, 1946.

5

Economic Theory, Economic Reality, and the Fate of the Poor

BARRY F. BLUESTONE

Economists often work with abstract models of "perfect" economies which obey strict mathematical laws. In some cases this serves to sharpen the focus of empirical research. Yet, if the abstractions neglect reality and play on the minutiae, the theory can make for disastrous practice. Such is the case with modern labor theory and manpower policy.

"Bourgeois" economics begins with the premise that individuals attempt to maximize their "utility" or welfare subject to economic constraints. Consumers, for instance, maximize their welfare by choosing a bundle of commodities constrained only by their income and product prices. Firms maximize profit subject to the constraint of cost structures and demand conditions. Likewise, labor theory assumes that workers maximize their welfare by investing in themselves and choosing between work and leisure subject to the limitations of time and the costs of schooling and training. In the abstract there can be little doubt that this analysis is uncommonly succinct, insightful, and logically correct. In practice, however, it often leads economists to propose the wrong policies for the wrong people. The problem lies not in the framework, but in the emphasis placed on its separate parts. Economists tend to focus attention on the maximizing behavior of individuals and neglect the real economic constraints before them. This is especially true with regard to the poor.

Traditional economic theory requires competitive product markets, adequately mobile labor, and sufficient labor market information. Without these assumptions much of the traditional theory falls apart. As a result, economists tend to de-emphasize barriers between labor markets, the inadequacy of labor market information, and unequal opportunities afforded different groups in society. Competition among firms and individuals supposedly distributes workers so that the more skilled earn higher wages. It follows that those who earn less *must* be less skilled. Each worker is paid only what he is "worth."

The policy implication is clear cut. Economists conclude that the only way to help the economically disadvantaged is to change them. The poor must be equipped with more education, more training, better health, incentives to move,

117

and industrial discipline. *Because* the poor have low incomes, they *must* be unskilled, unhealthy, or lack the proper work attitudes. The only way to improve the chances of the poor is through a multitude of manpower programs designed to take care of one or another personal trait which contributes to unemployment or low wages. The poor are thus blamed for their poverty. While society may be responsible for not educating, training, or providing a healthful environment, the poor bear the brunt of any changes necessary to achieve a decent standard of living.

What economists overlook is the glaring fact that the economy does not create enough good jobs, and consequently many people with adequate skills are denied adequate employment. Because of racism, sexism, regional immobilities, and the risk attached to geographic and employment mobility, millions of workers have no jobs. Millions more are trapped in jobs which fail to pay a living wage. The basic structure of the economy is such that it creates good jobs and bad ones and then parcels them out on the basis of race, sex, and luck. More often than not, the economist's role has been to justify this distribution of opportunities, not change it. Rarely is the structure of the economy considered at fault for the poverty of the poor. And even less frequently do economists propose solutions aimed at the structure of the labor market rather than the characteristics of its victims.

A Historical Review of Labor Economics

While it is true that economists seldom defend the economically disadvantaged, it is not true that economists have always ignored the structural characteristics of individual labor markets. The currently accepted view of labor economics, that associated with the "human capital" school, is not the only view of labor market dynamics. Although it presently holds sway among academicians and policy makers, other labor market paradigms exist and new ones are being developed. The policy implications of the conflicting paradigms are at such variance that they deserve more attention.

In the 1940s and 1950s, labor economists recognized the importance of differences in the quality of labor. However, they also recognized the importance of barriers to mobility and the inadequacy of labor market information. Many institutional factors were observed to impinge on the wage determination process: e.g., government regulation, minimum wage legislation, unionization. Even the founders of the neoclassical analysis were "troubled by the 'peculiarities' of the labor market – the fact that the worker sells himself with his services, that his immediate financial need may place him at a disadvantage in negotiating with employers, that he is influenced by non-pecuniary motives, that he has limited knowledge of alternative opportunities, and that there are numerous objective barriers to free movement of labor."[1]

Thus by 1951 Lloyd Reynolds observed the following:

Most economists would agree that the notion of a "perfect labor market" is a highly abstract concept useful mainly for normative purposes. We can make a step forward, then, by avoiding any debate over this straw man and by relegating it to its proper role as a norm for welfare discussions. *This narrows the range of controversy to genuine issues: what are the most significant sources of imperfection in labor markets? how important are these imperfections in checking the play of market forces? what can be done as a practical matter to improve labor market structure?*[2] (emphasis added)

These were the important questions in 1951; twenty years later they are, if anything, even more critical. During the 1950s labor economists, including Harold Levinson, Arthur Ross, Clark Kerr, Sumner Slichter, and Lloyd Reynolds, pursued research which asked, "What is it about *different industries, different regions* of the nation, and *different labor markets* which accounts for the wide variance in employment and wage rates?" Others wondered why individual labor markets make for large differences in unemployment and underemployment? These economists were studying the differences in industrial structure which were correleated with wage differentials, asking questions about the effect of unionization and minimum wages, and indirectly posing the right questions about the determinants of income distribution. The critical variables were on the demand or industry side of the wage and employment equation: unionization, profitability, government attitude toward collective bargaining, the firm's ability to pay, the capital intensity of production, and the racial and sexual composition of the workforce. It was assumed, more or less correctly, that the skills required for most production jobs and many white-collar clerical occupations did not vary greatly *between* industries, firms, and regions.

The conclusion of much of this early research was summed up in Sumner Slichter's "Notes on the Structure of Wages." His research and that of others led him to conclude "that wages, within a considerable range, reflect managerial discretion, that where managements can easily pay high wages they tend to do so, and that where managements are barely breaking even they tend to keep wages down."[3] Harold Levinson slightly modified this conclusion with the observation that it is the existence of a "permissive economic environment" in the form of high profits, monopolized product markets, and spatial limitations which allow unions to gain strength and take advantage of high wage opportunities for their members.[4] The important differences in wages paid to individuals, and indeed in the labor force status of working-class employees, were shown to be related to industry attachment and region. Whether a person lives in Appalachia or Chicago has a great deal to do with the probability of locating employment; working in the steel industry vs. a drycleaning establishment pretty much determines income. Differences in education, training, skills, and "discipline" were taken to have some effect on labor force status, but were by no means the only variables or even the most critical ones.

Although much of the early research failed to focus on *who* got into *what* industry and who lived *where,* it was assumed that economic minorities — blacks, chicanos, Indians, teenagers, and women — would be restricted to the less skilled occupations *regardless* of the skill level of the worker. The individuals in these groups would have their employment possibilities limited to those firms (and industries) which operate in a "repressive" rather than permissive economic environment. Employment status and wage level were shown to be related to race, sex, region, industry, unionization, profits, and capital/labor ratios rather than determined exclusively by "human capital" traits.

Much of this research was related to the key question of the day: "What is the effect of unions on the efficiency of labor markets?" Consequently some of the more far-reaching implications for public policy were ignored. Based on their research, however, it is clear that social policy is needed to deal with market barriers and industry structure. The creation of alternative job opportunities to combat both unemployment and low-wage employment is certainly implied by their work.

But the 1950s came to an end and a new development in labor economics was soon to push much of the research of the decade off to the side and purge it from the leading economic journals. In 1960, T.W. Schultz, Edward Denison, and Gary Becker were beginning to develop a coherent "human capital" economics to replace the fragmented institutional and neoclassical theories which had prevailed to that point. By calling nearly everything that comprises worker productivity "human capital" these theorists were able, with a single semantic stroke, to explain all variance in employment status and wage rates in terms of one parameter.[5]

Correctly enough, the human capital school observed the strong correlation between education, training, skills, and competencies of the workforce and the incomes which individuals and families receive. They noted that physicians have more education (human capital) than janitors and that doctors are better paid. Based on so simple an observation, the human capitalists extrapolated their finding to cover all labor force research. Treating labor as shells into which human capital is poured, in greater or lesser amounts, this school was able to "explain" the wages and employment of all individuals. Those who invest more in themselves will (almost automatically) find employment more often, reap higher wages, and benefit from greater economic security.

But the extrapolation of the global finding to each and every segment of the labor force inevitably leads to critical errors and misconceptions. These in turn point to dangerously mistaken policy implications. Based on their reasoning and on the assumption that labor markets are workably competitive, the human capital school concluded, in essense, that those who earn little, those who are involuntarily employed part time, and those who end up with no employment at all are unskilled and unproductive *by definition*. That the economic structure itself may be to blame for their condition is, at best, relegated to obscure passages and footnotes.[a]

The key variables studied by those who embrace this paradigm include formal education, institutional and on-the-job training, health, and migration. The labor market is assumed to be perfect enough that once the human capital of an individual is raised, he or she will be able to rise up from low wage employment, underemployment, or joblessness. *The solution to the poverty problem resolves into a technical exercise of finding the right combination of manpower programs or human resource development schemes to lift each individual from personal disadvantagement.* Unfortunately, this school of thought neglects or obscures a critical factor: many of those who suffer from low wages and unemployment *have* a considerable amount of human capital. They fail to find jobs which pay a living wage becuase of racism, sexism, economic depression, and uneven economic development of industries and regions. Compared with some workers who have found steady employment in the high wage industries, these workers have, in many cases, even more human capital, but happen to be the wrong color or sex, too young or too old, or live on the wrong side of town or in the wrong part of the country. The inadequacy of the economic system is a more important cause of poverty than the inadequacy of people. Yet the human capital school attempts to immunize the patient when it should be eradicating the disease.

Admittedly, the labor market theorists of the 1950s underestimated important elements on the supply or human capital side of the wage and employment process. But the disregard of the demand side by the human capital school has also been in error, and dangerously so, since it puts the onus of poverty reduction on those who suffer it rather than the economic system which promulgates it. A labor market paradigm is needed which understands the strengths and weaknesses of both positions and begins to analyze both sides of the labor market process. This new paradigm is now being developed, some of the preliminary results are in, and more definitive conclusions will soon be forthcoming.[6]

Glimpses of the first results confirm the suspicion that both sides of the labor force equation are important. Both human capital and economic structure variables are critical in understanding wage determination and differential unemployment rates. Wachtel and Betsey have shown in a sophisticated multiple classification analysis that, after controlling for human capital variables such as

---

[a]This criticism, of course, does not apply to all labor economists of the "human capital" school. Some economists who embrace this approach, including Lester Thurow, are not blind to the extensive economic, political, and social barriers which limit the extent of correlation between human capital and economic status.

education and job experience, industry structural variables are still highly significant in explaining the wage rates of full-time workers. Using 1967 data they find that unionization, broad industry-occupation group, region, and city size are all important in determining the wage rate of individuals.[7] After extensive research, my colleagues and I have found that within education groups, controlling for race and sex, there is large variance in wage rates across industries.[8] In yet unpublished regression analyses it has also been discovered that after controlling for human capital variables, the critical factors explaining inter-industry variance in wage rates are profits; unionization; the sex composition of the workforce; the percentage of the industry's product exported or sold to the federal, state, and local governments; and the capital/labor ratio in the industry. Workers who obtain employment in an industry which is highly profitable, unionized, capital intensive, and supported by government purchases will receive higher wages, even if their training, education, health, and discipline are average or below average. Workers who are trapped (primarily because of sex and race discrimination) in unorganized, less profitable industries, operating with little capital per worker, and gaining little support from government or foreign purchases will be lowpaid, even if they are well-educated and have an adequate supply of human capital. An extremely extensive multivariate analysis is now underway using a massive set of data compiled on individuals, their occupations, and the industries in which they work.[9] Hopefully this study will answer some of the more critical questions about the significance of individual variables in explaining wage differentials, especially for the working poor and low-wage workforce.

Low Wages and the Working Poor

A good deal of this research grows out of the recent awareness that the majority of the poor in America work for their poverty. The evidence indicates that over 50 percent of the very poorest families have household heads and often additional family members who work. Sometimes this work is only part time and interrupted by periods of involuntary unemployment. Yet in at least *one poor family in four,* the household head is employed full time throughout the year.[10] In a significant number of additional families, the head of household may not be employed full time, but someone else is and the family still remains poor.[b] In millions of other families not counted in the official poverty statistics,

---

[b]The "sexist" nature of our society often creeps even into the way statistics are computed. The Census Bureau assumes automatically that if a husband is present in a household, he is the head of household, whether he is the primary breadwinner or not. A family with an unemployed husband and full-employed wife is considered as "unemployed." Therefore the statistics on the working poor are probably grossly underestimated because of poor families in which the husband is disabled or simply cannot find work, but the wife is employed.

at least one person is working full time at extremely low pay. Full-time wages are low enough in some occupations and industries that an individual with a moderate-sized family can work forty hours a week, fifty-two weeks a year and still face the bleakest poverty. In New York City alone, there are approximately a quarter of a million families whose breadwinners are working at full-time jobs for wages so low that their families are eligible for Public Assistance Income Supplements under New York State's Home Relief Program.[11] Throughout the United States this unfortunate situation is repeated over and over. In 1968, there were 2¼ million families with nearly ten million individuals living below the low-income cut-off who had family heads working year round full time.[12]

Special tabulations from the 1967 Survey of Economic Opportunity clearly indicate that the low-paid are not necessarily uneducated or unskilled.[13] Over 17 percent of all white males with full-time regular jobs earn $2.25 or less an hour and even one in eight of those who have some college earn this little. For minorities the figures are much higher. Two out of five black male high school graduates earn below this low-wage figure, while nearly six out of ten white women and seven out of ten black women with the same amount of education fall into the same wage category. Even one-quarter of all white female college graduates working full time all through the year earn less than this wage. At the other extreme, a significant number of white males without a high school education earn adequate incomes because they have landed in profitable industries.

For many of the low paid, low wages are not due to lack of education or human capital. Low wages are mainly the result of entrapment in low-wage nondurable manufacturing firms, retail trade establishments, service industries, and to some extent wholesale trade. Being black, brown, or female is often sufficient to narrow industry choice to a low-wage firm within one of these peripheral industries and narrow occupational choice to a low-wage clerical, operative, laborer, or service position. Few alternative job opportunities are available, especially for those living in depressed regions of the country. Since these workers are crowded into industries (which already have a reduced *ability* to pay) wages are forced even lower by the sheer fact of an "oversupply" of labor. Given the opportunity to escape to the high-wage sector, many low-wage workers would perform admirably. Without years of extra education, without massive doses of institutional and on-the-job training, without learning a new "industrial discipline," many low-wage workers could fit into a unionized, profitable, capital-intensive industry and begin to earn a living wage. High-wage firms which have waived credentials to hire high school dropouts and even the hard-core unemployed report that with little special training, these new workers assume a productivity and an industrial discipline characteristic of their normal hires.[14]

Manpower Programs in the Sixties

Nevertheless, until very recently, the core of antipoverty strategy consisted of manpower training and human resource development. The human capital school had dominated in the choice of social policy. At best, the results from following this policy direction have been mixed. For those who completed MDTA training, only three out of five advanced in pay during the middle sixties, and the increased earnings were quite small. According to the largest study of MDTA involving over 100,000 institutional training graduates, the average wage for males *after* training was only $2.06 per hour, 27 percent higher than the average pretraining wage rate. For females the posttraining wage was boosted to $1.53, less than 20 percent above pretraining average earnings.[15] These results are for people who actually finished the program *and* found jobs. Thousands of others failed to complete programs and still others finished training, but were unable to find suitable employment. Another of the federal manpower programs, on-the-job training (OJT), has provided more people directly with jobs, but the training component appears to be a subsidy for specific job training that the employer would normally have provided. The federal government's General Accounting Office (GAO) found that:

OJT contracts had served primarily to reimburse employers for OJT which they would have conducted even without the government's financial assistance. These contracts were awarded even though the intent of the program was to induce new or additional training efforts beyond those usually carried out.[16]

The important point is not that manpower training is irrelevant to improving the condition of the economically disadvantaged, but that for many workers, the major problem is the total lack of good jobs, not lack of human capital. The major policy thrust must be in the direction of creating adequate jobs for people to fill, not training people for nonexistent ones.

New Social Policies for the Seventies

Several events have led to a reevaluation of poverty strategy: (1) Manpower programs are failing. (2) The welfare system is overtaxed. (3) Unemployment is rising. (4) And last, but not least, the administration needs to attract votes in 1972. Consequently a raft of legislation has been prepared over the past two years to deal with the situation. The Work Incentive Program gave rise to the Nixon Family Assistance Program (FAP). Both were designed to encourage welfare recipients to find employment. The concept of changing welfare into workfare has found stiff resistance from civil rights groups and the National Welfare Rights Organization, since it would force welfare mothers to find employment or lose benefits. Senate and House liberals have recently attacked the program for legislative loopholes which would reduce current benefits in several states and for the low floor on guaranteed income: for a family of four, $1,600 without food stamps, $2,400 with.

In contrast to the FAP program, several revenue-sharing bills have been prepared in an effort to develop a "new federalism." These proposals are aimed at urban and rural problems arising from state and local government insolvency, inadequate public services, and rising unemployment. Such legislation would shift federal tax revenue to the states and cities to use as local public officials deem best. Praised by its supporters for putting money and decision power where it is needed most, it is damned by its critics who argue that the funding is inadequate to begin with and that uncontrolled funds in the hands of local officials will be squandered and used primarily for political ends.

A variant of the "fiscal federalism" programs, the Manpower Revenue Sharing Act, supposedly would solve all problems. It shifts tax revenue to state and local governments, it encourages needed public services, it will help provide manpower training for people who can benefit from it, it bails out bankrupt cities, and it also provides employment opportunities for the disadvantaged in paraprofessional and service jobs. Public employment, making government the employer of last resort, has excited policy makers more than most other programs. According to the Labor Department, public service careers will (1) help eliminate institutional, individual, and environmental barriers that have prevented the employment of the disadvantaged in the public sector; (2) improve the "efficiency" of government and assist public agencies in delivering their services "effectively"; and (3) support the competitive merit system.[17]

Whatever their claims, the development of all of this new legislation has an ambiguous promise. On the one hand it could, if liberally written, provide the foundation for solving many urban and rural finanical ills and create meaningful well-paying jobs for many of the disadvantaged. Or it could turn out to be the ultimate bane of the impoverished. It all depends on the level of funding, the form of encouragement or coercion to find employment, and the types of jobs provided in the public sector.

In tandem an ill-formed Family Assistance Program and a half-funded Manpower Revenue Sharing Act could lead to meaningless low-wage public sector employment which welfare recipients must either accept, or decline at the expense of further assistance. The low-wage jobs developed in this manner will neither do much to meet the shortage of public services in the city nor provide an opportunity for the poor to escape their impoverishment. The legislation which is passed will probably not be this bleak. But given the sentiment in Congress and the veto power of the president, whatever legislation is passed will at best make some marginal improvements in a post-marginal situation. Some added public services will be provided, the red ink in local budgets will be less profuse, unemployment will rise at a slower rate, and some new jobs for a few of the disadvantaged will be developed. The problems of poverty and the urban environment will continue.

Nevertheless, the concept of public service careers for the disadvantaged has a brilliant, but normally ignored, potential. This chapter earlier argued that (1) the poor are much more skilled than often assumed; (2) the unemployment problem is primarily due to an inadequate supply of jobs, not skills; and (3) the reason for low wages among millions of workers is the lack of alternative employment opportunities. Minority workers are concentrated in industries which have little ability to pay. Furthermore they are "crowded" into these industries by the lack of alternative employment opportunities and this forces wages down close to subsistence. *The remedy to this situation is a large "oversupply" of meaningful well-paying job opportunities available to all members of the labor force, but especially to the economically disadvantaged.* An enlightened public service career program, funded at a high level, can provide this "oversupply."

Aggregate demand policies of creating employment through tax cuts and general public expenditure increases have never been able to develop the right kinds of jobs for the right people. In the past, reliance on private sector employment and massive injections of public funds has created an "over-demand" for highly skilled professionals and technicians, but created little in the way of alternative job opportunities for the disadvantaged workforce. The result has been continued unemployment and low wages for the poor *and* employment bottlenecks which cause inflation for everyone. Mismanaging the economy through such aggregate policies has promoted the coexistence of rising unemployment and rising prices.

In contrast, the development of, let us propose, $30 billion worth of public service career opportunities will have a number of effects. In the first place, it will provide a set of public services desperately needed in the urban and rural areas of the nation. Second, it will provide *primary* job opportunities for millions who are now unemployed or underemployed. And, finally, the creation of millions of *alternative* employment opportunities will have the *indirect* effect of significantly raising wages in the peripheral industries of the private sector, thus aiding many of the working poor. The elimination of the oversupply of *labor* to the peripheral sector through the development of an oversupply of *jobs* in the public sector will have the long-run effect of redeveloping the low-wage segment of the economy. Firms in the periphery will be forced to rationalize their production techniques and capital-intensify their technology in order to meet the competition for labor. Many firms will fail, but others will be able to resurrect themselves as part of the core economy. A by-product will be an increased efficiency in production.

But the major effect of public service employment of this magnitude will be to give the disadvantaged worker an alternative opportunity to unemployment or a low-wage job. Given this choice, the real standard of living of the poor will rise as the underpaid workforce finds employment either in the public sector or in the new higher paying private economy. Manpower programs will still be necessary to provide the opportunity for upgrading.

A note of pessimism is in order however. Given the politics of the day, such legislation has small chance of being passed or implemented. In the first place, there is little money left to spend once the defense budget is appropriated. Also the wealthy in this country have become accustomed to the services supplied by cheap labor and have little desire to pay decent wages for such things as laundered shirts and garbage collection. Finally, it is sad, but probably true, that many economists will rush to Washington to testify that such a program would be an assult on economic efficiency and the competitive ethic.

Notes

1. Lloyd G. Reynolds, *The Structure of Labor Markets* (New York: Harper and Brothers, 1951), p. 2

2. Ibid.

3. Sumner Slichter, "Notes on the Structure of Wages," *Review of Economics and Statistics* 32 (1950): 80-91.

4. Harold M. Levinson, "Unionism, Concentration, and Wage Changes: Toward a Unified Theory," *Industrial and Labor Relations Review* 20, 2 (January 1967).

5. For an extension of this concept, see the excellent monograph by David M. Gordon, *Economic Theories of Poverty and Underemployment* (Lexington, Mass.: Heath-Lexington Books, 1972).

6. See Howard Wachtel and Charles Betsey, "The Determinants of 'Working Poverty'," chapter 3 of this volume; Lester Thurow, *Poverty and Discrimination* (Washington: The Brookings Institution, 1969); Albert Rees and George P. Shultz, *Workers and Wages in an Urban Labor Market* (Chicago-: University of Chicago Press, 1970); Barry Bluestone, Mary H. Stevenson, and William M. Murphy, *Low Wages and the Working Poor* (Institute of Labor and Industrial Relations, University of Michigan-Wayne State University, 1971) unpublished manuscript.

7. See Wachtel and Betsey, "Determinants."

8. See Bluestone, Stevenson, and Murphy, *Low Wages.*

9. For more detail, see my dissertation, "The Personal Distribution of Earnings: Individual and Institutional Determinants," (Department of Economics, University of Michigan, Ph. D. dissertation.)

10. Computed from, "Work Experience of Family Heads by Poverty Status of Family, 1968," Table 1 in *Manpower Report of the President,* March 1970, p. 121.

11. "The Working Poor," in *Coalition News,* the newsletter of the New York Urban Coalition, Vol. 11, No. 5., p. 8-9.

12. *Manpower Report of the President,* March 1970, p. 121.

13. These special tabulations were made from the Survey of Economic Opportunity, 1967, conducted by the Office of Economic Opportunity and the Bureau of the Census.

14. The Ford Motor Company, following the 1967 Detroit rebellion, waived normal credentials and hired more than 5,000 poor workers for regular employment. In a sample of 2,000 of these workers, 75 percent were high school dropouts. These new workers were evaluated by Ford at the end of their first year with the company. They were found to meet previously set standards in terms of retention, absenteeism, and capactiy to adjust. Similar results were found in the special program developed by IBM in Bedford Stuyvesant. See Bennett Harrison, "National Manpower Policy and Public Service Employment," *New Generation* 53, 1 (Winter 1971): 6.

15. "The Influence of MDTA on Earnings," *Manpower Evaluation Report,* No. 8, December 1968, U.S. Department of Labor, Manpower Administration, p. 18.

16. U.S. General Accounting Office, *Improvements Needed in Contracting for On-the-Job Training Under the Manpower Development and Training Act of 1962,* (Washington: General Accounting Office, 1968.)

17. Jules Cohn, "Public Service Careers: The Need for Realism," *New Generation* 53, 1 (Winter 1971): 17.

6

Congress and Public Service Employment

WILLIAM J. SPRING

Despite the rhetorical commitment (beginning at least with Franklin Delano Roosevelt's request to Congress on January 4, 1935, for a program to "provide jobs for all those willing to work"), the country has failed to bring that promise even near reality. In fact, between the time of traumatic collapse of the entire economy in the Great Depression and the employment crisis of the 1970s, few Congressmen saw pressing need for a job creation effort beyond Keynesian fiscal and monetary policies.

The nation is now paying the price through two decades of catastrophic rates of unemployment and underemployment in the poverty neighborhoods of its great cities, crime, welfare, despair, and the collapse of urban civility, if not of society itself. Chronic poverty, violence, and crime — issues one might suppose inevitable only in the explosively growing urban areas of underdeveloped nations with unemployment rates of 20 percent or more — these issues are the most important domestic concerns of the richest nation the world has ever known.

The nation has been willing to adopt direct action to assure jobs — a public service employment program — only during times of extraordinary crisis, and then only on a small-scale emergency or "transitional" basis. As late as 1967 a domestically liberal Democratic administration actively lobbied against a modest public service employment proposal.

It is important to remember that the peaceful March on Washington in the summer of 1963 — where Reverend Martin Luther King proclaimed his dream of reconciliation in America — was for *jobs* as well as for freedom. The riots in successive summers, Watts in August of 1965, Chicago in July of 1966 and then the explosions in more than eight cities in the summer of 1967, including the dreadful two weeks of July in which sixty-six persons were killed in Newark and Detroit, have been claimed to be direct outgrowths of discrimination, poverty, unemployment, and underemployment.

A Harris poll taken after the riots indicated that 66 percent of whites and 91 percent of blacks interviewed favored a massive public service employment program as preventative for riots.

But in October of 1967, with cities in ruin, and national unemployment at only 3.8 percent, an effective coalition in Congress of moderates and conservatives, led by the administration, defeated by a vote of 42 to 47 a very modest public service employment program offered by Senators Joseph Clark and Robert Kennedy.

Since 1967, opinion has begun to change. In the fall of 1970 the Congress adopted an Employment and Manpower Bill including authorization of $9.5 billion to create 310,000 public service employment jobs over a three year period. The month the bill cleared Congress – December 1970 – unemployment stood at 6.2 percent of the workforce, with 5.1 million unemployed.

That bill was vetoed December 16, 1970, but in April 1971, with unemployment at 6.1 percent, the Senate voted 62 to 10 for the Emergency Employment Act, a bill that became law with the president's signature on July 12.

To what extent the change in Congressional support, between 1967 and 1971, for public service employment legislation represents a genuine commitment to full employment for all Americans, including the residents of the inner cities, is open to some question, for the modest public service employment program ($1 billion and 130,000 jobs) was approved by Congress on an "emergency" and "transitional" basis. Like Roosevelt's 1935 Emergency Relief Appropriations Act, the Emergency Employment Act of 1971 was passed in a period of national unemployment crisis. The earlier crisis was the collapse of the entire economy, with unemployment levels approaching 25 percent of the work force. In 1971 the crisis, while much less severe nationally, was extraordinarily severe and rising in some cities (Seattle, 12 percent: Wichita, 10 percent) and directly tied to the loss of government contracts in defense and space expenditure and a deliberate slowing down of the economy. Laid-off aerospace engineers and the unemployed Vietnam war veterans both staked claim to special federal treatment.

The first public service employment program was launched in the bitter winter of 1933-34, when a quarter of the American work force was on the streets.

It was launched under Harry L. Hopkins' vigorous leadership without benefit of specific Congressional authorizations. Hopkins had been lured down from New York the previous May to become Federal Relief Administrator. The money for the Hopkins effort – nearly a billion dollars during the short, three-and-a-half-month life of the program – came out of funds already appropriated to Harold Ickes' Public Works Administration.

Here let me digress for a moment into the alphabetical underbrush that has obstructed comprehension of New Deal programs. The Ickes agency, the Public Works Administration (PWA), concerned itself with massive construction projects, like Boulder Dam, not with low overhead labor-intensive projects. The Public Works Program was enacted into law, with a $3.3 billion authorization, as part of the National Industrial Recovery Act during the "100 days." Title I of that act authorized the National Recovery Act. Public Works money under Title II was to act as a significant stimulus to improve the desperate economic situation. However, Ickes, in his curmudgeonly honesty moved so slowly in getting money spent that by the fall of 1933 very few projects had been started.

Roosevelt then simply assigned a billion dollars of Ickes' appropriation to Hopkins for the crash job creation program.

Between December and March, Harry L. Hopkins hired over 4 million Americans at a cost of some $933 million to teach, build roads, airports, and recreation centers. He also hired some 3,000 writers and artists in Federal Arts projects and unemployed rabbis to compile a Jewish dictionary.

The reception the program received seems to have set a pattern for congressional attitudes toward public service employment.

The word "boondoggle" was coined by opponents of the program to describe some of the Hopkins projects. The idea that direct federal appropriations could never provide a real job was very prevalent in 1934 and durable enough to be employed by Nixon in his message of December 1970 vetoing the Employment and Manpower Act of that year.

The program was very unpopular with many conservatives, especially those who had become reliant on cheap labor, and who feared the program would rot the moral fiber and disrupt the economy of the country. Governor Talmadge of Georgia forwarded to F.D.R. a letter from an irate plantation owner who claimed that work relief made it impossible to get cheap black farm labor. "I wouldn't plow nobody's mule from sunrise to sunset for $.50 a day when I could get $1.30 for pretending to work on a DITCH".

Support for the program came from participants who actually got work. Lorena Hickock, a field investigator for Hopkins, reported: " . . . and did they want work? In Sioux City they actually had fist fights over shovels . . . " Even some normally conservative Republicans came out in support of the effort. Governor Alf Landon of Kansas, for instance, said: "This civil works program is one of the soundest, most constructive policies of your administration, and I cannot urge too strongly its continuance."

The issue of state and/or local vs. federal control was also raised. The National Association of Manufacturers and the U.S. Chamber of Commerce organized businessmen to urge returning welfare exclusively to the states. Of thirty-seven governors replying to their questionnaire, only Georgia's Talmadge agreed. Senator James F. Byrnes of South Carolina said: "Turning federal funds over to the states for administration would mean more politics instead of less politics in administration."

Despite the program's success, and the continuing need, Roosevelt let the program die in the early spring of 1934. He listened to conservative critics, and his budget advisors who still sought with him the grail of a balanced budget.

The legislation that led to the Works Progress Administration (WPA) was not enacted until the following year – April 8, 1935, to be precise. One wonders what happened to the 4 million so briefly working for the government in the winter of 1933-34 during that year. Certainly the rate of unemployment did not markedly slacken during those months.

After the Democratic sweep of the 1934 Congressional elections, Roosevelt committed himself for the first time to the proposition "that Washington should try to give every employable worker a job through a massive public-works effort, costing perhaps $5 billion the first year and less in succeeding years . . . "[2]

In a January 4, 1935, message to Congress, Roosevelt asked $4.86 billion to put 3.5 million to work at a so-called "security wage." The Emergency Relief Appropriations Act of 1935 passed the House quickly and the Senate more slowly. The American Federation of Labor was opposed to wages below the prevailing rates. Senator Pat McCarran attempted to raise the wage rates, but a presidential veto threat — not the last such threat to affect Congressional public service employment policy — defeated the effort.

The WPA was one of three agencies set up to administer the new program. Under the aggressive Hopkins, it just about ran away with the show. The Works Progress Administration, and its variants, carried on until World War II took over responsibility for job creation. The summary statistics are very impressive: Over $10 billion spent between 1935 and 1943, over 600 thousand miles of roads constructed, nearly 78,000 bridges and 35,000 public buildings, among other things. In 1939 there were over 4 million Americans engaged in federally subsidized work in one program or another.

Between the death of WPA in 1943 and the Emergency Employment Act of 1971, the nation was without a major federal job creation program.

As the end of the war approached, Roosevelt, in his 1945 State of the Union Message, rededicated himself to "an American Economic Bill of Rights."

Of these rights the most fundamental, and the one on which the fulfillment of the others in large degree depends, is the right to a useful and remunerative job . . . Full employment means not only jobs — but productive jobs. Americans do not regard jobs that pay substandard wages as productive jobs.

To maintain high employment we must, after the war is over, reduce or eliminate taxes which bear too heavily on consumption.

He proposed a program of cooperation between government and private enterprise to provide "a decent home for every family" and "to make a frontal attack on the problems of housing and urban reconstruction." He also proposed more major public works:

. . . The T.V.A. which was constructed at a cost of $750 million — the cost of waging this war for less than 4 days — was a bargain. By harnessing the resources of (other) river basins . . . we shall provide the same kind of stimulus of enterprise as was provided by the Louisiana Purchase and the new discoveries in the West during the nineteenth century.

But inflation, not depression, marked the American economy after the war. And the great-hearted program that Roosevelt envisoned — including tax cutting and major public construction undertakings — was laid aside.

The proposed Full Employment Act of 1946, after passing the Senate, was gutted in conference by conservatives who wished no part of any more government control or participation in the economy than was absolutely unavoidable.

Instead of "full employment" the conference-approved bill only pledged the government to:

Use all practicable means consistent . . . with other essential considerations of national policy . . . to coordinate and utilize all its plans and resources . . . in a manner calculated to promote free competitive enterprise . . . conditions under which there will be afforded useful employment opportunities for those able, willing and seeking to work . . .

The Senate bill had simply declared it to be the responsibility of the federal government to maintain full employment and to assure at all times sufficient opportunities for all Americans to exercise their *right* to continued full employment. The statement of the managers made it explicit: "The term 'full employment' is rejected, and the term 'maximum employment' is the objective to be promoted."[3]

The first major training legislation to pass in the 1960s — the Manpower Development and Training Act of 1962 — was based on the assumption that help should be provided for those with an attachment to the work force who found themselves without jobs due either to automation or declining industries and regions. There was little in the original bill to help the poor, and no public service jobs at all.

But then poverty was being rediscovered in America. Michael Harrington's *The Other America*,[4] preceded by Professor Robert Lampman's obscure 1959 study for the Council of Economic Advisors and the Joint Economic Committee,[5] set off a round of journalistic and political interest in the plight of the poor. Before his death, Kennedy had planned to build his domestic program for 1964 around an attack on poverty, according to Schlesinger.

What strategy would be followed? Daniel Patrick Moynihan tells the story of a heated cabinet meeting at which W. Willard Wirtz made the case for public service employment, a jobs strategy to fight poverty. But he lost.[6]

How then could the poor be given "opportunity"? Through access to education, housing, health, legal, child care, and other *services* available to wealthier Americans, but denied the poor. The community agencies were to "mobilize" the resources of the community to meet these service needs in the hope that the good will of informed, organized Americans would meet the needs of the forgotten poor. Needless to say, there was very little talk as the bill moved through Congress of control by the poor of federal dollars and programs.

At the heart of a services strategy is the idea that the economy (and the supply of jobs) is fundamentally adequate. The way to help the unemployed is not through an increase in the supply of jobs (very expensive that), but through training programs, and the provisions of related "supportive" services, such as day care, and education for the young (so that they will not grow up to be unemployable).

In 1965 a modest form of public service employment amendment – Operation Mainstream, mostly for older men in rural areas – was added to the bill.

Mainstream was based on a 1964 effort by Senator Gaylord Nelson of Wisconsin to establish a one billion dollar public service employment program through his Human Resources Act of 1964. That proposal never got serious consideration. However, Nelson gathered testimony from the Department of the Interior and from conservation officials from all states in the union. He used data gathered from these individuals to establish the existence of an enormous backlog of work in conservation and recreation projects to make already acquired parkland usable for mass recreation. Wisconsin, for instance, reported 14,000 man-years of work to be done. On the other hand, Nelson gathered statistics on unemployment to demonstrate the great "unused natural resource" the unemployed represent. Moynihan refers specifically to the Nelson legislation in his discussion of Wirtz's efforts within the cabinet.

By the summer of 1966 it was clear to the Labor Department that the MDTA and the other manpower training programs were not reaching the hard-core unemployed, that they were, to use the jargon of the manpower trade, "creaming" in the manner of an ordinary employer or dean of admissions who seeks to most promising applicants for a job or a class.

Wirtz also found that very few statistics were available on the extent of job-related poverty. How serious is unemployment in poverty neighborhoods? To what extent do people work, but still live in poverty because of low earnings from jobs available to them? National unemployment and earnings information was available. But small area data were almost entirely lacking. To devise programs – and to justify funds to pay for them – Wirtz had to document the need.

Wirtz organized a special survey of the inner city areas of ten metropolitan areas on November 11, 1966. Out of that survey he developed a "subemployment" index which provided a startling statistical look at the economic reality of slum life. Among inner city residents, 35 percent were not able to earn above poverty wages in the ghetto labor market. In the slums of New Orleans, for instance, while the labor market area rate of unemployment was 3.3 percent, the subemployment rate – those unemployed, working only part time, discouraged workers, and those working full time, but earning only poverty level wages – stood at 45.3 percent of the poverty area work force. In East Harlem, the comparable rates were 3.7 and 33.1 percent.

Based on this information Wirtz wrote a memo to the President in January 1967, which said that:

If a third of the people in the nation couldn't make a living . . . there would be a revolution. This is the situation — and the prospect — unless action is taken in the nation-within-the-nation, the slums and ghettos.

He also stated:

The main reason for this [34.7 percent subemployment rate] isn't the economy. It's the condition and position these people are in — uneducated, untrained, with health problems, police and garnishment records, fatherless children, and so forth . . .

Wirtz recommended a program of concentrating federal training, support and day care efforts in the target areas of the largest cities (a proposal that eventually became the Concentrated Employment Program (CEP), announced by President Johnson on March 14, 1967, and launched a major effort to enroll American business in providing jobs for the hard-core disadvantaged — the Job Opportunities in the Business Sectors or JOBS program announced in January 1968 and gotten underway in March 1968.

Commenting on the success of the Kennedy tax cut proposal — not enacted into law until 1964 — Secretary Wirtz said:

It took the reversal — through the tax cut legislation of 1964 . . . of almost two centuries of political-economic theory and practice to produce a period of unprecedented economic growth that has meant jobs for millions of people who wouldn't otherwise have had them. Jobs are the live ammunition in the war on poverty . . . But it must be recognized that the gains have been least in the slums, and will be even less in the future. Most of those who are jobless there won't get jobs even if the economic growth rates go on up . . . . At the same time . . . any worsening in the economy would turn the slums riots into revolutions. Any proposal to 'cool off the economy' . . . if it means increasing unemployment [would be] a fatal *retreat* in the war on poverty. (In memo to Lyndon Johnson, January, 1967)

Although Wirtz's study documented the shortage of jobs at decent pay in poverty areas, he did not draw from this information any conclusions critical of job supply in the economy as a whole. He spoke rather of "jobs going begging." Nor did he mention the shortage of public services in poverty areas. Therefore, the conclusions he drew did not lead in the direction of a major public service employment program, but rather in the direction of redoubling efforts in job training and opening up of "opportunities." His aim was not more jobs, but a more equitable distribution of the nation's 3.5 percent unemployment.

The riots of the summer of 1967 led to the first congressional test of sentiment on public service employment since the 1930s. Senators Clark of Pennsylvania, chairman of the Poverty subcommittee, and Robert Kennedy had conducted a long "Examination of the War on Poverty" during the spring and summer of 1967. A bill to extend the program through 1969 had nearly cleared committee when the riots occurred. Senators Clark and Kennedy proposed at a committee executive session the Emergency Employment Act of 1967 as a new title to the OEO extension. The proposal would have granted to the Secretary of Labor $1 billion for fiscal year 1968 and $1.5 billion for fiscal year 1969 "to provide financial assistance to public and private agencies for programs to create employment opportunities," with emphasis on "employing those in areas with a chronic labor surplus . . . in such fields as health, public safety, education, recreation, streets, parks, housing, neighborhood improvement, conservation and beautification." In a collection of background papers on public service employment assembled by the committee staff, heavy emphasis was placed on documenting the need for public services and the potential of hiring the poor to carry them out.

A study done for the Office of Economic Opportunity in 1965 by the highly respected consulting firm, Greenleigh Associates, found 4.3 million needed jobs in public service employment, more than enough to absorb the 3.5 million then unemployed, if funds could be found to carry out the work. The Commission on Technology, Automation, and Economic Progress, concerned mostly with the danger of the elimination of jobs through automation, also recommended a major public service employment program. The Automation Commission pegged the figure at 5.3 million potential jobs. The Clark Committee report also included the information on a public opinion poll showing that 66 percent of whites and 91 percent of blacks favor large-scale federal employment projects as effective in preventing riots.

The Administration was in adamant opposition to the plan. The specter of the dread "boondoggle" was raised. White House aide Joseph Califano is reported to have written the strong letter denouncing the Emergency Employment Act to the members of the Senate Labor and Public Welfare Committee arguing that the jobs would be "make-work." It is more than a little ironic that the Johnson Administration, the Administration that declared a "War on Poverty," should be opposed to moves toward providing adequate jobs for the poor. The administration was under budgetary pressure, the cost of the Vietnam war having already forced a drastic scaling down of plans to expand the war on poverty.

As the time to bring the bill to the floor approached, it was clear that strong bipartisan support was essential if an Emergency Employment Act was to pass the Senate. Therefore, the principal sponsors agreed to support a substitute sponsored by Senator Winston Prouty of Vermont, a senior Republican on the Labor and Public Welfare Committee, and the Republican leader Senator Hugh Scott. The Prouty-Scott substitute contained little in the way of jobs. Instead of the $1 billion for public service employment, it provided a program in which over 37 percent of the funds could have gone to "human investment training programs" by private industry and another 20 percent for on-the-job training under MDTA. Even this modest plan was defeated 42 to 47, with the help of Democratic majority leader Mansfield. The Emergency Employment Act itself was then knocked out of the bill 54 to 28. Many of those speaking *for* the Prouty substitute took care to disparage "make-work" such as the Clark-Kennedy bill proposed, "as warranted only for those who have reached a point in life where further education and training could not qualify them for productive jobs."

Apart from the score or so of certified liberals in the Senate in 1967, there was little support for even emergency public service employment legislation, or understanding of the need for a dramatic increase in the number of jobs available at decent wages in poverty areas. Even among the liberals there was little understanding of the critical nature of the problem.

Kennedy understood. In July he had told the Senate:

To be without (work) is to be less than a man — less than a citizen — hardly . . . to have any identity at all. . . . . More than segregation in housing and schools, more than differences in attitudes or life style, it is unemployment which marks the urban poor off and apart from the rest of America.

Support for public service employment did continue to grow. The Kerner Commission recommended in March 1968 that Congress enact immediately a program that would create one million new jobs in the public sector in three years, 250,000 in the first year.

Emphasis should be placed on employing trainees to improve rundown neighborhoods and to perform a variety of other socially useful public services which are not "make-work," including Community Service Officers in police departments, as recommended by the President's Commission on Law Enforcement and the Administration of Justice . . .

The Urban Coalition in 1968 asked Dr. Harold Sheppard of the Upjohn Institute to survey the public service job creation potential as seen through the eyes of local public administrators and officials. His findings were: there were 300,000 potential jobs, 150,000 of them available for unskilled workers, in cities of over 100,000 population — if funds could be found to pay salaries. Sheppard's data have been cited earlier in this volume.

In the winter of 1961, with unemployment at its lowest level since the Second World War (3.3 percent in February), the persistance of very high rates of unemployment in poverty areas, especially among young people, led many in Congress to advocate public service employment programs.

Congressman James G. O'Hara of Michigan, an expert on manpower programs, introduced a comprehensive manpower act, including in its Title III a public service employment program for eligible unemployed persons. With strong labor support, the bill gained over 100 sponsors. The bill did not include a dollar authorization.

Many other Congressmen introduced variations on the full employment, public service employment theme; for instance Congressman Conyer's H.R. 3338, the "Full Opportunity Act."

Among liberal and labor-oriented Congressmen, the concept of public service employment — even during the time of near full employment for the economy as a whole — had gained wide acceptance.

Meanwhile the administration, redeeming a campaign pledge, moved to cut $100 million, about half of its total, from the Jobs Corps budget. The administration argued that major expansion of the JOBS program would more than take up the slack in job opportunities.

In testimony before the Senate Manpower Subcommittee George P. Schultz, then Secretary of Labor, said the administration would commit $420 million to the JOBS program in fiscal year 1970, enough to assure 140,000 jobs for the disadvantaged in the private sector.

The failure of this JOBS effort — the administration was able to spend only $21 million of that $420 million during the fiscal year (July 1969-June 1970) and to employ only 46,723 persons in the program through July 1970 — played a major role in convincing the Congress that the private sector, even with substantial subsidy (an average of $3,000 was spent per JOBS enrollee, half for training and half for salary subsidy) was unable to provide sufficient jobs. Between the time of Schultz' announcement in April 1969 and July 1970, unemployment went from 3.5 percent (2.8 million unemployed) to 5 percent (4.1 million unemployed). This fact alone is probably adequte to explain the failure of a program designed to provide preference for disadvantaged workers.

In August of 1969, President Nixon proposed a major reorganization of the job training or manpower programs in a three-part domestic package including revenue sharing and welfare reform. The president sought to simplify manpower administration — some 10,000 local sponsors were dealing directly with the Department of Labor — by turning the programs over to states and large cities for basic administration.

Senator Nelson, chairman of the Senate Subcommittee on Employment, Manpower, and Poverty, responded on Labor Day with a pledge to hold hearings on manpower reform and employment to build support "for a major program to create hundreds of thousands of public service jobs. He cited both the need for expanded public services and the commission findings that such jobs were suitable for the unemployed poor.

The promise of America is a fraud unless it is backed up with the promise of a job. This world owes no man a living, but this nation owes every citizen a genuine chance of a job at a wage which will support his family. A nation that can afford to reach the moon can afford to provide a fair opportunity for all its citizens. Indeed, it cannot afford not to.

Nelson pledged to hold hearings in cities all across the nation. The first hearings in December, 1969, gave the Committee an opportunity to explore the

Administration's attitude toward public service employment. The first witness was Secretary Schultz.

Senator Nelson asked him: "...at what stage, if any, [do] you think we ought to be providing public service employment?"

Mr. Schultz: "...we feel that there is a role for such jobs in solving manpower problems ... [but] our belief is that for the most part the problems that we have can be worked with by getting people into regular jobs, and that the economy is producing more and more jobs at a very rapid rate ... the processes of operation of a healthy economy do produce an ever-increasing number of jobs, both private and public, and it is to those jobs that we think we ought to get people moving."

Senator Nelson: "You arent't saying that every single person in the country who is able to work, that there is a job open for him are you?"

Mr. Schultz: "I think that is a reasonable expectation. We ought to have that kind of situation, yes. We have a lot of job openings right now, as well as unemployed ... "

It was, of course, a political occasion. The answers were not precisely on point. Shultz did not say there was no level of unemployment at which public service employment on a significant scale ought to be put into effect. He did not actually say that there was a job available for "every single person." But the thrust was in that direction.

In Shultz' view the American economy is basically healthy, producing a resonably good supply of "regular" jobs. If there is a temporary shortage, it is the responsibliity of the central government to expand aggregate demand through government spending until the supply is adequate again. Of course, during a time of high inflation a little additional unemployment will just have to be accepted in the interest of the greater good.

The committee held hearings in Los Angeles, San Francisco, Corpus Christi, Cleveland, and Milwaukee. In city after city witnesses told the following story: There are not enough training slots for those who need them. In Los Angeles it was estimated that 240,000 training slots were needed and only 24,000 were available. It was further established that the training programs that existed were not working very well primarily because there was a lack of jobs. Reggie Collins, a 24-year-old black Watts resident, testified that he had been in four different training programs and had never been able to land a decent job. What was a decent job? Collins said he was hoping for work that paid $2.00 an hour. In the minds of most witnesses the lack of jobs overshadowed the weaknesses of the organization of manpower training programs. The Democratic senators came to view public service employment as the key to making manpower training work.

In May of 1970, Professor Charles Killingsworth of Michigan State University testified before the committee. Killingsworth had been one of those who had urged during the Kennedy administration that structural problems as well as the lack of aggregate demand were key to persistent unemployment. Killingsworth testified that during the late 60s, the space program and Vietnamese war spending had lowered unemployment to below 4 percent. But the problems of severe unemployment in the inner cities had not been helped very much. He said the basic problem of unemployment had not been solved at all: a significant part of unemployment had been masked by a change in the way unemployment was calculated, and much of the remaining employment change could be traced directly to war.

If jobs were the key, the question still remained in many minds as to whether the private sector could somehow be induced to solve the problem of the unemployed poor. The administration and the National Alliance of Businessmen had been boasting of the effectiveness of the JOBS program. In April of 1970 the Nelson subcommittee issued a report on the results of an intensive study of JOBS showing that the target of jobs for 1970 — 140,000 jobs within a year — had not been met. In addition, the subcommittee uncovered a number of extremely questionable contracts in which private manufacturers and consulting firms were making money from the JOBS program, hiring men on federal subsidies to do unskilled low-paid work and not providing the remedial training contracted for. If the private sector could not provide jobs even with substantial subsidy, then public service employment seemed the only answer. By September 1970 the unemployment rate had reached 5.5 percent and the Employment and Training Opportunities Act of 1970 passed the Senate 68 to 6, providing for major manpower reform and authorizing a total of $9.5 billion to create 310,000 public service jobs over a three year period. Efforts by conservatives to weaken the public service employment provisions were decisively defeated. An amendment by Senator Dominick to limit public service employment to temporary two year jobs, and to pay only 80 percent of prevailing wages, was defeated 43 to 29. Back in 1935, President Roosevelt had threatened to veto his own emergency employment act if an effort by the Federation of Labor to pay prevailing wages was successful. The WPA program began by paying a "security wage" above welfare, but below prevailing wages.

The administration had been threatening to veto the Employment and Manpower Act since June on various grounds. It objected to the continuation of so-called "categorical programs" such as the Job Corps, Neighborhood Youth Corps, and Operation Mainstream that existed in Title I of the Economic Opportunity Act. It desired major program responsibility to be left with governors at the state level. Most importantly, the administration was opposed to earmarked funds for a public service employment program. In the Conference on the Emergency Employment Act, the issue of categorical programs was resolved by continuing the programs, but not requiring that any specific amount of money be spent on them. The issue of state control was compromised by providing major technical assistance for states and providing that, where requested by local communities, a state could step in to help run manpower programs. But on the issue of public service employment, conferees and the administration reached an impasse. The administration had proposed that individuals employed under public service employment program be paid wages below the market (the defeated Dominick amendment) and in conference they insisted that the jobs themselves be temporary and transitional. The conferees were unwilling to take so restrictive a view of public service employment. The Senate-House conference report in December of 1970 provided for "an annual review by an appropriate agency of the status of each person employed in a public service job under this title" and that "maximum efforts shall be made to locate employment and training opportunities . . . and the participant shall be offered appropriate assistance in securing placement in the opportunity which he chooses after appropriate counseling". The Administration had requested the authority to cut off funds to cities that did not move a specified percentage of their public service employment employees off the PSE payroll.

On December 16, 1970, President Nixon vetoed the Employment and Manpower Act. He stated: "The conference bill provides that as much as 44 percent of the total funding in the bill go for dead end jobs in the public sector. WPA — type jobs are not the answer for the men and women who have them, for the government which is less efficient as a result or for the taxpayers who must foot the bill. Such a program represents a reversion to the remedies that were tried 35 years ago. Surely it is an inappropriate, an ineffective response to problems of the 1970s." However, the president did say "transitional and short-term public service employment can be a useful component of the nation's manpower policies."

In January the unemployment rate for December was published, showing 6.2 percent of the workforce unemployed, a total of 5.5 million Americans. With the rising rate of unemployment, the pressure within Congress to act in some way to recognize the pressing need for jobs was clear. It was determined to introduce an Emergency Employment Act keyed to those words "temporary" and "transitional" in the president's veto message and designed for quick congressional passage. The measure was based on a small provision in the administration's original manpower training act. The administration had proposed that during times of high unemployment — over 4.5 percent for three months — an additional $200 million would be "triggered" for training. The Emergency Employment Act (introduced as S. 31 on January 5) expanded that trigger concept into a major public service employment proposal providing for $500 million in federal funds for public service jobs when unemployment reached 4.5 percent for three months and an additional $100 million for each increment of one-half of 1 percent. The bill was sponsored by thirty-four senators, including the Republican minority leader, Hugh Scott of Pennsylvania. On February 8, the first day of hearings on S. 31, mayors from fourteen cities, gathered by the U.S. Conference of Mayors, appeared to testify. They included Lindsay of New York, Daley of Chicago, Uhlman of Seattle, Tate of Philadelphia, Alioto of San Francisco, Massell of Atlanta, and Driggs of Phoenix.

Never before had such an impressive panel of witnesses been lined up to testify before the Senate for any manpower legislation, let alone a bill proposing public service employment. The mayors told a chilling story of urban areas suffering under the twin blows of rising unemployment and declining public services, of unemployment highly concentrated in the most volatile areas of our society, the inner core of our large metropolitan areas. Mayor Gribbs of Detroit stated that there were 800,000 unemployed in his city, 24 percent of the inner-city poor. Mayor Daley of Chicago said "The problems were not created by the mayors. They were not created by the cities. They were created by a sudden movement of people and we think we are entitled to ask your immediate help." The Republican mayor of Phoenix, John D. Driggs, said, "We have had more than a 60 percent increase in unemployment this past year. In the inner city it is approximately 20 percent. We have 10,000 urban Indians in Phoenix and their unemployment rate is 50 percent." They also testified that even as thousands of their citizens were idle by lack of work, the cities found themselves unable to maintain the most basic public services because of lack of funds to fill job slots. Mayor D'Alesandro of Baltimore stated, "The work is there, the jobs are there, we have the plans, we don't have the financial resources to follow through. We have a municipal hospital, one of the finest in the country, yet the amount of registered nurses, the amount of nurses' aides are at a minimum." Mayor Lindsay of New York estimated "that we could use an additional 50,000 to 75,000 public service jobs tomorrow morning . . . in areas such as sanitation and services to augment police services, educational aides in public schools, nurses aides, licensed practical nurses in our hospitals." Mayor Burke of Louisville said, "Simply in health and hospital needs we could use whatever share of public service employment our city could get . . . We can say almost the same thing in the fields of solid waste disposal, housing, building inspection and air pollution control."

Mayors and representatives of other cities told the story of the serious decline in the aircraft industry with unemployment rates of more than 10 percent in Wichita, Kansas, and 12 percent in Seattle, Washington.

With the Emergency Employment Act moving through the Senate, the administration changed its basic position on public service employment. In testimony before the House Ways and Means Committee, the administration requested an authorization of $800 million for public service employment programs under the Family Assistance Plan. Meanwhile the House was considering a similar public service employment measure that provided 100 percent federal funding and a veteran's preference. The Emergency Employment Act passed the Senate in record time on April 1, 1971. The vote was 62 yea against only 10 nay.

Meanwhile the administration had changed signals on the manpower reform issue. In August 1969 the administration urged a major reform in the manpower "delivery system" so that Washington would have to deal with fifty state and a few hundred large city applications rather than 10,000 local contractors. Then in 1971 the administration included manpower funds in its "special" revenue-sharing plans, asking Congress to approve the dispersal of $2 billion dollars in manpower funds with no applications or plans filed with the Labor Department at all.

Fighting a rearguard action against the rising support for public service employment in Congress, the administration was willing to allow states and localities to spend manpower revenue shared funds for public service employment if they wished. But it remained firm against the only kind of legislation that could provide substantial funds for public service employment, legislation that would recognize the need for public service employment apart from training programs. The administration let it be known that if the Emergency Employment Act passed, it would almost certainly be vetoed. It attempted unsuccessfully to have its Manpower Revenue Sharing proposal — introduced only in March, and as yet unconsidered in hearings or committee — substituted for the Emergency Employment Act on the House floor.

The conferees representing the House and the Senate met in late June to consider the differences between the two houses' versions of the Emergency Employment Act. The feelings of the Senators and congressmen crowded into a small out-of-the-way room in the Capitol were somewhat downcast. Senator Javits said that in his view there was a 60-40 chance the bill would be vetoed. Congressman Albert Quie of Minnesota, a frequent spokesman for the administration's point of view in conferences, said, no, the chances were more like 90-10.

Suddenly, however, the administration was willing to at least sit down and discuss the situation. Then in an unusual series of triangular bargaining sessions, between House and Senate conferees and the administration, a compromise was hammered out — the administration insisted that the Senate's word "transitional" be sprinkled freely throughout the bill — and the bill was enacted and signed.

How is it possible that a Senate, which had defeated forty-seven to forty-two, only three years before, a moderate, watered-down version of an emergency employment act could have voted so overwhelmingly for a major public service employment program in 1971? Among the factors to be considered are certainly the following. First in 1967 the Democratic administration opposed public service employment. Administration opposition would be enough by itself to explain more than enough votes to defeat the plan. When the administration and the Congress are controlled by the same party, as they were in 1967, congressional leaders are most reluctant to develop legislative initiatives that will embarrass their own administration. In contrast, in 1971 a Republican administration downtown enabled Democratic Congressmen and committees to take a much more critical view, and to develop comprehensive alternative proposals.

Of most crucial importance, perhaps, was the unemployment rate. In 1967 the national unemployment rate was 3.4 percent of the labor force. In 1970 it was 5.5 percent of the labor force, and by April 1971 it had averaged over 6 percent for three months. Not only were a greater number of people unemployed, but the composition of unemployment was sharply different. In 1971 there were an estimated 400,000 aerospace workers unemployed. In this group were approximately 60,000 unemployed scientists and engineers. From December 1959 to December 1970, the number of California aerospace workers declined by 82,000. In the same period in the state of Washington, 40,000 aerospace workers lost their jobs. In addition to aerospace workers it was estimated that 600,000 employees lost jobs due to the general defense cutbacks during this period. Unemployed veterans became a major issue by the spring of 1971. As the Senate committee report stated, "It is a tragedy for an individual to be unable to find a job in order to support himself and his family, but when that individual has just spent 12 months or more risking his life in support of his country being unemployed is an unconscionable injustice." Military separations had increased from 565,000 in 1966 to 1,000,000 in 1969 and 1,120,000 in 1970. For the first two months of 1971, the unemployment rate among veterans 20 to 29 years old was 10.2 percent, while the unemployment rate for nonveterans in the same age group was 6.8 percent. Congress recognized a clear responsibility to unemployed veterans and to defense and aerospace workers thrown off the jobs because of defense cutbacks. In contrast, the Emergency Employment Act of 1967 was concerned with unemployment among the inner-city poor. It was the riots in those inner cities that had prompted Kennedy and Clark to propose legislation in the first place. While concerned with inner-city unemployment in 1967, the Congress felt no sense of special obligation to solve that problem through public service employment. In 1971, however, Congress did feel an obligation to make at least a gesture toward providing jobs for those people thrown out of work in direct consequence of federal policy. In 1967 it was the position of the administration that the purpose of manpower programs was to provide training to enable individuals to compete in the open market with jobs. Long before the national unemployment crisis of 1971, the inadequacy of training programs by themselves for inner-city residents was clear. The Labor Department had made a major commitment to provide jobs for inner-city residents through the private sector, the JOBS program. By the spring of 1970, following the Employment, Manpower, and Poverty Subcommittee's study of the JOBS program, the idea that one could rely on the private sector was open to serious question. A former ambassador, George C. McGhee, testifying for the Urban Coalition, told the committee "It would not be reasonable to expect the private sector to do the whole job. The jobs are just not there." With unemployment standing at over 6 percent, the Senate overwhelmingly passed the Emergency Employment Act.

In conference with the House, a veteran's preference provision was quickly accepted. A provision to make funds available to small areas of particularly high unemployment even afer the national program was phased out was also accepted. This "special employment assistance program" authorized $250 million a year to provide public service employment jobs in areas of "substantial unemployment" as small as inner-city neighborhoods or areas within rural counties. Chinatown and the Mission District in San Francisco, Watts in Los Angeles, and Bedford Stuyvesant in New York were specifically mentioned in the conference report.

The Emergency Employment Act provided jobs for all who were unemployed, the same terms upon which jobs were offered in the first emergency program run in that dread winter of '33 and '34 by Harry Hopkins. The Emergency Employment Act provides wages no lower than the federal minimum and ranging up to $12,000 a year. In fact, no more than 30 percent of the first people hired under the Emergency Employment Act were poor.

For those who are concerned about the potential of a major public service employment program as a way of meeting the needs of the inner-city poor and those in rural backwaters for whom the free enterprise economy provides little hope of a secure life through decent employment, the Emergency Employment Act is a hopeful, but not entirely satisfactory piece of legislation. Senators Clark and Kennedy back in 1967 were concerned about the chronic shortage of jobs in the inner city and the disaster that it spelled, not only for the individuals involved, but for their cities and for the nation as a whole. They painted a graphic picture of declining employment in rural areas (Mississippi lost half of its agricultural work force between 1950 and 1960), individuals streaming hopefully into the cities of the North only to find few jobs and fewer at decent pay.

Labor Secretary Willard Wirtz documented in his subemployment studies of ten ghettoes in 1966 that over 35 percent of the inner-city work force was unable to earn even poverty wages in the inner city — even when national unemployment stood at only 3.7 percent. The small-scale Labor Department public employment programs such as Operation Mainstream and New Careers demonstrated that many considered "hard-core unemployed" could be trained for semi-professional duties if real opportunity following training was available. The JOBS program showed that there was only a limited potential for the disadvantaged in private industry. When Congress finally passed a major public service employment program into law, it was designed not for the hard core or even the inner-city poor or rural unemployed, but as a general measure to help all of the unemployed. Supplying 150,000 jobs in public service, the most generous estimate made by the supporters of Emergency Employment Act, would not have provided jobs for anything like the 500,000 hard-core unemployed identified by Wirtz in his study. And dropped into the ocean of the 5.5 million unemployed men and women in the spring of 1971, it could hope to make hardly a ripple.

Of the original aims of Kennedy and Clark, all that remained was the special employment assistance program which holds promise of providing public service employment funds to poverty neighborhoods after the national program has been phased out. This section of the legislation holds the greatest promise for those who hope to use public service employment as a weapon in the fight against chronic poverty. Another weapon in the legislation is the requirement that local jurisdictions seeking funds will "undertake analysis of job description and a re-evaluation of skill requirements at all levels of employment including Civil Service requirements and practices relating thereto, . . . "It can be hoped that this section will lead to greater access to public service employment jobs under regular Civil Service both for those employed through the Emergency Employment Act and for the poor in general.

From 1967 until November 1971, the Bureau of Labor Statistics continued research on the unemployment problems of poverty neighborhoods attempting to establish a subemployment index, such as Secretary Wirtz had published, as a regularly reported statistic. The work has now been terminated by the Nixon Administration. However, the "underemployed" are written into the legislation, eligible for jobs under the Emergency Employment Act. The underemployed are defined as "persons who are working part time but seeking full-time work and persons who are working full time but are receiving wages below the poverty level" as determined by the Office of Management and Budget. It can be hoped that this legislative recognition of the existence of underemployment may lead to a regularly published index and thereby to a wider understanding of the role of underemployment and its concentration in inner-city and poor rural areas in the persistence of poverty in the country.

On July 12, 1971, President Nixon signed the Emergency Employment Act in San Clemente. In signing the bill he emphasized that it would provide jobs for veterans and for youth and that the jobs will be "transitional."

It is interesting to note that just prior to signing the Emergency Employment Act, the president had vetoed an accelerated public works bill which was adopted in record speed by Congress during this spring of 1971. Thus the old controversy between Harold Ickes' Public Works Administration, with its heavy construction approach to unemployment, and Harry Hopkins' WPA small labor-intensive "publice service" projects has persisted until the present.

As encouraging as is the passage of the Emergency Employment Act and as widely accepted as the public service employment program seems to be, we still have little reason to believe that the nation accepts responsibility to provide decent employment for all Americans as a serious imperative. The Constitution requires that the government promote the general welfare and provide for the common defense. Back in 1961, when Labor Secretary Goldberg urged President Kennedy to pursue a public works program to get the nation moving again, Kennedy is quoted as saying that "defense will have to be my public works". Kennedy is also quoted as stating that in England when unemployment goes over

2 percent they storm Parliament and when American is at 6 percent nobody seems to care. Schlesinger, in discussing the problem of poverty, makes an interesting remark in his book on the Kennedy administration, *A Thousand Days.* Schlesinger says "that most of the unemployed are not poor and most of the poor are not unemployed." The implication is that poverty and jobs were separate porblems. It was this perception which led to the Kennedy's administration formulating an antipoverty strategy, planned in detail and carried out by the Johnson administration, based on providing services to the poor. Until there is wider recognition of the relationship between the pay a man receives from his job and the persistence of poverty, and until Congress and the nation take seriously the responsibility to provide jobs for all Americans, we will solve neither the problem of jobs nor the problems of poverty.

Congressional action of 1935 through 1971 shows that Congress is willing to adopt direct job creation legislation during times of acute crisis responsibility to act to increase the job supply. There is not as yet evidence that Congress is willing to enact major public service employment legislation designed to assure an adequate job supply of decent wages for those unable to find adequate opportunities in the private sector.

Notes

1. Robert Sherwood, *Roosevelt and Hopkins* (New York: Harper & Bros., 1950, p. 60)

2. Arthur Schlesinger, Jr. *The Policies of Upheaval* (Boston: Houghton Mifflin, 1947)

3. *Conference Report on Employment Act of 1946,* Report No. 1520, House, 79th Congress, 2nd Session, Feb. 5, 1946.

4. Michael Harrington, *The Other America* (New York: Macmillan Co., 1963).

5. Robert Lampman, *The Low Income Population and Economic Growth,* Joint Economic Committee, Study Paper 12, December, 1959.

6. Daniel P. Moynihan, "The Professors and the Poor", *Commentary,* August, 1968, pp. 19-28.

Appendix

Provisions of the Emergency Employment Act of 1971

THE NATIONAL CIVIL SERVICE LEAGUE

On July 12, 1971, the president signed into law the Emergency Employment Act of 1971. This is the first major piece of legislation creating federally-financed public service jobs since the New Deal. Although this act is considerably less ambitious in its scope and provisions than the Comprehensive Manpower Act which President Nixon vetoed in December 1970, it nonetheless marks the passage of a milestone in national manpower policy, and establishes a precedent for continued federal subsidization of the wages, salaries, and benefits of state and local public employees.

Observers expect Congress to fund the new measure within the next few weeks. In the meantime, the Department of Labor will be developing guidelines and application forms for jurisdictions wishing to take part in the programs of the Emergency Employment Act of 1971.

Funding

The EEA contains two different "funds." The first provides $750 million for fiscal year 1972, and $1 billion for fiscal 1973. This "regular national program" is "triggered" whenever the national unemployment rate reaches or exceeds 4.5 percent for three consecutive months – a condition almost certain to continue during the two year tenure of the EEA. A minimum of 85 percent of these monies is earmarked for the wages, salaries, and benefits of public service workers. Up to 15 percent may be used by the Secretary of Labor for training and related activities. Up to 1 percent may be allocated by the Secretary of Labor for research and program evaluation.

The second "fund" provides $250 million for fiscal 1972, and another $250 million for fiscal 1973. This "Special Employment Assistance Program" is available for job "creation" in any area – including an urban ghetto or Model Neighborhood[a] – which sustains an unemployment rate of at least 6 percent for

---

Reprinted from the National Civil Service League, *Exchange*, 1,5 (July 1971).

[a]The EEA specifically defines eligible areas as "any area of sufficient size and scope to sustain a public service employment program and which has a rate of unemployment equal to or in excess of 6 percentum for three consecutive months as determined by the Secretary [of Labor]." Moreover, "it is the understanding of the [House-Senate] conferees that areas within cities . . . such as Chinatown or the Mission District in San Francisco, Uptown or Lawndale in Chicago, Watts or East Los Angeles in Los Angeles, portions of Seattle [and] Harlem or Bedford-Stuyvesant in New York City will be so designated by the Secretary." U.S. House of Representatives, *Emergency Employment Act*, Conference Report, 92nd Congress, 1st Session, Report No. 92-310, June 28, 1971, p. 15.

149

three consecutive months, *regardless* of the national rate. This condition is, of course, all too easily met in the central city ghettos of American cities.

Eligible Applicants

Any unit of federal, state, and general local government, *any public agency or institution which is a "subdivision" of state or general local government,* and any Indian tribe on a federal or state reservation, is eligible to apply for public service wage subsidies. After much debate, the Senate and House conferees definitely prohibited private nonprofit agencies (including private Community Action Agencies) from being "eligible applicants" (or what used to be called "prime sponsors"). No such prohibition was made against City Demonstration Agencies (i.e., Model Cities Agencies), since they are of course an integral part of city government.

Regional Allocation

A minimum of 80 percent of the total funds must be allocated among the eligible applicants according to a formula (to be designed by the Secretary of Labor) which will give weight to each applicant's state's share of national unemployment, subject to the constraint that the eligible applicants within *each* state (including, of course, the state government itself) *must* receive at least $1.5 million among them. The Secretary of Labor may allocate up to 20 percent of the monies according to any other criteria.

Eligible Workers

The EEA defines two categories of eligible workers. The *unemployed* are persons currently without jobs, or adults who (or whose families) receive public assistance ("welfare") and are either (1) without jobs; or (2) working already in jobs which provide insufficient income to allow them to become independent of welfare.

The *underemployed* are defined as persons working part time but seeking full-time work, or persons working full time but earning only a poverty-level wage (currently about $4,000 per year).

The act frequently uses the term "transitional employment" to describe the jobs created under its authority. The *Conference Report* on the act seeks to define what the congressmen and senators meant by this term:

. . . the word transitional describes, first of all, the limited duration of the authorized program, in that this Act expires on June 30, 1973, and the fact that funds for the principal program [but *not* the Special Employment Assistance Program] cease to be obligated when the national rate of unemployment recedes below 4.5 percent.

Second, for individuals employed under the program, it is the intention of the conferees that public service employment jobs lead wherever possible to positions not supported under this Act in the Public or private sector . . .

All of this language is intended to make it crystal clear that public service employment shall not be of the dead end, make work sort that is feared by the critics of public service employment.

It is the clear intention of the conferees that the program not be administered in such a way as to make of the jobs simply training slots with stipends . . .

However, the conferees agreed that the word "transitional" as used in this act —

does not in any way limit that length of time an individual can stay on a specific public service employment job during the term of this Act — and no regulation may require any such limitation;

does not limit the kinds of jobs to be made available under the program; specifically, jobs are not to be limited to those which are inherently temporary; jobs to be funded under this Act are to include such jobs as policemen, teachers, nurses, firemen, and other jobs widely recognized as necessary and permanent in nature;

does not prohibit the re-employment of those who have been laid off regular public service jobs because of fiscal problems at the local level. In fact, the conferees expect that many localities will rehire such employees. *(Conference Report)*

Wage Provisions

Eligible applicants are required to pay whichever is the higher of

- the federal minimum wage (currently $1.60/hour).
- the state or local minimum wage (if any).
- the "prevailing rate of pay" for persons employed in similar public occupations by the same public employer.

In their *Conference Report,* the conferees are quite explicit about this pay comparability requirement:

To illustrate, in the case of a city using Federal funds received under this Act to employ nurses in municipal hospitals, the prevailing wage would be that paid to other nurses in the same or similar jobs in municipal hospitals.

In addition, the applicant is required to pay "workmen's compensation, health insurance, unemployment insurance, and other benefits at the same levels and to the same extent as other employees of the employer."

Finally, the maximum annual wage or salary which may be financed in its entirety from these national funds is $12,000. If a jurisdiction wishes to pay a higher salary than that, the difference between that salary and $12,000 must be met entirely out of other funds.

The Application

The EEA requires an exceedingly comprehensive and specific application from jurisdictions or agencies proposing to sponsor public service employment programs.

Each application must address at least the following twenty points:

1. Identification of the agencies or institutions which will be involved in the program
2. estimation of the size, income, and employment status of the population and area to be served
3. commitment to jobs which, through on-the-job training, will enhance the skills of their incumbents
4. commitment to "special consideration" (but *not* absolute preference) for veterans of the Indochina and Korean wars
5. assignment of subsidized workers to jobs in expanding (as opposed to "dead-end") occupations
6. consideration (but, again, no absolute preference) for manpower trainees or graduates unable to find jobs
7. "description of the methods to be used to recruit, select, and orient participants, including specific eligibility criteria"
8. "a description of unmet public service needs and a statement of priorities among such needs"
9. description of the jobs to be filled, the work to be performed, and the skills required
10. the wages, salaries and benefits to be paid each subsidized worker, "and a comparison with the wages paid for similar public occupations by the same employer"
11. description of the education, training, counseling, health care, day care or other supportive services to be provided (where appropriate)
12. plans for training and utilizing supervisory personnel
13. "a description of career opportunities and job advancement potentialities for participants"
14. commitment to provide the Secretary of Labor with program data as per Section 11(a) of the EEA

15. *commitment to the undertaking of job descriptions, analysis of skill requirements and civil service system problems* [emphasis ours] (e.g., excessive reliance upon written exams, excessive use of educational credentials)
16. development of linkages with upgrading and other local manpower programs
17. "assurances that all persons employed under any such program, other than necessary technical, supervisory, and administrative personnel, will be selected from among unemployed and underemployed persons"
18. *"assurances that the program will, to the maximum extent feasible, contribute to the elimination of artificial barriers to employment and occupational advancement, including civil service requirements which restrict employment opportunities for the disadvantaged"* [emphasis ours]
19. assurance that not more than a third of the subsidized job slots will be filled by professionals (except for classroom teachers)
20. "such other . . . conditions . . . as the Secretary [of Labor] deems necessary.

There is also an additional — and quite interesting — requirement that

where a labor organization represents employees who are engaged in similar work in the same area as that proposed to be performed under any program . . . under this Act, such organization shall be notified and afforded a resonable period of time in which to make comments to the applicant and to the Secretary [of Labor].

Reports

The draftors of the EEA were very concerned about allowing for the provision of sufficient data to permit evaluation of the federally-subsidized public service employment concept. The act therefore requires each jurisdiction receiving support to submit "periodic reports" to the Labor Department, covering:

1. age, sex, race, health, education, and *previous* wage and employment experience of all participants
2. follow-up on participants for at least one year after they leave the subsidized slot, with a comparison profile on similar individuals employed by the jurisdiction whose jobs were *not* subsidized
3. "total dollar cost per participant, including breakdown between wages, training, and supportive services, all fringe benefits, and administrative costs."

The Secretary of Labor is, in turn, required to submit to Congress at least annually a report on the progress of the program, including the reporting of that data given to him by the participating jurisdictions. He will publish this by state, region, and nationally.

A remarkable historical document on the public works and related programs of the 1930s is John Kenneth Galbraith and G.G. Johnson, Jr., *The Economic Effects of the Federal Public Works Expenditures, 1933-38* (Washington, D.C.: U.S. Government Printing Office, 1940). For a striking set of photographs depicting work activity under the WPA, the reader is referred to *City,* the journal of the National Urban Coalition, October-November 1970. Perhaps the most well-known chronicler of the manpower and economic development programs of the 1950s and the 1960s is Sar A. Levitan; cf. *Federal Aid to Depressed Areas* (Baltimore, Maryland: The Johns Hopkins Press, 1964), and *The Great Society's Poor Law* (Baltimore: The Johns Hopkins Press, 1970). The Manpower Administration of the U.S. Department of Labor is currently preparing a monograph surveying the experience of the first ten years of the Manpower Development and Training Act programs. Two journal articles which are strongly critical of the "human capital revolution" in manpower policy are: Howard M. Wachtel "Looking at Poverty from a Radical Perspective," *The Review of Radical Political Economics,* Summer 1971; and Bennett Harrison, "National Manpower Policy and Public Service Employment," *New Generation,* Winter 1971.

Three economics text books which include a substantial amount of information on the manpower programs of the sixties are: Bradley F. Schiller, *The Economics of Poverty and Discrimination* (Englewood Cliffs, N.J.: Prentice-Hall, 1972); Clair Wilcox, *Toward Social Welfare* (Homewood, Illinois: Richard D. Irwin, 1969); and Sar A. Levitan, Garth L. Mangum, and Ray Marshall, *Human Resources and Labor Markets* (New York: Harper and Row, 1972), Part IV.

The principal source document for manpower legislation itself is, of course, the *Congressional Record.* A number of commentaries on selected pieces of legislation are published regularly in Washington; two of the best are the *Congressional Digest,* published by the Congressional Digest Corporation, 3231 P St., N.W. Washington, D.C. 20007; and the *Manpower Information Service,* a bi-weekly publication of the Bureau of National Affairs, Inc., 1211 Connecticut Ave., N.W., Washington, D.C. 20036.

Part III
The Measurement of Unemployment and Underemployment

"We do only what we measure," says Willard Wirtz, Secretary of Labor under President Johnson.

Without accurate and easily intelligible measures of labor market activity, it is difficult to organize public support for manpower programs which succeed, or public criticism of programs which fail. Indeed, it is nearly impossible to determine, without such measures, whether programs have succeeded or whether they have failed. The impact of a public policy on the environment (or on some "target population") has to be measured by comparing the state of that environment or population before, during, and following the termination of the program. Environmental changes are registered by *indicators* — or measures. In analyzing the effect of some medical treatment on a diseased patient, one common indicator of bodily response to the treatment is a change in the temperature of the patient. A farmer measures the effect of the application of a new kind of fertilizer by changes in crop yields, the incidence and severity of crop diseases, and so on.

For many years, economists and policy makers have measured the state of labor markets — both nationally and locally — by one principal indicator, the rate of unemployment:

$$\frac{\text{number of persons looking for work but not working}}{\text{number of persons working or looking for work}} \times 100$$

This particular indicator measures the percentage of those persons looking for work (i.e., the "labor force") who have apparently been unable to find it (the so-called "unemployed").

The government computes and publishes monthly unemployment rates for the nation as a whole and for 150 "labor market areas," which consist of major cities and their suburban and exurban "hinterlands." These statistics are compiled by U.S. Training and Employment Service branch offices from the records of those workers covered by Unemployment Insurance (about 40 percent of the nation's workforce).

Another set of unemployment rates is published regularly by the government. These are based upon direct household surveys, and tend therefore to be more comprehensive than the rates based upon "insured employment" alone. A number of statistical series have been developed from these data, including a quarterly report on the "poverty areas" of 100 large central cities, on the remainder of those cities, and (occasionally) on their suburbs as well. Regional figures are also made available periodically. Unfortunately, the size of the survey samples in any one city is too small to permit confident statistical inference. Therefore, individual cities are seldom identified by name in the government's publications. Occasionally, special surveys *have* been run which have permitted such identification, but these have been neither very broad (encompassing at most twenty cities or parts of cities, such as ghetto areas), nor continuous. Without *continuous* collecting and reporting of unemployment rates, it is of course not possible to measure *changes* in labor market conditions, just as a physician cannot measure a patient's reaction to a penicillin injection by taking the patient's temperature only once.

The unemployment rate is by no means the only indicator of labor market activity published by the government. Data are available — on much the same geographical basis as was discussed above — by which to measure full-time employment, wages earned, the duration of unemployment "spells," and many other indicators. Nevertheless, it is the unemployment rate which economists almost invariably put into their models as the "single best" measure of the strength of the demand for labor, which elected officials and their staffs most frequently refer to as a guide to their policy deliberations, and which the news media most regularly report as an indicator of "how things are going" in the American economy.

This primacy of the unemployment rate raises three kinds of important questions for manpower policy. *First*, how good *is* the conventional unemployment rate as a measure of the quantity of work available in the economy, and can it be improved? *Second*, can manpower policy continue to rely for guidance on national (or, at best, regional) unemployment rates, or must we begin to develop regularly-published local indicators as well? *Third*, is the measurement of the *quantity* of work in the economy enough? Don't we also need to examine the *quality* of that work — by industry, by occupation, and by location — if we are to be able to design manpower programs which will in fact improve the levels of living of the labor force?

These questions are especially relevant to a discussion of public service job development. The Emergency Employment Act of 1971 relies particularly heavily on the availability of both standard unemployment data and on indicators of *underemployment* to activate the legislation, to qualify jurisdictions (or parts of jurisdictions) for its benefits, and to permit evaluation of local public service programs. Moreover, a major argument in support of the EEA — an argument which determined the final votes of many Senators and congressmen — was the alleged inability of the private sector (particularly but not exclusively during a recession) to generate enough non-poverty jobs for all the people in the United States who want to work. In the past, this argument has been supported by "snapshot" studies such as the Department of Labor's 1966 Urban Employment Survey, which showed that even in the midst of the Kennedy-Johnson Vietnam "boom," perhaps 12-15 percent of the residents of central city ghettos were still unemployed, and as many as 50 percent were "subemployed" — locked into the low-paying, *truly* transitory work patterns of the secondary labor market. For the future, in deciding whether and how to continue the federal government's job development activities through programs such as public service employment, Congress and the Executive will have to know if and when the private sector can "carry the load," and *how much* of that "load" it can carry. To reach such decisions, legislators and program planners will need indicators of both the quantity and the quality of available work in both the public and the private sectors of the American economy.

At the third Upjohn Seminar, Professors Charles Killingsworth and Thomas Dernburg addressed themselves to the first question. How good *is* the conventional unemployment rate, which has come to be featured regularly on the evening news along with the stock market reports? Just what *does* the unemployment rate tell us about the "state of the economy"?

Killingsworth discussed the implications of two important changes in the official definitions, both of which tend to underestimate the seriousness of unemployment in the economy. The first of these changes was initiated in 1965, when it was decided that enrollees in most manpower training programs would henceforth be counted as "employed" (since the depression, when such programs were first instituted, the practice had been to count trainees as "unemployed"). Malcolm Cohen, of the University of Michigan, while still serving at the Bureau of Labor Statistics in Washington, estimated that — by 1967 — the direct effect of this definitional change had been to reduce the national unemployment rate by four-tenths of one percent. Using Cohen's methodology and data on the expanded training activities of the government since 1967, Professor Killingsworth reported that this effect has increased to .5 percent.[a]

Harold Goldstein, Assistant Commissioner of Manpower Statistics in the Bureau of Labor Statistics, defended the procedural change as being sensible, and pointed out to the Seminar that, in any case, statistics on manpower training program enrollments are readily available, so that the published unemployment rate could easily be adjusted by anyone preferring

---

[a]Recall the definition of the unemployment rate given on p. 159. Defining trainees as employed rather than unemployed leaves the denominator unchanged, but reduces the numerator. Thus, the ratio falls.

the pre-1965 categorization.

Harold Sheppard noted that this was not the first time that changes in government programs have affected the unemployment rate. The lowering of the retirement age by the Social Security Administration, from 65 to 62, was followed by a significant reduction in the labor force participation of men aged 62-64, resulting in a decline in the aggregate unemployment rate.

The second definitional change discussed by Killingsworth is more subtle. Prior to 1967, individuals were asked by the Census or Employment Service interviewer a set of simple questions amounting to this basic query: "Were you employed, unemployed, or not looking for work last week (or month)?" In the early 1960s, a committee of distinguished economists and statisticians (the "Gordon Committee") had criticized this procedure, on the grounds that many men not actually in the labor force would nevertheless report that they were "unemployed," since — in a work-oriented society — they felt that they were *expected* to be looking for work if not actually working. To overcome this hypothetical flaw in the procedure, the Gordon Committee recommended the introduction of a "check list" designed to ascertain whether or not those who were not actually employed had or had not tried to find work in the previous week (or month). Those who "passed" the "check list" were to be classified as "unemployed." Those who "failed" it — who could not demonstrate that they had actively sought jobs — were to be categorized as "not in the labor force."

These changes went into effect in January 1967. It was now possible for an individual who genuinely wanted to work, but who had not tried to find a job through orthodox channels (or who had given up looking altogether out of discouragement), to be counted as "not in the labor force," and therefore not part of the unemployment statistics at all. The larger such a group, the more seriously does the published unemployment rate understate the severity of joblessness in the economy.[b] Killingsworth estimates that the net effect of this change in the definition has been to underestimate aggregate unemployment by about .2 percent.[c] Moreover, the effect may be even more serious during recessions. With general expectations of unemploy-

---

[b]Letting L = labor force, E = the employed, and L-E = the unemployed, we want to know how the rate (L-E/L) changes when L changes. Differentiating the unemployment rate with respect to L gives

$$\frac{d}{dL}\left(\frac{L-E}{L}\right) = \frac{d}{dL}(1 - EL^{-1}) = \frac{E}{L^2} > 0$$

When L increases, the unemployment rate increases. When L falls, the unemployment rate falls.

[c]In rebuttal, Goldstein indicated that half of this estimate (.1 percent) is probably attributable to the removal of 14-15 year old persons from the sample.

ment being higher, more people may give up looking, even though they want to work and would take a job if one were offered.

Taken together, these estimated changes of .5 percent and .2 percent lead Killingsworth to the conclusion that the existing unemployment rate understates national aggregate joblessness by at least .7 percent. In 1969, when "full employment" (3.5 percent) had allegedly been achieved, the nation was actually experiencing 4.2 percent unemployment – a difference of some 600,000 workers! During the 1970-71 recession, when unemployment averaged about 6 percent, the "true" rate may have been closer to 7 percent.

The effect of these definitional changes has been greater on the unemployment rates of certain sub-groups in the population than on others. Blacks, for example, have a much higher proportional membership among manpower trainees, discouraged workers, and workers aged 14-15 than do whites. This may have led to what now appears to have been a temporary decline in the ratio of black to white unemployment rates from its long-term trend value of 2.0 to a 1970 level of 1.7. Killingsworth and Robert A. Gordon (chairman and namesake of the Gordon Committee) have studied this apparent closing of the black-white unemployment "gap," and found that it is due entirely to a sharp reduction in the labor force participation of black workers!

Killingsworth offered two proposals to the Upjohn Seminar. He urged the participants to be wary of comparisons between post-1965 and pre-1965 unemployment rates. He also urged the congressional staffs to count workers hired under the Emergency Employment Act as "not in the labor force" for the purpose of computing the national unemployment rate to which the bill would be "triggered." This suggestion was subsequently incorporated into the Emergency Employment Act of 1971.

Such a dual definition – one for the purpose of this particular program and another for conventional usage – is bound to create confusion in the future. Yet is is difficult to see a way of solving the dilemma. For programs which involve training without the guarantee of a post-training job, the pre-1965 approach is clearly the most sensible: trainees should be counted as people looking for work, and therefore "unemployed." But for job development programs such as that mandated by the Emergency Employment Act, classification of participants as "unemployed" deprives the program of the opportunity to demonstrate its effectiveness; the purpose of the EEA is precisely to reduce unemployment! Yet to count participants as "employed" could – as Killingsworth reminded the Seminar – actually de-activate the "trigger" and shut off the program!

Professor Thomas Dernburg of Oberlin College reported to the Seminar on his studies of the behavior of the unemployment rate over time. "It appears," he said, "that since the beginning of 1967, one of our leading indicators — the one that we most often pay attention to — namely, the rate of unemployment, has become a woefully inadequate measure of the level of prosperity. It has gone up when we expected it to go down. It has gone down when it ought to be going up, when other things indicated that it ought to be going up."

For example, unemployment in 1966 (a very prosperous year) averaged 3.8 percent. The first half of 1967 "just missed being classified as a recession" as the unemployment rate rose to 3.9 percent. In 1968, the rate finally began to fall, and did not begin to rise until a year later — even though the economy had already started to slow down after the middle of 1968.

What happened? Apparently, whenever the number of jobs in the economy rose, the number of people looking for jobs — the labor force — also rose, in nearly a "one-for-one lockstep basis."

The increase in employment would tend to lower the unemployment rate, the increase in the labor force would tend to raise it; if anything happened from month to month or from quarter to quarter, it would tend to be a consequence of random noise. So we really didn't get any indications at all of what was going on.

Dernburg estimated that, during this period, the "elasticity" of labor force participation with respect to employment equalled .96. In other words, an increase in employment of 100 percent was followed by an increase in the size of the labor force by 96 percent. Thus, "there was absolutely no correlation whatsoever between the overall unemployment rate and the growth of employment."

The policy implications of what Dernburg and others call "hidden unemployment" are particularly relevant to the design of a job creation program such as public service employment. In the past, the government would set a target rate of unemployment (such as the Kennedy Council of Economic Advisors did, using 4 percent), observe the current magnitude of unemployment, and compute the number of jobs needed to get from "here" to "there," assuming a fixed labor force. If, however, increases in employment are accompanied by significant increases in people looking for jobs (an *increased* labor force), then the computation will underestimate the number of new jobs needed. To get a "correct" estimate, this elasticity of labor force participation — this phenomenon of "hidden unemployment" — must be measured and accounted for in planning job creation programs.

In an earlier collaborative study with Kenneth Strand, Dernburg had found that the elasticity of labor force participation over the period 1953-62 had averaged .43, a much lower figure than the one describing the post-1967 period. One of the key differences between the two periods (and the two sets of figures) has been the greatly increased volatility in the labor force participation of prime working-age men, especially black men. Dernburg believes that this dramatic change may be the result of those definitional changes instituted in 1967 and discussed earlier by Killingsworth. "What appears to have happened is that whether you pass or fail that check list is now a function of the degree of prosperity in the economy." When the economy is healthy, men *do* "check with the Employment Service," "answer advertisements," etc. But when the economy is depressed, why bother? Thus, where it used to seem (from the indicator used) that unemployment varied while labor force participation was more or less constant, it now appears to be true (from the "new" indicator) that labor force participation fluctuates from month to month, while unemployment *doesn't* move very much!

Bennett Harrison, acting as chairman of the Seminar, suggested that such volatile labor force participation is quite consistent with the theory of economic dualism presented at the first two sessions. From this interpretation, the Gordon Committee procedural and definitional changes actually succeeded in capturing the presence of the secondary labor market. [d] From the perspective of conventional macroeconomics (with its model of a unified economy), this fluctuation in labor force participation was indeed bizarre. To a dual economy theorist, it was altogether to be expected.

Dernburg's solution to this problem is to urge policymakers to "forget this global unemployment rate and look at the sub-groups."[e] Insofar as even sub-group (or sub-area) unemployment rates become misleading because of "hidden unemployment," Dernburg advocates the use of "adult full-time employment" as an indicator of labor market behavior. This statistic is readily available (although not yet on a regular small-area basis), and its wide promulgation by economists and government officials would seem to be a constructive activity.

Harold Goldstein reported to the Seminar that the BLS has been engaged for several years in a number of experimental programs to develop small-area labor market indicators and measures of the quality as well as the quantity of employment.

The first of these experiments was the eight-city, ten-ghetto 1966 Urban Employment Survey, from which was produced an index of "subemploy-

---

[d]The effect of the change in the categorization of the "unemployed" is to make that classification a function of the "job hunt." Sometimes secondary workers "look" for (legal) work, and sometimes they do not. Thus, labor force participation appears to be unstable.

[e]BLS Assistant Commissioner Goldstein agreed that policy-makers should concentrate on "the unemployment situation for particular groups in the population — for black workers as compared to whites, for people in particular communities, for people with particular levels of skill or education. This is really where you get the insights."

ment." This indicator included the conventionally unemployed, those who were working part time because they were unable to find full-time work, people earning at a rate below the national minimum wage, and half of the male non-participants aged 20-64 (on the grounds that approximately this proportion might have been "discouraged" and not actually unable to work). The index also included an adjustment for the notorious "male undercount," first discovered in the 1960 Census, where it was learned that large numbers of men who *should* appear in ghetto samples (based upon the actual number of women found in the ghetto, and the ratio of men to women found outside the ghetto) avoid the Census-taker. The "subemployment" rates calculated from these surveys yielded estimates ranging from 25 percent in the Roxbury section of Boston to nearly 50 percent in the *Chicano* slums of San Antonio.

The second experiment was reported in the 1968 *Manpower Report of the President.* A simpler, but still controversial "subemployment" rate was developed for the national economy. Individuals with at least some work experience during the year were counted as "subemployed" if they had fifteen or more weeks of unemployment or if they earned less than $3,000 for full-time, year-round work. The first published estimates referred to 1966; in a year during which national unemployment averaged 3.8 percent, national subemployment measured about 10 percent. By 1968, this subemployment rate fell to 7.3 percent, and in 1969 — with national unemployment at 3.5 percent — national subemployment fell still further, to 5.2 percent.[f] Although this index has not been calculated for the 100 sets of inner-city poverty neighborhoods (a calculation which the congressional aides attending the Seminar agreed would be "very useful"), Goldstein indicated that such a series might be developed in the near future.

A third program to measure the "quality" of employment has in fact been underway for some time, and is no longer "experimental." The BLS publishes regular statistics on "involuntary part-time employment": the number of people who work part time but have sought and continue to seek full-time jobs. "In March 1971, there were about two and a half million people in this category," said Goldstein.

A fourth effort — thoroughly experimental — consists of attempts to measure "underemployment" in the sense in which the classical economist

---

[f]It may be observed that, since this national subemployment indicator is *not* adjusted for variations in labor force participation attributable to "hidden unemployment," it is subject to the same criticisms leveled by Killingsworth and Dernburg at the conventional unemployment rate. In other words, it probably understates the severity of "subemployment."

uses the term: individuals working beneath their *potential* productivity.[g] The definitional and measurement problems here are enormous. The Gordon Committee had suggested an "operational" definition: "people working below their current highest skill or at wages below what that skill, if fully utilized, would normally earn." Goldstein noted the difficulty of developing a hierarchy of skills ("who is to say that the electrician who is working as a carpenter is working below or above his highest skill?"). Moreover, to ask a worker to indicate his "highest skill" if he is not currently practicing that skill invites potentially enormous response errors ("is the man who reports that he is 'really' a concert violinist really a competent, qualified concert violinist?"). Nevertheless, the Urban Employment Survey Group and its chief, William Milligan, has tried to develop procedures and questionnaires for measuring such "underemployment" among those whom the conventional statistics record as being "employed."

The fifth and final BLS experimental program reported by Goldstein represents an attempt to measure the key variable: non-participation induced by "discouragement" (including those who — in Dernburg's words — "fail the checklist"). Since 1967, the Current Population Survey has included a series of BLS questions for all those who report themselves (or are allocated by the Census representative to the category of) "not in the labor force." Goldstein summarized these questions:

We asked: When did he (or she) last work? Why did he leave that job? Did he lose his job? Or did he just quit? Was it personal reasons, or was it because of slack work — the economic situation? Does he intend to look for work within the next twelve months? Does he want a job now?

In 1967, of the more than fifty million people of working age (sixteen and over) who were not in the labor force, nearly five million said they did indeed "want a job now." Others — particularly female household heads — indicated that they might look for work if child care facilities were available. Finally, in 1967, 700,000 people admitted that they had stopped looking for work because "they believed no work was available." That number fell to 500,000 in 1969, but rose again to 800,000 by the first quarter of 1971. Blacks represent about a quarter of that total (even though they constitute only 11 percent of the labor force). "What we are

---

[g]Joan Robinson used as a prototype of underemployment the situation of skilled British workers during the Great Depression who were forced to sell match boxes in the Strand.

getting at," said Goldstein, "is the beginning of a sensible measurement of this notion of discouragement." These statistics are now published quarterly.[h]

In the discussion that followed these presentations, the congressional aides made it clear: (a) that the aggregate unemployment rate — even were its imperfections to be somehow removed — is becoming increasingly inadequate as a guide to the formation of public policy; (b) that the BLS' experimental programs would be more useful if they could be expanded sufficiently to permit the identification of individual labor market and poverty areas; and (c) that it would be particularly useful if the BLS would aggregate the various measures (involuntary part-time employment, poverty-level work, labor force discouragement, etc.) into a single, composite indicator of "subemployment" such as was done in the 1966 Urban Employment Survey, but not since then. (See Chapter 9 in this volume). Several aides also asked why the 1968-70 Urban Employment Survey, conducted in the ghetto areas of six cities and in the non-ghetto ("control") areas of two, had been discontinued. Goldstein replied that the program had been extremely expensive, and had therefore been terminated by its sponsor, the Manpower Administration. (Relatively little of the enormous amount of information collected in this most recent U.E.S. has been analyzed, and even less has been published.) A sixty-city "Census Employment Survey," utilizing the U.E.S. questionnaire, *was* appended to the 1970 Census operation, however, and should yield results in the near future.[i]

---

[h]This indicator would be substantially improved by asking respondents to distinguish between their perceptions of the availability of *any* kind of job and the availability of a "decent job at decent wages." The six-city 1968-70 Urban Employment surveys did in fact ask respondents to state their "reservation wage" — the minimum wage rate they would accept for (legal) work. In their study of the *Job Hunt* (Baltimore: Johns Hopkins Press, 1966), Harold L. Sheppard and A. Harvey Belitsby found that 69 percent of blue-collar workers recently or still unemployed had a "reservation wage," with the average, on a weekly basis, of $65.00 (as of 1964).

[i]As this book goes to press, a study of the 1970 Census Employment Survey has just become available. It estimates urban subemployment rates of from 33 percent (using $2/hr as the threshhold of "adequate wages") to 62 percent (Using $3.50/hour, the equivalent of the B.L.S. Lower Level Recommended Budget for an urban family of four). See William J. Spring, Bennett Harrison, and Thomas Vietorisz, "Subemployment and the Urban Crisis", *The New York Times Magazine,* Sunday.

7 Changes in the Definition of Aggregate Unemployment

CHARLES C. KILLINGSWORTH

I have emphasized on several occasions and also want to emphasize again that there were two rather substantial changes in the set of concepts that we utilize in attempting to measure unemployment in the monthly Labor Department surveys. It is my feeling that these changes in definition have been generally ignored in discussions of the unemployment problem and that in particular – and in this year's legislative proposals especially – the changed definitions are having a significant impact on the shape of legislation.

But now about the definition changes in 1965. I should say that I am greatly indebted to the good fortune that sat me next to Harold Goldstein at a luncheon in New York City back four or five years ago; had it not been for that good luck, I don't think I would have picked up this really significant information.

But in 1963 or 1964, there had been some discussion of how to classify those people who were enrolled in the new manpower programs. There were several conferences and a good deal of debate, and this was conducted primarily at the technical level, not at the Secretary of Labor's level.

And finally a kind of agreement was reached, according to which the people in some of the manpower programs were to be classified as employed, those in some others were to be classified as unemployed, and those in still others – at least, one other program – were to be classified as not in the labor force.

Now those that were to be classified as employed were people who were enrolled in programs that, in my opinion, bore considerable resemblance to the WPA and the NYA programs back in the 1930s.

I certainly don't quarrel with the integrity of the technical decisions made, and I think that there is a considerable rational basis for the decisions that were made to classify people in these new programs – particularly NYA, College Work Study, and some others – employed. Nevertheless, in my view, this clearly did constitute a change in definition which was instituted in the early part of 1965, and which had a significant effect on the monthly figure is announced. ounced.

Now the simplest way of determining the impact of the change is simply to apply the definitions that had been followed previously, certainly the definitions that were applied in the 1930s, which classified the WPA and

NYA workers as unemployed. If those old definitions were applied, then, of course, you get a substantially larger figure for the monthly unemployment rate.

But there is another way to approach the problem, which is to ask the question, "What is the impact or what has been the impact of the manpower programs on the national unemployment rate?"

That is a more relevant, but very much more difficult way to deal with the matter, because it is necessary to make a series of assumptions concerning the prior employment status or prior labor market status of those people who became enrollees in these various programs, and then to make certain assumptions as to what their status would have been in the absence of the programs.

There is also a rather fundamental question as to whether you consider only the direct, immediate impact of these programs — that is, if you have a particular group in which a 20 percent unemployment rate was reported prior to the institution of the manpower program, do you consider only that unemployment has been reduced by this 20 percent of the group? Or do you take into account the fact that many of these people — say, Neighborhood Youth Corps enrollees — may have left jobs, which then were filled by people who were previously unemployed?

This set of problems was considered by Malcolm Cohen, who was in the Bureau of Labor Statistics for a time, and who undertook to determine the direct impact of these manpower programs on the unemployment rate. He gathered quite a mass of statistics from the various programs. By applying certain assumptions that, frankly, I regard as rather conservative, he reached the conclusion that by 1967, the direct effect of the manpower programs had been to reduce the national unemployment rate by four-tenths of a percentage point.

I have undertaken to gather more recent statistics and to apply the same assumptions in the calculation of the effect of the manpower programs. By 1969 the direct effect of the manpower programs comes to five-tenths of a percentage point — a slightly larger effect.

The second change in definition is, perhaps, a little more familiar to most of you, although if you haven't followed the statistics fairly closely it may well have escaped your attention. There was a set of changes in definition that were made effective as of January 1967. These again were fairly technical changes. Some of them had been recommended by the Gordon Committee back in the early sixties, and probably on balance they improved the quality of the unemployment statistics from a technical standpoint.

But their net effect was said to be approximately two-tenths of a percentage point — that is, to reduce the national unemployment rate, the reported rate, by roughly two-tenths of a percentage point. And that effect was estimated on the basis of a kind of parallel running of the old definitions and the new definitions in 1966, and then a calculation of the differences that were discovered between these two sets of definitions at that period in time, which, of course, was a period of relatively low unemployment.

Since one of the key changes in the definitions at this point related to the "seeking work" test, it is quite possible that in a period like the present, when we have a very much higher level of long-term unemployment, the overall effect on the unemployment rate may very well be larger than the two-tenths of a percentage point that was estimated as of 1966.

But be that as it may, the minimum estimate of the effect of the definitional changes in the last six years, as of 1969, is seven-tenths of a percentage point. In other words, the reported unemployment rate was 3 1/2 percent at the end of 1969; but without the manpower programs and without the 1967 changes in definition, the reported unemployment rate would have been 4.2 percent.

Now there are some interesting consequences of the changes in definition, particularly the first set:

There is, I think, a serious question about the validity of comparing the figures since 1965 with the figures before 1965, and saying, "Well, since the unemployment rate now is so much below what it was in 1963 or 1964 or whenever, we are really doing very much better."

I believe that the significance of the unemployment rate as a measure of labor market looseness has changed as a result of these changes in definition and changes in concept, and that it is really quite misleading to compare the figures before 1965 and the figures since 1965.

Perhaps that may be looked upon as something of a purist viewpoint. The difference is not huge, but I think that it is large enough to make a rather significant difference in the policy discussion.

But without getting too far into that, let me point out another interesting consequence of the 1965 changes in definition. That is the impact on the so-called "triggering" provision, which seems to be quite popular in legislative circles these days. Almost every proposal that comes along for a public service employment program has incorporated this innovative, imaginative, new device — the "triggering" device.

When the unemployment rate is 4 1/2 percent or higher for a period of three months or longer, then you throw in more money. And if the unemployment rate goes up another five-tenths of a percentage point, you throw in some more money, and so on.

It works the other way too, of course. This is very important. When the unemployment rate falls below 4 1/2 percent for three months, then you shut off the whole thing. You dismantle the program. And you assume that the economy now has really taken care of the problem of unemployment.

But as the definitions are currently applied, the public service employment program itself could quite conceivably trigger the mechanism that ends the public service employment program.

If you have an unemployment rate that is only two-tenths or three-tenths of a percentage point above four-and-a-half, and the public service employment program is large enough to bring it down to 4.4, the program itself has terminated the program and the termination of the program automatically raises the unemployment rate! So what you will have is a sort of a "yo-yo" effect!

I pointed out this anomaly a couple of months ago in some hearings before Congressman Daniels' Select Labor Subcommittee and, I suppose, in response to this, a provision was added to the Daniels' proposal under which people who are enrolled in the public service employment program are apparently counted as "unemployed" for the purpose of the triggering mechanism.

It is a little illogical, I think, to have one definition of unemployment for the purpose of one particular law, and another definition for general purposes.

Some of the discussion on this problem of measurement raises quite interesting questions about the difference between changes in behavior that are measured by a constant yardstick, and the differences in measurement that come out when behavior is unchanged, but the yardstick is changed.

Since 1967 we have had a different yardstick. We have applied — and it has been particularly significant with regard to the long-term unemployed — a tighter set of questions in determining whether or not a particular individual is actually actively seeking employment.

Many who were counted as unemployed prior to 1967 are not counted as unemployed today, the way these statistics are gathered. This has some effect, not only on the national unemployment rate, it has a significant effect on participation rates for particular groups. It has a much greater effect for some groups than for others. I think that we really haven't looked carefully enough into the effects of this set of changes in 1967 to be sure whether behavior has changed or whether what we are seeing is simply a reflection of the change in the set of definitions.

There are one or two other points that I just want to mention briefly, to illustrate this fundamental one about how important it is to try to figure out whether it is behavior that is changing, or simply the measuring rod.

A great deal has been made of the fact that the white/nonwhite unemployment rate ratio had dropped. Ever since 1953, you know, the nonwhite unemployment rate had been reported at just about double the white unemployment rate. If the white unemployment rate was 3 1/2 percent, then you could count on the nonwhite rate being 7 percent.

But in 1970 — I believe, the first part of 1970 — that ratio began to change, and the nonwhite unemployment rate fell to less than double. It got down to about 1.7, I believe, and seemed to stay there – and has remained there for quite some time. Without being excessively political, I will simply report that the Secretary of Labor in several special press releases hailed this as evidence of great progress in meeting the problems of black workers – the fact that their situation had improved relative to the situation of white workers.

However, I was a little skeptical about this, and so I checked the participation rates and found that virtually the whole change in this relationship is accounted for by a change, a drop, a rather large drop, in the participation rates for black workers.

Aaron Gordon has done detailed, careful work on this. He reported on his findings in a conference here in Washington early in 1971, and he confirmed my own impressionistic observations that this decline in the ratio is not really a change in relative welfare of these two groups nearly so much as it reflects simply a falling off in the participation rate of black workers, a much more rapid falling off for black workers than for other groups of workers.

On this matter of hidden unemployment, let me just make two very quick observations.

As Harold Sheppard has pointed out, many of the people, particularly the men who are not in the labor force, and who might otherwise be counted as discouraged workers – the hidden unemployed, et cetera – report that they are disabled or that they are ill.

Now I am going to advance a hypothesis which I cannot substantiate at this point, but which, it seems to me, should be borne in mind, and if possible, more carefully investigated. There have been various studies which indicate that when the rate of unemployment goes up, the rate of disabling illness tends to go up. Reported disabilities increase. When you have heavy layoffs in certain industries with disability plans, claims under the disability plans tend to increase.

There have been individualized studies, individual studies of plant shutdowns, which show that indeed even the prospect of unemployment, even of white collar workers – or perhaps one should say particularly of white collar workers – can induce genuine illnesses. Dr. Sidney Cobb, of the University of Michigan, has done some fascinating research on this phenomenon. There is a study based on the closing of the Studebaker plant, in which one poor fellow lost his hair, not once, but twice, in consequence of the impending shut-down of his plant.[1] So this high rate of disability among those who report themselves as not being in the labor force may not be wholly unrelated to the conditions in the job market.

I would not want to bet my life on that proposition, but I think that it is more than just a wild surmise. And I think that there is some evidence that has been accumulated that certainly points in this direction. So in classifying these people who are not in the labor market, I really think that we have to keep in mind this possibility — that some of these disability claims are induced by the job market.

A second observation is that the studies which have been made — and which, I agree, have been very valuable and illuminating — have tended to concentrate on the cyclical effects of changes in the unemployment rate on participation rates. I have felt for some time that another dimension really ought to be investigated, and that is the long-run changes, or the secular changes, the changes in participation rates for particular groups over fifteen or twenty years. And when you study that aspect of the matter, when you examine the record for various groups in the labor force for evidence of long-run trend, then some interesting patterns emerge.

Of course, I have been especially interested in analyzing these changes by level of education, and I have found that among male workers with less than the average education, the trend in participation rates, the long-run trend, has been very definitely downward, even in the so-called prime working years, thirty-five to forty-four.

And for people with very little education, there has been a sharp drop in participation rates over roughly a twenty year period, whereas among those males who are highly educated, in that same age group, there has been a slight upward trend in participation rates. So that the cyclical changes in participation rates don't really tell the whole story.

There are rather clearly, it seems to me, some long-run secular influences at work, and their effects are very different at different levels of skill and education in the labor market. And obviously — at least in the quite recent past — there has been a differential effect by color as well as by level of education.

Notes

1. Alfred Slote, *Termination* (New York: Bobbs-Merrill, 1969).

8

The Behavior of Unemployment 1967 - 1969

THOMAS F. DERNBURG

Without risk of exaggeration it is safe to say that the overall, or "global" unemployment rate is our most widely cited economic indicator. The unemployment rate also serves many other functions. Specific values of it are put forth as targets for macroeconomic policy. The famous "Okun's Law" utilizes the unemployment rate to estimate the gap between actual and potential Gross National Product. In its role as a proxy for labor market tightness, it serves as the foundation for much econometric wage and price forecasting, and it is the argument in so-called "Phillips curve" analysis. In that same role some analysts have used the unemployment rate as a predictor of labor force participation. Finally, the unemployment rate is frequently proposed as the measure according to which automatic federal expenditure and "formula flexibility" tax programs should be triggered.

Given the many roles that the unemployment rate has had assigned to it, it is important that we make sure that it is capable of performing these assigned functions in a reliable and systematic manner. Unfortunately, the movement of the global unemployment rate in recent years has been so erratic that it cannot be counted upon to perform any of these functions. It does not measure labor market tightness; it is a very poor index of prosperity; it is not correlated with the GNP gap as calculated by other means; and it certainly would be a poor guide to the initiation and termination of federal expenditure and tax changes. In particular, the unemployment rate behaved in an essentially random manner during the three year period 1967-69. Although its behavior during the more recent period of sluggishness has been more in line with expectations, it is possible for the 1967-69 episode to recur, and it is therefore important to examine this period. Accordingly, it is the purpose of this chapter to explore the nature of this behavior and to uncover its source.

It is a well-known fact that labor force participation responds to changing labor market conditions. Work by Bowen and Finegan, Dernburg and Strand, and by Tella confirms the predominance of the "discouraged

The author wishes to thank his colleague Hirschel Kasper for his careful reading and useful comments on an earlier draft. Robert C. Broadfoot and John Farmer rendered valuable research and computational assistance.

worker" effect over the "additional worker" effect.[1] Using monthly time-series data covering the years 1953-62, Dernburg and Strand found that an increase in employment of 1,000 would bring forth 454 additional labor force participants with the consequence that unemployment declines by only 546. The elasticity of labor force participation with respect to a change in total employment was found by these authors to be 0.431.

Inspection of the time-series for 1967-69 shows that this elasticity increased greatly; so much so that fluctuations in labor force participation sometimes caused the unemployment rate to move in a direction quite the opposite from what would have been expected, given the growth of employment and the pace of general business activity. The year 1967 furnishes an interesting example. Although the U.S. economy performed sluggishly in the first half of the year, with employment growth limited to an annual rate of 0.74 percent, and with real GNP growing only $3.5 billion between the fourth quarter of 1966 and the second quarter of 1967, the first half average unemployment rate of 3.80 percent was less than one-tenth of a percentage point higher than it had been during the second half of 1966. The revival of the second half of the year was then marked by a jump in employment growth to an annual rate of 3.22 percent and a real GNP gain between the second and fourth quarters of $12 billion. Yet despite this sharp revival the unemployment rate actually increased to an average of 3.89 percent (see table 8.1).[2]

Table 8.1

Rates of Growth in Gross National Product, Labor Force, and Unemployment Rates, 1967-1969

		Real GNP	Employment	Civilian Labor Force	Unemployment Rate
			(percentage rates of growth at annual rates)		(percent)
1967	I	−.90	0.80	1.05	3.76
	II	3.03	0.68	0.99	3.84
	III	4.42	3.90	3.91	3.84
	IV	2.80	2.54	2.97	3.94
1968	I	5.37	1.12	0.13	3.70
	II	7.54	3.14	2.57	3.57
	III	4.03	0.74	0.63	3.54
	IV	2.38	1.98	1.49	3.43
1969	I	2.76	5.02	4.68	3.35
	II	1.56	1.13	1.59	3.46
	III	2.00	2.79	3.45	3.61
	IV	−1.42	2.39	2.44	3.63

Sources: Real GNP, *Survey of Current Business,* July 1971; Seasonally adjusted civilian labor force, employment, and unemployment, *Employment and Earnings,* Vol. 17, No. 10, April 1971.

As subsequent events have confirmed, the weird pattern of 1967 is not an isolated instance. As can be seen in table 8.1 growth of employment was remarkably closely matched by labor force growth during the entire three year period under review. During this period, evidently, the elasticity of labor force participation with respect to employment jumped to a value close to unity. This is confirmed by the regression equation,

$$\overset{.}{\Delta} L = 0.0676 + 0.9565 \overset{.}{\Delta} E \qquad\qquad \overline{R}^2 = 0.868$$
$$(0.285) \quad (0.112)$$

where $\overset{.}{\Delta} L$ *and* $\overset{.}{\Delta} E$ are the percent changes in labor force and employment, expressed as annual rates, respectively.[a] The data used in the regression were taken directly from table 8.1 and cover the twelve quarters reported there.

If labor force participation and employment march together in lock step (plus allowance for random errors) movements in the unemployment rate will tend to be dominated by the random forces. In other words, in the ratio which defines the unemployment rate, $u = U/L = (L-E)/L$, growth in employment, E, is matched on a one for one (plus or minus error) basis by growth in labor force, L, so that very little of a systematic nature happens to absolute unemployment, U, and the unemployment rate therefore merely drifts down because of a trend in the denominator of the ratio of unemployment to labor force.[b] This is precisely what is confirmed by the

---

[a]The intercept in the above equation is not statistically significant. Homogeneous regression yields a slope coefficient of 0.9791 as compared with the 0.9565 obtained when the constant term is not suppressed. Standard errors are in parentheses.

[b]The unemployment rate is defined as $u = (L - E) / L$. Differentiating this equation with respect to E gives,

$$\frac{du}{dE} = \frac{(1 - u)}{L} \frac{dL}{dE} - \frac{1}{L} .$$

However, if labor force participation responds to changes in employment – for example if $L = a + bE$ – it would follow that, $dL/dE = b$, so that on substitution we get,

$$\frac{du}{dE} = \frac{(1 - u)b}{L} - \frac{1}{L} .$$

Clearly, if b is close to +1 there will be very little response by the unemployment rate to changes in employment. In particular if $b = \dfrac{1}{1 - u}$, there will be no response at all, and period by period changes in u will merely reflect random disturbances.

regression equation,

$$u = 3.6672 - 0.0050\dot{\Delta}E - 0.0343T \qquad \overline{R}^2 = 0.360.$$
$$\quad\;\;(.0823)\quad(.0330)\qquad(.0217)$$

In this equation u is the quarterly average global unemployment rate, and T is a linear time trend with $T = O$ in the second quarter of 1968. Inspection of this equation confirms the fact that over the period under review there was no statistical association between the growth of employment and the unemployment rate but that, as indicated by the statistically significant negative time trend, the unemployment rate drifted downwards gradually.

We must now attempt to identify the time at which the employment elasticity of labor force participation registered such a jump and also to attempt to identify the segments of the labor force that are responsible for the increase. Since our interest is primarily in the employment elasticity of participation, we resort to an extremely simple model that yields direct estimates of these elasticities. We begin by specifying,

$$\dot{\Delta}L_i = \alpha_i + \delta_i \dot{\Delta}E$$

where $\dot{\Delta}L_i$ is the percentage change in labor force participation in the ith population group and $\dot{\Delta}E$ is the percentage change in total civilian employment. To identify changes in the elasticity, δ_i, we introduce two interaction hypotheses. The first lets $\delta_i = \beta_i + \gamma_i T$, where once again T is a linear time trend. This hypothesis would allow for gradual changes in the coefficient of elasticity. An alternative hypothesis is to let

$$\delta_i = \beta_i + \gamma_i D_t$$

where D_t is a zero-one dummy variable that permits the elasticity to exhibit an abrupt change at a particular point in time. Experimentation showed that when a sharp break appeared to exist, it occurred at the beginning of 1967. This, of course, is as expected since the interviewing procedures used by the Current Population Survey (CPS) were changed substantially at that time. Further, the sharp-break hypothesis performed uniformly better – as measured by a comparison of adjusted R-squares – than the trend-drift hypothesis, in all but one of twenty-six groups studied. Thus it seems necessary to report only the sharp-break results.

To summarize: our hypothesis is,

$$\Delta L_i = \alpha_i + (\beta_i + \gamma_i D_t) \Delta E$$

where D_t is assigned values of zero for all quarters through the end of 1966, and a one for all subsequent quarters. Thus the parameter β_i measures the elasticity of labor force participation with respect to employment for the earlier period, while the sum $\beta_i + \gamma_i$ measures the elasticity for the later period.

The sexes were treated separately, each such group being divided by age and race. The labor force was also divided into full-time and part-time workers, and by major occupational groups. All employment and labor force data are seasonally adjusted quarterly values which, to suit the hypothesis, were transformed into one-quarter percentage changes. The data begin with the first quarter of 1963 and extend through the fourth quarter of 1969.

Table 8.2
Regression Results: Males by Age and Race

| | Coefficient | | | | |
	α	β	γ	$\overline{R}^2$	DW
All Males	.03115	.34813	.19611	.3937	1.826
	(.0727)	(.1196)	(.1005)		
16-19	−.3941	3.45955	−1.37623	.2169	1.447
	(.6978)	(1.1485)	(.9648)		
white	−.64138	3.97380	−1.49603	.2505	1.445
	(.7414)	(1.2204)	(1.0252)		
nonwhite	2.12424	−1.52005	.71135	−.0680	2.156
	(1.6044)	(2.6409)	(2.2185)		
Adult	.05818	.13620	.29446	.2294	1.351
	(.0877)	(.1443)	(.1212)		
white	.06216	.10632	.33975	.1897	1.740
	(.1041)	(.1713)	(.1439)		
nonwhite	−.18465	.62967	.14543	.0336	2.393
	(.2719)	(.4477)	(.3761)		

Table 8.3
Regression Results: Females by Age and Race

| | Coefficient | | | $\overline{R}^2$ | DW |
	α	β	γ		
All Females	−.10731	1.63902	.15294	.6134	1.939
	(.1699)	(.2796)	(.2349)		
16-19	1.16289	1.18282	−1.59286	−.0365	1.800
	(1.1486)	(1.8906)	(1.5882)		
white	1.30573	.91177	−1.60003	−.0404	1.795
	(1.1720)	(1.9291)	(1.6205)		
nonwhite	1.32368	4.94443	−.10713	.0369	2.053
	(1.8455)	(3.0376)	(2.5517)		
Adult	−.23414	1.67573	.34787	.5613	2.083
	(.2049)	(.3373)	(.2833)		
white	−.22765	1.71970	.33020	.5261	1.774
	(.2228)	(.3667)	(.3080)		
nonwhite	−.17626	1.18698	.57646	.1290	2.760
	(.4237)	(.6974)	(.5858)		

Table 8.4
Regression Results: Full-Time and Part-Time Labor Force by Age and Sex

| | Coefficient | | | $\overline{R}^2$ | DW |
	α	β	γ		
Full-Time	−.05113	.60621	.23704	.3570	2.757
	(.1216)	(.2001)	(.1681)		
16-19	.06806	.69902	.19001	−.0758	1.682
	(1.2863)	(2.1172)	(1.7785)		
Adult Male	−.05416	.32850	.16101	.1482	2.168
	(.1114)	(.1833)	(.1540)		
Adult Female	−.03420	1.17280	.37964	.3305	2.072
	(.2373)	(.3905)	(.3281)		
Part-Time	−.30786	3.17489	−.19657	.1652	2.449
	(.7556)	(1.2437)	(1.0448)		
16-19	−.50742	6.54687	−3.58739	.1884	2.733
	(1.4700)	(2.4195)	(2.0325)		
Adult Male	2.25491	−3.46743	3.59172	.1297	2.967
	(1.1890)	(1.9571)	(1.6441)		
Adult Female	−1.32696	4.43340	−.10231	.2183	2.433
	(.9408)	(1.5485)	(1.3008)		

Table 8.5
Regression Results: Major Occupational Categories

Group	Coefficient			$\overline{R}^2$	DW
	α	β	γ		
White Collar	.58307	.30993	.32161	.0459	1.947
	(.2073)	(.3412)	(.2866)		
Blue Collar	.17970	.29684	.30406	−.0068	2.487
	(.2630)	(.4330)	(.3637)		
Service	−1.47241	3.31991	−.69811	.4191	1.979
	(.4459)	(.7340)	(.6166)		
Farm	−2.81087	2.12523	.95364	.0245	2.149
	(1.1004)	(1.8112)	(1.5215)		

The regression results are reported in tables 8.2 through 8.5. The tables show the regression coefficients together with their associated standard errors in the first three columns. Column 4 of each table reports adjusted R-squares, and column 5 contains the Durbin-Watson statistic. Directing our attention first to table 8.2, we see that the β_i values are consistent with previous time-series studies in that male labor force participation prior to 1967 was sensitive to changes in employment among white teenagers and nonwhite adults, but not among white adults or nonwhite teenagers. Table 8.2 also provides the chief clue to our present puzzle — namely, a comparison of the interaction coefficient, γ_i, with its standard error shows that the elasticity of labor force participation for white adult males jumped sharply at the start of 1967 from a previous not significant value of .106 to a new value of .446. The effect on the overall male elasticity coefficient is to raise the pre-1967 estimate of .136 to a subsequent value of .431.

Table 8.3 reports the regression results for females. As expected, female labor force participation shows a high degree of responsiveness to changes in employment. Surprisingly, the data show that this responsiveness is greater for nonwhite adult women than for white women. The values of the γ_i coefficients relative to their standard errors suggests that there has not been a significant change in these relationships in the two periods under comparison.

Looking at the full-time vs. part-time results reported in table 8.4, we observe from the β_i coefficients that labor force responsiveness to changes in employment occurs both in the full-time and in the part-time categories, although, as one might expect, the elasticity of participation with respect to employment is much greater in the part-time labor force. The negative sign attached to the adult male part-time coefficient undoubtedly results from the fact that a rise in employment causes the part-time labor force to dwindle as these persons move into full-time occupations.

The interaction coefficients γ_i, focus attention on the part-time labor force. The positive coefficient for adult males is what one would expect from the results reported in table 8.2. Notice also that the negative interaction coefficient for teenage part-time workers, at 1.77 times its standard error, comes very close to being statistically significant.

Finally, when the labor force is divided into occupational categories we obtain the results reported in table 8.5. The table suggests that fluctuating labor force participation is most pronounced among service workers, although it provides no additional information about the increased elasticity of particpation after the end of 1966.

To summarize the results: After the end of 1966 there occured,

1. a sudden large jump in the employment elasticity of labor force participation among white adult males, and a concentration of this change in the part-time segment of the labor force;
2. an apparent decline in the responsiveness of participation among teenage part-time workers;
3. a continued high elasticity of labor force participation with respect to employment among adult women, with no evidence that the size of this elasticity differs in the two periods analyzed.

The fact that the sharp-break hypothesis for white adult males is supported by the data, and the further fact that the sharp-break yields a higher significance level than the time trend interaction, makes it reasonable to suppose that the increased elasticity we have been discussing is attributable to the change in CPS survey procedures rather than to any trend in the labor force participation habits of the population. The difficulty is in distinguishing active from inactive job seekers among the nonemployed. If a person had been actively seeking a job during the census week, he is counted as a member of the labor force and as unemployed. If, on the other hand, he had not been seeking a job, he is counted as out of the labor force and therefore also as not unemployed.

The task of identifying an active job seeker is a difficult one. Prior to the new procedures this was pretty much left to the discretion of the respondent himself. However, under the new procedures the respondent is given a check list of questions — did you register with an employment agency? did you answer a want ad?, etc. — that attempt to get a closer fix on actual labor market activity.

It seems likely that there exists a sizable number of unemployed males who, as a matter of necessity in a country dominated by the Protestant ethic, profess to be active job seekers even though their actual labor market activity is negligible or nonexistent. Under the old procedures these "active" job seekers would have been counted an unemployed and as labor force participants. However, under the new procedures, many of these persons fail to qualify under the check list and are therefore not counted as part of the labor force. It is this circumstance that may be responsible for the increasing responsiveness of male labor force participation to changes in employment.

The new procedures appear to have had two effects. First, they tend to reduce the unemployment rate for males because a sizable number of men are eliminated from the labor force. That this has in fact happened can be established by a comparison of the ratios of average unemployment rates for males to the average global unemployment rate. During 1960-66 the ratio of the average unemployment rate for males to the average global unemployment rate was 0.92. However, for the period 1967-69 this ratio dropped sharply to a value of 0.81. Second, the change in procedures seems likely to have caused labor force participation by *adult* males to appear to be sensitive to changes in employment, whereas previously it was not. This is because the number of those who previously were classified as active job seekers but who now flunk the check list, and are therefore excluded from the labor force, probably tends to diminish as employment opportunities improve. Put differently, under the old procedures adult males were either employed or classified as unemployed active job seekers, so that labor force participation was insensitive to changes in labor market conditions. The new procedures, on the other hand, cause the number of those classified as active job seekers to vary with the number of available job opportunities. Thus what we now observe is that the reduction in unemployment that accompanies an increase in employment is in part offset by an increase in labor force participation.

Our regression results for teenage females do not warrant any clear cut conclusions. Nevertheless, it does appear as if labor force responsiveness has diminished. Perhaps the opposite sort of phenomenon as that described above is at work here. It may be that there is a sizable number of young women who do not consider themselves as serious labor market participants, but who nevertheless undertake the kind of activity that qualifies them for inclusion in the labor force according to the check list. Under the old procedures many of these girls would have been counted as in the labor force only if they themselves indicated active participation. In contrast to adult men, their perception regarding active participation in the labor force is undoubtedly more sensitive to changes in job opportunities than is the actual activity that qualifies for inclusion via the check list. The result is that measured labor force participation by teenage women may now be less sensitive to changes in employment than it was in the past.

In concluding this discussion we should first note that the correlation between employment and labor force participation is far more imprecise and variable than it appears from the 1967-69 data alone. In 1970, for example, labor force behavior followed a substantially different pattern. While employment was practically the same in the fourth quarter of 1970 as it had been in the fourth quarter of 1969, labor force grew by a sizable 2.5 percent. The result, of course, was that the unemployment rate increased from 3.6 percent to 5.9 percent over this period.

During the extremely tight labor market conditions that prevailed in 1967-69, it may have been that the lock-step relationship between labor force and employment was attributable to the fact that gains in employment were constrained by supply limitations and therefore limited to increments to the labor force. If this is the case causality is reversed – it is the labor force that explains employment rather than the other way around. Further, if this is in fact the case, there may be a floor to the unemployment rate that is well above 3 percent. Once this critical rate is reached labor force and employment move together on a one for one basis, and the unemployment rate then becomes inelastic with respect to such variables as GNP, employment, and also with respect to wages and prices. It is this circumstance which undoubtedly explains the poor performance of econometric wage-price forecasting during recent years. Put differently, there may be a discontinuity in the Phillips curve at a critically low rate of unemployment at which point it becomes vertical whence the rate of unemployment becomes consistent with any rate of wage-price increase above a certain level.

We leave it as an open question whether the extremely high elasticity of labor force participation with respect to employment during 1967-69 was attributable to the supply hypothesis suggested here, the CPS procedures hypothesis advanced previously, or a combination of the two. In support of the procedures hypothesis, it is difficult to see how the supply hypothesis explains the extraordinary jump in the employment elasticity of participation among adult male part-time workers. Indeed, if the supply hypothesis were valid one would expect the increased elasticity to be a general phenomenon to be found in most segments of the labor force.

The fact of ultimate importance is that the global unemployment rate does not behave in a reliable or predictable way. Alternative indicators of those things that the global rate has been intended to measure must therefore be found. In searching for substitutes to improve on the performance of this versatile, though inadequate, player, it is appropriate to emphasize that these should be chosen with an eye to the particular position on the team they are intended to man. The unemployment rate for adult male full-time workers would appear to qualify as the best measure, among unemployment rates, of labor market tightness. This rate is free from variable labor force participation phenomenon and it reflects the situation in what might be called the guts of the labor force. It therefore is the appropriate argument in wage-price equations and in Okun's law type calculations.

On the other hand if our concern is with particular programs designed to assist specific segments of the population — women, nonwhites, teenagers, the aged, and so on — we certainly ought not to design or trigger these programs on the basis of the global unemployment rate. We should, rather, look at the unemployment rate of the particular group with which we are concerned. However, since labor force participation in many of these groups is highly sensitive to changes in business conditions, there is apt to be considerable hidden unemployment in these groups and an effort should therefore be made to adjust these group-specific unemployment rates to include the many unemployed persons who are discouraged and not presently looking for jobs. A procedure for making such adjustments is outlined in two earlier papers,[3] and other methods could undoubtedly be devised.

Finally, if the peculiar behavior of the unemployment rate during 1967-69 is to some extent attributable to the change in CPS procedures, we should nevertheless emphasize that this does not imply that we do not approve of these changes. It is, of course, ironic and unfortunate that a well-intentioned and careful attempt to improve the data may have generated certain misleading signals. Nevertheless the changes represent clear cut improvements that have greatly sharpened our information about the labor force. It is not the fault of the data gatherer if the user misinterprets the information and applies the various measures derived from it inappropriately. Hopefully that is where this chapter comes in — to assist the user to approach the data in a more sophisticated manner.

Notes

1. W. G. Bowen and T. A. Finegan, *The Economics of Labor Force Participation*, Princeton, 1969; T. Dernburg and K. Strand, "Cyclical Variation in Civilian Labor Force Participation," *Review of Economics and Statistics*, 46 (Nov. 1964):378-391; ----- "Hidden Unemployment 1953-62: A Quantitative Analysis by Age and Sex," *American Economic Review*, 56 (March 1966): 71-95; A. Tella, "The Relation of Labor Force to Employment," *Industrial and Labor Relations Review*, 17 (April 1964):454; ----- , "Labor Force Sensitivity to Employment by Age, Sex," *Industrial Relations*, 4 (Feb. 1965):69-83.

2. The data in table 8.1, as well as the other data utilized in this paper are so familiar that it scarcely seems necessary to cite sources. Seasonally

adjusted monthly and quarterly labor force, employment, and other household data are published in *Employment and Earnings*, U.S. Department of Labor, Bureau of Labor Statistics. The data employed here are the most up-to-date figures available, having been newly seasonally adjusted in early 1971. A few series were not available in published form. These data were made available through the prompt and courteous cooperation of Mr. Jack Bregger of the BLS.

3. Dernburg and Strand, "Cyclical Variation in Civilian Labor Force Participation," *Review of Economics and Statistics,* (Nov. 1964):378-391; ----- "Hidden Unemployment 1953-62: A Quantitative Analysis by Age and Sex," *American Economic Review,* 56 (March 1966):71-95.

9

Underemployment: The Measure We Refuse To Take

WILLIAM J. SPRING

Does the American economy provide those willing to work adequate opportunity to earn a living? Ask the average American and he will say yes, except, perhaps in extraordinary times like these. Is the impression true? No.

In 1966, according to Labor Department figures, while national unemployment stood at 3.8 percent, fully 30 percent of the urban poverty neighborhood workforce failed to earn more than poverty wages. But the subemployment index, published in 1967, has never been issued again, and the unemployment statistics we do get cast little light on the relationship between job quality and poverty. Despite attempts to quantify the public happiness — to measure job satisfaction, for instance — we do not publish regular data on the most important element in job satisfaction: Can a man earn a living from the job market? Public understanding of the crisis in our urban areas is badly hampered by the fact that such crucial statistical information goes scrupulously unpublished.

Thus, the cabdriver who drove me from La Guardia airport recently said: "... there are lots of $2.00 an hour jobs around ... it's just that the colored would rather loaf on welfare ... some get $10,000 on welfare while I'm lucky to make $5,000...." And the small lunber yard operator in the city of Hyden in Eastern Kentucky's poverty ridden, strip-mined mountains, urges that men be kicked off the Mainstream program to find "regular" work.

The President, in his veto of the Employment and Manpower Act of 1970, with its modest job creation provisions, ridiculed the concept of public service employment as "dead-end jobs": "WPA-type jobs are not the answer for the men and women who have them, for the government which is less efficient as a result, or for the taxpayers who must foot the bill...."

Listen to George P. Shultz, then Secretary of Labor, testifying before the Senate Manpower Subcommittee in November 1969:

Senator Nelson: "... at what stage, if any, (do) you think we ought to be providing public service employment?"

Reprinted from *New Generation* 53,1 (Winter 1971).

187

Mr. Schultz: "... we feel that there is a role for such jobs in solving manpower problems ... (but) our belief is that for the most part the problems that we have can be worked with by getting people into regular jobs, and that the economy is producing more and more jobs at a very rapid rate ... the processes of operation of a healthy economy do produce an ever-increasing number of jobs, both private and public, and it is to those jobs that we think we ought to get people moving."

Senator Nelson: "You aren't saying that every single person in the country who is able to work, that there is a job open for him, are you?"

Mr. Shultz: "I think that is a reasonable expectation. We ought to have that kind of situation, yes. We have a lot of job openings right now, as well as unemployed ..."

It was, of course, a political occasion. The answers were not precisely on point. Shultz did not say there was *no* level of unemployment at which public service employment on a significant scale ought to be put into effect. He did not actually say that there was a job available for "every single person." But the thrust was in the direction of the President, and the Hyden businessman and the anxious, bitter cabdriver: basically the American economy is healthy, producing a reasonably good supply of "regular" jobs. If there is a temporary shortage, it is the responsibility of the central government to expand aggregate demand through government spending until the supply is adequate again. Of course, during a time of high inflation a little additional unemployment will just have to be accepted in the interest of the greater good. So it goes.

It is against these easy assumptions that the information gathered by Labor Secretary Willard Wirtz, in his survey of subemployment in the slums of ten cities, crashes with such force. "If a third of the people in the nation couldn't make a living," he told President Johnson in a confidential memo, "there would be a revolution. This is the situation — and the prospect unless action is taken — in that nation-within-a-nation, the slums and ghettos.

The memo was based on facts gathered in a one-day survey — Armistice Day, November 11, 1966. In the tragic summer of 1967 the accuracy of Wirtz's analysis was brutally borne out.

The Wirtz subemployment index was based on a number of factors beyond raw unemployment data. Those working full time, but earning at the poverty level or below, those working only part time, but seeking full-time work, and those of working age who had dropped out of the labor force through discouragement were included. The hair-raising figures — 33 percent subemployment in Harlem, while city-wide rates ran well below 4 percent in 1966 — make policies aimed at deliberately increasing unemployment seem cruel. And they cast serious doubts on the training strategy of our urban manpower programs.

Table 9.1
Income, Unemployment, and Subemployment in 10 Urban Ghettos

Ghetto and city	Unemployment rates		Ghetto sub-employment rate[1]	Median individual weekly wage[1]	Median annual family income[1]	BLS minimum adequate family budget[2]
	Ghetto[1]	SMSA				
Roxbury (Boston)	6.5	[1]2.9	24.2	$74	$4,224	$6,251
Central Harlem (N.Y.C.)	8.3		28.6	73	3,907	
East Harlem (N.Y.C.)	9.1	[1]3.7	33.1	67	3,641	6,021
Bedford-Stuyvesant (N.Y.C.)	6.3		27.6	73	4,736	
North Philadelphia	9.1	[1]3.7	34.2	65	3,392	5,898
North Side (St. Louis)	12.5	[1]4.4	38.9	66	3,544	6,002
Slums of San Antonio	7.8	[2]4.2	47.4	55	2,876	(3)
Mission-Fillmore (San Francisco)	11.4	[1]5.4	24.6	74	4,200	6,571
Salt River Bed (Phoenix)	12.5	[2]3.3	41.7	57	2,520	(3)
Slums of New Orleans	9.5	[2]3.3	45.3	58	3,045	(3)

[1] November 1966.
[2] March 1967.
[3] Not available.

Source: Bennett Harrison, *Education, Training and the Urban Ghetto* (Ph.D. thesis, Univ. of Pennsylvania, 1970) to be published by The Johns Hopkins Press.

What if the number one problem in manpower is not the quality of the workforce but the chronic shortage of jobs at decent pay, near where people live, and at skill levels they can handle? If you have one hundred applicants for ninety jobs, you are going to have ten men unemployed. They will probably be the ten with the poorest ratings on whatever scale is being used, education, skill, age, work experience . . . or race. But the basic problem would not be their lack of training, but the lack of jobs. If there is such a "job gap," then the nearly exclusive concentration of manpower strategy of the 1960s on training was bound to fail.

When Wirtz launched the Slum Employment Survey in October, 1966, he already knew that the problems were serious, and that existing manpower programs were not making a dent. He also knew that the tough budgeting decisions are made in December and early January just before the submission of the budget to Congress. A determined department head, armed with impressive statistics, can make a real impact during this period. New programs for the inner cities would require new data that appeared to be precise and argued unmistakably both the necessity and the practicality of action.

But no such detailed data could be extracted from information available in the Labor Department. Wirtz would have to go out and gather his own. On a crash basis questionnaires were prepared and survey teams put together with representatives of various parts of the Labor Department and the Employment Service in different cities.

In the analysis of the data gathered in November there quickly developed an impasse between Wirtz and the economists of the Bureau of Labor Statistics. Wirtz desperately needed an easily understood scale to express the relationship between the job situation and poverty in the slums. The sensible answer was some measure of underemployment. Since most of those in the slums who could work did so, the raw unemployment data masked the situation, hiding behind the blanket category of "jobs" the disastrous facts of economic life as they confronted the urban poor.

But to the Bureau of Labor Statistics "underemployment" was a very slippery term, with a special meaning to economists. Manpower is considered by most economists to be a resource, a natural resource, like land. Underemployment to an economist means underutilization. For instance, using land in suburban Washington for farming when it would be more valuable in dollar terms as a shopping center would be underutilization. A farmhand, paid poverty wages in a rural backwater when he could be earning good money in a steel mill would then be considered underutilized, or underemployed. The process of industrialization could be considered in manpower terms as a process in which underemployed rural workers are drawn to industry in the cities where their labor is more fully utilized.

But what of a man who worked full time in the city, but was paid less than poverty wages? Should he be considered underemployed? Not, in the eyes of economists, if he is being paid what he is worth to the business. Of course, if a man with a Ph.D. can only find work as a $1.25 an hour janitor he would be recognized as underemployed. But the Bureau of Labor Statistics resisted very stronly using any income line as a measure of underemployment. After all, if a man is worth less than the poverty wage, that is bad for him, perhaps even bad for the nation, but in stark economic terms it might make hard sense. If you wanted to help him you would be talking about a welfare problem, not an economic problem.

Wirtz would not buy this line. And he personally devised the "subemployment" index used in analysing the results of the survey. The survey is easily the single most useful compilation of data on the employment problems of the inner city. It has been quoted and requoted whenever an attempt is made to compare the seriousness of the employment problems of the inner city with the general prosperity. But it has not been quoted much by professional economists.

From the study and memorandum came the Concentrated Employment Program — based on the idea that the problem, though catastrophic in intensity, was manageable in actual numbers and geographical scope — and the JOBS program — based on the same principle plus the great American faith that piety and the profit motive can always combine to get the job done.

Perhaps of equal importance for those who have tried to understand the complexities of the nation's failure to live up to the decent intentions of the Employment Act of 1946, the Wirtz survey provided first glimmers of the existence of a secondary labor market, of a world apart from the smooth functioning of the larger, primary, unionized, decent-paying job market that most Americans take for granted.

If 45.3 percent of those living in the slums of New Orleans were unable to make it in the system, while the labor market area as a whole had only a 3.3 percent unemployment rate, clearly training alone was not the answer; something fundamental was wrong. So Congressional staff members have been writing those 1966 figures into speeches pleading for a major public service employment program for five year now.

But the Wirtz figures have never been updated. Although the term "underemployment" has been incorporated into legislation that has passed the Congress (the Employment and Manpower Act of 1970, for instance) the Bureau of Labor Statistics does not issue statistics on either subemployment or underemployment.

In the winter of 1967 the Bureau of Labor Statistics, with funds from the Manpower Administration, set up the Urban Employment Survey task force under William Milligan, who had worked on the original Wirtz effort, to carry on the work of inner city surveying. It took the task force a year and one-half, until June, 1968, to get survey teams back into the field on an organized basis, this time in six cities. For the next two years the survey continued at a cost of about $1.5 million a year, with a staff of about 135 including enumerators, regional analysts, people at the Census Bureau and Milligan's own research and analysis team. The Urban Employment Survey gathered very detailed data through a process of continuous, weekly interviewing with quarterly, semi-annual and yearly analysis of data on labor force participation, income, unemployment, education, age and work experience.

Much fascinating information was developed. For instance, the survey found that in Houston and Atlanta fully 25 percent of the full-time workers earned less than $1.60 an hour, the federal minimum wage. In Atlanta and Chicago they found that 30 percent of the men and women not seeking work and therefore not officially counted in the labor force indicated they wanted a job "now." Jobless rates during the year – with the national rate at 3.4 – varied among the areas, but in Detroit it was 12.2 percent and in Los Angeles 10.3. For blacks in Los Angeles it stood at 15.2 percent. Whereas in the nation as a whole 70 percent of the men worked 50 to 52 weeks in the year, in Detroit's target area only 58 percent of the adult men had full-time year round jobs. But on the subemployment index itself no conclusive progress was made.

Then last June, the survey was abruptly terminated. The Urban Employment Survey field staff is no more. The end of Manpower Administration support came so suddenly that one particularly valuable tape containing follow-up interviews of people first questioned in 1968 who had then moved and been laboriously tracked down has not been tabulated at all for lack of funds, according to Milligan.

There are other statistical anomalies in Washington that serve ably to blind us to the extent of our poverty and underemployment problems. For instance, as Professor Charles Killingsworth testified to the Senate Manpower Subcommittee in 1970, changes in the way unemployment is calculated have reduced the published unemployment rate by .6 percent: "We made a great unheralded discovery in the 1960s. The quickest, surest way to reduce unemployment is to change the definition. We undertook two changes in the definition of unemployment which had the effect of reducing the published rate by six-tenths of a percentage point. . . . "

The changes include one made in 1965 to include enrollees in manpower training programs as either employed or not in the labor force. From the time of the WPA until 1965 people in federal manpower programs had been considered among the unemployed. That saved .4 percent unemployment. Then in 1967 the definition of seeking work was tightened up – reducing unemployment by another .2 percent according to Professor Killingsworth.

Our current unemployment rate, calculated by the pre-1965 measure is really 6.6 percent. You have to go back to 1961 to find a year when unemployment averaged higher than 6.6 percent (it was 6.7 in 1961 and 6.8 in 1958, the only years it has averaged over 6 percent since 1947).

The bite in Professor Killingsworth's testimony comes when he adds his estimate of Vietnam war-caused reductions in the civilian labor force (Army inductions plus a share of increased draft deferred college enrollments) to the "savings" in unemployment due to definitional change to reach a total of 1.1 percent reduction in the unemployment rate. Between 1964 and 68-69, he says, unemployment was reduced from 5.4 to 3.5 percent, a 1.9 percent drop. More than half of that drop, 1.1 percent, he attributes directly to definitional changes and the military draft, suggesting that we never really licked our chronic unemployment problem of the late 50s and early 60s, but rather masked it behind statistics and uniforms.

The poverty line — now at $3,800 for a family of four — is itself an enormously misleading figure. The story of its development by Mollie Orshansky from a Department of Agriculture estimate of the cost of a survival diet ($0.23 per person per meal) has a kind of crazy, Alice in Wonderland quality to it. It is enough to say that it is the most arbitrary kind of figure imaginable. And it serves to divide the interests of those labeled poor — and thus eligible for a vast array of meager programs — from their neighbors who are also quite poor, but slightly above the arbitrary line.

It is not as if we did not have some solid data on living costs. The same Bureau of Labor Statistics that is so reluctant to use any income line — regardless of how low — in judging job quality has done a very careful compilation of a minimum but adequate budget for urban families in various cities. In 1967 the minimum adequate budget was $5,500, fully $2,500 over the poverty line. Now the minimum adequate budget figure stands at $6,960, more than $3,000 over the official poverty line. Perhaps $6,960 as a minimum adequate income line is too high for political comfort. According to the December, 1970 Consumer Income report of the Bureau of the Census, 32.3 percent of America's families earned less than that — which calls to mind President Roosevelt's "third of a nation" speech.

The federal government's ridiculously low poverty line, the use of unemployment statistics to mask unemployment rather than make it clear and the refusal to measure the quality of work, at least in terms of earnings, through some subemployment or underemployment index are all examples of how we hide from ourselves the dimensions of our poverty problem.

Williard Wirtz deserves great credit for devising and publishing the first subemployment index. In his final annual report as Secretary of Labor in 1968, he pointed once again to the problem:

The definition and measurement of unemployment was not changed significantly during these five years [his tenure as secretary] — or during the past fifteen. More broadly, social indicators were not developed to complement the economic indicators; and since we *do* only what we *measure*, the measuring principally of economic facts continues to contribute to a distortion of program emphasis.

As long as unemployment statistics bear only a fractional relationship to the failure of the economy to provide support for its members through jobs, it will be very difficult to muster the public support necessary for a realistic manpower and job creation program.

The basic document on the definition of unemployment, including criticims of prevailing methods prior to the 1960s and recommended changes in those definitions, is the well-known Gordon Committee Report. A formal reference is: President's Committee to Appraise Employment and Unemployment Statistics, *Measuring Employment and Unemployment* (Washington, D.C.: U.S. Government Print Office, 1962). A critique of the Gordon Committee Report is contained in J.E. Morton, *On the Evolution of Manpower Statistics* (Kalamazoo, Michigan: The W. E. Uphohn Institute, December 1969), Part III. Several of the recommendations of the Committee were in fact adopted by the Department of Labor, and first instituted in 1967. A description of those changes actually implemented, and an analysis of the implications of the changes, is contained in Robert Stein, "New Definitions for Employment and Unemployment," *Employment and Earnings*, February 1967.

There is a growing literature on the nature of the "discouraged worker effect." In addition to the references cited in the first note to Thomas Dernburg's seminar paper, see T. Aldrich Finegan, "Labor Force Growth and the Return to Full Employment," *Monthly Labor Review*, February 1972.

The Bureau of Labor Statistics has published a series of monographs on subemployment in various cities across the country. These are available on request from the regional offices of the Bureau. The concept of subemployment is given prominent treatment in Bennett Harrison, *Education, Training and the Urban Ghetto*, (Baltimore: The Johns Hopkins Press, 1972), chapter 3. Since 1969, successive issues of the annual *Manpower Report of the President* (published by the Department of Labor) have discussed subemployment and/or some of its components, such as the extent of involuntary part-time work.

Part IV
Barriers to the Public Employment
of the Disadvantaged

Introduction to Part IV

The Upjohn Seminars were held during the spring of 1971, at a time when the Congress was debating legislation designed to provide cash subsidies to state and local governments to pay the wages and benefits of public service employees. By the time of the last Seminar, that legislation – the Emergency Employment Act of 1971 – had passed both Houses of Congress. Two weeks later, on July 12, the bill was signed into law by President Nixon.

It had been apparent for some time that certain aspects of civil service practices in federal, state, and local government were acting to "screen out" the black, brown, poor, the old, and those with modest general education. Probably the most serious of these practices was "credentialism": the requirement that job applicants possess certain educational credentials (such as high school or college diplomas) as preconditions for taking the civil service test which would determine their eligibility for a public service job. A second "barrier" to the employment of the disadvantaged in government jobs was the civil service exam itself. All too often, written ("pencil and paper") tests were required, the contents of which were patently unrelated to the work to be performed, while more relevant performance or other "unassembled" exams would have been more "valid," i.e., directly related to the tasks expected of the candidate.

By the spring of 1971, a small group of sociologists had already begun to study the extent and social costs of the practice of credentialism in both private and public employment. And at least one nonprofit Washington-based organization – the creator of the civil service system in the United States – had already been engaged for three years in studying and assisting concerned officials in the task of removing barriers to the public employment of the disadvantaged. The Upjohn Institute felt that this work should be represented at the Congressional Seminar. Without these civil service system changes, precious little of the wage subsidy money generated by the Emergency Employment Act – or by any other form of revenue-sharing, for that matter – would be likely to find its way into the pockets of the poor. Thus, in order to ensure minority and lower-class participation in public service employment programs, federal legislative efforts would have to be complemented by efforts at the local level to transform civil service procedures, wherever those procedures were found to be discriminating against the poor.

Dr. Ivar Berg began the evening's discussion with a summary of the results of his two year research project examining the popular assumption that "if better educated citizens earned more than their peers with modest educational achievements, it was simply because the better educated were

199

more productive. Else, why these differentials?"[1] Berg's interviews and data analyses, conducted in 1967 and 1968, were motivated by the suspicion that credential requirements for jobs were rooted not in "well-developed employer studies" of job tasks, but rather in uncritical retention of practices originating during the Great Depression and subsequent recessions, when the excess supply of labor was so great that government personnel offices were encouraged to "use educational screening devices as a convenient [but not necessarily accurate or relevant] way of sorting out applicants."

Berg's study consisted of three separate investigations. The first of these used Census and Labor Department data to compare educational requirements for jobs with actual educational attainments of the labor force. Requirements were obtained from Bureau of Employment Security data on "4,000 jobs, representative of almost the entire American job market," for 1956 and 1966.[a] These were compared with the actual educational distributions recorded in the 1950 and 1960 censuses. Observing the relationship between the 1950 (attainment) - 1956 (requirements) pairings, and the 1960 (attainment) - 1966 (requirements) pairings, Berg found that "we probably passed the matching point in the American economy of just the right balance of requirements and achievements sometime between 1956 and 1966. We are at the point now where the educational achievements of the work force are surpassing the economy's requirements."[b] There is, in other words, no evidence to support the most frequently proffered argument for the use of educational credentials as prerequisites for employment: the increasing technical sophistication of job tasks in the American economy.[c]

The second stage of Berg's research consisted of interviews with corporate managers, to solicit direct information on hiring and credentialing practices. These interviews led Berg to conclude that "the managers were fingering a rosary. I did not sense that they had any evidence in support of their insistence that they were, 'of course', judicious in raising educational

---

[a]From a decomposition of each "job" into its various functional "tasks," B.E.S. and the employers who consult it were able to assess the kind and extent of preparatory training needed to enable an individual to perform each task at an "average level of competence." Berg himself then translated these "general educational requirements" into equivalent years of schooling, using a variety of techniques and assumptions.

[b]In his remarks to the Upjohn Seminar, Berg emphasized that he was addressing himself *only* to the relationship between schooling and labor productivity. He "was not dealing with the cultural, social or political benefits of an educated population in a democratic industrial society."

[c]See the evidence on the alleged "skill twist" in the previous papers by Bluestone, Harrison, Killingsworth and Wachtel.

requirements." With one exception, the managers simply *assumed* that schooling and productivity were positively correlated.

In the third phase of his research project, Berg collected raw data on the performance and schooling of employees in many different kinds of establishments — a hosiery mill in Mississippi; a textile mill in the same state; the nation's largest insurance company; the leading firm in the paper industry; a large New York City department store; an automobile assembly plant in Westchester, New York; New York City's power company; Bell System employees in offices across New York State; the six largest electrical equipment manufacturers; the Armed Forces; and a 5 percent sample of the Federal Civil Service. As indicators of performance (or productivity), Berg used whatever measures the employers themselves were using, e.g., for purposes of promotion or pay increases. These indicators included supervisors' evaluations, absenteeism, turnover, and results of performance tests ("could the Armed Forces trainee dismantle a truck and reassemble it within some time limit?"). The question to be explored was always the same: "In a given job category, do better educated employees perform better by management's own standard than employees doing the same job with less education?"

In nearly every case, Berg found either that there was *no* significant difference between the job performance of workers with different educational backgrounds, or that education and productivity were actually *inversely* related. For example, "Among 620 scientists and engineers working in the six largest heavy electrical equipment manufacturing companies, I discovered that — whatever management's criteria for evaluating performance — the less educated employees earned at least as good (and, more often than not, *better*) evaluations than the group with more education." Yet the better-educated employees were receiving substantially higher salaries. "Employers were apparently rewarding the higher degree; evaluating more positively those with fewer credentials, but paying them less." *Education and wages were found to be positively correlated, but education and productivity were not.* Attempts to predict performance (or productivity) from information on education were fruitless; "years of formal schooling predicted absolutely nothing. As a matter of fact, it got in the way, becoming noise in almost any kind of statistical analysis."

The inverse correlation between education and performance was found to be especially common when turnover was used as the performance indicator. Milton Millon, Deputy Director of the National Civil Service League, observed that this phenomenon was particularly noticeable in the civil service. Jurisdictions, unable to explain why turnover was so high, would make the entrance examination *more* difficult in an effort to "get better people, i.e., people who would stick with the job." But this would only *increase* the quit rates! Millon suggested that the difficult exams were screening in workers who were relatively *overqualified* for the tasks to be performed. Overqualification breeds boredom, disinterest, and — finally — high turnover. Since the ability to take tests has been shown to be highly correlated with years of schooling ("those in school for a long time get more experience in taking tests than those who drop out of school relatively sooner"), the same hypothesis could explain Berg's findings.

Berg told the Seminar that employers probably continue to practice credentialism because they "sincerely believe it to be based upon a valid premise: that educated workers are better workers." Bennett Harrison explained the theory of "statistical discrimination,"[2] and offered it as a refinement of Berg's explanation of employers' propensity to practice credentialism. If employers believe that a positive relationship between education and productivity holds on the average, then a risk-averting personnel officer will minimize long-run profit losses for his firm by ranking prospective job candidates according to their educational attainments. This is a *cheap* screening device (assuming that the premise upon which it is based is correct). Even where the next candidate to appear for an interview may be capable and skilled, it is cheaper to judge him *not* by his own, individual capabilities, but rather by reference to the *average* (or "expected") capabilities of his peer group. Thus, if he belongs to the class of "high school dropouts," profit-maximizing employers will attribute to him the *expected* behavior of a high school dropout: poor performance.[d]

By letting the school system do the job of ranking future workers,[e] employers' propensity to practice credentialism does indeed appear to be efficient from the point of view of the stockholders. However, if the average relationship between schooling and productivity is *not* positive (as indicated by Berg's results), then credentialism is *not* efficient after all. In particular, high turnover resulting from the overqualification generated by credentialism increases personnel costs and cuts into profits.[f]

---

[d]The same theory can be used to explain at least part of what is usually called "racial" discrimination. A historical correlation between skin color and job performance can lead non-racist, but conservative, profit-maximizing, risk-averting employers to use race itself as a statistical indicator of expected performance. The most important implication of the theory of statistical discrimination is that *past* discrimination (in education, employment, accommodations, etc.) will almost inevitably translate into *continued* discrimination.

[e]Or determining one's place in the job queue, to use Peter Doeringer's very apt expression.

[f]Even if the premise of a positive average relationship between schooling and productivity *were* correct, this would not justify the practice of credentialism by *public* employers. The "stockholders" of government "firms" are the public itself — including those very individuals against whom the credentialing procedure discriminates. And, in any case, governments are not supposed to be profit-maximizing employers.

The Congressional aides then asked Professor Berg to present his policy conclusions. These he summed up in one statement. Neither educational credentials nor passing scores on written exams testing for general educational experience are good predictors of on-the-job performance. To the extent that there is past or present discrimination in the education system, moreover, such "credentialism" discriminates against certain groups in the society. Therefore, the use of educational credentials and written test scores as employee selection instruments should be eliminated. Probably the only truly "fair" precedure would be to *hire* on a "first-through-the-door" or "random selection" basis, followed by an intensive probation period with supervisors' evaluations and other performance criteria determining whether the worker would be promoted to "permanent" status.

In fact, the federal courts are rapidly moving toward the same conclusion. In a series of District Court cases, judges across the country are awarding victories to plaintiffs suing both private and public employers for "discriminatory practice" through the use of "invalid" examinations – exams for which correlation between the substance of the test and the tasks to be performed on the job has not been demonstrated. On March 8, 1971, the U.S. Supreme Court decided 8-0 in the *Griggs V. Duke Power Co.* case that the use of unvalidated examinations and general educational credentials was in violation of the Civil Rights Act of 1964.[g] This is expected to become a major precedent in the growing legal battle against credentialism.

Experimental programs are currently underway whose objective is to study the personnel practices of various state and local government employers and to recommend institutional and procedural changes which, by modernizing local civil service, would also expand employment opportunities for the disadvantaged.[3] These programs are being implemented by the U.S. Office of Economic Opportunity, the Department of Labor, and the Model Cities Program of the Department of Housing and Urban Development. Most of these experiments are being conducted with the help of the National Civil Service League.[h] Since 1968, teams of personnel specialists from the

---

[g]Dr. Berg's study was part of the evidence considered by the court.

[h]Organized in 1881 by national leaders including Theodore Roosevelt and Carl Schurz, the League founded the civil service system and encouraged Congress to pass the Pendleton Act – the first national civil service law – in 1883. Since that time, the League has acted as a clearinghouse for information on public sector employment. Its five model civil service laws have served as the models for the local legislation of hundreds of jurisdictions across the country. Since 1968, it has become an active promoter of civil service system change through its several programs concerned with "public employment and the disadvantaged."

Part IV – contains three major inputs of NCSL's activities: (1) an adaption from its report on overcoming civil service barriers; (2) a Department of Labor summary of the League's PROJECT PACE MAKER (Appendix A); and (3) a report on court decisions about testing and credentialism (Appendix B)

League have visited more than 125 jurisdictions across the country. These site visits have led to the identification of both specific barriers to and potential opportunities for employment of the disadvantaged in the public sector. The findings of the League's field and research staffs played a major role in the congressional debates which led to the enactment of the Emergency Employment Act of 1971.

Members of the National Civil Service League's professional staff were therefore invited to address the Upjohn Congressional Seminar, to present some of their findings on the use of credentialism and other discriminatory personnel practices in state and local government. NCSL Executive Director Jean Couturier, in introducing his associates, emphasized that much of the discussion about "merit" systems requiring written exams in order to avoid the risk of permitting "patronage" appointments was misguided. "There are only two requirements that the League has ever demanded of a truly meritorious civil service: (1) the use of an open, objective, apolitical system of employee selection, and (2) the provision of tenure, to protect employees from the vagaries of "elections." Couturier noted the League's conclusion from its recent field studies that there appears to be "almost no need for change of a local or state civil service law to create job opportunities for the disadvantaged under merit principles. Almost all of the changes that are needed are eigher in *attitudes* or in unstated *administrative* policies and on rare occasions in rules and regulations. But almost never is there need for a change in law."

The first of two presentations by the staff of the National Civil Service League consisted of a simulation of a "confrontation" between the leaders of a Model Cities Agency and a Personnel Director (or Civil Service Commissioner) in the jurisdiction. With the promulgation in November 1970 of an order from HUD to all cities receiving "supplemental or other HUD funds" to incorporate "model neighborhood" (i.e., ghetto) residents into the jurisdiction's regular civil service system within not more than two years, Model Cities Agencies have had a mandate to attack the administrative barriers to public employment of the disadvantaged. The administrative procedures at issue were identified in the simulated "confrontation"

It became immediately clear that the conventional personnel practice of placing announcements of new job openings on Civil Service Commission or other City Hall bulletin boards was considered inadequate by Model Cities officials. To the extent that the city's central administrative labor force was already nearly entirely white (or non-poor), such limited advertising of vacancies would at best lead to information diffusion by word-of-mouth – to other whites. Model Cities officials demanded "outreach" recruiting programs; deliberate attempts to acquaint ghetto residents with information about jobs through the location of posters, announcements, and recruiters themselves in places frequented by the poor, such as community centers, churches, taverns, and pool halls.

The excessive reliance upon educational credentials as job prerequisites was also identified by the Model Cities representatives as a major source of difficulty in implementing the new HUD mandate. One "citizen board chairman" recommended the experimental substitution of experience for education. The "personnel director" rejected this suggestion. "After all," he observed, "there are lots of people out there with college degrees whom we can draw from before we have to fall back on those who didn't get beyond high school," implying that the possession of the credential was a clear indicator of superior potential performance.

Written examinations were also critized, both in substance ("you don't have to ask who was the third President of the United States!") and on procedural grounds ("many black kids have had unpleasant experiences in an educational setting. They are bound to tighten up when returned to that setting to sit down and write for two hours. If the job 'doesn't require 'sitting, reading, and writing,' why test their ability to sit, read, and write?"). One Model Cities personnel expert quoted his jurisdiction's civil service rules on the subject of testing:

As the Personnel Director may determine, examinations may consist of any one or a combination of the following types of tests: oral performance, written, physical, medical or psychological, evaluation of training and experience, or any other forms designed to test fairly the qualifications of applicants.

Clearly, it is administrative inflexibility and not inequitable rules which constituted the problem here.

More than any other single objective, Model Cities officials sought *tenured appointments* for their constituents. The agency's "director" explained:

Without tenure, you are not in the system; you have no career. You might spend five years as a Clerk Typist I. A Clerk Typist II position opens up, and you must go and stand in line for it, perhaps even take a test for it. Your experience counts for nothing. It is as though you never worked at all, never contributed to the operation of the city.

It is true that even tenured employees are subject to layoffs, when budgets do not permit continued operation at existing force levels. However, even in such (relatively rare) instances,[4] those with tenure have first priority in being reemployed.

The second of the League's presentations to the Seminar consisted of a roundtable discussion by members of the staff of Project PACE MAKER, an Office of Economic Opportunity demonstration program under which state and local governments formally ask OEO for an intensive site visit by personnel technicians provided by NCSL. Eighteen of these comprehensive field studies had been completed by the time of the Fourth Upjohn Seminar.

PACE MAKER project director William Williams echoed an earlier analysis by Ivar Berg in telling the Seminar that

Most merit systems in the country today were founded during the 1930s when we had a period of economic depression. A system was needed to screen large numbers of highly qualified people for a very small number of jobs. The credentialing system accomplished just that – it was a "screening-out" device. Unfortunately, it still is.

The staff then reported on the nature and extent of five prevalent institutional barriers to the employment of the disadvantaged in the public sector: irrelevant qualifications and requirements, excessive use of written tests, inadequate outreach recruiting, reactionary or recalcitrant attitudes by civil service officials (frequently despite a strong desire on the part of elected officials to integrate the civil service workforce), and an unfavorable image of the system among the disadvantaged. Changes would be required in all of these areas if progress was to be made.

A number of particularly dramatic examples of unrealistic job requirements were given. In one PACE MAKER jurisdiction, a truck driver candidate was required to have a high school diploma and two years of full-time paid employment experience. He could, however, substitute for the experience requirement with "training in a recognized or accredited business school"! Cooks, carpenters and auto painters in this jurisdiction were also required to be high school graduates.

These requirements clearly discriminated against the unlettered; others – such as height minimum of 5'8" for entry level firemen – served to "screen out" Chicanos in one Southwestern city. As one particularly angry Chicano organizer told the NCSL staff: "Well, you know, we have fires in Mexico, too – but of course, they build their buildings closer to the ground!"

In its field studies, the PACE MAKER technicians noted a common failure on the part of jurisdictions to distinguish between general and specific education. "If the job calls for a biologist, then requiring a biology degree is relevant." Yet, in one state, fifty-four of a total of sixty-seven job classes required high school and/or college diplomas – regardless of specialty.

Some of the most amusing – and at the same time most tragic – stories concerned patently obsolete job requirements established decades ago and simply never reexamined thereafter. The PACE MAKER staff recounted the origins of the famous expression: "bite the bullet." Even today, some 90 percent of all police departments in the United States have as a physical requirement that the job candidate have natural teeth in his upper and lower cuspids. False or missing teeth are grounds for automatic rejection.

This provision was first introduced in the 1860s, when bullets were commonly encased in a wax sheathing to prevent them from rusting. Before loading their revolvers, policemen had literally to "bite the bullet"! Needless to say, ballistics technology has changed radically in the last hundred years. Yet, the vast majority of American police are still required to be able to "bite the bullet."[i] Clearly, disadvantaged persons and other people who tend to have poor teeth will suffer disproportionate rejection rates as applicants for police jobs.

Many other inequities were cited. Job application forms often requested information on whether the candidate had ever been arrested (regardless of whether or not a conviction was obtained). Examinations often tested for knowledge totally unrelated to the tasks to be performed (*janitors* in one jurisdiction were asked to "select the best of the five following antonyms to the word 'alleviate'," *charwomen* were asked to state whether or not "common colds are contagious," and urban development community relations advisors were asked whether or not it was correct to define hardening of the arteries as aphasia).

In all of these examples, administrative "hardening of the arteries" was the problem — not inflexible rules and not outmoded laws.

In the ensuing discussion among the Seminar participants, the crucial interrelation between civil service procedural changes at the local level (whether or not funded by the federal government) and legislative attempts to promote such changes through national guidelines was explored. The Emergency Employment Act of 1971 contains several stipulations with respect to the use of outreach recruiting, task-related exam design, relevancy in credentialing, and a general concern for absorbing the poor and the "uncredentialed" into state and local government. All the participants attending the Fourth Upjohn Seminar urged the congressional aides to strengthen these requirements in future legislation, citing the landmark Griggs case as a mandate for tougher federal statutes.

In addition to Ivar Berg's presentation to the Seminar, we have included Bennett Harrison's "Public Service Jobs for Urban Ghetto Residents" — primarily because it presents, in an empirical fashion, some of the policy implications of Berg's theme, especially the "good-job" potentials of public service employment for a major segment of our unemployed and underemployed population. This paper was originally written for NCSL.

Notes

1. Ivar Berg, *Education and Jobs: The Great Training Robbery*, (New

---

[i]It was pointed out that the District of Columbia police department only eliminated this requirement in 1970.

York: Praeger, 1970). See also S.M. Miller, *Breaking the Credentials Barrier,* Ford Foundation, 1967; S.M. Miller and Marsha Kroll, "Strategies for Reducing Credentialism," *Good Government,* Summer 1970.

2. See Michael J. Piore, "The Dual Labor Market: Theory and Implications," in David M. Gordon (ed.), *Problems in Political Economy: An Urban Perspective* (Lexington, Mass.: D.C. Heath, 1971).

3. See, for example, U.S. Department of Labor, *1971 Manpower Report of the President,* April 1971, pp. 171-78.

4. On the remarkable secular stability of public service employment, see Bennett Harrison, *Public Employment and Urban Poverty* (Washington, D.C.: The Urban Institute, June 1971), Paper No. 113-43, pp. 29-32.

10 Education and Work

IVAR BERG

The proposition that the "quality" of manpower, defined in large measure in terms of educational achievement, is an important factor in economic development and growth may not be dismissed. Nor may one reject casually, out of hand, the related proposition that the individual's opportunity for obtaining one or more challenging and well-paid jobs in a working career is a function of educational accomplishments.

Accordingly, economists, unsettled by the difficulty of accounting for variations in national economic growth rates, and for longitudinal changes in growth rates within a nation, by attending to investment only in physical capital, sought for a number of years after World War II to determine the economic returns to human capital. They sought to do this as they had previously sought to discover the returns to investment in more conventional forms of capital.

And the results seem to prove the point that the return on efforts to improve the stock of human capital were not small, though they tended to vary from one study to another, depending on a variety of assumptions about such things as discount rates in the calculation of lifetime earnings. And the results were heralded with considerable fanfare as the economic fraternity pointed with pride to the power of the particular analytical and estimating tools used in their work.

In one sense the results were not altogether surprising. After all, subway posters, guidance counselors, government spokesmen – particularly the latter – have long pointed to the relationships to be observed in regular cross-tabulations of educational and income data, in the context of advice that all Americans go to school, stay in school, and continue their educational pursuits.

In these analyses, and in the advertisements for education, it was assumed that education and earnings were linked by our old friend, productivity, which is to say that if better educated citizens earned more than their peers with modest educational achievements, it was simply because the better educated were more productive. Else, why the systematic differentials between the incomes of these groups?

American ideology about individual worth and individual reward reinforced such a view, and the emphasis on education, (during the years that we should have been fighting a war against poverty and were instead fighting skirmishes against the poor) helped to make popular the belief in the esoteric formulations and mathematical equations that were mobilized in support of the human capital concept.

Closer inspection of the education, productivity, and income equation, however, may give one some reason not to dismiss propositions about the economic benefits of education, but to suggest that these propositions require some considerable corrective qualification.

Because some of us felt that there was something incomplete about these analyses, we sought in 1967 and 1968 to examine whether, in fact, education and credentials for jobs were rooted in well-developed employer studies of their actual requirements for employees, or whether the unemployment rates of the pre-Kennedy boom had simply encouraged uncritical managers to use educational screening devices as a convenient way of sorting out applicants. The examination consisted, essentially, of three prongs:

First, we examined the educational achievements of the work force as reported in the 1950 and in the 1960 Censuses. And we compared these enumerations of the educational achievements of the entire work force with educational requirements for jobs by translating trait data on 4,000 jobs representative of almost the entire American job market that were collected by the Bureau of Employment Security in 1956 and 1967. Thus we had 1950 and 1960 educational achievements juxtaposed with 1956 and 1967 educational requirements for jobs based on studies by the B.E.S.

The method was crude, as Sidney Fine, of the Upjohn Institute, knows better than I. He has been more than a little bit sensitive to the difficulties one encounters in making translations of the concepts used by the Bureau of Employment Security. Thus, B.E.S. graded this extraordinary number of jobs in the economy in accordance with breakdowns referred to as General Educational Development and Special Vocational Preparation. B.E.S., itself, eschewed any effort to translate "General Education Development," a qualitative scale, into years of education.

But we did make the translation of these General Educational Development requirements for jobs into years of formal schooling. We did it in a variety of ways, however, to protect the integrity of the findings against the charge that we had only looked critically at the uses made of education by employers. And we were accordingly able to avoid some – in fact, most – of the pitfalls that go with a translation of the B.E.S. methodology in dealing with these materials. Because it is an important question, I feel an obligation to urge caution upon the readers, and invite them to examine the detailed methodology in our original report.

The results, when we compare 1950 achievements with 1956 requirements, and 1960 achievements with 1967 requirements, suggest that we may quibble, in fact, over the precise date, but that we probably passed the "matching point" in the American economy of a balance of educational requirements and achievements sometime in the period between 1956 and 1967. If one wants to take the average manager's point of view, we are at the point, now, and not earlier, when the educational achievements of the workforce surpass the economy's requirements, not narrowly, but fairly broadly conceived, for the adequate and even good performance of work in the economic sector.

I should emphasize here that I was dealing, throughout this analysis, only with job requirements, and therefore only in a narrow sense with the economic benefits and returns of education. I was *not* dealing with the cultural, personal, social, and political benefits of an educated population in a democratic industrial society.

As an educator, I am not prepared to bite the hand that feeds me any more than I am willing, as a scientist, to lick the hand that would applaud mounting investments, particularly in higher education, without a substantial and critical look at the broader consequences of such support.

The second stage of the inquiry required a systematic study of employer practices with respect to hiring and educational requirements, and the logics that managers would mobilize in support of their practices. We stopped after only twenty interviews at the upper reaches of American corporate society very simply because I felt that the managers were fingering the rosary of the conventional wisdom.

We did not sense that they had any particular kind of evidence that they could mobilize in support of the repeated affirmation that, of course, they were judicious in raising educational requirements; it should be perfectly obvious, they argued, that the quality of the workforce would be significantly enhanced if managers screen out the less-educated people at the hiring gate.

We quit, after twenty interviews, simply because we were not getting anywhere. As a matter of fact, of the twenty firms, the only one that even understood what I was talking about was Inland Steel – hardly surprising since it is a corporation with a long history of sensitivity in the general area of manpower planning and manpower policy. They understood what we were saying. They had not undertaken to do the cross-tabulations regarding education and performance that we would have wished, but they did have week-old computer printouts on the educational achievements of the work force, and were at least prepared to cross-tabulate these data with such performance indicators as absenteeism, and with data on piece work grievances and the like.

We then began, in the third phase, collecting raw data on performance and education and skill – performance measured in terms of salary or wages, and in terms of employer evaluations, supervisor's evaluation, absenteeism – whatever the employers, themselves, were using as measures of the adequacy of individual performances for purposes of promoting or of increasing the merit pay, of employees. Always the question was the same one: "Do better educated employees, in a given job category, in fact, perform better, by management's own standards, than the employees doing the same job with substantially, or significantly less education?"

Hoping that one could, by this kind of strategy, get some sense of whether or not education, from the manager's point of view, has some kind of a short-run, middle-run, or long-run payoff, we looked at a hosiery mill in Mississippi. We looked at a textile mill across the state in Mississippi, at the nation's biggest insurance company's debit agents (in all of the regions in which it is operating as a national company); at one of the nation's leading paper company's technicians; at all of the sales personnel in one of New York City's largest department stores; at the production workers in a G.M. assembly plant in Westchester; at all of the technical personnel in New York's Con Edison apparatus; at technical and clerical personnel in the New York Bell System.

We looked at turnover data that had been ground out by researchers before us, in a variety of different industries. We looked at 620 scientists and engineers working in the six largest heavy electrical equipment manufacturing companies. Systematically, when we compared the better with the less-educated populations performing at the same job level, in this extensive rather than intensive kind of research, we discovered that, whatever management's criteria, the less-educated employees earned at least as good, and more often than not, better evaluations from management as judged by promotions and earnings, than the population group doing the same job with more education.

It became apparent that it would be judicious to have a look at the Federal Civil Service, and we were able to examine a 5 percent sample of the entire Federal Civil Service. We discovered for federal employees, up and down the Civil Service structure, from GS-4 to GS-17, education is the least potent of the kinds of variables anyone might extract, from any kind of an analysis, in an effort to try to predict success in the Federal Civil Service.

In a sub-sample of the F.A.A., I took all of the GS-14 and 15 Tower Controllers. We found that about half of the population group responsible, in the nation's largest air terminals, for getting passengers into the air, through the air, and down out of the air, have graduated from no more than a high school academic program. If we translated them into the private sector, these jobs would clearly be the kinds of jobs that would require perhaps as much as a master's degree – given the responsibility, given the supervisory obligations, and given the sheer pressures, technical and otherwise, involved in the transportation and safety of millions of flight passengers.

We also did a fairly wide-reaching study of the performance of personnel in the Army, the Navy, the Air Force – and the Marines. Here, again, it turned out that in any military training program in which one could get measures of performance acceptable to critical readers – that is, not just test scores coming in at the tail end of a six weeks' program in motor mechanics, but significant measures of performance – that education was, at best, a third-order predictor. This analysis did show that selected *courses* in academic programs, as well as on-the-job experience, accounted for most of the variance in the performance of people in these training programs. And the programs ranged from motor mechanical and clerical programs, to highly sophisticated exposures like those familiar in World War II, as the "Eddie" Program at Great Lakes, requiring some considerable intelligence.

Numbers of years of formal schooling predicted absolutely nothing. As a matter of fact, it very nearly got in the way! Data on education became "noise" in almost any kind of statistical analysis of the data. It got in the way of variables that were more significant, which were obscured by education – other things such as, perhaps, aptitudes, which are hard to distinguish from educational achievements, since there are some correlations between aptitudes and educational achievements.

It may be of interest to note that the consequences of the underutilization of educated manpower is not cost free. Thus, when we examine the satisfactions of employees who have high levels of education in jobs requiring modest skill with those who have relatively modest educational achievements, but hold high skill jobs, we discover the predictable. In the process one obtains some sense of the underlying layer of disenchantment and alienation that doesn't receive much attention in American society, work dissatisfaction of the so-called silent majority.

Even if we control for age we hardly reduce the dissatisfaction of employees who sense that they have been led, through their educational exposures, to expect all manners of reward, gratification, and challenge in the job. There is no evidence, meantime, that the American economy has suffered any untoward consequences of the processes by which less-educated people have, in so many instances, received a crack at decent, well-paying, challenging, exciting jobs. The cost consequences for the firm, in a society in which we pride ourselves on a management apparatus that responds to the microeconomic parameters that presumably should govern in decision making, and thereby lead managers to produce lower-cost products with maximum efficiency, are not trivial.

It is interesting to note that in the sample of 620 engineers and scientists, those with advanced degrees started off at higher salaries than those with more modest degrees, but when the employers were asked to rank the best of these scientists and engineers, it turned out that the correlation between evaluation and education was lower than the relationship between education and salaries. Which is to say that these employers were apparently rewarding education more often than performance. One may, of course, not wish to take as seriously the job dissatisfactions of scientists and engineers as the plight of those who are "credentialed" out of jobs or who would be useful members of the work force but for lack of schooling, that would be underutilized in the work setting. But the issues do deserve consideration, as do the consequences for an educational apparatus that becomes a handmaiden of malpractice.

One can hardly disallow the genuine possibility that the malaise that we sense on our campuses among our young people is related to this more generic process — young people who are not sure whether they are being educated for jobs, and if they are, what kinds of jobs can they get. Many, of course, feel that education should serve other kinds of purposes.

One possible implication of the results I have outlined is that we examine very, very carefully the investments that we are *not* making in public education through the first twelve grades of school.

One senses that we are producing a threefold culture in American society, as a consequence of some of the things that are going on behind these data: We are producing a small, highly educated, scientific and cultural elite. We are producing a very frustrated group of middle-income families, who simply cannot afford the rising cost of education — and they are mounting. It is not clear that we can sustain higher education at current levels, for large numbers of people, without extraordinary increases in public outlays.

The third population group is the group that stands outside of this credentialling fence entirely. Unless we start exploring opportunities for employment, and unless we find a way of getting around the inflation problem, while producing larger numbers of stimulating job opportunities for larger numbers of people, I think that we are headed for disaster. It is almost impossible to deny that there are racist implications inherent in arrangements whereby we fight inflation with unemployment and allocate so incredibly many jobs on the basis of formal education.

We, in the educational fraternity, have unwittingly joined in league with those who have tried to sell education, by overselling ourselves. I think our product has deteriorated. I think we have misled ourselves. We are trying to be all things to all people. I think we have lost control over the meaning of higher education in the process of trying to put everything we do so systematically to work in an economy that isn't producing these kinds of jobs.

11

Overcoming Civil Service Barriers To Employment In The Public Sector: The Case of Model Cities

NATIONAL CIVIL SERVICE LEAGUE

Introduction

The National Civil Service League, under the authority of the U.S. Department of Housing and Urban Development, has been engaged in a comprehensive program to provide in-depth technical assistance (T/A) to Model Cities programs across the nation in the area of public employment of the disadvantaged. The technical assistance provided has been both direct and indirect.

Direct T/A was provided to some twenty cities in 1970, and an additional twenty cities will receive direct T/A in 1971. As a result of this intensive exposure to the multifarious problems facing City Demonstration Agencies (CDAs) in their thrust to develop maximum employment opportunities for the disadvantaged — Model Neighborhood Residents (MNR) — NCSL has been able to also prepare indirect T/A materials.

This paper is one of the League's indirect T/A efforts. It is designed to inform CDAs of the many successful approaches to overcome barriers to MNR employment.

The text of this paper includes recommendations and potential strategies dealing with basic problem areas which include: recruitment, selection, promotions and transfers, rule changes, and problems and potentials of interagency cooperation. This paper is merely intended to point out possible strategies to CDAs. Obviously, all of the recommendations will not apply to every CDA. Every locale will find itself faced with problems that are particularly indigenous to it and it alone. It is hoped that the contents herein will provide CDAs with an overview of the problems as they exist nationwide. CDAs which have problems that are similar to those dealt with in this paper should be able to utilize the strategies and suggestions that are applicable.

Adapted from National Civil Service League, "How to Overcome Civil Service Barriers to the Employment of Model Neighborhood Residents," Washington, D.C., 1971.

215

I. Rule Changes

In general, merit systems are established within jurisdictions by the passing of a law or statute. Said law or a statute is usually very general in nature, setting forth only broad principles of operations. The law establishes an independent body (council, board, commission) and delegates to it the authority to establish detailed rules for the operation of the system. These rules are administered by the staff of the parent body under the direction of the executive officer of the independent body. This staff, in the course of implementing the rules, by necessity, interprets the rules accordingly — the vaguer the rules, the more flexible the interpretation. Thus, the system functions at three basic levels with the corresponding levels of responsibility:

Level	Responsible Body
I. Statute, Law, etc.	City Council, State Legislature
II. Rules which prescribe operating procedures	Council, Board, Commission
III. Administrative interpretation of laws and rules	Merit System Director and Staff

For purposes of systems change, it should be noted that it is easiest to induce rule changes at level III. Changes at levels I and II require formal action (amendment) by the responsible body. This can be very time consuming.

The following set of recommendations are very general in nature and are applicable to virtually every jurisdiction. Before any intensive effort to change formal rules and regulations for the benefit of the CDA, it is essential that the following procedures, or some variations thereof, be employed.

1. Training and briefing sessions should be held in which CDA staff members review and study intensively, civil service rules and regulations of the city and/or state so that they are in a better position to negotiate with the civil service system. Such sessions might also include the director of the personnel department, as well as a Civil Service Commission member (where applicable).

2. CDAs need to know and understand the power(s) of their local legislative bodies. Since it is generally recognized that state or local legislative bodies have almost unlimited control over civil service, an examination of local charters and ordinances can help in determining the scope of

legislative authority with regard to civil service. (Overruling personnel department, discretion to change powers and functions of personnel agency, fiscal authorization for positions, etc.)

3. Each phase of the personnel program should be examined for changes, adjustments and recommendations that will enhance employment opportunities for model neighborhood residents, and at what level (legislature, Civil Service Commission, personnel director) it will probably be easier to secure these changes, adjustments and recommendations.

4. Local legislative bodies should adopt a policy specifically geared towards the hiring of disadvantaged and require a periodic report showing progress in this area, and where there has been no progress, why.

After efforts to implement the above have been conducted, those specific rules and regulations which have been identified as potential barriers to MNR employment can be dealt with specifically. The CDA should develop a total picture of the entire system before attempting to address itself to any component. Once the target has been identified, several strategy options are available.

5. Whenever possible, efforts to change rules and regulations should be directed first at the personnel director or whomever is performing a similar function. Most civil service rules are written to allow for "loose" interpretation. This will circumvent the need for time-consuming formal amendments and/or ordinances.

If the personnel director is sympathetic to the concerns of the CDA, oftentimes the rule-change effort ends at this point. As mentioned earlier, it is easiest to induce changes at level III, as no formal legislative action is required. If, however, the personnel director is not in accord with the CDA's concern, it becomes necessary to seek formal changes.

6. In cases where the only means open to the CDA with respect to rule changes is via the amendment or ordinance route, success is contingent upon the organization of the process. It is essential that the responsibility for the initiation of the proposed changes falls jointly upon the shoulders of the citizens' governing body (citizen participation component) *and* the CDA director. Together they must promote an atmosphere of understanding among MN residents.

The people must also be aware of the importance of the proposed rule changes with respect to how they will benefit from the changes. In this manner, they will be able to present a unified front and are then able to negotiate from a position of strength. Further the mayor as well as the city council should be made aware of the desires of the people.

The following recommendations are designed to provide the CDA with an organized procedure to follow when seeking rule changes. It is essential, however, that the recommendations made earlier (1-4) be acted upon first. Rules that the CDA opts to change or eliminate should be reworded etc. to the satisfaction of the CDA.

7. Prepare resolutions for city council adoption. This resolution should be recommended to the council by the citizen's governing body.

8. After adoption of an employment policy, a recommendation for the precise wording of each rule should be given to the mayor for his approval and presentation to the Civil Service Commission.

9. All preparations for the city council and mayor should be backed by research conducted by the CDA legal staff, the citizen's governing board's technical assistant as well as the CDA's manpower and personnel staff.

10. At no time should this action be discussed with the Commission by anyone less than the mayor.

All of the above suggested strategies are set forth to provide the CDA with an organized attack on the system that they are seeking to change. For the most part these recommendations are universally applicable.

The next set of recommendations are devoted to specific rules that serve as barriers to MNR employment. Inasmuch as the content of local rules and regulations vary widely from jurisdiction to jurisdiction, the following suggestions are directed towards the restrictive rules that are most common across the nation. Further, they are addressed to the general intent of such rules, as specific wording also varies widely. Obviously, via the process outlined in the preceding pages, other restrictive rules will be identified. Chances are, however, that most local rules will also include the following barriers as well.

Rule: Moral Character — "Every applicant must be of good moral character, etc."

Problem: "Good moral character" is an ambiguous phrase. It can serve as a "screening-out" mechanism, inasmuch as it allows the selection authority to determine whether a person is qualified for a position on their individual or collective assessments of what is "good moral character." Reliance upon such subjective criteria is a very dangerous procedure. Since there are no clearly defined standards of "good moral character," this rule is inconsistent with merit principles.

11. All references to "good moral character, etc." should be clearly defined in behavorial terms with respect to position, or the rule should be deleted.

Rule: Examinations — "The written examination will be administered by the personnel director . . . "

Problem: It is commonly recognized that written examinations are discriminatory to minority groups. Most examinations used today are not culture-fair and are lacking in validity. As a result, they are, in effect, serving to "screen out" MN residents.

12. All references to "*the* written examinations" should be eliminated from the rules. They should be replaced by statements which permit the personnel director to employ oral and performance examinations which have more validity with respect to minority groups. (See section on selection.)

13. An option available to the CDA during the negotiation process is to include a rule which allows for the weighting of the test battery so that the written part of the examination is de-emphasized, while the oral and/or performance examination is stressed. This will give MNRs a better opportunity to pass the examination. (See section on selection.)

Rule: Certification of Appointment.

Problem: Most jurisdictions' rules allow for appointments to be made from a list of eligibles via either the "rule of three" or the "rule of one." Neither method allows for preferential treatment of MN residents primarily because MN residents don't usually reach the top of an eligible list.

14. For positions which require "knowledge of the MNA" the rule of one or three should be waived to allow for the appointment of MN residents. Rules permitting *selective certification* would satisfy this recommendation.

The use of selective certification is one of the most effective means of "screening-in" MNRs. This procedure has been used extensively at the federal government level in cases where a person with very specific skills is needed. For example, there may be twenty-five people on the eligible list with the minimum qualifications in the area of administration. However, if the position calls for a person with experience in the administration of programs dealing with Spanish-speaking people, the appointing authority can use selective certification as a means of selecting a person irrespective of his rank on the eligible list. The same methodology can be employed to hire MNRs if the qualifications are so structured as to require "knowledge of the MNA."

Recommendations 11-14 address themselves to common restrictive rules. Again it is incumbent upon the CDA to analyze the rules that apply to its jurisdiction for purposes of developing systems-change strategies.

II. Recruitment

Lack of sophisticated and innovative recruitment methods is one of the most prevalent problems observed by NCSL in its T/A activities. Personnel directors often claim that they have tried to recruit applicants from within the MNA with little success. Much of the blame for this failure lies in the fact that recruitment in many instances merely means the posting of position vacancy announcements on the City Hall bulletin board (which is often found in an obscure place), or the placing of announcements in the local classified advertising section of the newspaper (which many MNRs do not read).

Experience has shown that ordinary recruitment methods, such as those referred to above, are irrelevant with respect to MNRs. Positive recruitment methods are necessary to reach the disadvantaged.

This being the case, an effective recruitment program must take into consideration the life styles of the people it is designed to reach.

The following recommendations are examples of innovative and contemporary methods of reaching a target group of disadvantaged people, i.e., MNRs; "hard-core unemployed," etc.

It should be noted that all of these recommendations may not be directly applicable to local situations. The CDA should, however, employ any of the following, or variations thereof, to develop a positive recruiting plan. Once such a plan has been developed and finalized, efforts should be made to "persuade" (if necessary) the personnel director to employ the plan in the future. Also, the CDA should use the approach when recruiting for all CDA and delegate agency positions. Finally, to maximize resident employment, the CDA should make the plan available throughout the city. (See section on interagency cooperation).

15. Recruiters should know the people in the target community and preferably be a part of that community.

The traditional method of recruitment alluded to earlier is impersonal and, in effect, serves to place the initiative upon the applicant. Positive recruitment calls for the initiative to be placed upon the recruiter. The recruiter, if he is a part of the target community will better be able to relate to his peers, and explain the nature of the opportunity in language that is easy to comprehend.

16. Recruitment should be performed by people who know what agencies, what type of jobs, and what education and training opportunities are available.

Another advantage of using peer-group recruiters who are involved in the program and otherwise informed of the total job picture, is that they will also be able to speak to the other aspects of the opportunity, i.e., education and training, etc.

17. Use outreach workers who contact people through neighborhood centers, settlement houses, schools, welfare agencies, police and correction departments, and CAA's and also seek help and advice from presently employed model neighborhood residents, who can sell the program.

It is necessary to employ all of the outreach facilities within a city to conduct an exhaustive recruitment program. Agencies which are involved in community work are excellent resources. They will be more than happy to assist in the process, because it will be they who will be adding to their credibility in the community when they "find" jobs for people.

18. Establish working relationships with agencies outside of the project to insure that those agencies which are referral sources are aware of the need to recruit potential applicants having the characteristics desired by the projecct.

It is wise to maintain a solid working relationship with *all* grassroots type organizations. Outside agencies should also be able to explain the nature of the duties of the vacant positions.

19. Utilize recruitment efforts via mass media such as newspapers, radio, and television to help influence community attitudes. Attempt to utilize free or nominal cost public service time.
Prudent publicity is also a good technique. Care should be taken to insure that said publicity is of a form that will be understood by the target community.

20. Simplify and make job announcements more attractive.

The job announcement should be drafted in such a way as to immediately hold a potential applicant's attention. Avoid use of fine print and technical language. It is often good to use contemporary jargon such as "Dig it" or whatever is fashionable slang. However, care should be taken to insure that the jargon is being used correctly, otherwise, it will serve to annoy the person. When in doubt, it is best to stick to simple, understandable language. The use of cartoons or caricatures has been proven to be an effective mechanism. If possible, colors should also be used.

21. Job announcements should be reviewed to determine if they indicate, in addition to traditional items, training opportunities, salary increases, and mobility opportunitiees.

As is the case with recruiters, the job announcement should also point out the additional opportunities available.

22. Include a provision in all examination announcements that appropriate volunteer experience will be noted on the same basis as paid experience: Amend the application form to request applicants to list volunteer work.

This kind of inclusion will serve to induce the applicant to think in terms of how he can improve his chances of getting the job.

23. Prepare and issue a publication that graphically shows examples of career ladders for the disadvantaged in state employment.

Emphasis should be placed on the security involved in public service jobs. Applicants who have experienced short-term jobs followed by long-term lay-offs, are no doubt receptive to the potential for long-term employment. This is a strong selling point.

24. The CDA should provide a service to potential applicants in the form of assisting them in filling out formal job applications to insure that it is done correctly and completely.

Experience has shown that many applicants' chances are hurt because they did not complete their applications. Also, an experienced person (Employment Counsellor) will be able to tell the applicant the best way to answer questions on applications.

Recruitment methods, if they are to be successful, must address themselves to the life styles of the target community. Job announcements, handouts, etc. should be posted conspicuously in places of frequent contact — food stores, liquor stores, churches, etc.

Care should be taken, however, to keep in mind the number of vacancies available. If there are only one or two open slots, a massive, full-scale recruiting program can be damaging. If 50-75 people respond to the recruiting effort, and only 2 can be hired, those that are not hired will be further frustrated and embittered.

In conclusion, there are no standard guidelines for recruiting. Different situations call for different approaches. Perhaps the primary prerequisite is merely to be certain that the situation that prevails locally dictates the type of recruiting approach. Clearly, the ultimate objective is simply to motivate the target community to respond to job announcemtns and to submit applications for review by the persons responsible for selection.

III. Selection

The selection process is very much related to the recruitment process. Any effort to revitalize the recruitment procedure must be followed by an assault upon the selection mechanism. It would be ludicrous to successfully recruit MNRs as desired, only to have them, in effect, "screened-out" by an overly rigid selection mechanism. It is, therefore, incumbent upon change agents to conduct an interrelated attack on both components of the system. Care should be taken to ensure that the changes being sought with respect to selection are consistent with those being sought with respect to rule changes and recruitment.

The selection process refers to the utilization of examinations to determine whether an applicant meets the minimum criteria established for a particular position. There are, however, many types of examinations that may be used. The most prevalent types of tests in use today are: the written test, performance tests, oral interviews, psychological tests, and physical examinations, etc.

Also inherent within the selection process are the minimum criteria established with respect to qualifications. Usually, these standards are incorporated into the civil service rules and regulations. These must be attacked in the manner described in the section on Rule Changes. To achieve maximum employment of MNRs, it is necessary to change these rules so that they are relevant with respect to the life styles of the MNR.

This section consists of recommendations which are designed to use the selection process as a "screening-in," rather than a "screening-out" process. While the recommendations are not exhaustive, they are intended to be benchmark suggestions. Again, local situations will dictate the ultimate strategy. It is incumbent upon the CDA to select those suggestions it regards applicable, and to incorporate them into its overall strategy.

25. Selection should not be in the hands of one individual, but should be a team effort.

As mentioned in Section I, it is very dangerous to allow one individual to choose whomever he regards as the most qualified for positions. Inasmuch as most civil service rules are intentionally vague, there is a great deal of room for interpretation. This allows subjective judgment to be a factor. A team of three or four persons with responsibility for selection is a good safeguard against subjectivity. If at all possible, the team should be composed of a representative number of persons who are from the MNA. In this manner, they will be able to consider the factors of environment when making decisions.

26. Hire or reassign minority group personnel to all personnel offices that are responsible for interviewing applicants and for performing other technical personnel functions.

People who are familiar with a particular life style are better able to assess an applicant's qualifications equitably.

27. Testing as part of the appraisal process should be utilized with caution and should not be to "screen out" applicants.

28. Standardized tests should only be utilized to meet a specific need to supplement information required for selection, and under no circumstances should all applicants be processed through identical, restrictive, and rigid series of tests.

Experience has shown that the disadvantaged traditionally have a fear of examinations – of any form. The standardized test particularly causes a great deal of apprehension. This is probably a carry-over from the classroom, and the applicant's experiences (usually negative) in that scenario.

29. Eliminate the use of written tests, except for those positions where the written test is actually a performance test, such as for the position of typist, etc. Where written examinations must be used, insure that all questions have a direct bearing on the duties of the positions for which the examinations are held.

Written examinations have been the single, most commonly employed device to "screen-out" MNRs. Except in cases which are rare, the MNRs' capacity to pass written examinations is inadequate because of the inadequate education he has received. This is no secret. Also, as mentioned above, his negative experiences with written tests are a serious psychological impediment. In cases where written tests must be used, the CDA should take every precaution to insure that the tests are culture-fair, and have validity.

30. Do not use written examinations unless they have been validated to show that there is a correlation between test scores and job performance.
This is the best method of testing the validity of an examination. Persons already employed in a position for which there is a vacancy should be given the same examination. If the person who is judged to be the most competent on the job scores the highest on the test, and the second most competent person scores second highest on the test, then the test can be regarded as valid. If not, then some adjustments are in order.

31. Devise tests using a simplified format and simplified arrangement and spacing of items. Make more use of nonverbal items. And provide ample time for applicants to answer questions on all sections of examinations.

Experience has shown that the format of written tests is very important. Complicated, lengthy examinations are unnecessary. Also, if more time is allowed, or the number of questions is decreased, MNRs are likely to perform better.

32. Examinations for all professional and para-professional positions should be oral, with the oral examination having not less than an equal weight to that for experience. Examining boards where Model Neighborhood residents are involved (CDA generated jobs) should have representation from CDA staff and the Model Neighborhood area staff.

The written test is relevant with respect to determining the qualifications of professionals (Planners) and para-professionals (Planner Aides). Experience is an important factor, but should not be all that is considered. The oral interview (examination) is the best mechanism for obtaining an overall picture of an applicant's relative qualifications. It is also the best method of matching the specific duties of a position with a particular applicant.

33. When examinations are weighted with major emphasis on the written section, weights should be changed so that the least amount of weight is given to the written part of the examination. This will give minority groups better opportunity to pass the examination.

In many jurisdictions, a series of tests are employed (test battery), one of which is usually written. The written test should be de-emphasized, while the oral interview should be emphasized.

34. Adopt the practice of evaluating most competitors on the basis of experience and training. Where specific experience is not required to qualify for a particular position, evaluate candidates through oral interviews by using ad hoc panels composed of employees or persons familiar with the required duties.

Persons responsible for selection should be thoroughly familiar with the nature of the duties to be performed. The most important qualification sought in an applicant is his ability to do the job. Experience and training are the best indicators of this ability.

35. Develop and utilize performance tests where it is not practical to evaluate applicants on the basis of length of experience and training.

The performance test is an excellent means of testing ability to do the job. This kind of test is best used in positions in which machines are used, or the nature of the work is not abstract, e.g., typists, stenographers, mechanics, writers, switchborad operators, draftsmen, etc. Positions requiring decision making, or policy setting are not practical for performance tests.

36. Change experience requirements when they are unrealistic and merely screen out applicants and are not essential to job performance.

In an effort to get the most qualified persons for positions, experience requirements are often excessive. This is particularly true in the case of professional positions. Qualified MNRs are, no doubt, already employed. If the target population is characterized by unemployed people, chances are they will be unable to meet overly excessive requirements. Experience requirements should be job-related and realistic.

37. Eliminate all unessential educational requirements. Where it is necessary to specify education, set requirements at levels which will be in accord with the duties to be performed.

Educational requirements are one of the most common "screening-out" mechanisms. In many instances, they are unnecessary, and simply serve to foster credentialism. All educational criteria should be reviewed to determine whether they are job-related and absolutely essential. The percentage of MNRs who hold college degrees is very minute.

38. Accept successful completion of training programs as qualifying for positions, without further examinations.

39. For entry level training positions, qualifying should be based on ability to participate in training programs rather than performing the task of the positions.

Training programs provide MNRs with an excellent mechanism for entering the system. CDAs should negotiate to secure substitution of experience and/or education requirements with completion of related training programs.

40. Age qualifications should be removed from all requirements.

Experience has shown that the median age in most MNAs tends to be very low (17-22). The next largest concentration of population lies in the 45+ category. Hence, there is generally a large number of young and old people. However, most systems prefer applicants between 21 and 35. Age should not, under any circumstances, prevent a person from being appointed to a position for which he meets the other qualifications.

41. Do not reject applicants when conviction records have no real bearing on the duties to be performed. Give consideration to the degree of gravity that conviction records have in direct relation to the types of duties to be performed when deciding to reject or accept applications.

Many jurisdictions' rules still prohibit anyone who has a criminal record of any kind from obtaining a public service job. MNRs have, as a rule, a higher percentage of arrests per 1,000 people than any comparable segment of the population. While it may be prudent to allow appointing authorities to exercise discretion in the hiring of past offenders, care should be taken to insure that they are given every possible consideration for the job sought.

The preceding recommendations relating to selection should be regarded as central to the goal of employment of MNRs. Again, each of the sections above are interrelated, and the CDA's thrust for change should be internally consistent.

IV. Promotions and Transfers

Among the barriers to the promotion of individuals in the civil service, the following are probably the most prevalent. Although these barriers do not restrict the promotional opportunities of the employee with a "disadvantaged" background only, they would be more severe for the disadvantaged than for regular employees and probably would be encountered by the disadvantaged at a comparatively lower level of the career ladder.

A. Excessive use of written tests.
B. Rigid requirements (overly strict interpretation of rules and regulations)
C. Poor or limited advertising of promotional opportunities.
D. Lack of well-defined career ladders.
E. "Dead-end" jobs.

Possible solutions to the problem of limited mobility are:

42. Civil service coverage for model neighborhood residents. Exemption from the civil service system limits career and promotion opportunities due to the limit on the number of positions within the CDA and delegate agencies.

43. The creation of career ladders and lattices through the use of job restructuring. Career ladders and lattices should be both meaningful and realistic. Extra job classes should not be created just to establish a ladder. Assurance should be made that each step on the ladder has identifiable duties that are increasingly more difficult and responsible in performance requirements.

44. Career ladders should not have large skill or educational gaps.

45. Clerical careers should be based on entry training levels for each class. Promotion should be based on successful completion of training and/or probationary period as well as satisfactory performance when entry is not the issue.

46. Whenever feasible, position training or completion of training should be used for promotions up the ladder.

47. Time should be given off the job for career development.

48. Contractors should be required to offer training programs to up-grade employees.

49. Identifiable linkage should be established between professional and non-professional positions.

50. Credit for experience in a given occupational area should be substituted for credentials or academic credits whenever possible.

51. Promotion should be based on past performance instead of tests.

52. Single general classes should be established where practical to provide a career ladder. For example:

General Service Worker	I
(Journeyman Class)	II
Working Foreman	III
Gen. Service Supv.	I
Gen. Service Supv.	II
Gen. Service Supv.	III
Division Chief	

53. As some series of classes may be limited in promotional opportunities, the personnel director should encourage the development of a transfer program and establish policies for horizontal transfer and diagonal.

54. To facilitate horizontal or diagonal transfer, corresponding or like classes should be identified in the several agencies or departments within the jurisdictions.

55. Where like or identical classes do not exist the basic skills for particular classes should be compared to determine the opportunity for lateral transfer, e.g., health aide in the Health Department and social welfare aide in the Welfare Department may require the basic core skills of outreach, the ability to relate to the same clientele, etc.

56. An individual within the CDA staff and preferably within each agency should be designated as staff development officers with the task of informing all employees of promotional transfer, and training opportunities.

12

Public Service Jobs For Urban Ghetto Residents

BENNETT HARRISON

I. Introduction

There are at least seven million men and women in America who are labor force participants and yet who are poor. In the congested ghetto areas of our central cities, even the *most* stable families – those with both parents present and with the male head working full time – are unable to earn more than an average $82 a week in the market-place. Most earn considerably less.

For many years, we have operated elaborate social welfare programs which are often founded on the misguided principle that the poor are incapable of the rational management of their lives, and therefore require services in kind in addition to (if not in lieu of) money income. Where cash transfers are made, the urban poor have often been forced to submit to humiliating and degrading administrative procedures and "consultations." At the same time, those capable of working find that they are unable to earn enough to remove their families from the welfare rolls. As we shall see, the large majority of the urban poor who are able to work *do* work, a fact which the "conventional wisdom" simply refuses to accept. But the jobs to which they have access are of poor quality and pay low wages. And the compensatory welfare payments and programs made available to them are incapable of raising their family incomes even as high as the barely adequate minimum budgets recommended by the federal government.

The urban poor thus find themselves enclosed in the most vicious of all circles. As Camus wrote of Sisyphus, "There is no more dreadful punishment than futile and hopeless labor." Recently, however, concerned citizens – professionals and laymen alike – have begun to question the fundamental validity of our urban poverty programs. Out of these discussions, there appear to be emerging two simple but nonetheless important propositions: *an incomes policy ought to distribute money rather than services,* and *an employment policy ought to develop jobs as well as aspirations.* Too many ghetto housewives have been advised for too long on the "proper" composition of the family budget, while the size of that budget remains grossly inadequate. And far too many ghetto workers have been recruited and trained for jobs that disappear like a will-o'-the-wisp after the federal

Reprinted from *Good Government*, Fall 1969.

subsidies run out, or after "civic-minded" private employers encounter the season's first frost.

The National Civil Service League has undertaken the important task of stimulating public employment of the disadvantaged under merit principles at state and local levels. There is a precedent for such an antipoverty strategy. The federal civil service has for several years pursued an active policy of developing aide and technician occupations within federal agencies. According to the 1969 *Manpower Report of the President* (p. 103), more than 100,000 workers — nearly 10 percent of the total federal white-collar labor force — are paraprofessional aides or technicians in the sciences, engineering, medicine, and education.

The case for a local public service job development program for the poor is based not only on the income requirements of the poor themselves, but also and more fundamentally on the growing needs of *all* the residents of urban areas for expanded public services as Sheppard has already pointed out.

> ... there is a need for more workers in what has been called "public service employment." Unfortunately, this need has been obscured by the use of such terms as "government as employer of *last* resort," which implies that such employment should be advocated and provided only *after* private enterprise has failed to employ everyone; that these jobs with government agencies are only temporary, pending the rise in demand for workers in private enterprise; and that such jobs are not very desirable for the individual or useful and worth while to the community.
>
> But government is more than an employer: more accurately, its function is to provide services to citizens — such as education, health protection, national defense, park and recreation facilities, waste disposal, water services, construction and maintenance of highways and other transportation facilities, police and fire protection, etc.
>
> In living up to these and other obligations, the government obviously employs persons in jobs which are vital to the functioning of the society and the economy. The main point here is that *the need for the services to be provided is the underlying justification for public service employment.*
>
> ... The present level of services in all these categories is inadequate to meet public needs; an expansion of services would provide more jobs. Furthermore, it can be argued that these public services facilitate growth in the private sector, and that if the latter is to prosper, it requires an "infrastructure" of the public service facilities, provided by public service employees.[1]

In the following pages, we will examine in detail the case for a local public service job development program. For the present, we shall concentrate on programs addressed to urban ghetto residents, for the simple reason that the pressure which is building in these areas is rapidly approaching critical mass and desperately requires relief.

We shall start by examining the past, present, and most likely future course of the growth in demand for urban public services and the "derived demand" for public service workers. We may then turn to the "supply side" of the problem and consider the ghetto labor force as a potential source of supply of public service workers. At this point we should remind ourselves that such a program as advocated here will require a commitment from local officials to abolish the discriminatory hiring and wage practices presently found in many government agencies.

Finally, we will develop a preliminary sketch of the costs and the potential benefits of a public service job development program. This section will focus on two models — one at the state and one at the national level — which have already been in operation for several years.

II. The Demand for Public Services in Urban Areas and the Derived Demand for Public Service Workers

The Gross National Product represents the value of all the goods and services actually produced in the economy. Figure 12.1 shows the post-war growth patterns of real GNP and its principal components. Clearly the demands for goods and services have grown at much the same rate — about 3.9 percent per year.

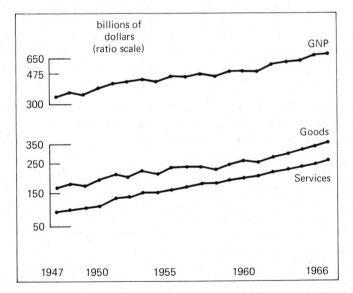

Figure 12-1. Growth of U.S. Output by Type of Product: 1947-1966. (Figures are in constant 1958 dollars) Source: National Industrial Conference Board, *Economic Almanac, 1967-68*, (New York: Macmillan, 1967), p. 121.

In order to produce this output, private and public enterprises and agencies must purchase resources or "inputs," the most important of which is certainly labor. And here we encounter a dramatic contrast. Between 1953 and 1963, manufacturing employment actually *fell* by better than 4 percent, while among the principal components of the service sector – business services, medical and health services, and state and local government – employment increased over the same period by 131 percent, 73 percent, and 77 percent respectively![2]

This remarkable phenomenon, which lies at the roots of many aspects of the current "urban crisis," is explained by rapid post-war technological progress which has introduced a panoply of labor-saving production processes into the goods-producing sector of the American economy. The service industries – requiring as they do a high degree of personal contact with consumers and an amount of record-handling which grows faster and faster as the population to be serviced expands – continue to employ labor-*using* "techniques of production." As we shall see in a moment, there is every expectation that this contrast will grow stronger during the last third of the twentieth century.

These developments have been especially pronounced in the cities.[3] Figure 12.2 displays the growth patterns of employment in New York City since 1950. In terms of absolute numbers of jobs added to the city's economy, local government has been the most important of the service-producing sectors. Between 1958 and 1967, local governments provided nearly 100,000 new jobs for New York's workers. This was nearly twice the number generated by the next "best" sector, business services. During the same period, New York City lost nearly 160,000 manufacturing jobs.[4]

Service employment is now the principal source of jobs in all of the nation's cities, and an increasingly important source of incomes. And of the various sectors producing these urban services, government is quantitatively the most important of all. Table 12-1 shows the percentage contribution of both total services and government to overall 1967 employment in twelve large metropolitan areas. The table also illustrates the direct impact of this growth in government services on the residents' personal incomes since 1950. Notice that the orders of magnitude of these indicators of the primacy of public employment do not differ significantly, even though the twelve urban areas have been selected from all regions of the United States.

Who are the employers in this large and growing market for urban public service workers? We have already seen that, among the three broad levels of government (federal, state, and local), the latter has been numerically the most significant in terms of new jobs created. "Local" government includes a whole host of jurisdictions, from counties and municipalities (including the city itself) to townships and "special districts" (such as local school districts). The 1950s was the period of most rapid growth in the *number* of such governments; by 1957, there were more than 18,000 among the

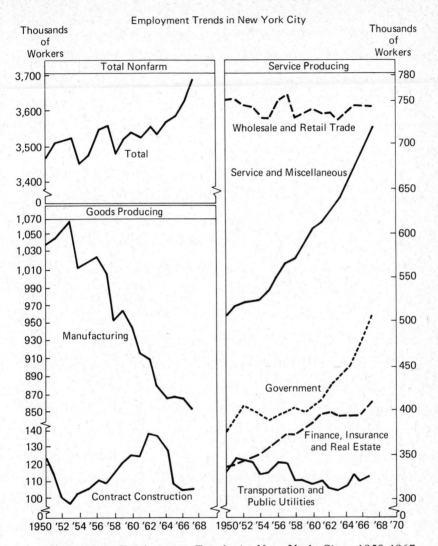

Figure 12-2. Employment Trends in New York City: 1950–1967. Source: Bureau of Labor Statistics, U.S. Department of Labor, Middle Atlantic Regional Report Number 10, *Changing Patterns of Employment, Income, and Living Standards in New York City*, June, 1968.

Table 12.1

The Relative Contribution of Service-Producing Industries to Income and Employment in 12 Selected Urban Areas

	Services as percent of total 1967 employment[a]		Wages and salaries earned in government as percent of total personal income[b]	
	All Services	Government	1950	1962
Baltimore, Maryland	66.3	16.9	11.16	13.81
Birmingham, Alabama	63.5	12.7	5.12	7.49
Boston, Massachusetts	n.a.	14.8	9.88	10.90
Cleveland, Ohio	57.4	12.4	3.88	5.11
Columbus, Ohio	69.7	21.8	9.81	14.39
Hartford, Connecticut	n.a.	11.2	5.18	6.74
Nashville, Tennessee	70.6	17.9	8.68	10.21
New York, New York	68.1	13.8	7.28	8.88
Philadelphia, Pennsylvania	61.5	14.3	7.06	10.27
Pittsburgh, Pennsylvania	59.9	11.8	4.04	6.58
Portland, Oregon	n.a.	17.0	7.91	10.50
Providence, Rhode Island	n.a.	13.3	6.29	9.86

Sources:

[a]Juan de Torres, *Economic Dimensions of Major Metropolitan Areas,* National Industrial Conference Board, Technical Paper Number 18, 1968, table 8. Data are from the March, 1967 *Current Population Survey* of the U.S. Department of Commerce.

[b]Robert E. Graham and Edwin J. Coleman, "Personal Income in Metropolitan Areas: A New Series," *Survey of Current Business,* Office of Business Economics, U.S. Department of Commerce, May, 1967, table 3.

nation's metropolitan areas, each an individual employer offering many different kinds of jobs to local residents. Figure 12.3 shows the distribution of local governments by type in six large urban centers in 1957, and gives us some additional impression of the diversity in this new labor market.

And what of the jobs themselves? Table 12.2 contains a listing of selected jobs in various local government agencies in twelve metropolitan areas in January 1969, together with current average salary ranges. For two other cities (Baltimore and Washington, D.C.), we have tabulated the mean salary increases which public employees in these two municipal governments currently receive by the end of five years of service (see table 12.3). The jobs run the gamut from *account clerk* and *typist* — whose duties are more or less well known — to more unusual and innovative positions such as

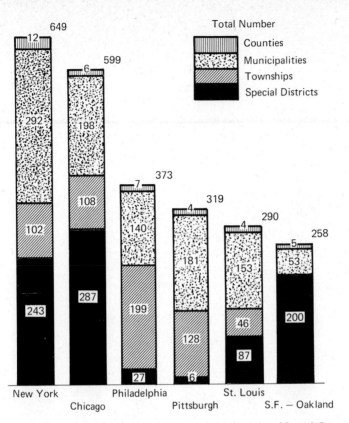

Figure 12-3. Metropolitan Areas Contain a Multitude of Local Governments. Source: *Census of Governments, 1957.*

recreation leader (responsible for organizing playground and recreation center activities), *nursing assistant, engineering aide* (performing field surveys, making simple computations and drawings, and maintaing survey equipment), and *teacher's aide.*

Compare these salary ranges with the median estimated monthly wage incomes earned by a sample of workers in ten urban ghettos who were interviewed in November, 1966 by the U.S. Department of Labor (see table 12.4).[5]

Are the trends which we have been reviewing expected to continue into the future? The answer is an unqualified "yes." The technological changes since World War II appear to have developed an internal dynamic which insures continued innovative generation of labor-saving industrial processes. Expanding leisure time and increasing personal incomes will in turn be translated into effective demand for an increasingly larger and more varied

Table 12.2

Representative Salary Ranges in Selected Public Service Occupations in 12 Metropolitan Areas: January, 1969[a]
(Dollars per Month)

					Occupations			
	Typist	Account Clerk	Keypunch Operator	Computer Operator	Recreation Leader	Engineering Aide	Clinical Lab Technician	Nursing Assistant
Atlanta	355-438	457-563	386-476	497-612	476-587	370-457	—	—
Boston	329-422	476-630	357-459	456-600	—	405-524	422-548	446-550
Chicago	385-467	404-491	404-491	540-656	445-540	445-540	491-596	367-445
Cleveland	338-484	407-556	338-484	467-645	($6/hr-$11/hr)	407-558	—	—
Detroit	442-457	598-639	488-532	733-791	669-721	576-604	681-730	570-574
Houston	234-399	444-668	234-399	392-601	234-399	496-733	—	—
Newark	300-375	325-417	392-467	—	—	650-742	392-458	—
New Orleans	281-358	325-415	310-395	415-530	—	—	395-505	358-458
New York	363-480	383-511	363-480	500-666	625-774	429-549	429-549	454-544
Philadelphia	394-438	481-583	392-473	521-633	591-721	463-560	501-608	417-503
St. Louis	364-442	442-537	382-464	512-622	401-487	720-875	442-537	299-364
San Francisco	400-488	488-593	476-578	578-703	653-795	—	721-876	476-578

Source: Public Personnel Association, *Pay Rates In The Public Service,* January 1969.

[a] Average of county, municipal and special district jobs

Table 12.3
Entry-level and Five-year Wage and Salary Benchmarks in Selected Occupations in Baltimore and Washington, D.C. — November 1968[a]

Occupation	Baltimore City Government		Washington City Government	
	Entry Wage	After 5 Years	Entry Wage	After 5 Years
Account clerk	$4321	$5469	$5145	$5829
Telephone operator	4321	5469	—	—
Clerk typist	4525	5743	4600	5214
Computer operator	6637	7991	6981	7913
Computer programmer	9621	11137	10203	11563
Keypunch operator	4741	5743	4600	5214
Teacher's aide	($1.59/hr)	($1.97/hr)	($2.47/hr)	($2.80/hr)
Engineering aide	4525	5469	4600	5214
Library aide	4321	4741	4600	5214
Sanitation worker	($2.40/hr)	($2.62/hr)	($2.54/hr)	($2.78/hr)
Auto mechanic	($3.31/hr)	($3.65/hr)	($3.37/hr)	($3.73/hr)

Source: Local Government Personnel Association, *Washington-Baltimore Metropolitan Area Wage and Fringe Benefit Survey,* November, 1968.
[a]average wages in municipal government positions

Table 12.4
Median Monthly Wage Earnings of Workers in Households with Male Head or Female Head

Ghetto	Male Head	Female Head
Roxbury (Boston)	$324	$240
Central Harlem (N.Y.C.)	300	264
East Harlem (N.Y.C.)	288	220
Bedford-Stuyvesant (N.Y.C.)	320	268
North Philadelphia	284	188
North Side (St. Louis)	296	200
Slums of San Antonio	236	140
Mission-Fillmore (San Francisco)	328	272
Salt River Bed (Phoenix)	256	160
Slums of New Orleans	264	140

Source: U.S. Department of Labor, *1966 Urban Employment Survey,* unpublished data files, author's calculations.

number of service-producing jobs.[6] Indeed, some economists refer to the emerging system as the "post-industrial economy."

The U.S. Department of Labor, for example, expects an increase of 12.4 million jobs in the service-producing industries between 1965 and 1975, as against 2.7 million jobs in the goods-producing industries. Government alone is expected to contribute nearly a third of the new service jobs.[7]

In the spring of 1968, the National Urban Coalition solicited from the mayors of fifty large cities (populations of 100,000 or more) information on public service job needs in their municipal agencies.[8] The Coalition asked the mayors to estimate the numbers of *additional* personnel needed to improve the delivery of such urban public services as antipollution enforcement, education, health, traffic control, housing inspection, police, fire, recreation, urban renewal (including Model Cities), sanitation, welfare and general administration, assuming that the usual budgetary constraints were somehow relaxed (e.g., by tax transfers from the federal government). The mayors were then asked how many of these new jobs could be filled by people without technical or professional training, particularly those from the "inner city."

From a sample of thirty-four completed questionnaires, Dr. Harold L. Sheppard of the W.E. Upjohn Institute has projected the potential new municipal job demands of the 130 American cities with populations of at least 100,000. (See Tables 1.9 and 1.10 of this volume, pp. 34-35). We may conclude that there are at least 140,000 public service jobs in the governments of just our *largest* cities which could be filled *now* by ghetto residents. Moreover, this is clearly a *minimum* estimate. Dr. Sheppard reminds us that the projection covers only the very largest cities, only the municipal agencies of these cities, and only those urban functions which have already been institutionalized. In fact, "not only do we have a *backlog* of unmet public service needs: there is also a vast amount of *unanticipated* and *unplanned* needs for which little preparation has been made."[9]

The most comprehensive manpower projections undertaken in consideration of explicit social development goals are those generated by the National Planning Association for the U.S. Department of Labor's Manpower Administration. According to NPA, "the fields for which rapid [employment] growth is projected tend to be associated with the pursuit of four goals — education, health, research and development, and transportation."[10] All are social goals toward whose attainment the public sector will certainly play a leading role. What kinds of occupations are associated with these "growth industries" of the future? NPA's list of occupations for which projected demand is expected to increase by at least a third between now and 1975 include: personnel and labor relations workers; social, welfare, and recreation workers; technicians; cashiers; office machine operators; secretaries, stenographers and typists; stock clerks; engineering aides; hospital attendants; and practical nurses and nurses' aides.[11]

Table 12.5 shows the proportion of new jobs which NPA expects to be located within the public sector, distributed by broad occupational category. In relative terms, the fastest growing category will probably be professional and technical employment, which may be expected to provide a significant number of new jobs for urban *males*. In absolute terms, the most important category will continue to be clerical workers, largely a *female* occupation.

Table 12.5
Recent and Projected Proportions of Total U.S. Employment Located in the Public Sector, by Occupation

Occupation	% of total with jobs in the public sector		
	1964	1970[a]	1975[a]
Professional, Technical and Kindred	7.2	8.6	9.5
Managers and Officials	5.2	5.4	5.5
Clerical	13.2	13.4	13.5
Craftsmen and Foremen	3.2	3.5	3.7
Operatives	0.9	0.9	1.0
Other Service Workers	10.4	11.5	11.9

Source: Leonard Lecht, *Manpower Requirements for National Objectives in the 1970's* (Washington, D.C.: National Planning Association, Center for Priority Analysis, February 1968), pp. 292, 294, 298.
[a]Projections assume that GNP will grow at an average annual rate of 4.5% between 1964 and 1975.

Even without a conscious, planned effort at expanding government employment opportunities for minority workers, the public sector will inevitably become a more important source of jobs for them. Simple "straight-line" extrapolation of past nonwhite employment trends yields the projections of demand for nonwhite workers (shown in table 12.6), distributed over those occupations which we have already predicted will be among those in greatest demand in the next decade.

In the sections that follow, we shall explore the feasibility, costs and potential benefits of deliberately *increasing* this public demand for nonwhite workers — especially those clustered in the ghettos of our central cities — through public service job development programing. The overwhelming evidence of the materials examined above points to this as a sensible strategy for integrating ghetto workers into the urban labor force.

Table 12.6
Projection of Demand for Nonwhite Workers Distributed Over Predicted High-Demand Occupations

Occupation	1964 (thousands)	1975 (thousands)	Percentage Change
Professional and technical	488	789	62.0
Personnel and labor relations	3	5	67.0
Social, Welfare, and recreation	33	59	79.0
Medical technicians	21	34	62.0
Cashiers	34	54	59.0
Office machine operators	33	52	58.0
Secretaries, stenos, typists	108	233	116.0
Hospital attendants	147	292	99.0

Source: Leonard Lecht, *Manpower Requirements for National Objectives in the 1970's* (Washington, D.C.: National Planning Association, Center for Priority Analysis, February 1968), p. 75.

Note: Table assumes an average annual percentage growth rate of GNP between 1964 and 1975 of 4.5%. Numbers are extrapolated from the 1950 and 1960 census and 1964/65 Current Population Survey data.

III. The Ghetto Labor Force: A Potential Source of Supply of Public Service Workers

In the last several years, Americans have been made increasingly aware of the existence and extent of poverty within their midst.[12] We have recently learned that the large majority of the poor who are able to work *do* work. This, however, is a "discovery" which the "conventional wisdom" simply refuses to accept.

In 1966, there were 2.3 million nonworking heads of "poor" families in this country, i.e., families receiving less than about $3,300 a year in income. But half of these were sixty-five years of age or older, 63 percent of the remainder were women, and 72 percent of the remaining 450,000 male household heads were either ill, disabled, or in school. The total number of working-age males who were in the labor force but who did not work at all in 1966 — both household heads and unrelated individuals — was probably not more than 86,000, a very small number.[13]

By contrast, about 1.7 million heads of poor households and 1.2 million poor unrelated individuals were involuntary part-time workers in 1966. About 1.1 million of these were males under sixty-five. Moreover, there were about 2.4 million family heads and 540,000 unrelated individuals who earned incomes under the poverty threshhold in 1966 *even though they worked full time.* Indeed, 45 percent of all poor families in 1966 had two or more wage-earners! In other words, in 1966, *close to six million men and women who sought full-time work and found at least some employment were poor nevertheless.*[14]

This is the national perspective. The employment problem in the urban ghettos is considerably worse. Table 9.1 of this volume (p. 189) summarizes the author's preliminary calculations from the Department of Labor's 1966 Urban Employment Survey (see footnote 5). The "sub-employment rate" is an index designed to measure the situation of the very large number of workers who *do* work, but hold marginal jobs, are involuntarily part-time employed, or earn poverty wages. Of particular interest is a comparison among the last three columns of table 9.1. In every case, the wages earned by ghetto workers during the survey week in November 1966, (even for families with multiple wage-earners), fell far short of the levels of income needed to maintain a barely adequate budget for an urban family of four, as estimated by the Bureau of Labor Statistics.[15] Even after welfare and other non-work incomes have been added in (column 5), there is still an average deficit of well over $2,500 a year below a minimum budget at which the family is assumed to live in rented quarters, own an eight-year-old automobile, and consume a diet consisting largely of dried beans.

The ghetto labor force clearly requires *good* jobs paying *adequate* wages. Programs intended to absorb the so-called "hard-core unemployed" into private industry are undoubtedly important components of an overall urban development strategy, but they are far too few in number and small in scale to score more than a small impact.[16] Moreover, as we have just seen, the heart of "The Problem" is *not* among the unemployed, but rather among those who do in fact work for a living, but who fail to receive a living wage. Training programs oriented primarily toward preparing blacks, Puerto Ricans, Mexican-Americans, and poor whites for industrial jobs are both inadequate and potentially dangerous, given the trends in goods-producing versus service-producing industrial growth which we examined earlier. And not only are such jobs of declining relative importance. We have also found them to be located far from the ghetto, relative to core city public service jobs. Thus far, experiments with planned "reverse commuting" to provide ghetto workers with subsidized transportation out to suburban industrial plants have met with a uniform lack of success.[17] (This does not, of course, mean that such experiments should be discontinued.)

The Nixon Administration is said to be considering offering tax incentives to firms prepared to build branch plants *inside* the urban ghettos. Quite apart from the very real risk of confrontation with ghetto leaders over the issue of local control of such facilities, there is substantial evidence that most firms' *location* decisions are relatively insensitive to tax concessions. Where such incentives have been successful in bringing new plants into depressed areas in the past, the firms which have been so attracted have tended to be marginal and of little benefit to the community, in terms of wage generation or anything else. Finally, in a period of possible tax reform, there is increasing opposition in Congress to creating additional tax "loopholes" which may be politically difficult to close later.[18]

It would seem to follow that, if ghetto workers are to find good jobs at accessible locations and paying adequate wages, they will have increasingly to look for these jobs in the public sectors of their respective cities.[19]

Can the ghetto labor force be recruited for employment in the public service? The potential supply of labor to any particular market will depend on the previous work experience of the labor force, the existence of competing uses of their time, prevailing wage rates, institutional constraints, and so forth. If the jobs entail the performance of unfamiliar functions, then workers' attitudes about training programs will surely enter into their labor supply decision.

We are now in a position to address at least a few of these considerations. Experience and attitudes about on-the-job training (OJT) of some 18,000 labor force participants in the ten urban ghettos surveyed in 1966 are tabulated in table 12.7. The workers in this sample range in age from fourteen to seventy-one. In every area, the large majority of those now in the labor force have already had some work experience, with the highest percentages reported in Central Harlem (almost entirely black) and the lowest in the slums of San Antonio (largely Mexican-American). About a fifth to a quarter of the workers have been or are currently employed in white-collar or craft occupations, in jobs where they have probably performed tasks similar to those associated with the public service jobs whose development we are advocating. At a minimum, therefore, something like three-quarters to four-fifths of the ghetto labor force will have to be trained for new job roles. From table 12.7, we see that most ghetto workers are prepared to accept such training (provided, of course, that it is associated with a *real* and not an illusory job).

There is now some evidence that the age structure of the populations of at least the older urban ghettos is becoming progressively more bimodal, with a preponderance of teenagers and persons over fifty years of age (especially the former).[20] In his study of teenage labor markets in 75 metropolitan areas, Edward Kalachek corroborated an earlier finding by William G. Bowen and T.A. Finegan that an increase in the teenage proportion of the population tends to be positively associated with the teenage unemployment rate. Kalacheck explains this by the "back-of-the-queue" hypothesis: employers generally prefer adult to teenage labor, so that "a higher teenage population is associated with more teenagers being grouped

Table 12.7

Job Experience and Attitudes Toward Training Among 18,345 Workers in Ten Urban Ghettos: November 1966

Ghetto and City	% never worked	Of those unemployed during the survey week		
		% previously employed as white collar or craftsmen	% willing to take OJT	% currently employed as white collar or craftsmen
Roxbury (Boston)	14.8	23.0	79.3	30.0
Central Harlem (N.Y.C.)	10.6	23.4	76.5	23.0
East Harlem (N.Y.C.)	17.7	20.2	75.5	21.5
Bedford-Stuyvesant (N.Y.C.)	23.0	15.1	83.6	27.5
North Philadelphia	22.5	17.4	76.7	19.7
North Side (St. Louis)	21.7	7.9	81.3	19.2
San Antonio	27.9	21.1	75.2	25.7
Mission-Fillmore (San Francisco)	16.2	32.3	76.3	37.7
Salt River Bed (Phoenix)	20.7	12.3	80.3	15.0
New Orleans	19.9	19.7	80.1	19.1

Source: U.S. Department of Labor, *1966 Urban Employment Survey,* unpublished data files, author's calculations.

toward the back of the hiring queue, where they remain unemployed until supplies of available adult workers are depleted."[21] Thus, even if there were no racial discrimination against minority teenagers, the recorded increase in the teenage proportion of the ghetto population leads us to expect to find a growing number of teens looking for work and being unable to find it. A new public service job program should be especially attractive to these young workers.

Another special category of ghetto workers (actual or potential) which can hopefully be attracted to such a program are the so-called "welfare mothers":

Welfare mothers, especially mothers of school age children, may be able to work full or part time. Even mothers of pre-school children may be able to accept employment if supervision is available for the children. A recent study of New York City's [Aid to Families with Dependent Children] cases found that 80 percent of the mothers on welfare have had some employment experience, while 70 percent would prefer employment to staying home. It would seem that there is a willingness and an ability by welfare mothers to work.[22]

Toward bringing this group into the public work force, it may be necessary to append a child day care center project to the overall program. Such a project could, of course, confer indirect benefits upon private urban employers as well, since the availability of such centers would undoubtedly increase the general female labor supply.

In fact, with the terms of the 1967 amendments to the Social Security Act beginning to be communicated to the welfare population by various citizens' organizations, and with Secretary of Health, Education, and Welfare Robert Finch advocating an even farther-reaching "Family Security Plan" with extensive built-in work incentives, an increasing supply of ghetto labor should be soon forthcoming.[a]

While the absolute numbers of ghetto welfare recipients who begin to search for work may turn out to be a good deal smaller than many have thought (more on this below), it would be at least expedient to develop a sufficient number of new urban jobs to absorb those who do offer their labor for sale as a result of these welfare changes.

In summary, ghetto workers badly *need* the higher quality employment which a public service job development program can provide. And there is every reason to expect that they would be *available* for placement and training in such new public jobs. Probably the greatest obstacle to meaningful public employment of ghetto residents will not be a lack of interest or ability among the latter, but rather the presence of racial discrimination in public hiring practices. It is to that unpleasant record that we now turn.

IV. Discrimination as an Obstacle to Meaningful Public Employment of Ghetto Residents

Recently, the U.S. Civil Rights Commission completed a survey of racial employment patterns in 628 public jurisdictions in seven major metropolitan areas.[23] Not surprisingly, "more than half of the Negro workers in State and local government were found to be employed by central city governments."[24]

The Commission further found that minority group workers usually hold the menial jobs of government. They are its street cleaners, trash collectors, janitors, hospital orderlies, elevator operators, and watchmen. Few achieve white-collar status. Those who do usually become clerks, typists, or low grade technical personnel in hospitals and related health activities.

---

[a]In N.Y.C., for example, the new regulations replace the old "100 percent tax" on earned income with a modest incentive arrangement according to which the welfare recipient may retain the first $85 earned per month and 30 percent of the balance, without jeopardizing his or her welfare payment.

Where blacks *were* found in white-collar jobs, the distribution was almost invariably skewed toward those requiring minimal contact with white clientele. Thus, "in both the North and the South . . . Negroes were most likely to hold white collar jobs in health and welfare and least likely to hold them in financial administration and general control."[25] Indeed, " . . . the director of finance for the city of Baton Rouge, when asked if he would hire a Negro certified as qualified by his city's civil service commission, replied: 'Would you steal a million dollars?' "[26]

The Commission found this maldistribution of public service jobs in every city studied. The technical functions of a clerical worker, for example, are highly independent of any specific government agency's mission. "Yet, in Detroit, Negroes filled 80 percent of the clerical jobs in welfare compared to 30 percent of the clerical jobs in general government." And in Memphis, blacks held 33 percent of the clerical positions in public health but only 1 percent of the clerical jobs in public utilities![27] "Generally, departments which conduct much of their business with the Negro community employ larger numbers of Negroes."[28]

As compared with other workers, blacks were relatively more highly concentrated in the semi-skilled and unskilled jobs of government. Table 12.8 shows the percentage distribution of black and "all other" (almost entirely white) employees by occupation and function for each of four central cities (excluding employees of the educational system). By far the largest proportion of black public service workers are engaged as laborers for community development agencies and public utilities. On the other hand, the nonblack workers are distributed far more evenly among the various occupations and functions. Note the *extremely* small proportion of blacks employed in public safety or as uniformed police, never much more than 5 percent of all black public employees. This in cities with very large black populations and highly strained police-community relations.

Table 12.9 demonstrates even more vividly the extent to which public personnel officials treat black and white workers separately. There, we see the modal *entry-level* monthly salary ranges for a selected set of San Francisco public service jobs, recorded in 1965. Each of the selected positions is one in which the percentage of black workers is relatively high. In several of these jobs, blacks even hold the majority of the posts. Yet the salaries paid to incoming whites are higher than those paid to incoming blacks in eight of the fifteen cases shown. The gap in modal entry-level salary ranges from zero to as much as $450 per month. The mean difference between black and white entry-level salaries among the eight categories where a positive difference was recorded is about $135 monthly.

This sobering examination of racial discrimination in local public employment reminds us of a critical constraint on the job development program advocated by the National Civil Service League. Unless state and local

Table 12.8
Percentage Distribution of Black and "All Other" Central City Public Employment by Occupation and Function: March 1967[a]

	ATLANTA		HOUSTON		MEMPHIS		BATON ROUGE	
	Black[c]	All Other	Black	All Other[b]	Black	All Other	Black	All Other
Occupations	100.0	100.0	100.0	100.0	100.0	100.0	100.0	100.0
Officials and Managers	0	1.6	1.2	4.6	0.3	7.2	0	5.8
Professional and Technical	0.9	9.3	1.9	11.2	9.5	15.3	1.5	13.5
Office and Clerical	0.7	10.0	2.6	14.4	3.2	14.3	0	15.2
Craftsmen and Operatives	12.6	29.7	19.1	14.2	4.6	20.5	24.5	19.3
Laborers	69.8	4.9	60.8	2.6	53.9	1.3	64.8	5.4
Uniformed Police	3.9	18.4	3.0	20.4	1.0	12.6	3.4	16.6
Uniformed Corrections	0.3	0.9	0	0.2	0.4	0	—	—
Uniformed Fire	5.3	18.7	2.9	20.6	0.3	16.7	2.4	19.5
Civilian Public Safety	1.5	3.2	2.2	8.4	3.9	7.0	0.3	3.5
Other Service	5.0	3.3	6.4	3.3	22.9	5.2	3.1	1.2
Functions	100.0	100.0	100.0	100.0	100.0	100.0	100.0	100.0
Financial Admin. and Control	0.6	7.4	0.8	10.2	0.8	4.7	0	19.8
Community Development	30.2	23.4	44.6	27.9	14.0	8.7	66.4	21.6
Public Welfare	—	—	—	—	—	—	—	—
Police Protection	5.1	20.7	5.0	27.8	4.0	17.7	3.4	19.8
Corrections	0.3	1.2	0	0.3	1.2	1.5	—	—
Fire Protection	5.6	19.3	3.0	21.7	0.5	17.1	2.8	19.8
Health, Hospitals	—	17.6	4.2	5.3	31.9	17.4	0	0.1
Public Utilities	53.7	17.6	37.9	1.9	47.6	32.9	20.5	8.8
Other	4.6	10.5	4.5	5.0	—	—	7.0	10.1

Source: U.S. Civil Rights Commission
[a] does not include employees in education
[b] Mexican-Americans are not included

Table 12.9

Entry Level Salary Scales of Negro and White Public Service Workers in San Francisco City and County: October 1965 (Selected occupations and functions) (dollars per month)

	Semi-Professional	Professional	General Service	Service-Promotional	Building Services	Clerical	Horticultural
Board of Education							
Percent Black				17.8	43.0		22.7
Modal Black Salary				$451-500	$451-500		$651-700
Modal White Salary				$501-550	$451-500		$651-700
Juvenile Court							
Percent Black		22.0			57.1		
Modal Black Salary		$551-600			$401-450		
Modal White Salary		$751-800			$501-550		
Non-Uniformed Police							
Percent Black					47.4	6.5	
Modal Black Salary					$451-500	$351-400	
Modal White Salary					$451-500	$401-500	
Public Health							
Percent Black	46.9		78.6	76.2	75.5	11.4	
Modal Black Salary	$401-450		$401-450	$451-500	$401-450	$351-400	
Modal White Salary	$801-850		$401-450	$451-500	$401-450	$451-500	
Public Utilities							
Percent Black					65.3		
Modal Black Salary					$451-500		
Modal White Salary					$501-550		
Recreation and Parks							
Percent Black		31.6					29.1
Modal Black Salary		$601-650					$451-500
Modal White Salary		$601-650					$551-600

Source: Human Rights Commission of San Francisco, *Racial and Ethnic Employment Pattern Survey of the City and County of San Francisco Governments*, October 1965, courtesy of the U.S. Civil Rights Commission.

public personnel officials are prepared to relax this constraint, the benefits from a public service job development program for ghetto residents will at best be sharply reduced. At worst, the entire program might be of no benefit whatsoever.[b]

V.   The Structure and Costs of a Public Service Job Development Program

We have now reached that point in our survey where it becomes necessary to define more precisely just what kind of job program we want.

Essentially, there are two competing (although not mutually exclusive) strategies or "models" for the definition of new public service jobs. The first involves "breaking down existing professional or skilled jobs and generally separating out the simpler tasks. The second is a developmental approach starting with the definition of public and/or technological needs, and followed by the design of tasks to meet those needs."[29]

Each of these strategies has been implemented recently, the former at the national level and the latter in New Jersey. While there may be other examples of public service jobs programs operating around the country, these are the two with which we are most familiar. Moreover, the contrast between these two programs is sufficiently sharp to enable the reader to develop his own preliminary impressions about the relative merits of the "job spinoff" versus the "job development" strategies. Thus, the following discussion is intended to be suggestive rather than critical. In particular, it does not constitute a formal evaluation of either sample program.

The "job spinoff" strategy was institutionalized in a 1966 amendment to the Economic Opportunity Act introduced by Rep. James H. Scheuer

---

[b]As disenchanting as the performance of the local public sector may be, it is still superior to the performance of the *private* sector as an employer of black workers, at least in the cities studied by the U.S. Civil Rights Commission and the U.S. Equal Employment Opportunity Commisssion in 1966 and 1967:

Blacks As Percent of:

S.M.S.A.	Population	State and Local Employment	Federal Employment	Private Employment
San Fran.-Oakland	8.6	12.7	20.4	8.0
Philadelphia	15.5	30.6	25.1	12.2
Detroit	14.9	29.5	30.6	14.8
Atlanta	22.8	24.5	21.2	15.2
Houston	19.5	18.7	20.3	11.8
Memphis	37.9	38.6	27.2	25.5
Baton Rouge	31.7	7.3	n.a.	17.4

Source: U.S. Civil Rights Commission Report, 1969, I, p. 4.

(D-NY), and generally known as the "New Careers" Program. Originated and developed by Dr. Frank Riessman and his associates at the New Careers Development Center of New York University,

The New Careers Program aims to serve two objectives simultaneously — to relieve shortages of professional personnel in human service activities and, in so doing, to meet the need of the unemployed and underemployed for meaningful jobs with career-ladder possibilities. The program prepares disadvantaged adults for paraprofessional jobs in public and private nonprofit agencies in such critically undermanned fields as health, education, welfare, neighborhood redevelopment, and public safety. To a greater extent than other [training] programs . . . this one includes classroom training, either before or along with on-the-job training. The agencies providing the training guarantee jobs for enrollees upon its completion.[30]

During fiscal 1967, the "Scheuer New Careers Program" was funded at $33 million, to be distributed by the Department of Labor to "any state or local agency or private organization to pay all or part of the costs of adult work training and supportive services." During calendar 1968, some 6,500 persons were enrolled in New Careers projects around the country.

At the request of the Department of Labor, AVCO Economic Systems Corporation undertook a detailed evaluation of New Careers projects in eleven cities. AVCO's interviews were conducted over the period 11/67-6/68. The corporation's teams of experts found the same general organizational structure in each city they visited (figure 12.4, a flow chart for the Houston project, is quite representative). A New Careers agency directed the recruitment of adult ghetto workers (mostly female heads of households aged 26-35), arranged for them to receive basic prevocational training, and helped to place them in various "user agencies" in the local city government, where they received on-the-job training, with the promise (not always realized) of a permanent job in the agency attendant upon the successful completion of training. Various supportive services from dental care to transportation subsidies were occasionally provided by charitable organizations in the community. In most of the projects, part of the trainee's week was spent off the job in a classroom setting, sometimes at the local state university.[31]

AVCO's conclusions about these eleven New Careers projects were quite negative. There was a critical shortage of counsellors; the trainee-to-counsellor ratio varied from a manageable 17 in Burlington, Vermont to an impossibly high 201 in Minneapolis. Many of the promised services, especially child day care centers, were never provided.

But more important than any of the foregoing is AVCO's evaluation of the *quality* of the jobs: " . . . the agencies look on their enrollees as merely 'free' labor, a kind of 'adult' Neighborhood Youth Corps. Far too many of the agencies (especially the smaller agencies) offer only 'dead end' jobs.[32]

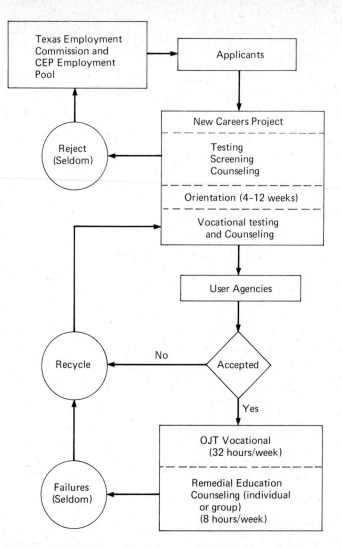

Figure 12–4. Flow Chart of Enrollees in Houston, Texas, New Careers Project.

This is the chief risk in pursuing the strategy of spinning off "subprofessional" jobs from existing professional positions. If the jobs thus created do not fill legitimate personnel needs of the user agencies, then there is a real danger that the new income streams generated by the development program may eventually dry up. Are "careers" such as "hospital pharmacy aide," "patrolman aide," "safety patrol aide," and "housing project patrol aide"[33] really *careers?*

Equally risky and objectionable to many critics of this strategy is its explicit identification of the trainees as a group apart. The "New Careerists" are given special training, special supportive services, and even special job titles. For the poor, this may perpetuate their sense of inferiority, an attitude which public programs should do everything within their power to dissipate. Moreover, from the point of view of the regular (largely white) public labor force, this special treatment of the ghetto poor may engender discontent which could lead to serious labor relations problems later.

By May 31,1968 — nearly nine months after the inception of the program — the eleven projects evaluated by AVCO had managed to graduate only 338 of the 2,635 ghetto residents who had been enrolled, a throughput of about 14 percent.[34] By contrast, 726 trainees (or over a fourth of those enrolled) had dropped out of the program altogether by Memorial Day, 1968. Moreover, the costs during the first year of the program were quite high. Table 12.10 displays the principal items for the set of eleven projects. *Planned* unit costs were reasonably high to begin with, ranging from a low of $4,139 per trainee per year in Harrisburg to $7,259/trainee/year in Minneapolis.

Under actual operating conditions, however, only the Burlington project was able to recruit *and hold* a sufficient number of the "disadvantaged" to be able to operate at full capacity. The other ten projects all operated with some excess capacity, the opportunity costs of which — when translated into realized unit cost figures — are revealed to have been quite expensive indeed. Realized unit costs ranged from $4,557/trainee/year in Harrisburg to $7,695/trainee/year in Paterson, New Jersey; the mean was $6,097 (or about $508 per trainee per month). Paterson's unit cost overrun attributable to excess capacity was more than $3,000; the mean overrun among all eleven cities was almost $1,300.

Table 12.11 exhibits the costs for the entire nationwide program for calendar 1968 (6,455 trainees). Given the AVCO analysis, we are entitled to suspect that the Department of Labor's overall unit cost figure of $4,223/trainee/year is perhaps a *target* rather than a statistic.

A working "model" employing the second job development strategy is provided by the example of the New Jersey Public Employment Career Development Program. Quite unlike the New Careers approach, the New Jersey experiment brings the poor "into the mainstream of public employment, rather than being segregated into certain categories of jobs reserved only for them."[35] Moreover, it operates within the state's civil service structure. Indeed, its most important long-run contribution may well be the development of creative change in civil service procedures and requirements as they affect the poor in New Jersey.

The Career Development Program is currently operated as an integral part of the New Jersey Department of Civil Service, and is directed by Richard

Table 12.10
Total and Average Operating Budgets for 11 New Careers Projects, 1967/68

Project	Total Budget FY 1968	Planned Enrollment Capacity	Expected Unit Cost	Enrollment on May 1, 1968	Realized Unit Cost	Capacity Utilization —%—	Unit Cost Overrun
Burlington	$ 231,820	50	$4636	50	$4636	100.0	0
Columbus	1,127,000	226	4986	153	7366	67.7	$2380
East St. Louis	667,970	135	4948	111	6018	82.2	1070
Harrisburg	1,490,270	360	4139	327	4557	90.8	418
Houston	1,101,360	250	4405	218	5052	87.2	647
Huntington	288,180	68	4237	52	5541	76.5	1304
Miami	561,940	130	4323	88	6385	67.7	2062
Minneapolis	1,502,680	207	7259	201	7476	97.1	167
Newark	1,158,633	250	4634	67	6937	66.8	2303
Paterson	531,000	120	4425	69	7695	57.5	3270
Providence	459,600	97	4738	85	5407	87.6	669

Source: AVCO, Volume 1, p. 29.

mean realized unit cost = $6,097
mean unit cost overrun = $1,295

Table 12.11

New Careers Budget for Calendar 1968, U.S. Department of Labor (Average enrollment = 6,455 persons)

Item	Total Cost	Percentage	Average Cost
Wages and fringe benefits	$18,193,481	66.7	$2819
Supportive services, including transportation and day care centers	1,840,314	6.7	285
Recruitment	45,174	0.2	7
Counselling, training, supervision, remedial education and other staff activities	2,420,053	8.9	375
Job development, placement, referral and follow-up	437,045	1.6	68
Administrative and other overhead	4,319,344	15.9	669
	$27,255,411	100.0	$4223

C. Darling. It began, however, as a project of the New Jersey Office of Economic Opportunity, under the direction of Frederick A. Schenk. Initially, a team of career development specialists was assigned to the chief personnel officers in the various state agencies. These specialists reported to their respective agency heads, but were to a large extent responsible (and responsive) to the Program director. Their role in the strategy was a central one, for it was their job to identify personnel needs in the various agencies as they arose, to analyze entry and promotional requirements of various job classes, to design modifications of existing job specifications, to create new job titles, and to recommend new entry requirements — all within the corpus of the civil service system. Thus, the Public Employment Career Development Program was designed to act not only as a special employment service or broker for the poor, but to "help to create the openings it [was] trying to fill."[36]

The Program's achievements since its inception in the fall of 1966 have been many. More than 2,000 job specifications have been reviewed and over 183 job titles either revised or added to accommodate the skills and education of the poor. The apprentice painter civil service exam is now given in Spanish as well as in English, opening up for the first time in New Jersey public employment for Puerto Rican and other Spanish-speaking residents. In 200 cases (for example, with the state Department of Transportation), a far more relevant and less restrictive work performance test has been substituted for the written test. Together with the state Departments of Civil Service, Labor and Industry, and Education, the career development staff has set up two clerical training centers for the poor. Finally, as of February, 1968, the Program had placed 301 slum and migrant workers into state civil service jobs.[37]

But probably the most significant of all the Program's achievements has been the agreement with the state Civil Service Commission to eliminate formal education requirements for certain jobs, substituting in their place "an ability to read, write, and follow directions." Specially designed civil service exams offered in core city areas such as Newark's Central Ward are another innovation directly resulting from the Career Development Program's activities. And throughout the Program, the fundamental principle is never lost sight of: "we identified areas where the agencies themselves had the greatest needs and addressed our service capabilities in this direction."[38]

Mr. Schenk firmly believes that the resources exist for transforming *existing* state institutions into functional components of a public service job program that could ultimately absorb as many as 120,000 additional workers into the state civil service system. As director, he took great pains to articulate his experiment with the various activities of MDT offices, the Neighborhood Youth Corps, and — most important of all — the local CAPs, whose credibility *inside* the ghetto is quite possibly the War on Poverty's greatest victory.

Even the ostensibly mundane business of advertising and administering the civil service exam is turned to good use. For the clerical trainee exam, Schenk hired some "dudes" to recommend a set of examination sites located in the ghetto. Some 900 people showed up for the examination held in a school in Newark's Central Ward, more from that neighborhood than had participated before. The examination monitors also came from the local population.

Together with his preference for working with (although hardly within) existing structures, Schrenk insists that the poor ought not be singled out for special attention once they occupy permanent public service jobs. The Career Development Program recently opened up seventeen maintenance and construction apprenticeships to ghetto applicants. The names assigned to these new jobs are instructive: "carpenter," "electrician," "machinist," "plumber," and so forth. In a similar spirit, Schenk advocates training and frequent promotions for regular as well as for disadvantaged workers. This is not only a question of morale; a career "ladder" for the poor leads nowhere if the middle "rungs" are not at least periodically accessible, i.e., vacant.

The New Jersey Career Development Program has no formal provision for providing supportive services to its clients. The justification offered (if indeed it is not just a rationalization of the usual budget constraint) is that services are essentially fringe benefits. To commit the Program to the provision of such services would in Schenk's opinion sensitize the unions, and set in motion a bargaining process which could have an ultimately undesirable impact on the poor themselves.

The New Jersey Public Employment Career Development Program is operated, of course, on a considerably more modest scale than is the New Careers Program. Complete *ex post* cost figures are currently available for only one "job title," the *clerical trainee* project. In this project, the trainee learns typing, shorthand, and filing. "The opportunity is thus provided for permanent employment in government, satisfying our manpower need on the one hand and providing badly needed jobs on the other."[39] So far it has been possible to accept only fifty persons (forty-nine of them female) for enrollment in this particular project.[40]

The first set of costs incurred were those associated with program design (or what the staff refers to as "Idea Costs"). Fundamentally, these included the costs of job title and examination modification, and overall project pre-planning, which took place over the period of April to October 1967.

Salaries of four career development specialists	$ 7,400
Clerical staff	3,000
Executive advice	1,000
Subtotal	$11,400

The first civil service exam under the new system was held on Saturday, October 7, 1967 at seven centers throughout the state. A total of 4,376 persons applied for the exam,[c] of whom 2,810 appeared and 1,166 passed. All of the latter were placed on the Civil Service Clerical Trainee Employment List. Of these, fifty were selected for training at the Trenton Center, performing actual daily work tasks for the state government along with other regular workers. Three classes, each of six months' duration, were conducted.

The "pre-employment costs" associated with administering the exam and arranging for subsequent placement were:

---

[c]We have no figures on the cost of outreach, although Schenk has indicated that considerable attention was given to this program element.

Personnel	$6,150
Materials	465
Administrative Overhead	890
Subtotal	$7,505

Finally, the costs of training fifty persons had to be incurred. Since all training was performed on the job, the staff refers to these as "post-employment costs." Supervisory cost is valued at approximately two half days per week of time released from normal supervisory duties, or $336 per trainee per six-month course:

Personnel

Supervisory (see text)	$16,800	
Instructors	10,937	
Clerical Trainee		
salaries/6 mo. @ $1,684	84,000	
Office staff	4,222	$115,959
Materials		1,775
Fixed Cost and Other Overhead		$ 17,100
Subtotal		$134,834

Summarizing these costs, we have:

Program Design Costs	$ 10,400
Pre-Employment Costs	7,505
Post-Employment Costs	134,834
Total Cost	$152,739

It remains now to estimate the costs per trainee. Clearly, the first and third components should be allocated over the fifty persons who actually received training. For the second component, however, 1,166 people (i.e., all those who passed the exam) received services which would otherwise not have been forthcoming in the absence of the Program. Consequently, it is appropriate to estimate the average annual costs per trainee of the New Jersey Clerical Trainee Program at:

$$\frac{10,400}{50} + \frac{7,505}{1,166} + \frac{134,834}{50} = \$2,915$$

This now appears to be a remarkably low estimate, relative not only to the

New Careers data assessed earlier but also to most of the figures emerging from other programs such as Job Corps (around $8,000 – but including a large travel component) and the JOBS Program of the National Alliance of Businessmen ($4-5,000).

With these two ongoing programs as examples, how, then, shall we "cost out" a public service job development program for residents of the urban ghetto? Most of the training given to these new workers has been and will probably continue to be of a "general" nature. That is, the skills learned are more or less readily transferable from one job and one employer to another. There are many economists who believe that the costs of this kind of training program should be estimated by the extra *earnings* foregone by workers during their training, i.e., by the difference between the trainee's earnings under the program and the wages which he could have earned in some alternative employment, *without* training. This approach assumes that the trainee will be paid a wage which is net of most of the costs of training him. In other words, a program providing general training is as-sumed to make the worker pay for his own training, since presumably he can take the new "bundle of skills" invested in his person to other employers. Thus, he could earn a relatively higher *present* wage by fore-going training and accepting employment elsewhere.[41]

In our examples – and generally in a policy of public employment for the disadvantaged – these assumptions are not satisfied. Whether or not an implicit subsidy is involved (and probably it is), the New Careers and the New Jersey Career Development trainees generally receive the regular entry-level wages prevailing in the agencies to which they are assigned. Even more important, it is questionable whether the trainees would be able to find *any* alternative employment, let alone jobs paying higher wages (see the discus-sion on pp. 239 and 243 above). Indeed, the explicit objective of a public service job development program is to provide jobs for those who are out of work or only marginally employed. Such programs are *not* designed to compete with other public and private employers for those workers who are already successful.

Therefore, at this introductory stage of the National Civil Service League's investigation of these issues, it seems advisable to employ the more traditional concept of program cost: the administrative budget. In these terms, it appears that a public service job development program can prob-ably "deliver" a trainee within the period of a year or less for an average cost of between $3,000 and $7,000.

VI.   The Benefits from a Public Service Job Development Program

The major quantitiable social benefit from a public job program is the present value of the *extra* GNP contributed over some future period of time by the newly trained worker.[d] From Commerce Department data on GNP contributed by government workers and on total employment in all governments (in America) for the period 1946-1965,[42] we may project the future level of GNP per public employee to any given future year, with the additional man-power being supplied by ghetto residents.[e] For our purposes, we shall assume that a jobs program implemented in 1969/70 will enable its graduates to contribute extra GNP at the projected rate up until 1975, after which prediction is not feasible since new technologies in service delivery may by that time require the worker to undergo retraining. Figure 12.5 shows the historical and projected rates at which public service workers contribute to GNP. The shaded band which we have established around the locus of projections serves to allow for the inevitable uncertainty involved in predicting the shape of any future event from previous experience.

These future returns to the social investment of job training must now be *discounted back* to the present, in order to make them directly comparable to the costs which are, after all, born in the present and not in the future. By discounting, we mean that all decision makers have some relative preference for present as against future income, some subjective notion about the relative urgency of receiving income now rather than later. Economists call this "discounting the future," and the rate of interest which expresses this "feeling" in quantitative terms is called the "rate of time preference." Formally, the present value of a current investment which yields returns R in future years $1, 2, \ldots, n$ is equal to

$$\frac{R_1}{(1 + r)^1} + \frac{R_2}{(1 + r)^2} + \ldots + \frac{R_n}{(1 + r)^n}$$

where r is the rate of discount. Obviously, the larger the value of r we select as an expression of our "rate of time preference" or "feeling about the future," the smaller will be the present value of the investment.

---

[d]Because of the accounting conventions of the Department of Commerce, this will also equal the *extra* wage incomes earned by the new workers, i.e., the difference between their wages in the new public service jobs (after training) and their wages in previous private or public employment (if any).

[e]This procedure requires that we make two key assumptions:
(a) full employment of "non-poor" labor so that if the disadvantaged worker were *not* trained and placed, the economy would have to forego the incremental GNP that he is capable of producing.
(b) the necessary complementary capital (equipment and all other resources) will in fact be available. Predicting the future contribution to GNP of disadvantaged workers by reference to the benchmark of *all* public service workers' previous contribution critically depends upon the former being given "equal access" to the capital — human and material — which permitted the latter to "produce."

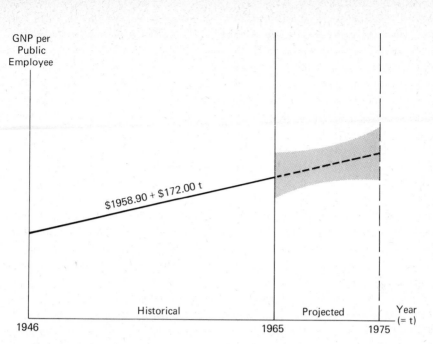

Figure 12–5. Historical and Projected Rates at Which Public Service Workers Contribute to GNP.

In private industry, or in the long-range budgeting decisions of an individual family, it is both natural and sensible that a relatively *high* rate of interest be used to discount future expected income. For the individual, a dollar earned today *is* worth a good deal more than a dollar which may be earned next year, not only due to inflationary phenomena, but because of the risk that next year's dollar may never actually materialize! For governments, however, the situation is altogether different. The government will certainly be here a year from now — or ten years from now — to collect on its current investment. The risk of default is less than for the private decision maker. The very size of the national economy makes it possible for the government to absorb the remaining risks without jeopardizing its "credit."

Thus, in discounting future contributions of new workers to GNP, we will use alternative interest rates: 4 percent, 6 percent, and 8 percent. The upper rate is probably relatively more appropriate to private than to public decision makers, while the converse is true for the lower rate. Moreover, in making the GNP-projections themselves, we will make varying assumptions about the magnitude of the contribution per new worker. In terms of the shaded band in figure 12.5, expected extra GNP per new public employee in each of the years 1970-75 will be assumed to take on the values associated with the lower limit, the midpoint, and then the upper limit of the band, each in turn. It will be convenient to refer to these as the "pessimistic," "neutral," and "optimistic" projections respectively.

The results for each of the nine possible estimates of the present value of the extra GNP per worker expected during the period 1970-75 are shown below. These estimates are:

Projected Contribution to GNP

		Pessimistic	Neutral	Optimistic
Rate of	4%	$33,642.70	$34,961.10	$36,279.50
Time	6%	$31,511.30	$32,748.10	$33,984.80
Preference	8%	$29,581.50	$30,744.10	$31,906.80

Thus, the program may have a payoff of from about $29,600 to $36,300. These numbers represent the 1969 value of the extra GNP which each new public service worker may be expected to contribute to the national economy over the next six years.

There are several potentially important *indirect benefits* which a public jobs program has the potential for generating. While we will not attempt to assign any quantitative dimensions to these benefits in the present paper, they deserve to be mentioned briefly.

In Section II above, we alluded to the post-war out-migration of manufacturing and wholesale plants from the central cities to their suburban "rings." However, as Herbert Bienstock, Middle Atlantic Regional Director for the Bureau of Labor Statistics, has observed for at least one large American city:

Emphasis on overall manufacturing employment trends has tended to obscure the fact that a substantial proportion of the "manufacturing" workers in New York City are indeed a part of the City's important office worker force. N.Y.C. is a headquarters city and few would argue that the retention of headquarters offices is not a matter of crucial concern to its economic health.

... in contrast to the general ... flight of jobs and industry from N.Y.C ... the data – at least for the manufacturing sector – indicate that ... on balance jobs in N.Y.C. administrative offices of manufacturing companies increased by 3,600 during the period from 1962 to 1967, rising to some 82,000 in the latter year.[43]

If New York's experience is at all a barometer of general urban trends in this particular respect, then there is an important potential "sidewise link-age" between the public and private sectors in the cities. Previously unem-ployed or subemployed ghetto residents may be given on-the-job training in local government offices, after which they may eventually move into basically similar positions in the administrative offices of the city's private firms. In this way, a public service job development program is potentially capable of generating important external benefits for the *private* employers in the urban economy by performing outreach, placement and training functions on their behalf.

A second and much-discussed indirect benefit of a jobs program is the potential reduction in public welfare costs which might result from previous welfare recipients moving "from the relief roll to the payroll." It is hard to say how large these potential savings are likely to be. New York City's Department of Social Services, for example, estimates that only 9 percent of that city's adult welfare population is employable.[44] It would probably be a good idea not to expect much relief here, and certainly not tax relief. The incomes of the ghetto poor are so low already that it may be necessary for some time to continue several different income supplement and jobs programs simultaneously. This is the price we must pay for so many years of neglect.

VII. Summary and Conclusions

We have estimated the present value of the *direct* social benefits from a public service job development program to be between $29,600 and $36,300 per new worker employed, and the cost of training him to be $3,000-$7,000. The limiting benefit-cost ratios are thus:

$$\frac{\$29,600}{\$\ 7,000} = \$4.23 \qquad \frac{\$36,300}{\$\ 3,000} = \$12.10$$

In other words, considering only the direct impact of a public jobs program on GNP over the next five years, a dollar invested now in a new worker from the urban ghetto may return anywhere from $4.23 to as much as $12.10 in extra GNP.

On these "efficiency" grounds, the policy would seem to represent a *sound* social investment. That it is also a *desirable* investment there can no longer be any doubt. We have seen that the urban economy is rapidly generating increased demands for public services which cannot be met by the existing labor force alone. We can, in other words, no longer afford the waste of productive resources which the underutilization of ghetto labor represents.

Yet, after all the data have been analyzed and all the computations performed, perhaps the strongest argument for a public service job development program is a bluntly political one. In the United States, no improvement in the black man's access to the legal and material benefits of full citizenship has even taken place without the support – indeed, without the initiative – of government. There is not the slightest indication that the private sector is going to be any more willing in the future than it has been in the past to actively seek black Americans as co-workers, neighbors, or employees. Thus, if the provision of jobs for ghetto residents is not accepted as a public responsibility, their intolerable employment status will probably remain essentially unchanged.

Nearly 100 years ago, the nation found itself confronted with a major political crisis. A newly emerging industrial economy required an entirely new breed of public professionals to manage its growth. The old spoils system was incapable of supplying the new kind of specialized, educated, permanent personnel demanded by the new system. At this critical juncture in American history, it was the National Civil Service League which, more than any other body, helped to institute the merit examination system, thereby enabling the American economy to realize its potential.

Now the nation is again in crisis. The economy is faced with acute unemployment. The cities that propogate our culture are deteriorating more and more rapidly, largely because of our discriminatory practices in housing and employment. And the younger and stronger members of that race against whom we have practiced *apartheid* and worse for more than 300 years have told us – bluntly, passionately, and violently – that they will no longer accept these arrangements.

It is appropriate that the National Civil Service League should be the organization to once again identify and commit itself to supporting a public policy designed to help resolve a political crisis. As with the earlier policy innovation, so the present one – public employment of the disadvantaged under merit principles – is proferred as a strategy for enabling American society to prepare itself for entry upon a new age. In the post-industrial era, no nation – even the wealthiest – will be able to afford the luxury of a predilection as internally divisive and debilitating as racism.

Notes

1. Harold L. Sheppard, *The Nature of the Job Problem and the Role of New Public Service Employment* (Kalamazoo, Michigan: W.E. Upjohn Institute, January 1969), pp. 19-20.

2. Harold L. Sheppard and Herbert E. Striner, *Civil Rights, Employment, and the Social Status of American Negroes* (Kalamazoo, Michi-

gan: W.E. Upjohn Institute, 1966), pp. 77-78. These are "full-time equivalents" computed by Striner.

3. The traditional sources of jobs for new immigrants to the cities have been those manufacturing and wholesaling industries which most intensively employ blue-collar workers. Since World War II, the substitution of horizontal-space-intensive for vertical-space-intensive techniques of production and freight handling have induced firms to move from the older central cities out to their suburban rings, where land assembly is both cheaper and easier. This decentralization of goods-producing industry is facilitated by and in turn reinforces the increased substitution of private for public transportation — yet another technological change which has had a major impact on modern urban life. The historical record of "suburbanization," and its implications for black workers whose residence is still effectively restricted to the urban core, are discussed in: John F. Kain, "The Distribution of Jobs and Industry," in *The Metropolitan Enigma*, ed. James Q. Wilson (Cambridge: Harvard University Press, 1968); John F. Kain, "Housing Segregation, Negro Employment, and Metropolitan Decentralization," *Quarterly Journal of Economics*, May 1968; John R. Meyer, John F. Kain, and Martin Wohl, *The Urban Transportation Problem* (Cambridge: Harvard University Press, 1965); Dorothy K. Newman, "The Decentralization of Jobs," *Monthly Labor Review*, May 1967; Thomas Vietorisz and Bennett Harrison, *The Economic Development of Harlem* (New York: Frederick A. Praeger, forthcoming), especially Chapter 6.

4. Bureau of Labor Statistics, U.S. Department of Labor, Middle Atlantic Regional Report No. 10, *Changing Patterns of Employment, Income, and Living Standards in New York City,* June 1968, Tables 2 and 3.

5. U.S. Department of Labor, *1966 Urban Employment Survey,* unpublished data files, author's calculations. The Harlem component of this ten-city survey (whose sample size was over 37,000 ghetto residents) is analyzed in Vietorisz and Harrison, *The Economic Development of Harlem,* Chapter 1. The entire sample is examined in some detail in Bennett Harrison, *Education, Training, and the Urban Ghetto* (Baltimore: The Johns Hopkins Press, 1972), Chapter 3.

6. See the various reports of the National Commission on Technology, Automation and Economic Progress. These have been condensed and summarized in *Automation and Economic Progress,* eds. Howard R. Bowen and Garth Mangum (Englewood Cliffs, New Jersey: Prentice-Hall, 1967).

7. U.S. Department of Labor, *Manpower Report of the President,* 1967, Table E-9.

8. Harold L. Sheppard, *The Nature of the Job Problem,* pp. 22-28.

9. Ibid., p. 28.

10. Leonard Lecht, *Manpower Requirements for National Objectives in*

the 1970's (Washington, D.C.: National Planning Association, Center for Priority Analysis, February, 1968), p. 75.

11. Ibid., Table 3-3.

12. The recent public recognition and discussion of poverty can probably be traced to President John F. Kennedy's "discovery" of Michael Harrington's *The Other America* (Baltimore: Penguin Books, 1962).

13. Sheppard, *The Nature of the Job Problem,* pp. 1-2.

14. Ibid., pp. 2-4. The nonwhite poor made an even greater effort in 1966 to improve their family incomes than did the white poor. Sixty-three percent of nonwhite families headed by a male had two or more wage earners, compared with only 39% of similar white families. The percentages for female headed families were 55% and 38% respectively.

15. Bureau of Labor Statistics, U.S. Department of Labor, *Three Standards of Living for an Urban Family of Four Persons: Spring 1967* (Washington D.C.: Superintendent of Documents, 1967), Bulletin 1570-5.

16. Sheppard, *The Nature of the Job Probleem,* pp. 17-19; Samuel M. Burt and Herbert E. Striner, *Toward Greater Industry and Government Involvement in Manpower Development* (Kalamazoo, Michigan: W.E. Upjohn Institute, September 1968). After a little over a year of activity, the National Alliance of Businessmen had managed to place some 118,411 workers in member corporations with subsidies from the Department of Labor's MA-3 program; Jean White, "Business Needs Help in Aiding Ghettos," *The Washington Post,* Sunday, January 12, 1969, p. E4. By March of this year, the total had risen only to about 125,000 workers, distributed among some 12,500 companies for an average of only ten new workers per company; *Business Week,* March 8, 1969, p. 62. Ghetto workers are traditionally the "last hired but the first fired" in private labor markets. Thus, by the middle of March, the Ford Motor Company was announcing the closing of two special hiring centers in central Detroit and the layoff of several hundred newly hired workers from the ghetto; *Business Week,* March 22, 1969, p. 41.

17. Carol S. Greenwald and Richard Styron "Increasing Job Opportunities in Boston's Urban Core," *New England Economic Review,* Federal Reserve Bank of Boston, January-February, 1969, pp. 30-40. See especially the discussion on pp. 34ff. A detailed investigation of urban transportation strategy from the point of view of the ghetto (including reverse commuting) is found in Oscar Ornati, *Transportation Needs of the Poor,* (New York: Frederick A. Praeger, 1970).

18. William Cris Lewis, "Tax Concessions and Industrial Location: A Review," *Reviews in Urban Economics,* Fall, 1968, pp. 29-45. See also the final report of the National Commission on Urban Problems (Sen. Paul H. Douglas, Chairman), released December 14, 1968. The most highly pub-

licized of the "branch plants" has been Aerojet-General's tent-manufacturing facility established in Watts in 1966. By May of this year, however, and despite Labor and Defense Department subsidies and contracts totalling well over $2 million, the project had lost "several hundred thousand dollars" and employment had been cut back from 500 to 300 ghetto workers. John Herbers, "Economic Development of Blighted Inner-City Areas is Running Into Snags," *New York Times,* May 4, 1969.

19. Indigenous ghetto economic development may be a different matter altogether. The number of "inside jobs" created by local community corporations through the instrumentality of new businesses and cooperatives would of course be necessarily small. Nevertheless, they could be an exceedingly important piece of the overall mosaic, generating a catalytic effect on the community. Such efforts could easily be designed to articulate with a public job development program, for example with the ghetto development corporation providing the outreach and recruitment functions for government personnel administrators. Most important of all, young black activists in the ghetto *want* ghetto economic development. See Bennett Harrison, "A Pilot Project in Economic Development Planning for American Urban Slums," *International Development Review,* March 1968; Thomas Vietorisz and Bennett Harrison, *The Economic Development of Harlem.*

20. Andrea Beller, "Demographic Trends," in: Development Planning Workshop, Harlem Development Project, *The Economy of Harlem* (New York: Columbia University, September 15, 1968), volume I, p. 20; and Bennett Harrison, "The Distribution and Scale of Commercial Activity in the Urban Ghetto," Dept. of Economics, University of Maryland, Jan. 1972, mimeo.

21. Edward Kalachek, "Determinants of Teenage Employment," *Journal of Human Resources,* Winter, 1969, p. 17.

22. William A. Johnson and Robert Rosenkranz, "Public Assistance," in *Cities in Trouble: An Agenda for Urban Research,* ed. Anthony H. Pascal (Santa Monica: The RAND Corporation, August, 1968), RM-5603-RC, p. 98.·

23. *For All the People . . . By All the People,* 1969. The cities surveyed were: San Francisco-Oakland, Philadelphia, Detroit, Atlanta, Houston, Memphis, and Baton Rouge. Data are for the payroll period including March 12, 1967.

24. Ibid., Chapter I, p. 5.

25. Ibid., I, 2.

26. Ibid., I, 3.

27. Ibid., I, 2.

28. Ibid., I, 15.

29. Sidney A. Fine, *Guidelines for the Design of New Careers* (Kalama-

zoo, Michigan: W.E. Upjohn Institute, September, 1967), pp. 13-14.

30. U.S. Department of Labor, *Manpower Report of the President,* January, 1969, p. 102.

31. Division of Research and Evaluation, AVCO Economic Systems Corporation, *Pilot Evaluation of Selected New Careers Projects,* U.S. Department of Labor, Manpower Administration, Office of Manpower Policy, Economic Opportunity Act Contract #61-7-002-09, 2 volumes, submitted August, 1968. (Hereafter AVCO)

32. AVCO, Volume I, p. 27.

33. U.S. Department of Labor, Manpower Administration, *New Careers: Position Descriptions – A Sourcebook for Trainers,* University Research Corporation, 1967.

34. AVCO, p. 32.

35. Judith G. Benjamin, "Civil Service and the Poor: Some New Developments," July, 1967, mimeographed, pp. 26-27.

36. Ibid., p. 18.

37. Department of Community Affairs, New Jersey Office of Economic Opportunity, *Public Employment Career Development Program,* Trenton, various documents, dated 1967-1969.

38. Ibid.

39. Ibid.

40. Ibid. There is, of course, no way of knowing to what extent if any the New Careers Program also tended to practice "creaming."

41. T.W. Schultz, "Investment in Human Capital," *American Economic Review,* March, 1961; Gary S. Becker, "Investment in Human Capital: A Theoretical Analysis," *Journal of Political Economy,* October, 1962 (supplement); Jacob Mincer, "On-the-Job Training: Costs, Returns, and Some Implications," Ibid.

42. Office of Business Economics, U.S. Department of Commerce, *The National Income and Product Accounts of the United States, 1929-1965, 1966,* Tables 1.7 and 6.4 Figures are in constant 1957-59 dollars.

43. Bureau of Labor Statistics, *Employment, Income and Living Standards,* pp. 11-12.

44. Johnson and Rosenkranz, "Public Assistance."

Appendixes

Appendix A – Project PACE MAKER

U.S. DEPARTMENT OF LABOR

The Office of Economic Opportunity is implementing a new program, called Project PACE MAKER (Public Agency Career Employment Maker), which provides technical assistance to state and local governments interested in removing the legal, administrative, and psychological barriers to employment of the disadvantaged.

Upon request of the individual jurisdiction to OEO, a team of personnel technicians from the National Civil Service League makes an intensive analysis of the local civil service system. Those interviewed include the chief officers of the jurisdiction, personnel and civil service officials, user agency directors, line supervisors, rank and file employees, and community organizations attempting to place disadvantaged workers in local government jobs. The laws and administrative rules of the jurisdiction are examined, and an estimate is made of the legal feasibility of institutional change. Finally, the survey team's findings and recommendations for change are documented in a confidential report to the chief elected officer of the jurisdiction.

It will not be possible to evaluate the impact of Project PACE MAKER until the eighteen jurisdictions which have received technical assistance have time to study the reports, solicit independent opinions from other sources, and assemble the resources needed to implement the recommendations of the League. Nor can the findings for particular governments be revealed, under the terms of their contracts with OEO. It can be said, however, that they testify to the widespread existence of the previously mentioned barriers to employment of the disadvantaged in state and local governments.

For the most part, these barriers can be attributed to civil service rules, other administrative procedures, and attitudes toward the hiring of the disadvantaged and are therefore susceptible to administrative correction. To the extent that administrative changes such as those proposed by PACE MAKER can be initiated, the capacity of local jurisdictions to effectively carry out federally assisted manpower programs will be increased. Several experiments in actual institutional change (as distinguished from information gathering) are, in fact, already underway.

Reprinted from U.S. Department of Labor, *Manpower Report of the President,* (Washington, D.C.: U.S. Government Printing Office, 1971).

269

Appendix B – Recent Federal Court Decisions on Testing and Credentialism

NATIONAL CIVIL SERVICE LEAGUE

The cases cited in this article address the following questions and problems:

1. What is required for validation of tests?
2. Can a high school diploma be used as a prerequisite to employment?
3. What is the role of "good intentions" in discrimination cases?
4. "Business necessity" is the key to validity.

The cases presented are divided into two groups, those involving public employers, and those involving private employers.

Public Employer Cases

In cases involving public employers, arguments based on the equal protection clause of the United States Constitution and the Civil Rights Law of 1964, have been used successfully in employment testing cases.

A. In *Carter* vs. *Gallagher,* Case No. 4-70 Civ. 399, United States District Court, Fourth Division of Minn., (1971), the court was presented with statistical data that showed that only six out of a total of 24 blacks who had taken the firefighters examination since 1948 had passed; and for various reasons none of the six who passed were ever hired. The complaint further alleged that the test and testing method used by the Civil Service Commission for firefighters discriminated against certain minority groups, in that it denied said groups an equal employment opportunity. The court granted the following affirmative relief:

1. Enjoined (prohibited) the use of the current firefighters examination until it can be validated according to the "Guidelines on Employment Testing Procedures" issued by the Equal Employment Opportunity Commission on August 24, 1966;
2. Required that references in applications for employment regarding "arrests," as such, be eliminated i.e., such reference must refer to "convictions" as opposed to mere "arrests," and that the circumstances surrounding any conviction should be considered;

Reprinted from *Something Else: The Model Cities Manpower Newsletter,* published by the National Civil Service League, vol. 2, no. 2, May 1971.

3. Eliminated the requirement for a high school diploma or GED for "entry level" firefighter's positions; however, the court felt that the high school diploma or GED could be used as a requirement for successful completion of the probationary period;
4. Required affirmative action in the recruitment of minorities;
5. That the next 20 firefighters positions that become vacant be filled by minority applicants without regard to their place on the list of eligibles.

B. In *Penn* vs. *Stumpf,* 308 F. Sup 1238 (1970), the United States District Court, Northern District of California, recognized the right of black applicants for patrolman positions to seek relief from the allegedly discriminatory hiring practices of the Oakland, California Civil Service Commission, in its administration of the examination for patrolmen. The court allowed the action to be brought against "the Commissioners of the Oakland Civil Service Board of Commissioners; the Personnel Director of said Board and his agents; and the Chief of Police Department and his agents, in their official capacity, under the Civil Rights Act of 1964. The court by allowing suit to be brought against these public officials in their official capacity, in effect held that the Civil Rights Act of 1964 could be used as the basis for relief in certain cases involving public employers, i.e., cities. municipalities, etc. The court stated that "where the relief sought is . . . in the nature of a declaratory judgment and/or injunction, no sound reason presents itself for immunizing municipal officials from suit under the Civil Rights Act." *Penn* vs. *Stumpf,* suggests that in cases involving discrimination in employment, relief can be sought against public employers under the Civil Rights Act, at least in those cases where only injunctive relief (as opposed to monetary damages) is being sought.

C. The Court, in *Arrington* vs. *Massachusetts Bay Transportation Authority,* 306 F. Sup. 1355 (1969), summed up the problem in the following way:

"A hiring practice [test or diploma requirement] related to ability to perform is not itself unfair if it means that disadvantaged minorities are in fact adversely affected. However, if there is no demonstrated correlation between scores on an aptitude test [or high school diploma?] and ability to perform well on a particular job, the use of the test in determining who or when one gets hired makes little business sense." If the effect is to discriminate, intentional or in fact, "then it becomes unconstitutionally unreasonable and arbitrary."

D. In *United States* vs. *Frazer,* Civ. No. 2709N, July 28, 1970, N.D. Ala., the United States District Court affirmed the right of the United States government to enforce, through legal proceedings, the terms and conditions of federal grant-in-aid programs. In this case, certain departments of the state of Alabama were recipients of federal grant-in-aid funds. These departments continued to practice racial discrimination in their hiring practices, notwithstanding the fact that the federal government has set and monitored merit system standards in state programs receiving federal funds since 1939. One standard required by the government is that the federal grant-in-aid funds be "administered by persons selected on the basis of their merit and fitness," and not race or color. The court found that:

1. Out of 1,000 clerical personnel employed by the defendants only one was black;
2. Only 26 out of a total of 1,104 case workers were black, and that those blacks employed were assigned, with few exceptions, exclusively black case loads;
3. That the defendants had "participated in procedures by which the cafeterias in buildings in which their employees work are operated on a racially discriminatory basis;"
4. That the defendants had been racially discriminatory in their *recruitment* practices. They found that while the defendants had actively recruited at predominantly white schools and had advertised through radio and newspaper, *"There are no mailings to newspapers or radio stations with predominantly Negro clientele. Furthermore, the defendants have not sought to hire graduates of predominantly Negro schools!"* [Emphasis added]

The court concluded that the above facts showed a "systematic refusal to appoint qualified Negro applicants," which "constitute unlawful racial discrimination."

Private Employers

In *Willie S. Griggs et al.,* vs. *Duke Power Company,* 91 S. Ct. 849 (1971), black employees in a class action suit sought to prevent the employer from allegedly violating the Civil Rights Act of 1964 by requiring a high school diploma and achieving a "satisfactory intelligence test score" for certain jobs. The jobs in question had been previously limited to white employees. The plaintiffs alleged that the requirements of a high school diploma and a "satisfactory" score on the intelligence test had the effect of preserving the "effects of the employer's past racial discrimination." Chief Justice Warren Burger set forth the unanimous opinion of the Court:

. . . the Civil Rights Act prohibits an employer from requiring a high school education or passing of a standardized general intelligence test as a condition of employment in or transfer to jobs when:

1. neither standard [high school diploma or passing of a general intelligence test] is shown to be significantly related to successful job performance;
2. both requirements operate to disqualify Negroes at a substantially higher rate than white applicants; and
3. the jobs in question formerly had been filled only by white employees as part of a long standing practice of giving preference to whites.

The Court went on to say that the Congressional intent or objective in enacting Title VII of the Civil Rights Act of 1964 "was to achieve equality of employment opportunities and remove barriers which operated in the past to favor an identifiable group of white employees over other employees. Practices, procedures, or tests neutral on their face, and even neutral in terms of intent, cannot be maintained if they operate to freeze the *status quo* of prior discriminatory practices." In that regard, the Court stated that "good intent or absence of discriminatory intent does not redeem employment procedures or testing mechanisms that operate as 'built in headwinds' for minority groups and are unrelated to measuring job capability." The Court held that the employer has the burden of showing that a "given requirement has a manifest relationship to the employment in question." The Court held that Section 703(h) of the Civil Rights Act of 1964 was properly construed by the Equal Employment Opportunity Commission in its *Guidelines on Employee Selection Procedures* (29 CFR Secs. 1607.1-1607.14), as permitting the use of only job-related tests.

It should be noted that the Court did not proscribe the use of testing or measuring procedures per se. What is proscribed is giving these devices and mechanisms controlling force unless it can be demonstrated that they measure job performance. "If an employment practice which operates to exclude Negroes cannot be shown to be related to job performance, the practice is prohibited." A showing of "business necessity" is required to establish the validity of an employment practice in these cases.

Annotated Bibliography to
Part IV

There are a growing number of excellent theoretical and empirical studies of the technological and behavioral relationships between education, training and worker productivity. The most accessible – and by far the most influential – has been Ivar Berg, *Education and Jobs: The Great Training Robbery* (New York: Praeger Publishers, 1970). See also Hirsch S. Ruchlin, "Education as a Labor Market Variable," *Industrial Relations,* October 1971; Daniel E. Diamond and Hrach Bedrosian, *Hiring Standards and Job Performance* (Washington, D.C.: U.S. Department of Labor, 1970), Manpower Research Monograph No. 18; Herbert Gintis, "Education, Technology and the Characteristics of Worker Productivity," *American Economic Review,* May 1971; and Lester Thurow and Robert E. Lucas, Jr., *The American Income Distribution: A Structural Problem* (Washington, D.C.: U.S. Government Printing Office, March 1972), U.S. Congress, Joint Economic Committee Print.

On the problem of excessive use of educational credentials by employers, see S.M. Miller, *Breaking The Credentials Barrier* (New York: The Ford Foundation, 1969); S.M. Miller and Marsha Kroll, "Strategies for Reducing Credentialism," *Good Government* [the journal of the National Civil Service League], Summer 1970; and Arthur Pearl and Frank Reissman, *New Careers for the Poor* (Glencoe, N.Y.: The Free Press, 1965). A series of articles on recent federal court cases involving credentialism is published in *Good Government,* Winter 1971.

The National Civil Service League periodically publishes a model public personnel administration law designed to aid state and local governments in formulating local merit system rules and guidelines. The most recent "model law" gives considerable attention to the problem of credentialism as a barrier to equal employment opportunity in the public sector; copies are available on request from NCSL, 1825 K Street, N.W. Washington, D.C. 20036.

The U.S. Civil Service Commission publishes an annual report on minority employment in the federal government. The best statistical study of minority employment in state and local government, although somewhat dated, is still U.S. Commission on Civil Rights, *For All the People . . . By All the People* (Washington, D.C.: U.S. Government Printing Office, 1969). This voluminous report is summarized in "Minority Employment in State and Local Governments", *Monthly Labor Review,* 1969.

Part V
Public Sector Manpower Planning and
the Financing of Public Service Jobs

Introduction to Part V

It has been apparent for quite some time that America is both lacking in public services and chronically short on jobs, especially for the unskilled. The public sector is also the fastest growing source of jobs in the economy. So when the problem of unemployment is discussed, the possibility of providing jobs in the public sector for the unskilled unemployed makes sense.

Objections are frequently raised, however, by those who believe that the very lack of skills that makes many of the unemployed unattractive to private industry will make them unable to perform truly vital public services. This charge underlies the common accusation that public job creation programs will amount to no more than a new form of "make work" or "boondoggle." It is a serious charge.

Even assuming that the unskilled poor *are* capable of performing competently in the public service, others have suggested that the best administrative procedures for "creating" those jobs would not be through another federal employment program, but rather through the transfer of additional federal revenue to states and localities to expand their services.

The fifth session of the Upjohn Seminar series considered these two questions: Are there jobs for the unskilled in expanded public service? If so, how should those jobs be financed: through revenue sharing, or through direct public service employment programs?

On the first point, Jacob Rutstein of the National Civil Service League presented strongly supportive evidence to the Seminar. Rutstein asked officials of operating agencies in the city of Chicago and the state of Connecticut to estimate their need for additional public service employees over the next three years. Given the tendency of employers to practice "credentialism," we should expect such an open-ended question to lead to answers which – if anything – are biased in favor of skilled workers. In Chicago, where some 41,000 are now employed, officials expressed a need for an additional 35,000 employees, an 85 percent increase. In Connecticut officials estimated an additional 50 percent increment above the 19,000 now working for the state. These figures in themselves are no surprise. The interesting fact is that Rutstein found that over half the new jobs in Chicago, some 17,000, are jobs whose tasks are such that many could almost certainly be filled by unskilled workers. The percentage distributions of desired incremental employment in the two jurisdictions are as follows:

	Chicago	Connecticut
Aide, attendant and assistant	50.1	21.6
Paraprofessional	2.7	11.2
Clerical and office	11.5	12.7
Administrative, technical and managerial	18.9	18.9
Professional and legal	9.1	20.3
Skilled and semi-skilled	3.1	3.8
Custodial and unskilled	4.6	11.5
	100.0	100.0

Note that the city, which currently has twice as many employees as the state, proposes to allocate a substantially larger share of its new jobs to the unskilled/semi-skilled categories than does the state. The only category where this relationship is significantly reversed is paraprofessionals; Rutstein told the Seminar that the state could absorb almost five times as many of these workers as the city because of the health services which the state alone provides.

The aide, attendant, and assistant jobs for which many unskilled workers are undoubtedly prepared include the following:

career development aide, ambulance attendant, case worker aide, children's welfare attendant, community aide, clerical aide, community coordinator aide, community health aide, correctional aide, education aide, environmental aide, food service aide, foster grandparents, health aide, health education aide, hospital helper, house parents, maintenance aide, mental health aide, neighborhood assistants, nurses' aide, nutrition aide, occupational education aide, parent education aide, teacher aide, playground assistant, and senior aide.

In developing staffing guidelines for these jurisdictions, toward the objective of facilitating employment of the disadvantaged, Rutstein emphasized the need for significant changes in civil service procedures. In Chicago, for example, applicants for regular civil service positions must pay a $3 fee in cash at City Hall for the privilege of taking a qualifying exam, the results of which are seldom announced in less than six months.

If a worker with relatively little education is to have a fair chance at a decent job and the opportunity for promotion within the civil service, it is essential that the requirements for the job be fully understood by the personnel officials themselves, and that an effort be made to divide the work in a jurisdiction into specific tasks which provide a scale graduated for difficulty: a "career ladder" that a man or woman may hope to climb. According to the Upjohn Institute's manpower task analyst, Dr. Sidney

Fine, "The whole system – certainly in the public service area – has to be examined, reconsidered and, to a certain extent, reorganized."

Following the presentation by Rutstein (whose guidelines for staffing local public service employment agencies are reproduced in Chapter 13), Fine described to the Seminar a method (which he has helped to develop) that allows some degree of objective "designing" of jobs. The fruit of this methodology has been the development of the Labor Department's well-known (and periodically revised) Dictionary of Occupational Titles, in which some 4,000 jobs in the private and public sectors are "rated" along several scales of difficulty.

At the center of Fine's methodology is the task statement. Fine's taks analysis includes seven scales, broken down into three groupings: Each task requires some involvement with *things*, with *data,* and with *people.* Dr. Fine scales the task both on the degree of competence required in each of these areas and on the balance between them. Tasks are also scaled on the basis of the *reasoning, math,* and *language* achievements needed to perform them satisfactorily. And finally, Dr. Fine scales the task on the basis of its balance between *prescription* and *discretion,* the extent to which a person performing that task is simply following orders (prescription) and the amount of decision making (discretion) the task entails.

Fine emphasized the difference between a task statement and an ordinary job description. He analyzes the task required for an organization to function, not necessarily the specific jobs into which those tasks may be momentarily divided. Using these tasks statements, Fine gave the Seminar an example in terms of welfare administration. The identification of specific tasks makes it possible to design jobs with relatively modest skill requirements, in order to produce more jobs for unskilled and semi-skilled individuals, and generally to provide the first "rungs" of a career ladder. "In Utah, for example," Fine said, "we have already designed social worker aide jobs for women, AFDC mothers. They have been hired and are working out extremely well." (One unexpected problem was created when – after the Utah jobs were announced – college graduates began applying for them! This was, of course, a period of very high national and regional unemployment).

As indicated in the Introduction to Part II, we have included in the present part a detailed account by Earl Wright, who was intimately involved in the early and subsequent planning for one community's participation in the program of public service employment created by the Emergency Employment Act. His account is unique to this volume, since it provides us with "what it really is like" at the grass-roots level – of determining agency estimates of numbers and types of jobs; priorities and goals for distributing a limited number of jobs for a large number of applicants (and in an equitable manner); and the coordinated involvement of disparate community groups – both public and private.

Having identified the latent demand for labor in state and local government, having found that a solid proportion of these jobs would be available for the unskilled, and having learned that a technology exists for designing and redesigning jobs to provide even greater opportunity for the unskilled through career ladders, the Seminar's attention was then turned to the question of how best to provide the funds for the jobs themselves.

Dr. Selma Mushkin of Georgetown University presented the case for revenue sharing. She pointed out that the growth in civilian employment has been nearly four times as great in state and local government as in the work force as a whole during the period 1962 to 1970 – 12.1 percent vs. 3.4 percent – and that state and local governments deliver the bulk of civilian public services. The national government spends somewhere on the order of from $20 to $25 billion each year, whereas state and local components spend at least $130 billion on public services. "Basically all of the public services that we *care* about are provided by the states and localities," she said.

Revenue sharing is needed because the expansion (let alone the maintenance) of these services requires additional resources which local governments simply do not possess. Resort to the federal tax system is sensible because, Dr. Mushkin said:

the federal tax system is clearly superior. It is superior because we live in a national economy, and the federal government is the only government we have with a *national* tax base. It is superior because it costs less to administer, and it costs less for the taxpayer to pay his tax dollar. It is superior, too, in that it happens to be a little fairer and more equitable as far as income classes are concerned.

Now while the taxpayer clearly prefers – and if I were a corporation, I would greatly prefer – to rely on the federal tax system, we seem in the country to prefer the services to be locally administered and locally designed. With that kind of division, we have got to find some way to get the federal tax dollar into the state and local governments.

Granted that the dollars must be federal, what role should the federal government play in the administration of the program? Professor Mushkin believes that the spending should be left nearly entirely to the local jurisdiction, and that jobs ought to flow from local attempts to meet public service demands, rather than be designed as part of a federally-controlled manpower or "job development" program. She told the Seminar that she feared that any effort to give priority to the hiring of the unskilled would mean, in practice, hiring such workers in preference to others better able to do the job, resulting in shoddy work and a further loss of public confidence in government. (Participants in the Seminar argued vigorously – partly on the basis of Rutstein's earlier remarks – that the unskilled unemployed were perfectly capable of doing excellent work given a real opportunity. The problem is not creating special opportunities for inferior workers, they claimed, but of providing enough jobs for all workers and eliminating artificial barriers — such as credential requirements that do not relate to the functions to be carried out — that block many from a fair share of such opportunities as do exist.)

Professor Melville Ulmer, of the University of Maryland, while agreeing that it is essential for us to spend more money in the public sector at the state and local level, argued for the contrasting view that the program *should* be controlled from Washington. First, to be useful during times of rising or high unemployment — as a counter-cyclical measure — it is essential that the funds be triggered on and off by Washington. A permanent, institutionalized "pass-through" formula would lack this counter-cyclical structure. Then, the new or additional service must "relate to our highest national priorities, among those the production of innumerable public goods that most of us would agree are sadly lacking today."

This requires that the federal government retain control over this program, a central control, including not only its overall dimensions but also the specific character of the project involved, the types of employment involved, in short, the provision of federal standards.

In other words, the considerations that I have outlined would rule out, at least for this purpose, the revenue sharing plan that Miss Mushkin has spoken about, in which you remember, that state and local governments would be entirely free to use federal funds exactly as they wished, with no restrictions.

Ulmer pointed out that most revenue-sharing schemes would reward all states more or less equally, whereas the difference in state expenditures on public services is often a function of "their willingness and social consciousness, their political, administrative, and moral maturity, rather than their incomes." Florida and Wisconsin, he pointed out, have the same per capita personal incomes. But Wisconsin pays an average benefit of $185 a month to its welfare families, Florida pays $95. Florida pays 25 percent less per pupil in its primary and secondary schools — $700 per pupil vs. $900 per pupil in Wisconsin.

In a multiple correlation study, I found that income differences among the fifty states account for less than one-third of the observed differences in the amounts they spend on education per pupil. I found no correlation at all between their income levels and their tax efforts.

If the states differ so widely in those intangibles of morality, ethics, responsibility and the rest, how can we logically suppose that all or even most public service employees would be put to socially effective use, if the states were free to use them as they wished, and if they were costless too?

In the discussion following this exchange of views between Professors Mushkin and Ulmer, the point was made that the kinds of problems which Jack Rutstein had found in Chicago — the kind of civil service rigidity which makes it difficult for the poor and unskilled to obtain jobs in the first place, and to have promotional opportunities once they acquire those jobs — can only be overcome with a considerable degree of federal control of the program to insure that local jurisdictions undertake the kind of civil service procedural reform and job redesign necessary. Critics responded with the observation that, while the federal government (e.g. through the U.S. Civil Service Commission) *could* exert its power and influence on behalf of civil service reform, there was no reason to expect that it would actually be willing to do so.

Evaluations of the Emergency Employment Act of 1971 will hopefully shed some much-needed light on this, and other, questions.

13 Staffing Guidelines for Local Public Employment

JACOB RUTSTEIN

Introduction

The Emergency Employment Act of 1971 intends the most rapid possible absorption of unemployed and underemployed people into the public service. To meet this urgent goal of immediate employment, eligible state, county, and municipal governments and other public employers must be prepared to shift their personnel systems into high gear. Such an emergency public employment program requires the identification of the most expeditious means by which large numbers of new employees may be taken on board. Therefore, consideration must be given to such basic factors as:

1. Identification of the kinds and numbers of positions to be used,
2. Knowledge of the characteristics of the eligible participants,
3. Priorities among the potential positions that meet program requirements for employment of the unemployed and underemployed,
4. Job standards and qualification requirements that provide a desirable "match" between the participants and the public service positions established for transitional employment.
5. Choice of civil service or othrer public employment procedures that permit the quickest screening, examination, and hiring to meet identified priorities in terms of specific designations of the unemployed and underemployed participants, and public service needs.
6. Expediting the administrative process involved in the recruiting, screening, selection and organizational placement of transitional public service employees.

   In the start-up phase of the program, time is of the essence. Nevertheless, a relationship exists between the method of hiring on an emergency basis now and the potential for long-term employment placement of transitional employees at a future stage. What is done in the short run can affect the long-run use of these positions as "transitional" stepping stones for movement of emergency employees into permanent positions in the public and private job sectors. The more closely the existing employment system is adhered to in meeting the short-run priorities of immediate, rapid, and large-scale hiring of a new labor force, the more efficiently that process will be able to move these employees into the regular permanent system at a later date.

The following suggestions relate various methods which might prove helpful to an employing agency in meeting program goals in the initial hiring phase of the Public Service Employment program within the context of civil service and other public employment personnel systems.

Determining the Number and Kinds of Public Service Positions Needed

The first major issue is to decide on *how many and what kinds of positions* should be established for the first run of the Public Service Employment Program.

In some part, the *kinds and levels of public service activities* that should be performed to improve governmental service and the *skills and abilities needed* to do the work will provide some answers. But, the major basis for determining how many public service jobs will be filled will very likely be directly related to the amount of federal money made available. In practically every jurisdiction, the staff that handles the budget function, given an approximate amount of money, can quickly come up with the number or numbers of positions that can be filled under the Public Service Employment Program.

The basic problem is to decide what *kinds of positions* are needed and *how many* should each department or operating program get to meet its needs. Depending on local circumstances, there are any number or combination of ways which can be helpful. For example:

The Annual Budget. Comparison between departmental budget requests and fund authorizations could point out positions in vital public services that could not be established or funded because money was just not available.

Impact of Cut-Back or Freeze Orders. Study of documents such as personnel records, reduction-in-force directives, lay-off notices, position ceiling orders, etc., could give direct information on how many positions have been abolished or left unfilled within the current or immediate past years because of lack of public funds.

Meeting with Heads of Departments. Group meetings with heads of departments or program officers which directly approach the issues of what public service programs within their responsibility are not being adequately performed because of lack of people; how many additional positions or people will they need to "beef-up" or expand their activities to satisfactory levels; how many transitional public service participants can they use and put to work immediately; and how much will be needed in the way of salaries and other related costs.

In meetings of this nature the need is for fast but realistic "guess-timates" to get the Public Service Employment program started, rather than comprehensive manpower planning activities.

Urban Planning, Economic Development and Other Research and Reference Organizations. In some states and general local government jurisdictions research and development organizations such as Economic Development Committees, City Planning Commissions, Planning and Development Departments, University Research Groups, CAMPS, etc., may have already surveyed the unmet public service needs and developed some personnel projections.

If such has happened, then reports and the background experience of staff could provide both relevant data and logical impressions of public service needs, position requirements and manpower projections.

Questionnaires and Report Forms. Simple, direct forms requesting information on *program priorities* and the *number of additional positions and people* needed immediately, and for the next six months or so, can be very useful in getting basic information quickly and in a format readily translatable for cost estimates and personnel planning.

None of the above suggested methods are mutually exclusive. They can be used by themselves or in various combinations. In addition, there are other methods that governmental jurisdictions may find more effective locally in getting the Public Service Employment Program off the ground in the shortest possible time. For example, depending on the Personnel Department, the Office of the Manpower Coordinator, or the Office of the Chief Executive to arbitrarily determine the first quota of public service positions on the basis of past experience in program operations and the unemployment situation; or designating a knowledgeable public official to conduct a rapid survey of position and person requirements through telephone and personal contacts; or, instructing operating departments to request the Personnel Office to provide them with transitional public service employees up to 1 percent, 5 percent, or 10 percent of their current work force, depending on the size of their departments in proportion to the total public employee work force.

However, even in developing position and personnel requirements in the most expeditious manner, certain objectives of the Emergency Employment Act of 1971 should be kept in mind:

1. Public Service employment programs should be designed to provide transitional employment in jobs providing needed public services.
2. Special consideration should be given to filling jobs which provide sufficient prospects for advancement or suitable continued employment by providing complimentary training and manpower services.
3. Public service jobs, to the extent feasible, should be provided in occupational fields most likely to expand within the public or private sector as the unemployment rate drops.
4. The program must not result in the displacement of currently employed workers, or in partial displacement such as reduction in non-overtime hours, wages, or employment benefits.
5. Public service jobs should not be substituted for existing federally assisted jobs. (Employing agencies will be required to maintain or provide linkages with upgrading and other manpower programs to help transitional public service employees find regular upward careers in the same or other fields of work.)

Determining the Extent and Characteristics of the Unemployed Population

The overriding objective of the Emergency Employment Act of 1971 is to hire the *unemployed and underemployed* in jobs providing needed public services. Knowledge of some basic facts about *how many* and *what kinds* of persons are out of work, and available for employment, would be very helpful to a Public Service Employment Program, even in its earliest stages. In particular, even general information about the major breakdowns on such factors as Vietnam military service, age levels, ethnic composition, and sex groupings could help shape the types and numbers of public service positions to be filled on the first go-around.

Current information on the numbers of unemployed, with some major breakdowns on demographic factors, are readily available to states and most large cities through official federal government sources. However, since the scope of the federal government's unemployment statistics primarily is focused on the nation as a whole, the states, and the Standard Metropolitan Statistical Areas, information on the unemployment situation may not be as readily available for the smaller cities and counties.

These smaller governmental jurisdictions may then have to look to sources other than federal government agencies for the basic unemployment data most useful for developing the initial phases of their Public Service Employment programs. Some of these other sources are:

1. *Local offices of the State Employment Service,* which may be able to provide a basic approximation of the number of persons out of work, and available for work, in the area, with some breakdown as to veteran status, sex groupings, ethnic characteristics, and manpower training enrollments.
2. *Community manpower agencies (i.e., Model Cities, CAMPS, etc.).* The outreach offices of such agencies could provide both general and detailed information on applicants and referrals for work or training opportunities. In particular, information from these sources could be most helpful in defining the unemployment situation among the disadvantaged and "hard-core" unemployable segments of the population.
3. *Veteran organizations and local draft boards* might be possible sources of information on Vietnam era veterans.
4. *Welfare offices* can provide data on the number of persons in the area receiving welfare because of unemployment and who may be available for work.
5. *Labor unions* can provide information on union members who are out of work.
6. *Local government personnel office* can provide data on the number of persons applying for public employment.
7. *Quasi-Public agencies* (i.e., the Urban League, National Alliance of Business-men, Opportunities Industrialization Center, Settlement Houses, etc.), can provide information on numbers and characteristics of disadvantaged unem-ployed job-seekers.
8. *Specialized government organizations* (e.g. Committee on Urban Oppor-tunity, Veterans Departments, Concentrated Employment Program, Depart-ment of Human Resources, etc.). Previous studies and reports may provide information on general and specialized unemployment situations within inner-city or urban poverty areas.

Some of the above listed sources could be very helpful in providing readily available unemployment information and data that can be used in the initial "start-up" phase of the Public Service Employment Program. Others of the sources would, perhaps, be more useful in planning and implementing long-range program objectives and goals.

Another possibility in developing the "start-up" program is the use of official statistics from the Bureau of Labor Statistics and the Bureau of Census on a extrapolated basis, for example, estimating the labor work force and the number of kinds of unemployed in the jurisdiction in proportion to the labor work force and the number and kinds of unemployed in the state or the closest Standard Metropolitan Statistical Area.

Getting the Unemployed and Underemployed Person
on the Public Service Rolls

The major objective in the Public Service Employment Program is to bring the unemployed or underemployed persons into public service as rapidly as possible. The question is *how to do it* within the flexibilities of the local civil service merit system with *the least possible adverse impact* on both the regular personnel system and the regular government employees. This major issue is made up of a number of individual, yet interlocking, subordinate issues such as:

1. What system should be used to *hire* the eligible persons for transitional employment?
2. What should be done to *publicize* public service job openings under the program and *recruit* transitional public service employees?
2. How do we *examine* the applicants and *select* from among the eligible participants?
4. Who should be responsible for *selecting and appointing* the transitional public service employees?

Civil service rules, policies, and regulations will, for the most part, govern how each state and general local government will meet these issues. [a] However, there is generally sufficient flexibility in any civil service system to consider and apply alternative methods and processes to help meet the dual objectives of: (1) Moving fast to get the Public Service Employment Program started with the first allocations of federal money; and (2) Hiring the first group of transitional public service employees within the spirit of the applicable public personnel management system.

Some examples of alternatives possible with the flexibility of civil service or personnel mangement systems are:

1. The system for hiring

   a. Hiring the initial group as "temporary" or "provisional" employees, outside the competitive appointment system.
   b. Within the competitive system, hiring transitional public service employees under "indefinite term appointments."
   c. Consider all transitional public service appointments as "emergency" appointments, using special established provisions for the rapid hiring of eligible participants.

---

[a]See Guidelines issued by the U.S. Civil Service Commission for Reevaluation of Civil Service Requirements and Practices to Eliminate Artificial Barriers to Employment and Advancement.

2. The position structure

   a. Using already established job classifications such as administrative trainees, clerical assistants, etc., to serve as the entrance point for rapid appointment.

   b. Establishing new basic classifications with minimal basic qualifications within the established structure which can be used for initial job appointments.

   c. Using general job descriptions in the major work categories, such as: clerk; public service aide; assistant; supervisor; paraprofessional; etc., for initial appointment.

   d. Establishing an entirely new classification group for transitional Public Service employees which provides for initial entry into public employment in an emergency situation.

   e. Adding additional positions to existing regular career classifications to be filled on a non-competitive basis.

3. Reaching potential participants. The problem will *not* be to find sufficient participants for this program. It will be to give proper priority to those for whom the program is primarily designed. Care should be taken not to so generalize the publicity that persons not meeting basic criteria will be asking for consideration. With the above in mind basic criteria will be asking for consideration. With the above in mind any or all of the following could be helpful in reaching the target segments of the unemployed population:

   a. Contact former laid-off employees (who have been out of work for at least thirty days) either by telephone or by letter.

   b. Issue local newspaper release which ties in with national picture, but emphasizes local consideration on the number and kinds of job openings, and the opportunities for *special veterans, unemployed* graduates of manpower training programs, etc. To be even more helpful to applicants the contact point for further information could be identified, such as: personnel or reception office, Public Employment Service Office, and representatives of community organizations.

   c. Develop contacts with such cooperating agencies as: State Employment Service, Welfare Department, community outreach offices, Manpower Training activities, unions, and veteran organizations.

   d. Have the personnel office or government office performing similar function keep data on applicants that appear to meet the criteria for public employment participation, or refer all inquiries to one central point in the governmental organization.

4. The selection process. There are at least three major problems involved in the selection process. *First,* there are apt to be more applicants for transitional public service employment than there are jobs available. *Second,* there are a

number of provisions included in the Emergency Act of 1971 which limit the choice of selection, such as: all transitional public service employees except for necessary technical, supervisory, and administrative personnel shall be selected from unemployed or underemployed persons; and, special consideration will be given to certain groups — Vietnam veterans, older workers, non-English-speaking persons, disadvantaged young persons eighteen years or older entering the labor force, etc. *Third,* applicants for public service employment under most state, county or city systems must meet certain basic legal requirements such as citizenship, residence, minimum age and other age limits.[6]

It is almost certain that, regardless of the personnel system, preliminary screening would be necessary in determining who among the crowd of applicants should be selected. Which preliminary screening methods could be used effectively depends on local situations and governing rules and regulations. Some of the alternative methods that governmental organizations can find helpful, either by themselves or in various combinations are:

a. Application forms. These are probably the most common method now in use for preliminary screenings. Since most application forms are used for a great variety of jobs in the organization, the addition of a *supplemental form* focusing directly on such factors as unemployment, time, and location of active military service, and training taken at any of the manpower programs could prove to be a useful tool.

On the other hand, some jurisdictions may find a *form specially constructed* for the Public Service Employment program to be more effective in the screening of applicants for transitional public service jobs.

b. Oral interviews. Fast preliminary screening can sometimes be done by oral interviews, either by individual interviewers or by group panels. This method could be most effective when the interviewers are well trained, stick to a well-prepared question list, are objective in attitude as well as expression, and are not overwhelmed by hordes of applicants. Conversely, lengthy period of waiting for the interviews can be frustrating and irksome to both applicant and interviewer.

c. Other organizations. To help relieve the pressure on the employing organization and enable it to carry on with its normal flow of business, other *public or quasi-public organizations,* closely related to significant segments of the target population, can be used to do the preliminary screening in conformance with prerequisite requirements, for example: local employment services — veteran referrals, registered applicants, etc.,

---

[b]Citizenship and age limits are not requirements under Part 55, 29 U.S. Code, Grants under the Emergency Employment Act of 1971.

Welfare Department — welfare recipients who meet the criteria for participation; public manpower agencies (such as Model Cities, CEP, Public Service Careers, WIN, etc.) — inner-city residents, manpower training enrollees, economically deprived, etc; government agencies — Veterans Administration, U.S. Civil Service Commission, OEO offices, etc.; community and private organizations — unions (for laid-off union members), Veteran Organizations (for Vietnam and Korean vets), manufacturing firms (for laid-off workers), Urban League and similar outreach organizations (for disadvantaged, chronically unemployable, part-time workers), etc.

d. Testing methods. Virtually all state and local government systems use a variety of testing procedures to both "screen-in" and "screen-out" potential applicants for public employment. Most common procedures are: written tests, oral tests, performance tests, unassembled tests (reviews of education and experience listed in application).

Variations of all such testing procedures can be useful in the initial start-up phase of the Public Service Employment program, particularly in the screening of large numbers of applicants. How, where, and what kinds of tests should be used will depend on how fast they can be administered and rated, their relationship to the really important elements for adequate job performance, and their impact on the predominant groups of unemployed or underemployed persons applying for transitional public service employment.

5. The appointment process. Normally, the head (or his delegated representative) of the employing organization (unit, section, department, bureau, etc.) selects the candidate for appointment to the position from among a list of pre-screened candidates certified or referred by the Personnel Office. Usually, the appointing authority reviews all the documentation, interviews all the candidates and, based on his best judgment, makes his final selection in compliance with local governing civil service rules and regulations. This method of selection is at its best when sufficient time is available to make well-considered, deliberate judgements on the relative strengths and weaknesses of each prospective candidate. When faced with very short deadlines, urgency of processing demand, and need to place persons on government rolls as soon as possible, some other methods may be more practical, such as:

a. The personnel office (or similar unit in the organization) pre-screens and interviews all applicants and makes the final selections for certain kinds of positions, for all positions below a certain salary level, or for all positions to be filled;

b. Interdepartmental panels interview all candidates referred by the personnel office (or similar organization), and the individual representatives make final selections for the employing organization;

c. Chronological selection. The first qualified persons to apply for the positions are selected. Variations of this method also can be used giving due consideration to special groups such as Vietnam and Korean vets, etc.

d. Outside agencies. Providing outside agencies such as local state employment offices, community action groups, welfare departments, etc., with job orders and qualifications for specific types of positions and having them refer final candidates for job placement.

e. Direct selection by departments. Give heads of departments authority to recruit, screen, and appoint eligible participants to transitional public service positions within their departments. Information then about who was appointed, positions filled, and dates of entrance on duty are given to the personnel office for administrative processing.

The above list of alternative methods are neither exclusive or complete. The staff of many governmental personnel organizations drawing upon their understanding of the local situation, past experience and knowledge of applicable laws, rules, policies, and regulations can very likely develop other methods within the confines of the personnel merit management system that can serve them equally as well (or better) in the rapid employment of eligible participants.

Placing the Newly-Hired Transitional Public Service Employees Within the Governmental Organization

After hiring the public employee, the general practice is to have him report for duty to assigned supervisors in the employing department, after completing the necessary physical examination and administrative processing. Normally, the employing department is prepared for the new employee with respect to space, equipment, and availability of supervisory personnel. However, in the emergency situation of hiring many new employees within a very short period of time, the normal process may not always be useable.

The employing departments may need more time to get the necessary work equipment, or space will not be available for a week or two, or supervisors are tied up with other projects for the next few days. Under these conditions, the natural tendency would be to hold off putting the new employees on the rolls until all conditions are satisfactory. But, with the commitment to get the Public Service Employment program started almost immediately, and to get the new public service employees on the rolls by a certain date, there will be little possibility that delaying the actual entrance on duty until optimum conditions are met will be feasible.

Again, in a situation of this nature, consideration of other alternatives such as the following might be necessary:

1. Establishing a totally new Department of Emergency Manpower within the governmental organization with the major function that of a "reception and holding" unit. The transitional public service employees hired during the emergency period can be directly assigned to basic positions in that department. Operating organizations throughout the government jurisdiction can supply a complement of supervisory help and necessary equipment. During the first few days of employment the new employees could get general orientation to the operations, functions and procedures of the organization. In addition, the personnel people could check over the abilities, skills, capacities, etc., of the new employees for more effective position assignment to the various operating departments. Then, as the target or assigned positions open up for operation the new employees move out to their regular assignments.

2. Designating one established office or department in the organization to serve the "reception and orientation" unit for the first (and succeeding) group of transitional public service employees until the regularly assigned offices and departments are ready for them. Such an office could be the personnel office, the Office of Manpower Coordinator, or the Department of Human Resources.

3. Designating a unit within the operating department to serve for "reception and orientation" for the new employees coming to that department until the employees can be assigned to their designated positions under the regular supervisors.

14 Job Task Analysis

SIDNEY A. FINE

The administration is very concerned now about day care and homemaking. And as my dear wife is fond of pointing out, the "Dictionary of Occupational Titles" assigns the lowest conceivable skill level to a foster mother and nursery teacher aide. So here we are on the verge of sending perhaps a million mothers into the labor market, and presumably, somebody is going to have to take care of their children, and we are prepared to have them cared for by workers the Dictionary considers less skilled than a dog trainer.

The Dictionary notwithstanding, there *is* a technique to being a homemaker or a foster mother; there is something to know about it. Knowledge, technology, tools, and skills are needed. Not everybody can be a homemaker. Just as not everybody can be a job analyst, a career developer, and a job developer. Merely monkeying with job descriptions and changing words like "taking instructions" to "coordinating" to get a higher grade doesn't make a job developer.

That is the situation. It is not just a *word* game. There is something more to it.

Our point of departure at Upjohn, in relation to this whole problem, is that we look upon the government as a very logical place for career opportunities, for the government to be the employer of first opportunity.

The government has merit systems. It has a long tradition of careers, of promoting people, and of giving training. Maybe it hasn't always been the best, but it is a logical place for this kind of thing to begin.

Public service careers make a lot of sense. We all know of the great need for many of these occupations. But they are not going to work if all we are going to do is hire people at the very bottom — a situation which we now have in many places — and then keep them there in dead-end jobs. We can't repeat that situation again.

At Upjohn we faced this problem, and tried to deal with the current happenings the best way we knew how. We felt that the existing knowledge, with all of its limitations — and we don't really know enough — could be organized into a technology, so that career developers, job developers, people assigned these responsibilities, could acquire this technology and thereby know what they were doing when they started designing jobs in welfare agencies, in nurseries and day care situations, in antipollution programs for people entering the labor force.

One of the fundamental elements we teach is that you cannot make this opportunity idea work if you think only in terms of careers for the disadvantaged or some peripheral group of that nature. It is careers, new careers, for everybody.

The whole job system — certainly in the public service area — has to be examined, reconsidered and, to a certain extent, reorganized, so that not only is room made for people who have been kept out of the mainstream, but that actually new life is injected into the very jobs that do exist. There is a tremendous, so to speak, traffic jam in the existing structure.

With all due respect to Phil Rutledge, who is head of the Human Resources Agency in the District of Columbia[a], using the technqiue we have developed to study some of the agencies in the District, we found, for example, that there was very little difference between the jobs of so-called Grade 5's and Grade 7's and Grade 9's and Grade 11's except for seniority. Functionally, they didn't differ very much. And this creates a deterioration of morale; this creates a very sick situation. Where are you going to bring the new people? What are they going to do? How are they going to grow? Where are they going to move? The people who are there, right now, are not moving, they are not going anywhere.

This is not only characteristic of the District. It just happened that the District was handy when we studied those jobs. It is characteristic of merit systems throughout the country — federal, local, state. It is an endemic situation. So when I say "a new career for everybody," I mean precisely that. The reconsideration has to be made.

I want to go briefly into a few of the elements of a career opportunities system, and then I am going to show you a tool. Technology should have some tools. I am going to show you a tool that we have developed. It looks gimmicky. In fact, it is gimmicky. But you shouldn't keep your eye on the gimmick. Don't look at the hole; look at the doughnut, in other words!

But first, let us consider what are the elements of a career opportunity system. We take the position in this training that Upjohn gives that the units of the technology of job design tasks and that the tasks themselves are expressed as statements which specifically relate worker behavior to organizational objectives. These two things, worker behavior and organizational objectives, must be tied together in a very controlled way. These statements are controlled for reliability and for validity by seven scales — six of which were originally developed in the Department of Labor in connection with the new "Dictionary of Occupational Titles," which I had something to do with, and another one which I developed subsequently, a scale of instructions.

These controlled task statements enable one to develop the essential ingredients of a career opportunity system, whether it is a ladder or a lattice,

---

[a]Since the time of the Seminar, Mr. Rutledge has become Deputy Administrator of HEW's Social and Rehabilitative Services.

namely, training requirements, qualifications, performance standards, and instructions. A few words about each of these follows.

Training Requirements. - Training requirements for each task are described as functional and specific. By functional training we mean that which provides general ability, such as the ability to manage the language, the ability to type, the ability to operate machines. By specific content training we mean that which has to do with the particular plant, its particular situation, its particular procedures to produce its product and make it marketable — two special, different kinds of training.

We identified the functional training with general education, and we identified the specific content training with specific vocational training.

We think that the one is properly the business of a general educational system, and the other is the proper business of the institution — the work organization itself, the public service organization, if you will.

Qualifications. - In the matter of qualification we are functionally oriented, not credential oriented. All of our scales describe what a person has to do and what he needs to know in functional active terms. They don't say you need eight grades or twelve grades or ten grades or a bachelor's degree or anything like that; if a worker knows it and has done it, that's it.

The qualifications scales are in terms of reasoning, which is concerned with how many variables, concrete or abstract, a worker can handle; with mathematics; and with language. And these are all expressed in functional terms.

Performance Standards. - The third essential ingredient of a career opportunity system is the matter of performance standards. We defined these in terms of descriptive performance standards, which are the ones that you usually hear from the supervisor — in other words, "Get this job done as fast as you can," or "Be as neat as you can," and numerical standards, which are like, "I want this job done here by the close of business today."

Now these are two different kinds of standards, and they each have different purposes. They both can be developed from an explicit task statement of the kind that I have described.

Instructions. - The fourth and last consideration that is contained in this kind of material is the mix of prescribed and discretionary content in jobs. This formulation is a British formulation by a man whom some of you may know, Elliott Jaques, who has written books called *The Measurement of Responsibility* and *Equitable Payment*. These concepts have to do with those aspects of a job in which a person can exercise discretion, as opposed to those which are prescribed for him. We see in this concept, particularly discretionary as opposed to prescribed content, the leading edge of growth, and growth, of course, is an essential ingredient in a career opportunity system.

Consider that a career opportunity focuses not only upon what the person can do to give a service, to contribute to productivity, but what he himself can do to grow in the situation. What is the leading edge of growth for an individual? It is the discretionary duties in the job.

These then are the elements that go to make up a career opportunity system.

I say there is a technology to all this. There is something to know. When you apply these techniques, you produce task statements, and then you put the task statements and their elaboration into a storage and retrieval system. We use cards, notched around the edges; a very elementary system, a storage and retrieval information system. They contain the task statements and all of the information is on the card. Those of you who were in World War II will remember that a Form 21 controlled our destinies.

Each card represented a person in those days. Here each card represents a task, and all of the information that I have mentioned to you is punched at the edge of the card. Now don't get upset with the idea that there needs to be a card for each task in the universe of work; there are not that many tasks in this world. It turns out, using these techniques, that there are a given number of modular tasks in any given field.

Let's say that in the welfare industry, where we have concentrated, or in the mental health industry, another one in which we have worked, there may be 250 or 300 modular tasks. There are then many other tasks, maybe 1,000 more, which reflect different degrees of specific content, but functionally they are the same kinds of tasks. The difference between an eye doctor and an ear, nose, and throat doctor performing certain examining tasks is the specific content. The functional nature of the task will remain quite the same. That is what I mean by the difference between a modular task, and a variation in specific content.

For example, there are approximately 100 tasks that are modular for various aspects of the welfare industry. On each there is a task statement. Here are the performance standards. Here is the training content, as I have described. And now you can begin to design jobs because the cards are basic units. These units can be organized in terms of similarity in training, similarity in standards, similarity in complexity of functional level, or some essential variation.

Knowledge of these units gives a supervisor, a manpower planner, a great deal of know-how, a great deal of flexibility. And if this same material is in the hands of the merit system person, the staff training person, the organizational planner, and the supervisor on the county line trying to get the job done, they can then start communicating in some sensible way.

We have trained people as I have just described in over twenty-five states. It is slow going. It takes time. It is unfamiliar. But we have the system now going in approximately eight states.

In Utah, for example, we have already put together and designed social work aide jobs for women, AFDC mothers. Social agencies have hired them, and they are working out extremely well. That is, they are performing their functions expeditiously and demonstrating growth potential.

There are many problems, but most of the problems are with the agency — learning to absorb the new workers, learning to supervise them, learning to deal with the fact that they learn more quickly than it was expected they would learn.

We have the same program going on right now, on a fairly large scale, in Michigan, and Wisconsin, and in a number of other places.

In Utah we put together these elementary jobs that paid only $375 a month. For the mothers who came to work on them, it did not even mean an increase in income, incidentally, since some of them had five, six, or seven children. They gave up their health care, they gave up their nursery care — they gave up almost as much as they got.

But they did it willingly. They were very anxious to go to work. It was a tremendous lift to them. You had to see it to believe it, to hear their voices, as I have them on tape.

When the announcement was made for this particular job — Social Work Aide, Grade — I don't know, Sub-One, whatever they call it — college graduates applied for this position. And the big problem in Utah was, how do you discriminate against college graduates in this situation and really keep the jobs open for welfare mothers?

When we started this program about ten months ago, it wasn't so bad. But since then the unemployment problem has worsened. This is one problem that we don't know how to handle. In other words, college graduates who have been dis-employed from jobs paying ten to twenty thousand in one situation or the other are asking "Why shouldn't I get this job? I am qualified." So here is a problem that we haven't got the answer to, yet. But it is very interesting that we have this kind of competition for such jobs at the present time.

15

Planning a Public Employment Program:
The Kalamazoo Experience

E. EARL WRIGHT

Introduction

The county of Kalamazoo, a Standard Metropolitan Statistical Area (SMSA), and the city of Kalamazoo, the largest city within the county, were designated as program agents under the Emergency Employment Act of 1971. With the exception of participation as employing and cooperating agents under the Public Service Careers Program (PSC) and the Supplemental Training and Employment Program (STEP), neither unit of government had been previously involved to any major extent with federally funded manpower activities. The EEA program, therefore, posed a new and unique set of challenges to these governmental units concerning the planning, implementation, and administration of a relatively sizable public employment program.

Some Economic and Other Features of the Kalamazoo Area

The Kalamazoo situation is undoubtedly similar to that of other SMSAs — large and small — throughout the United States. The ability to finance improved and expanded public services is becoming increasingly difficult within the constraints of local revenues. In contrast to the past, relatively high levels of unemployment locally appear to be approximating a long-term rather than a temporary phenomenon. Although perhaps on a much smaller and less acute scale, governmental units in the Kalamazoo SMSA are beginning to experience some of the same basic problems encountered by the larger SMSAs.

Population, employment, and economic features of the Kalamazoo area have definite implications for a public employment program that is designed to be implemented within the jurisdictions of different governmental units within a single labor market area. The relatively large number of governmental units eligible to be designated as employing agents under the Kalamazoo EEA program and the distribution of employment and population within the area create additional problems that accentuate the need for a thoroughly planned and coordinated program between the county and city of Kalamazoo.

The Kalamazoo SMSA, with a population of 201,550, includes four cities, fifteen townships, and five villages. Within these governmental units are

303

numerous commissions and boards that could qualify as employing agents under the public employment program. The city of Kalamazoo accounts for 85,500 or 42.2 percent of the total SMSA population. The population of the other governmental units ranges from less than 1,000 for some of the villages to approximately 34,000 for the second largest city. Approximately 95 percent of the total SMSA population is white, with blacks accounting for most of the remainder of the population. Furthermore, over 80 percent of the black population is concentrated within the city of Kalamazoo.

Unemployment in the Kalamazoo area became a major concern during the second quarter of 1970. Since May of 1970, the unemployment rate for the Kalamazoo labor market area has been above 5 percent for every month. During the first six months of 1971, the unemployment rate ranged from 7.4 percent in January to 9 percent in June. Kalamazoo was thus classified as a substantial unemployment area during this period. This trend departs rather dramatically from the trend in unemployment for the area over the 1964-69 period, during which time the highest annual rate of unemployment was only 3.5 percent.

The high level of unemployment locally in 1970 and 1971 obviously reflects national economic conditions. During the past three years, however, the Kalamazoo economy has also experienced some marked changes in the distribution of its labor force. Over the period 1968-70, employment in manufacturing declined by 1,800 jobs. During the same period, however, nonmanufacturing and government employment increased by 2,000 and 1,800 workers, respectively.

The above paragraphs provide a general indication of some of the economic and employment features of the Kalamazoo area and suggest some of the considerations that had to be dealt with in planning and implementing the EEA program locally. Some of these problems were probably encountered by many of the approximately 700 governmental units that were allocated EEA grants with the probability that many different approaches were taken regarding the implementation of the EEA program. The remainder of this chapter is focused on the steps taken by the city and county of Kalamazoo to plan and implement a public employment program that could overcome a number of obstacles in a minimum of time to satisfy the overall objectives of providing needed public services and of reducing unemployment to the maximum extent possible with the federal funds provided. The experiences of these two local units of government should be applicable to smaller SMSAs throughout the nation.

EEA Funding for the Kalamazoo Area

Under grants allocated to governmental units with unemployment in excess of 4.5 percent (Section 5), $187,900 was designated for the city of Kalamazoo and $395,500 for the county. Following the announcement of the allocation of these funds on August 12, 1971, both the city and county submitted initial funding proposals that were intended to obligate 20 percent of their EEA grants and to allow program agents to begin hiring immediately.

Before full funding proposals for Section 5 funding were finalized, the governor of Michigan expressed interest in turning over to designated cities and counties the state's share of Section 5 allocations for areas where local program agents had been designated. Regional Manpower Administration representatives and the Governor's EEA Task Force met with Michigan's program agents on September 2 to explain the conditions under which the state would waive their funds to the cities and counties. The conditions that were finally set are summarized below:

1. Each program agent must identify the number, types, and cost of jobs to be created with the state share of the EEA allocations. The deadline established for submitting this information was September 9.
2. Each employing agent, if other than the program agent, must be identified. Decisions concerning the use of the state's share of funds must be based upon due consideration of the needs of local units and subdivisions of governments within their geographical boundaries, including school districts and tax-supported community colleges.
3. A statement of "goals" concerning the target groups to be hired with the state's share of the allocations must be submitted to the state. These goals should clearly indicate that priority in hiring would be given to veterans of Vietnam and Korea, persons on welfare, and minority groups.
4. If the aforementioned conditions were met, the state would waive 100 percent of its share of funds to the local program agents provided that all of the funds would be used for wages and fringe benefits of the EEA enrollees. Although the state would retain the right to review and monitor the cities' and counties' programs, the program agents would be responsible and accountable to the Regional Manpower Administration for the implementation and administration of their programs involving the state's share.

Both of the Kalamazoo area program agents were obviously receptive to the governor's proposal, although the county did have some concern over the establishment of goals for hiring without first determining its ability to meet the goals requested by the state. This concern was predicated on the fact that blacks and other nonwhites accounted for only 1.3 percent of the out-county population (county population excluding the city of Kalamazoo). Also, available information indicated that a relatively small proportion of the area's welfare recipients resided in the out-county area. The decision, however, was made by both the city and the county to meet the state's conditions to the extent possible and to apply for the state's share of Section 5 funds. This resulted in the city receiving an additional $253,800 and the county an additional $98,800. The

Kalamazoo program agents' Section 5 full-funding proposals, which were submitted by September 10, totaled $441,700 for the city and $494,300 for the county.

Under the EEA allocations to areas that had experienced 6 percent or more unemployment for three consecutive months (Section 6), the city and county were allocated additional funds amounting to $185,300 and $191,900, respectively. Considerable confusion centered around the allocation of these funds relating to their required application in the local areas. According to the Department of Labor guidelines, these funds were to provide jobs for residents of high unemployment areas within the program agents' jurisdictions. For the Kalamazoo area, however, estimates of unemployment existed only on an SMSA or countywide basis. The entire county, therefore, was designated as a high unemployment area. Following the allocations of these funds by the Department of Labor on September 21, the city and county met with Regional Manpower Administration representatives and had their concerns clarified regarding the requirements for Section 6 funds. Full-funding proposals, therefore, were submitted by the October 4 target date, and both program agents were then in position, contingent upon Labor Department approval, to begin implementing their programs which involved a total of $1.3 million for public service jobs.

Establishing the Administrative Framework for the Local EEA Program

The time span between the allocation of funds to designated program agents under the EEA and the date on which full-funding proposals were to be submitted for Section 5 funds was approximately four weeks. For many cities and counties, planning within this period for a new and unique employment program posed many challenges. The planning process was even more complicated because of the delays centering around the receipt of program guidelines and the changing interpretations concerning these directives from the Department of Labor. For the first two weeks technical assistance from the Regional Manpower Administration was for all practical purposes nonexistent.

As indicated on the following pages, however, the city and county of Kalamazoo had started making tentative plans for possible participation in some form of public employment program prior to their designation as program agents. Even with advance planning, which many areas probably did not experience, the establishment of the administrative framework and operative goals for the EEA program proved to be the most difficult, but perhaps most important, task encountered by local officials.

Planning Prior to Allocation of Funds

Prior to the passage of the Emergency Employment Act, the city and county of Kalamazoo actually began making plans concerning the anticipated PEP program. During the latter part of May 1971 staff members of the W.E. Upjohn Institute for Employment Research in Kalamazoo met with city and county officials to brief them on the status of the then pending legislation concerning public service employment and the possible implications of the anticipated passage of such legislation for the Kalamazoo area. Taking into consideration information provided by the Institute's Washington office, the local unemployment situation, and previous experience concerning the share of funds received by Michigan in other manpower programs, the Institute's local staff estimated that funding for the Kalamazoo area might be sufficient to provide public service jobs for between 125 and 175 unemployed workers. Although this estimate was made without adequate consideration given to a number of important factors, and by necessity involved many unknowns, it did serve the purpose of establishing parameters for initial planning purposes.

The purposes of the informational sessions that were held with local public officials were to provide them with the most up-to-date information available and to persuade them to begin planning for participation in some form of a public employment program. Although there were some reservations on the part of the local officials concerning the actual passage of this type of a manpower program and definite concern that smaller units of government would not fare too well in the allocation of funds, there was obvious enthusiasm for a public employment program and total agreement that initial planning should proceed immediately.

Subsequent to the initial meetings in May, the city and county began the process of assessing their public service needs, establishing priorities, and then translating the needs and priorities into possible job positions. The planning that took place prior to the actual allocation of funds also involved an ad hoc committee from the Kalamazoo Cooperative Area Manpower Planning Committee (CAMPS). During this period attention was focused on the possible relationship of a public employment program to other manpower efforts and on the administrative mechanics that would be required for the implementation of the program.

Although it was not possible to resolve all of the concerns, or perhaps even to identify many of the problems that might be associated with a public employment program, the time and effort that were expended during the preallocation period were judged to be quite beneficial to the local officials. For one thing, the local officials, together with the CAMPS committee, were provided current information on the directions that public employment legislation was taking. Second, this period served as an ideal time to orient local governmental officials and administrators to federal manpower programs. Third, the need for, and benefits of, a close-working relationship between the city and county became quite apparent. Fourth, and perhaps of the most importance, the planning enabled the units of government to consider seriously their public employment needs and to begin structuring priorities and possible approaches for meeting these needs.

Local Goals for Public Employment Program

After assessing the possible problems that could be encountered in implementing a public employment program and after reviewing the Department of Labor guidelines for the Emergency Employment Act, one of the major tasks of the local program agents was to finalize the administrative mechanics that would assure that local goals for public employment could be achieved within the EEA requirements. This task was obviously complicated because of the contradictory nature of the Emergency Employment Act legislation and guidelines. Furthermore, the local agents desired to accomplish certain goals, the attainment of which appeared to be limited seriously by certain aspects of the EEA guidelines. As attempts were made to secure assistance from the Regional Manpower Administration, it became quite apparent that federal officials would not be able to provide the necessary direction that was desired. The pressure to begin hiring immediately and the apparent lack of information provided to the Regional Manpower Administrator's office ruled out any in-depth technical assistance to local program agents. The establishment of specific local goals and objectives that could provide direction to the local program agents, and at the same time assure that the intent and spirit of the legislation could be carried out, therefore became a local responsibility.

Establishing priorities for distributing jobs to the unemployed. The requirement of hiring only unemployed and underemployed workers was obviously acceptable to local program agents, but was of such a general nature that it provided little direction. The delineation of certain groups that were to be given "special consideration" for employment only compounded the problem because of the large number of groups identified. The various groups – veterans, welfare recipients, minorities, persons under eighteen or over forty-five, workers displaced because of technological change, migrant workers, persons whose native tongue is not English, and other workers who come from socioeconomic backgrounds usually associated with substantial unemployment or underemployment – encompassed almost the full spectrum of the unemployed in the community. The guidelines, in specifying further that these persons are to be employed in proportion to their relative unemployment in the community, were of no help because such estimates of unemployment by target group are nonexistent for the Kalamazoo area. In this regard, the only goal that provided specific direction was a subsequent directive from the Labor Department indicating that program agents should attempt to hire one-third veterans. Beyond that point, the local program agents had little real direction regarding the distribution of jobs among the unemployed.

The only source of data that could provide any indication of the relative unemployment status of the specified target groups was recent job applicant data compiled on a areawide basis by the Michigan Employment Security Commission. It was recognized that the job applicant data fell far short of covering all of the unemployed workers in the area. As a first step, however, this information did provide a rough estimate of the unemployment status of some of the groups that were specified to receive special consideration for employment under the program. Without the intent of excluding any of the target groups, the city of Kalamzaoo established as a goal the hiring of at least 33 percent veterans, 25-30 percent minorities, and 15 percent welfare recipients. With the exception of the goal for hiring one-third veterans, the county's goals for these target groups were lower than the city's because of the different population composition within its jurisdiction and some concern of how it could achieve higher goals and still be consistent with the EEA guidelines concerning residency requirements. Furthermore, as a general consideration, both program agents preferred that their EEA jobs be allocated to those unemployed persons with the greatest employment needs.

The city and county were both interested in planning and implementing the EEA program within the framework of existing personnel policies and programs. For several years, the city had emphasized its affirmative action program, and the County Board of Commissioners had just recently enacted an affirmative action policy with the specified objective of increasing its number of minority employees as soon as possible. As noted earlier, the minority population in the Kalamazoo area is relatively small (out-county – 1.3 percent; city – 10 percent), and is comprised primarily of blacks and Spanish-Americans. Both program agents, however, wanted to apply their affirmative action policies under the EEA program. On the surface, this goal appeared to be consistent with the intent of the EEA, particularly since minority groups were one of the groups that were specified to receive special consideration for employment.

Other directives from the Department of Labor concerning the eligibility requirements for participants in the program, however, appeared to be inconsistent with the local program agents' objectives for hiring a relatively large proportion of minorities. The initial Department of Labor guidelines specified that participants should reside in the geographic area over which the program agent has jurisdiction. An interpretation of this requirement (which was later rescinded) from the Regional Manpower Administration indicated that the residency requirements applied even to the selection of participants by employing agents. The residency requirements for participants would seriously limit the county's ability to meet its affirmative action goals and were inconsistent with its current hiring policy. Although practically 100 percent of all county employees are residents of the county, hiring for county positions is obviously not limited to out-county residents.

The residency requirement, because of its adverse impact on one of the program agent's primary goals, accentuated the need for the two program agents to combine their programs in regard to the selection of enrollees and to establish mutually acceptable goals for hiring EEA participants.

Achieving an equitable distribution of funds among employing agents. As required by the Department of Labor guidelines, program agents were to distribute EEA funds on an equitable basis among city and county levels of government including public agencies that are independent of the supervision of the program agents. Other than indicating that consideration should be given to the size of population, the size and severity of unemployment, and the number of public service jobs at each level of government, the guidelines failed to provide specific directions and to delineate some of the factors that should be assessed before employing agents could be designated.

Because the general nature of the guidelines indicated that practically all local units of government within the city and county jurisdictions were eligible for participation in the EEA program, the local program agents were confronted with the problem of how to distribute funds in a manner that would create a maximum impact from the program. In simple terms, the choice was between parceling the funds out to units of government and local agencies based on the rather general considerations of population size and the number of public service jobs requested or distributing the funds on a more substantive basis.

The local program agents chose the latter approach, which necessarily involved more time and effort on their part, but which hopefully would lead to a more thoroughly planned and executed program. As an initial step, all eligible units of government and local agencies within the program agents' jurisdictions were provided copies of the legislation and guidelines and were requested to submit requests for funding as employing agents. Furthermore, it was specified that each unit should establish priorities for funding giving consideration to the public service needs within their area, the ability for the jobs to be filled from the ranks of the unemployed, and the units of government's ability to absorb the majority of those persons to be hired under the program into their regular work force.

The aforementioned procedure resulted in several of the program agents not requesting EEA funding. Some of the smaller governmental units were skeptical of the program with its involved and seemingly inconsistent requirements. Others were hesitant to create jobs and employ workers that in all probability they could not retain when funding for the program expired. In a few cases, it appeared that eligible employing agents were not interested in becoming involved in a federal program where they would be under considerable pressure for immediate performance accompanied by restrictive guidelines and federal monitoring and auditing procedures. It should also be noted that smaller units of government definitely have needs for additional public service personnel, but are frequently restricted from hiring such personnel even under grants because of the limitations of facilities, equipment, and supervisory personnel. The fact that such items could be counted as in-kind contributions is of little significance if local revenues are simply not sufficient to cover the cost involved.

All of the local governmental units that submitted applications were given consideration for participation in the program. In addition to establishing priorities for funding based on population size and the number of public service jobs within each unit's jurisdiction, the city and county established the following guidelines: (1) the relative need of the units requesting funding for financial assistance to create public service positions; (2) the ability of the requesting units to support adequately any EEA positions that would be funded; (3) the extent to which high priority public service needs would be met by the funds provided to the employing units; and (4) the ability of the units to provide jobs that would, in fact, be transitional for the majority of the unemployed to be hired; that is, the probability of the prospective EEA enrollees either being absorbed into regular positions or placed in a private sector in related work.

While the above criteria were somewhat less precise than desired by the local program agents and could be criticized on the basis of their subjectivity, they were generally accepted by the various units of government in the area and provided at least some framework of goals for selecting employing units. Although some exceptions to the above criteria may undoubtedly have occurred, it appears that the city's and county's primary goal of allocating funds to achieve the maximum impact of the program was achieved in a manner consistent with the legislative intent and the Department of Labor guidelines. Furthermore, employing units were designated without the occurrence of local disputes or criticisms that were encountered by program agents in other areas.

Selection of jobs to satisfy priority public service needs. The intent of the Emergency Employment Act – that positions to be funded should satisfy unmet public service needs – was quite clear. However, the number and type of public service areas encompassed by the legislation – law enforcement, education, public works and transportation, health and hospitals, environmental quality, fire protection, and parks and recreation – gave local program agents an open field in terms of the areas for which the EEA funds could be allocated. The rather general provision that program agents should create positions that involved the development of new careers, opportunities for a career advancement, and continual training and transitional public service employment did not narrow the field significantly in terms of the types of jobs that were eligible for funding under the program because of the limited time to consider the full implications of these factors.

Consistent with the above directives, the goal of the Kalamazoo program agents was to create positions that would satisfy the most urgent public service needs within their jurisdictions at the same time satisfying other requirements of the EEA program. The task, therefore, became one of identifying needs, assessing the relative importance and urgency of the needs, and developing priorities consistent with the intent of the EEA.

As an initial step, departments within each of the program agents and eligible employing agencies within the city's and county's jurisdictions were requested to identify their public service needs and to specify job requests on a priority basis that were consistent with these needs. This step was simplified to some extent because both program agents had given some consideration to their public employment needs prior to the allocation of funds under the program. For practically all of the potential subagents, however, the job of assessing and establishing manpower priorities was a new experience.

Because it was assumed that more positions would be requested than could be funded, local officials were guided by the following considerations in selection of public service positions: (1) the positions should be for services for which an identifiable need exists and currently is not being met; (2) the positions should be readily filled from the ranks of the unemployed with special consideration given to veterans, minority group members, and the disadvantaged; (3) the majority of the jobs to be created should require sufficient skill or training content to enhance the participants' movement into permanent employment, either within the public or private sector. Unfortunately, the severely limited time allowed for planning did not enable the local program agents to give adequate consideration to such factors as job restructuring and the training features of the EEA positions as they could be related to other manpower programs.

The county's approach for selecting jobs departed somewhat from the above procedure because of the relatively large number and different types of potential employing agencies involved. As noted earlier, the county was required to give consideration to other municipalities and agencies of local government that were not under its general control. Because of the diversification of the employing agencies involved and their lack of orientation to manpower planning, it was difficult to establish priorities except in somewhat of a hodgepodge fashion. The city of Kalamazoo, while encountering some difficulties in this area, was significantly less restricted in terms of establishing priorities because the majority of the EEA positions funded through the city's program were for city departments. The overall manpower and employment policies for these departments are established and administered centrally by the City Personnel Director.

Involvement of local community groups and organizations. The publicity that centered around the passage of the Emergency Employment Act and the subsequent designation of program agents created considerable local interest in the public employment program. The initial Department of Labor releases emphasized that hiring could be expected to proceed immediately in those areas funded in an effort to relieve local unemployment problems. Because information pertaining to the program was released through local news media before city and county officials were provided details of the program, there was a great deal of confusion concerning the possible impact locally and the role that local agencies – public and private – might play in the implementation of EEA. As could be expected, there was immediate interest among local organizations to determine if they could be designated as employing agents, how the effort would relate to existing employment programs, and what role, if any, they would have in the referral process and other aspects of the program.

As soon as local officials were provided with sufficient details, they were anxious to meet with individuals and groups in the community who were involved in manpower programs in general and who performed an advocacy role for any segment of the unemployed. Through such meetings, the local program agents sought to clarify any misunderstandings concerning the program and to extend an opportunity to existing manpower and related organizations to provide inputs for the planning of the EEA effort. Although sufficient time was obviously not available to allow for in-depth assessments and contributions, this approach was deemed desirable for a number of reasons. First, the city of Kalamazoo, particularly, previously had worked with several community organizations and wished to continue the good relationships that had been developed. Second, by developing a working relationship with such organizations, communications channels could be opened that would create a rather broad base of knowledgeable community awareness and support for the EEA program. Third, the involvement of groups that serve as advocates for veterans, minorities, and disadvantaged could extend the program agents' outreach and recruitment capabilities considerably. Fourth, by clearly articulating the scope and implications of the EEA funding, local officials could be better assured that the expectations of the unemployed would not be raised to unreasonable levels. In regard to this latter point, the Michigan Employment Security Commission had estimated that the unemployment level in the Kalamazoo area reached 7,100 in July 1971. In contrast to the large number of unemployed, the total EEA allocations for the Kalamazoo area would result in the creation of less than 200 jobs. Contrary to initial public understanding, the impact on unemployment would be relatively insignificant.

The first meeting with community and manpower organizations was held on September 1, 1971. This date actually preceded the final determination by the Department of Labor of the Section 5 allocations for program agents in Michigan. The following list of groups and agencies illustrates the extent of the local program agents' efforts to create positive community awareness and involvement in their programs.

Organizations Sponsoring Manpower Programs

Kalamazoo Community Action Agency
Kalamazoo County Chamber of Commerce
Lincoln Skills Center
  (Kalamazoo Public Schools)
Michigan Employment Security Commission
W.E. Upjohn Institute for Employment
  Research

Organizations That Perform Advocacy or
  Referral Functions

Brown Berets
City Community Relations Department
Douglass Community Association
Edison Center
Kalamazoo Community Action Agency
Kalamazoo County Department of
  Social Services
Michigan Veterans Trust Fund
Milwood Community Center
The Comstock Community Center
United Migrants Opportunities, Inc.
United Veterans Council
VFW Veterans Council

During the September 1 and subsequent sessions, representatives of the above-named organizations were provided the opportunity to recommend priority public service positions to be considered for funding and to explore ways in which they could develop a supportive relationship to the city and county programs. Although few suggestions were forthcoming during the short planning period, the city and county demonstrated their intent to plan and implement their EEA programs in a straightforward and equitable manner.

Optimum coordination between city and county government. Prior to their designations as program agents, both the city and county had explored to some extent the need for developing a close working relationship in any public employment programs that may be funded in the Kalamazoo area. Although substantial cooperation between city and county government had been rather sporadic in the past, the advent of a public employment program tended to crystalize the need for a better relationship. For one thing, the discussions that occurred during the preallocation period between local officials revealed that a greater commonality of goals and objectives existed than may have been anticipated by either unit of government.

Over the past few years, the city of Kalamazoo has made considerable progress in the employment of disadvantaged and minorities. This unit has also developed good working relationships with local manpower programs and groups that serve in advocacy roles for the disadvantaged. The city's background and orientation in these areas could be of obvious benefit to the county as well as to other units of government that may be involved in the EEA program as subagents. Although the county government's involvement in manpower development has not been comparable to that of the city, recent policies and programs of the County Board of Commissioners reflect their interest and intent to be more active in human resource development and affirmative action employment.

Even beyond the mutuality of goals currently being pursued by the two units of government, there were several other major factors that accentuated the need for coordinated programs. First, in a relatively small SMSA, the assessment and establishment of priority public service needs to be funded through the Emergency Employment Act could not be made successfully by either unit of government in a strictly autonomous manner. This was particularly true for the Kalamazoo area because of the probability that other units of government could qualify as subagents to both the city and county. Second, by coordinating efforts, the program agents would be in a better position to overcome barriers that were at least partially created by the ambiguous or inconsistent nature of the EEA legislation and guidelines. The best example of such a barrier is a residency requirement for EEA enrollees. In a labor market area the size of Kalamazoo, the requirements that program agents and subagents must hire unemployed workers who reside in their jurisdiction clearly constitutes an artificial restriction that would impede the county, particularly in meeting its local objectives as well as other requirements of the legislation. Therefore, it was necessary for the county and the city to develop a coordinated program that would allow them to exchange the residence requirements for specified numbers of job slots. Third, by coordinating efforts, the two units of government could expand their recruiting and outreach capabilities to assure that the specified target groups were employed in their respective programs. The approach that was followed by the program agents to develop and implement their programs in a coordinated manner is described below. While it is recognized that many alternatives exist for coordinating programs, the alternative chosen in Kalamazoo is unique in that it enabled the two program agencies to achieve most of the major advantages of having a single program and yet, at the same time, preserve their independent responsibility, authority, and accountability for their respective programs.

The Kalamazoo Consortium

Program agents in various parts of the nation have undoubtedly developed any number of arrangements in an effort to coordinate the operation of their PEP programs. The administrative framework that was established in Kalamazoo is probably similar in many aspects to the procedures followed in other areas. The Kalamazoo experience, however, might be unique in that a consortium was established that involved not only the city and county, but also a private nonprofit employment research organization. The two Kalamazoo program agents, together with the W.E. Upjohn Institute for Employment Research, entered into a consortium agreement that had two general objectives: (1) to enable the city and county to obtain assistance from the Institute in the administration of their responsibilities as program agents, and (2) to delegate certain functions among the respective parties in the consortium to minimize administration cost and to maximize the efficiency and effectiveness of the program.

A major feature of the consortium is that the city and county have combined their areas of geographic jurisdiction for the purpose of assuring an equitable inclusion of the identifiable groups of the unemployed. This feature of the consortium allows any eligible resident to apply for a job offered by either agent or any of the subagents in the EEA program. The city and county have agreed that there will be an equal tradeoff of job slots between them during the year's operation. Without this provision in the consortium, the city would be limited to hiring city residents, and the county would be limited to out-county resident participation. As pointed out earlier, adherence to such rigid residency requirements would seriously impede the inclusion of all eligible target groups on an equitable basis.

Some of the other major objectives and features of the consortium include the following:

1. Assistance by the Upjohn Institute in the planning and preparation of the Kalamazoo program agents' application.
2. Development of a coordinated system for recruiting and selecting EEA participants, including the establishment of procedures that assure uniform standards for the selection of applicants in conformity with the requirements of the Act.
3. Centralization of the distribution of information concerning the program operations and the provision for a central receiving point for comments and reactions from various individuals and groups in the community concerning the program.
4. Involvement of local groups in the community in order to promote understanding.
5. Development of linkages with existing manpower training programs in the community where such coordinated efforts are appropriate and feasible.
6. Establishment of a standardized, comprehensive data collection system that can serve as a basis for reporting both the effectiveness and financial status of the program.

7. Provision for the periodic monitoring and review of the program operations by the Upjohn Institute.

8. Evaluation of the program by the Upjohn Institute.

Under the consortium agreement, the city and county retain the control, responsibility, and accountability for the operation of their respective programs. With the exception of those functions that were specifically delegated to one of the parties or that involved a cooperative effort, all administrative functions required by the legislation and guidelines are the responsiblity of each program agent. Supportive services that are designed to contribute to the employability of the participants and to facilitate their movement into permanent employment are provided directly by the city and county or by education and training institutions in the community.

The attainment of many of the program's requirements and objectives in an efficient and effective manner is being facilitated because all of the subagents to the county and city are parties to the consortium. The employing agency agreement specified that the terms and obligations set forth in the consortium agreement are to be adapted by the subagent. Under the subagent agreement each employing agent is required to provide sufficient information necessary for the purpose of monitoring the employing agent's program and complying with the reporting requirements established by the Department of Labor.

One of the initial benefits of the consortium was the centralization and coordination of the recruiting and selection procedures for EEA participants. Under the coordinated recruitment procedures, the Michigan Employment Security Commission and over twelve other local manpower and community service agencies were notified of the number and types of jobs to be available under the program and were requested to refer unemployed and underemployed persons. The major recruiting effort was concentrated within a four day period at central locations, and maximum public awareness of the program among the unemployed and underemployed was achieved. Approximately 1,300 individuals applied for the EEA positions during this period. Thirty percent of the applicants were minority group members and 24 percent were veterans − two of the primary target groups for inclusion in the program. In addition, a large number of the applicants were receiving welfare of some type. The consortium is also expected to be beneficial in several other aspects of the EEA program, particularly in regard to planning for the second year of funding and efforts to move EEA participants to nonsubsidized employment.

Identification of Public Service Needs and EEA Jobs

Following the procedures described earlier, the program agents requested each eligible employing agent to identify his public service needs and to submit job requests accordingly. Following the requests for Section 5 funding, all departments of local government along with all eligible subagents were also asked to review the public service priorities and job requests established for Section 5 and to submit Section 6 job requests that reflected the impact of the first round of funding.

As could be expected, the number of job requests exceeded the number of positions that could be funded under the EEA grants. In all probability the number of positions requested would have been even larger if the eligible agencies had not been guided by the program agents' guidelines for judging the relative importance and need for public service positions. With priority given *primarily* to jobs that could be filled from the specified target groups of the unemployed and to those jobs that would have a greater probability of leading to unsubsidized employment, the number of potential requests was probably affected.

The positions that were requested during the initial period of the program for both Sections 5 and 6 are shown in table 15.1 by public service area. The public service areas – education, health and hospitals, law enforcement, etc. – indicate the principal governmental function performed by the department or organization to which the EEA participant would be assigned. A total of 414 requests were submitted to both the city and county for Sections 5 and 6 funding.

As shown in table 15.1 the job requests were fairly evenly distributed between the city and county, with the majority of the jobs relating to education, public works, law enforcement, and parks and recreation. In addition to these job requests, both program agents have received additional inquiries concerning potential EEA jobs. Most of these requests were submitted in hopes that additional positions could be created through "lapsed" funds.

The total number of positions funded through the Kalamazoo EEA program for both Sections 5 and 6 was 179, or approximately 43 percent of the total jobs requested. As indicated in table 15.2, the EEA positions are distributed within Kalamazoo County among fourteen separate city departments; twelve county departments, boards and commissions; seven municipalities, and six local school districts. The distribution of the 179 jobs by public service area and the specific positions that were created through the program are detailed in tables 15.3 and 15.4.

The process of designating employing agents and of selecting public service positions for funding was generally consistent with the city's and county's goals and guidelines. The Kalamazoo Consortium definitely provided increased flexibility to achieve some of the local objectives in accordance with federal EEA guidelines that could not have been accomplished if the two EEA programs were planned and implemented in an autonomous manner.

The planning and administrative framework established by the city and county should also have a positive impact upon the future operation of the public employment program. The relatively large number of job requests indicates that local governmental units are confronted with considerable pressure

Table 15.1
Number of Job Requests by Public Service Area, Kalamazoo EEA Program

Public Service Area	Total, all Sections – City and County	City of Kalamazoo		County of Kalamazoo	
		Sect. 5	Sect. 6	Sect. 5	Sect. 6
Total	414	176	36	125	77
Education	120	40	4	44	32
Public Works & Transportation	85	47	17	12	9
Law Enforcement	79	16	5	36	22
Parks & Recreation	40	33	4	2	1
Health & Hospitals	22	0	0	13	9
Social Services	25	9	6	8	2
Environmental Quality	18	18	0	0	0
Fire Protection	5	5	0	0	0
Administrative Departments (other)	20	8	0	10	2

Table 15.2
Distribution of EEA Jobs by Department and Subagents, Kalamazoo EEA Program

Program/Employing Agent	No. of Jobs
Total, City & County, Sections 5 & 6	179
City of Kalamazoo	
Section 5, Total	66
City Departments:	37
Community Relations	2
Police	1
Airport	2
Traffic Engineering	5
Parks and Recreation	2
Public Works	8
Assessor	2
District Court	1
Metro Transit	3
Treasurer	1
Computer Center	1
Personel	2
Auditor	1
Water	6

Employing Agents:	24
Kalamazoo Public Schools	19
Kalamazoo Valley Community College	5
Employed by City, But Assigned to Eligible Community Organization	5
Section 6, Total	23
City Departments:	18
Traffic Engineering	2
Parks and Recreation	4
Police	2
Community Relations	2
Airport	4
Metro Transit	4
Employing Agents:	7
Kalamazoo Valley Intermediate School District	4
Kalamazoo Public Schools	3
County of Kalamazoo	
Section 5, Total	65
County Departments, Boards and Commissions:	33
Public Health	7
Sheriff	6
Controller's Office	3
Juvenile Court	7
Equalization Office	1
Parks	2
Planning	2
Cooperative Extension	1
Mental Health Board	2
Soil Conservation District	1
Board of Commissioners	1
Employing Agents:	29
City of Portage	5
Ross Township	2
Portage Public Schools	5
Comstock Township	2
Cooper Township	1
Kalamazoo Valley Community College	4
Kalamazoo Public Schools	4
Kalamazoo Valley Intermediate School District	6
Employed by County, But Assigned to Eligible Community Organization	3

Section 6, Total	23
County Departments, Boards and Commissions:	9
Mental Health Board	4
Road Commission	5
Employing Agents:	14
Pavilion Township	1
Village of Richland	1
City of Portage	2
Kalamazoo Valley Intermediate School District	2
Schoolcraft Community Schools	2
Vicksburg Community Schools	1
Kalamazoo Township	2
Kalamazoo Valley Community College	1
Portage Public Schools	2

Table 15.3
EEA Jobs Funded by Public Service Area, Kalamazoo EEA Program

Public Service Area	Total, all Sections – City and County	City of Kalamazoo		County of Kalamazoo	
		Sect. 5	Sect. 6	Sect. 5	Sect. 6
Total	179	66	25	65	23
Education	56	24	4	20	8
Public Works & Transportation	42	15	10	10	7
Law Enforcement	20	2	2	14	2
Parks & Recreation	9	2	4	2	1
Health & Hospitals	11	0	0	7	4
Social Services	16	7	5	4	0
Environmental Quality	9	9	0	0	0
Administrative Departments (other)	16	7	0	8	1

Table 15.4
EEA Jobs Funded by Public Service Area, Kalamazoo EEA Program

Public Service Area and Job Title	No. of Jobs
City of Kalamazoo, Section 5	66
Education	24
Community School Aide	7
School Social Work Aide	2
Clerk-typist	1
Recreation Aide	1
School Activity Aide	2
School Media Aide	2
Learning Center Aide	1
School Community Relations Aide	2
School Social Work Aide	1
Personnel Technician	1
Custodian	2
Security Guard	1
Library Aide	1
Public Works and Transportation	15
Laborer	8
Traffic Aide	2
Draftsman	1
Dispatcher Trainee	1
Mechanic	1
Utility Man	1
Clerk-typist	1
Law Enforcement	2
Police Cadet	1
Microfilm Operator	1
Parks and Recreation	2
Account Clerk Trainee	1
Maintenance Repairman Trainee	1
Health and Hospitals	0
Social Services	7
Youth Coordinator	1
Neighborhood Aide	1
Community Planner	1
Youth Program Assistant	2
Clerical Supervisor	1
Secretary	1

Environmental Quality	9
Recycling Station Attendant	2
Recycling Station Leadman	1
Laborer	5
Labor Foreman	1
Other (Administrative Departments)	7
Clerk	1
Clerk-typist	1
Clerk-cashier	1
Junior Programmer	1
Personnel Technician	1
Personnel Aide	1
Account Clerk Trainee	1
City of Kalamazoo, Section 6	25
Education	4
Community School Aide	2
Custodian	1
Teacher Trainer	1
Public Works and Transportation	10
Maintenanceman	3
Custodian	1
Administrative Assistant	1
Mechanic	2
Utility Man	1
Traffic Aide Leadman	1
Parking Checker	1
Law Enforcement	2
Police Officer	1
Youth Bureau Aide	1
Parks and Recreation	4
Recreation Aide	4
Health and Hospitals	0
Social Services	5
Vocational Education Counselor	1
Neighborhood Aide	1
Day Care Worker	3
Environmental Quality	0
Other (Administrative Departments)	0

County of Kalamazoo, Section 5	65
Education	20
Placement and Follow-up Worker	1
Skills Curriculum Assistant	1
Audiovisual Aide	1
Printing Services Assistant	1
Custodial Matron	3
General Maintenanceman	1
Deliveryman	1
Administrative Aide	2
Group Worker	1
Investigative Aide	1
Special Education Teacher	5
District Educational Assistant	1
Cook	1
Public Works and Transportation	10
Janitor	1
Building Maintenanceman	1
Public Works Maintenanceman	5
General Maintenanceman	2
Clerk-typist	1
Law Enforcement	14
Jailer	3
Patrolman	3
Clerk-typist	2
Juvenile Caseworker	2
Cook	1
Juvenile Probation Aide	2
Psychiatric Nurse	1
Parks and Recreation	2
Park Caretaker	2
Health and Hospitals	7
Public Health Nurse	3
Sanitation Aide	1
Clerk-typist	1
Public Health Nurse Aide	2
Social Services	4
Community Counselor	1
Community Organization Trainee	1
Youth Coordinator	1
Administrative Assistant	1

Environmental Quality	0
Other (Administrative Departments)	8
Internal Auditor	1
Financial Auditor	1
Supply and Transportation Officer	1
Administrative Assistant	1
Draftsman	1
Planning Aide	1
Engineer I	1
Clerk-typist	1
County of Kalamazoo, Section 6	23
Education	8
Assistant Production Specialist	1
General Secretary	1
Community School Director	1
Maintenanceman	2
Audiovisual Clerk	1
Painter	1
Matron	1
Public Works and Transportation	7
Public Works Laborer	5
Public Works Maintenanceman	2
Law Enforcement	2
Police Officer	2
Parks and Recreation	1
Parks Maintenanceman	1
Health and Hospitals	4
Floor Supervisor (Rehabilitation Center)	1
Store Clerk Supervisor (Rehabilitation Center)	1
Bookkeeper	1
Clerk-typist	1
Social Services	0
Environmental Quality	0
Other (Administrative Departments)	1
Appraisal Clerk	1

to expand public services of practically all types. Because resources are not available to meet many of these needs, the local governmental units will be placing increased emphasis on manpower planning and on the identification and establishment of priorities for unmet public service needs.

16 Urban Finance: Problems and Perplexities

SELMA J. MUSHKIN

This chapter considers the three-pronged question: What are the fiscal requirements of the urban community, what are some major criteria for judging optional methods of meeting them, and what are those optional methods? The question of urban finance is described against a backdrop of several models of the urban economy.

The chapter focuses on financial aspects, but our basic concern is with the reality of the lives and hopes of those who reside, work, shop, and play in urban centers. We have grown accustomed to considering the urban crisis as a crisis of financial resources; it is more than a money matter. The urban crisis is a crisis of congestion, of poverty, and of unemployment, particularly among the young. It is a crisis of past educational neglect and restricted access to employment. It is perhaps a crisis born of the nation's dream of equality of opportunity and of cultural amenities at a time when growing affluence could bring the dream within reach, and does not, for the nation is riddled with the impact of war and unemployment.

We have heard with monotonous repetition: "The central cities of the nation are short of funds." Their financial plight is caused by the difficulty of gaining access to resources for public use — resources that are for the most part located in the nation's metroploitan areas. Barriers to access are essentially man made, and can be altered and adapted. But as we shall see, the city itself can do very little about the change.

Fiscal Requirements in the Central Cities

Expenditure by the cities has reached upward of $40 billion, yet it is a declining rather than increasing share of total public service outlays. For all local governments, spending has been constantly rising by about 8 percent per year over the past decade or so, but city spending is growing less rapidly than either the public sector as a whole or all local government. Much of this lag in city expenditures reflects the imbalances in the cities, some reflects the consequence of fiscal reform itself.

Functions of the urban community have been divided into two main categories — the category of functions that are fairly general or universal and for which outlays are relatively uniform between the rural and urban community,

327

and the category that calls for larger expenditures in more congested places. The second group we label "basic city services." The definition of "city expenditures" is derived from empirical data showing that for some services, expenditure on a per capita basis is two-and-a-half times or more higher in urban places than in rural ones. Among the major items of city expenditures are these: water supplies, police protection, fire protection, sewerage, parks and recreation, sanitation (other than sewers), and electric power generation. No one class or item of expenditure is as predominant at the city level as are the Big Three — highways, hospitals, and education (both direct for institutions of higher education and for state aids to local schools) — in the finances of the states.

Many of these municipal or city expenditures are of a character that generates added costs as the size of the population grows. While there may be economies of scale in the production of the services, these economies are less significant than is the broader scope of public activities required to accommodate problems of congestion and size.

The finances of the city today pose an intractable problem. We define two patterns of city finance here for purposes of contrasting the city today and that of years past.

The core dominated city. In the core dominated model of city structure and organization, the core is where all economic activity takes place. This core is surrounded by satellite or residential zones. Satellite areas are assumed for simplicity to be composed of households with identical tastes and income amounts, all earned in the city core. Further, in concept at least, we assume that all households are equally well off. Only rent differences can account for the varied settlement of households within the satellite area at different distances from the core. Each locational choice results in constant utility for consumers. Once the distribution of households (and of rentals) is determined, a price gradient for labor may be determined; it would measure the wage a firm has to pay at various locations in the satellite area to switch a given number of workers from their employment in the core to other places, but within the satellite area. The form of the wage gradient is not certain for all combinations of numbers of workers. However, if the numbers of workers in any particular plant are shown to be small relative to the population, the supply-demand relationship would yield a downward sloping wage gradient because of the saving in time and transportation costs. Other factor costs generally would tend to be equal in satellite areas and at the core.

The core dominated city of our earlier history follows this model fairly well. Various explanations have been given for the dominant position of the core. It has been argued for example that the high cost of moving goods within cities relative to the costs of moving people made for a dominant core center. Business location in satellite areas would, under these conditions, have involved moving away from the central goods-handling facilities of the city with the result of higher costs of transporting raw materials and finished products in the satellite communities than at the core. Such higher transportation costs for goods outweighed the lower costs of labor services in satellite areas. (Other theories have been advanced to explain the location of industry at the core of the city. These include the proximity to competitive firms thus generating a convenient market center such as a "clothing center," a "fur center," and also the proximity of firms that produce services and goods with complementarity of output.)

The core dominated city had relatively high fiscal capacity. Property values at the core tended to be high due to locational scarcity and high rents. In the satellite areas, in contrast, rents and property values were less and grew proportionately lower the farther the distance from the core. Thus the fiscal resources of the satellite area would tend to be characterized by lower income and lower property values compared to the core. The core city could raise as much if not more revenue than the satellite communities and could maintain a high level of expenditure at lower tax rates.

The history of city finances was just that — namely, higher outlays per capita, lower tax rates when computed as a share of the superior fiscal resources. Cities could grow and prosper without adverse tax incentives for their business firms and without undue deterrence to adoption of equal, or even higher, service levels than available to those outside the core.

The satellite dominated city. In the satellite dominated model of city structure, the major economic activity of manufacturing, wholesaling, and retailing takes place in satellite areas, and in addition, the satellite areas are where most of the residential zones are located. The satellite areas are assumed for simplicity to be composed of households with identical tastes and incomes earned in the satellite area. We assume all those in the satellite areas are equally well off. Rents would be similar throughout the satellite area, as employment places are uniformly distributed and equally distant from housing offerings. What would determine the activities (if any) at the core? If all economic producing activity were carried on in the dominant satellite zones, there would be either a further move of households from the core to satellite or the lowered wage and factor cost would provide incentive for industry to move back toward the core. This wage incentive to move back would be offset by the higher transportation costs of raw materials and of finished products and by other business costs such as added fire insurance premiums. If wages were lower and labor markets were unconstrained, some reverse movement might take place on job location and perhaps residential location.

The basic economics that relate (1) production location and costs to work place and earnings, (2) place of residence to place of work, travel time, and costs, and (3) rents and property values to classes of industrial, commercial, and residential property are adverse to the core under present circumstances. And this disincentive is intensified in many northern cities by the characteristic discrimination and concentration of blacks in core city areas. Many blacks cannot find housing that would permit them to move; some prefer not to move.

The core areas lose jobs and rentals. Resources for taxation are lower in the core city area than in the satellite community. Tax rates for equal per capita outlays would have to be higher than those in the satellites.

As a consequence of the demography of city life, one out of every three blacks now resides in the core of the largest metropolitan areas. Blacks represent 20 percent of the population of the core cities. In the central cities as a whole, 48 percent, or almost one out of two blacks, are nineteen years of age or younger, and two-fifths of the blacks are under fifteen years of age.

Past economic isolation of the blacks through job discrimination, discriminatory practices in education, and housing restrictions have contributed to the syndrome of black urban poverty. The proportion of blacks who are poor and live in the largest central cities is twice that of poor whites living there — 26 percent compared to 13 percent. When these figures are adjusted for the lower economic levels of the aged persons in general, the contrast between city poor who are blacks and those who are white (in the most economically productive years of life) becomes sharper.

The concentration of blacks and unemployed in the core helps to explain the higher expenditure requirements in the core at the same time that fiscal capacity is more restricted. Equal expenditures would require higher tax rates at the lower levels of property value and income; compensatory expenditures necessitate even higher outlays and higher tax rates. Incentive effects of those higher tax rates work to the economic disadvantage of the core.

But other factors also are contributory. Hawley, in 1951, made the interesting finding using 1940 data that the size and the percentage of the population in the metropolitan area outside of the central city is important in explaining the central city's per capita expenditures, while the central city's own population is not. Studies of political demand for public services suggest that core cities add to their fiscal burdens in some instances by financing services for the satellite communities. And in some of the major cities where black political power has grown there is a demand for improvement that calls for an accelerated pace of public service expenditure without the basic resources to finance additional outlays.

Criteria for City Support

A series of factors contribute to weakening the finances of the city, once strong as a consequence of the city's earlier dominant economic role. Fiscal attempts by the city to pull itself up by its bootstraps through added expenditures or business tax subsidies only accelerate further the speed of deterioration. We have seen the population in city after city grow poorer relative to the suburbs.

Cities can raise revenues within the competitive limitations of no higher rate of taxation than is imposed by the wealthier satellite communities. They can perhaps impose prices where such prices establish a market place for services or facilitate the equating of demand for services with supply by removing tax constraints. New program offerings such as home health services, meals for the elderly, and special language instruction perhaps fall into the class of service that may be financed through prices. We know less about the impact on location and interjurisdictional competition of differential prices for water supplies and trash collection.

Sizable additions to core city financing depend upon external sources. What could external funds be designed to do; or stated differently, what would be the purposes and what the results of external funding?

(1) External funds could be designed to keep effective tax rates equal in the core and in satellite communities. Without altering existing expenditure outlays, for example, the amount of external aid could be set so that extra taxing effort in core areas is replaced by reductions in taxes, and in place of those taxes are added grants-in-aid. With expenditure levels unchanged, how much added federal aid would be needed in the cities in order that their relative tax effort is equal to, but no more than that of surrounding communities? One estimate made some years back placed the figure of federal aid required at about $2 billion. More specifically, for 1965 it was estimated that in the 37 largest SMSAs, revenues were 7.63 percent of per capita income in the central cities, and 5.55 percent in the outlying areas of the same SMSAs. To bring the city tax effort down to 5.55 percent in those 37 SMSAs would have required an additional $54.33 per capita grant for the 37 million inhabitants of the central cities in those SMSAs. The $54.33 per capita amount would have required an additional $2 billion in federal aid. While this is not a large sum when viewed in the context of all governmental expenditure, it would involve more than a doubling of federal aid to city governments.

One approach, thus, is simple. Equalize effective tax rates between satellite and core city. The impact of this kind of approach would clearly be to remove the incentives within the tax structure for high income individuals or businesses to move out.

(Immediately the question is posed of the distribution of the tax load among groups in the population, both private families and business firms, because average effort may obscure the wide differences in load and burden of taxation.)

(2) The second approach to setting the amount of external funds would call for the evening out of expenditure levels. Instead of federal funding of differences in tax effort, this approach to determining the amount and kind of external funding would call for (a) the setting of public service expenditure

levels, (b) the determining of standards for those public services, and then (c) inquiring about the cost of equalizing. How much by way of added outlays would be required to bring expenditure levels in the core up to expenditure levels in the suburbs?

Expenditures do not, as suggested earlier, appear to be lower in the core than in the satellite communities for all services. On the contrary, they are often higher in the core. The variety of reasons that contribute to those higher expenditure levels include congestion costs, core city functions for satellite communities, and the impact on public service rates of discrimination in employment and housing.

(3) A third approach to setting the amount of external aid would call for federal funds sufficient to make the public service levels uniform. The question that arises is this: How much would it take in additional external aid to bring the quantity and quality of public services within the core area up to that of the satellite communities? What would it take by way of funds, for example, to have the streets as safe and as clean, the air as free from sulphur dioxide, the transportation of persons as quick and as free from traffic accidents? Costs of equivalent levels of services for those who are free to choose where they live is the dollar quantification that is being sought.

(4) Still a fourth approach concerns the amount of external aid required not only to equate quantity and quality of public services between satellite community and core for those with a locational choice, but also to gain equal services for those now barred from the choice of suburban or satellite communities by discriminatory practices. This approach calls for the financing of the extra costs of discrimination in employment and housing. There is a strong case for an indemnity payment to the city by the nation for those who have been encouraged by economic circumstances to move from the South to the North (and to the West) and who in that movement have not found the roots required to make the new communities their own. Blacks have come to the cities after a long period of neglect. They have come without the higher educational and other experience that would qualify them for living in complex metropolitan areas.

Neglect of service in the past needs to be compensated by more than equality of treatment now. It is important to understand that the problems of large concentrations of alienated people were unfamiliar to the cities and the resources needed were of a very different order and magnitude than the capabilities of the cities would permit or their higher income and industrial taxpayers would sanction.

Huge disparities within the metropolitan areas between the size of the public problems and the distribution of taxable resources point to use by the national government of its revenue system to channel the resources of the suburbs or satellite communities into the core areas. Service levels consistent with those of neighboring satellite communities at equal tax rates (on a truly effective basis) could be sought to stem the decline of the core city. But it is still not clear to what extent a decline can be stemmed by such equal tax and public service expenditure policy.

(5) Much greater incentives may be required. A reversing of the process of decline may necessitate (a) less than equal tax rates, (b) more than equal expenditures, (c) more than equal public service levels (measured by outputs), (d) a combination of lower rates and higher expenditures, and (e) compensatory steps to equalize social and economic conditions among special groups in the population locked into the core city by discrimination. Thus a fifth type of approach would be to reduce tax rates below the going level in the economic area or raise service levels.

Do the external funds restrain the forces that lead to dispersion of economic activities into satellite communities; do those external funds reverse the processes that have led to relative decline? The test of the amount and source of external funds would be the economic health in the core, produced as a consequence of external aids; economic health may be defined for this purpose as economic conditions compared to those prevailing in the satellite communities.

Effectiveness of external amounts thus is the relative economics of the core and the satellites, with the economics of the jurisdictions measured by relative family income levels (change in amounts and distribution), and unemployment rates (level and change).

Recent work that has been done suggests additional criteria for measuring external funds, namely, the social criteria that determine the quality of living – among them, safety, pleasantness, cleanliness, and the feeling of being free.

Once the problem of external aids is raised in this way, the means for external aids are broadened from the traditional categorical grant or any conditional aid to other forms of assistance and to other program mechanisms. For example, if the underlying causal factors determining the strength of the satellites in relation to the core are the costs of transporting goods to the core, then correction lies in the subsidization, perhaps, of transportation of major goods used in the city. For example, if the cost of transporting food is substantially less in the outlying areas than in the core, then the form of external aid might be directed toward such transportation subsidies as will overcome the disadvantage in the core. For each of the major factors affecting the relative growth of satellite and core, this approach to external aids requires the raising of the questions about what might be done to reduce or eliminate the outward movement toward the satellites and what might be done to gain incentives for relocation at the core. If, to use another example, cost of insurance is higher in the core than in the satellite communities, the external aid might take the form of an insurance subsidization to (a) equalize, or (b) give an advantage to the core. If the core survives because industrial interaction requires concentration of certain businesses such as financial establishments close to each other, then the economics of the core points to external aid that will subsidize and encourage this kind of business activity.

This same type of analysis applies to the more direct public policies as well as those less direct programs we have just discussed. If the economic disadvantage of the core is shown by unemployment, one can try to subsidize the types of industries that would reduce unemployment rates, or, optionally, the policy could be directed toward providing jobs through state and local governments to correct the existing high level of unemployment.

We have thus changed the sets of criteria by which funding in the city and the satellites is usually considered, and by the same token have broadened the options available to the nation and to the state in providing external assistance.

Program Options

What are the options and prospects then? Additional external aid in some form is the key issue, whether in loans or grants, program related general aids, supports for public service employment and for construction or payments through states or direct.

If the hypothesis is accepted that the limited resources of the cities do not permit them to raise the revenues required to (a) equalize taxes, (b) equalize benefits, and (c) make compensatory outlays evening out the costs of discrimination and other economic or social handicaps of the poorer persons or families, then external sources of funding become necessary. How are those external funds to be paid out? How are they to be financed? Who should pay? For how long a period of time?

The external funds may take a number of forms:

1. Direct national funding of nationally administered programs in the city – e.g., the DOD program for veterans returning to cities; the city post office.
2. National funding through general untied grants-in-aid to (a) state, (b) local government, (c) cities.
3. National funding through categorical aid to (a) states, (b) local governments, or (c) cities.
4. National funding through loans or loan guarantees.
5. National funding through wage and salary payments.
6. National tax credits as incentives for city taxation.

The advantages of national action compared to state are many, and include the nationwide scope of the national tax system in a national economy, the greater efficiency of the national tax system both in terms of administration and compliance, and the greater equity of that system.

Direct national programs in support of the city

The major program proposal now advanced in support of the city is H.R.1, or the Family Assistance Plan. That program is addressed to meeting the needs of poor *families* rather than poor cities, however.

Inadequacies of the present welfare program, particularly aid to families with dependent children, point to change in methods of providing public assistance. The proposed new program concentrates its payments in states that have large proportions of families with incomes below the poverty level, and that have had low levels of public assistance in the past, despite the high matching ratios offered by the national government. A major share of the proposed payments under H.R. 1 would go to the South and to rural persons.

The impact on city finances is not likely to be significant. A number of cities make no expenditure out of city budgets for cash assistance, and the fiscal "relief" to those cities that do finance cash payments is uncertain. As has been indicated, the Family Assistance Plan is addressed to increasing income where it is lowest; it is intended to remove the worst of the inequities and indignities. But the assured minimum income is below the present standards in many large industrial states; and for these states the outlook is higher welfare costs financed out of state or local tax sources, unless the relief provision is substantially enlarged or the minimum income assured through federal funding is raised. Thus, while the proposed program will do much to relieve the worst of the burden of poverty to black and white alike, especially in farm and rural areas where almost half the poor reside, it does not address itself to the plight of the congested urban community – the poor in those core areas.

National programs through untied grants-in-aid.

Initially, the main thrust of the administration's new fiscal federalism was toward an unconditional grant-in-aid program through which grants would go to the states in accordance with an allotment formula that called for allocations based on income and population. States under the initial administration proposals were required to pass through to local governments a part of the revenue share, with all general units of governments eligible to participate. Each local government would receive, as a minimum, that share of the state grant that is equivalent to the proportion that its own general revenue represents of the state and local own general revenue.

The amount of the revenue sharing is related to the income tax base and the percentage of sharing is stepped up over the period to 1 percent of taxable income. The amount of the revenue sharing for the first, but partial period was estimated in the budget at $4 billion, but the revenue share was calculated to reach about $5 billion.

Two sets of events appear to have had a major impact on proposals for general aid. The first is the consequence of the election of many additional new governors; many fewer state houses were "governored" by the same political party; general revenue sharing lost its strong state emphasis. The second event was the detailed criticism of revenue sharing in the course of congressional review. Political emphasis appears to have shifted away from the states to the cities. This change is apparent in the revisions made in formula proposals and in the allocations themselves.

Originally the administration's formula sought to maintain neutrality regarding government structures within the states. The result was a revenue sharing proposal that had the following characteristics: (1) it was not aimed at the large city problems, (2) it disregarded differences among local governments in relative ability to raise revenues from own sources, and (3) it lacked any incentives for improving patterns of local government to facilitate greater access of the people to government or improve efficiency in the use of public funds for effecting results desired in the urban community.

National categorical program aid to urban communities.

Several program approaches have been made to augment federal funds for the urban community through the route of categorical assistance. The administration's proposed special revenue grants for urban development and manpower training marked important turning points in that they encouraged the Ways and Means Committee to reconsider the proposed distribution of funds under General Revenue Sharing. The administration was proposing substantially augmented federal grants for urban communities through its special revenue sharing proposals. In addition, some distinguishing features of special revenue sharing were: (1) the absence of requirements for matching, (2) formula distribution of funds, distribution primarily or exclusively to local governments, and (3) wide discretion to the locality in using the funds.

The Model Cities Program enacted in 1966 followed a somewhat different program design. It was a categorical grant targeted at a special group and city area. It recognized that comprehensive planned attacks had to be made on the low income neighborhoods of major cities if the critical problems were to be addressed. But the program depended on bringing together existing federal aids (and state aids as well) with very little additional resource commitment. A broadening of the Model Cities approach would enable a city both to plan and to request appropriations for a total package of programs instead of seeking funds for an employment program from one federal agency, for a neighborhood health center from another, and so forth.

As a result of the discussions in the Ways and Means Committee on revenue sharing, a new pattern has emerged with emphasis on big city problems and programs. Mr. Mills indicated in his speech of September 27, 1971, before the California League of Cities: "If Federal aid is to be granted . . . then we must develop a new and fundamentally different approach that avoids the basic defects of revenue sharing." Need of local governments receives much emphasis in the Ways and Means Committee discussion and that need is being measured by income, or numbers of low-income families.

We have worked out one possible optional distribution formula targeted at city problems and intended to give as much support as practical to the large cities. Essentially, this formula calls for the use of an own revenue effort index. In brief, it seeks to meet three purposes:

1. To provide funds to the states in proportion to their own revenue efforts.
2. To help the states in their grant programs to local governments by giving federal support to the largest local governments with the heaviest expenditure requirements (large governments that make difficult the application of a uniform formula within states for state aid).
3. To reward those states that increase their aids to cities.

The formula design, in brief, would allocate revenue shares among states in proportion to population size and their own taxing effort. It would call for a separate allocation to large cities in an amount determined somewhat as follows: $10 per capita for each 1 percent of extra state aid effort — effort in excess of some established norm (set at, for example, 1/2 the own revenue effort of all local governments). The formula would provide additional amounts to states that increase their state aids to cities, with the amount of this reward calculated by the same formula as the allotments to the cities — that is, $10 per capita for each 1 percent of extra state aid effort. Extra state aid effort would be determined on the basis of incremental state grants as a percentage of city income.

While data now available are not fully adequate for such a formula, a research and fact-gathering effort would produce the data needed. The history of federal grants-in-aid is replete with similar data deficiencies that were corrected when the Congress determined that new data and estimates should be developed.

Still another possible approach is to grant each large city an amount equal to a fraction (e.g., 50 percent) of its city expenditures per poor person in the city. Per capita amounts would be determined by the average expenditures made by the city for the particular services and facilities it provides.

National funding through loans and loan guarantees.

Capital requirements for city development are large and include a wide range of facilities and types of equipment to facilitate, for example, pollution abatement, water and waste collection and disposal systems, reduction of recidivism among the population of correctional institutions, neighborhood centers.

A number of proposals have been advanced to provide financial assistance for capital outlays to the cities, such as Urbank, Community Development Banks, and extended authority for investment of certain pension or public trust funds in "municpals" — with the intent of reducing the cost of borrowing or enlarging access to borrowing. Among the methods are those providing new instrumentalities for municipal borrowing or the broadening of the market for municipal securities through federal guarantees and subsidization of interest.

Federal action through capital financing may have the effect of giving cities added incentive to construct new facilities, or to renovate older facilities; other options such as providing added city services, however, would be made more costly. Thus, a city deciding on whether to build a school or add personal services such as remedial reading could find the financing of school construction easier than paying additional teachers' salaries, and various allocations could be distorted from the path of greater efficiency by the relative access to funds.

From the perspective of the cities, the main drawbacks of a new federally sponsored development bank are: (1) the federal requirements and controls that would accompany federal assurances and subsidies, and (2) the need for — yet difficulties in arriving at — statutory criteria for rationing federal credit supports among eligible cities.

National funding of public service employment.

Congress has recently adopted a program designed to provide added employment opportunities in the public sector. The general notion of this approach to city finances is to pair two problems — the problem of gaps and inadequacies in public services, and the problem of unemployment in the center city. This pairing is a more direct approach to dual problem solving than general revenue sharing, yet in common with revenue sharing it can be construed as a noncategorical grant. If targeted where the unemployment is greatest and supported by adequate training and career-development mechanisms, it could help cope with major economic problems in the core cities. The problems are of several types: (1) assuring adequate supplementary funds for any matching requirements, (2) assuring add-ons to employment rather than substitutions, (3) safeguarding independent decision making in the city, (4) building in adequate administrative arrangements for supervisory services and upgrading, and (5) reducing the administrative overload and related costs.

National funding through tax credits.

Still an additional option is national use of the federal taxing authority to overcome revenue restraints on city governments by permitting taxpayers to credit city taxes against a federal tax levy. Usually tax credit proposals have dealt with the income tax and with state income taxation rather than city levies. It is doubtful that much by way of added revenues could be raised locally through a federal credit for local income taxes. Unless the federal tax credit approached 100 percent of the city tax, there would continue to be competitive pressures against adoption of the tax. Furthermore, some would urge that state rather than local use of income taxes should be fostered.

Who Should Pay, and For How Long?

The preceding discussion has focused on forms of external aid from the national government to the city. These forms generally involve additional national tax resources for the cities, and, by the use of the national tax system, an almost automatic enlargment of the share of city public services financed out of the generally progressive national income tax. Earlier it was suggested that one way of siphoning funds from satellite to core was through external aid from the nation to the city. The assumption underlying this statement is that the higher income groups would be taxed in support of the lower income core city residents.

How much external aid, and over what period, are matters for considerable economic analysis in terms of the industrial and manufacturing characteristics in satellite and core, SMSA after SMSA. If the amount and type of external aid is inadequate to reverse the basic economic forces that have led to the deterioration of the core relative to the surrounding areas, then the added external aid will not have achieved the purpose of such assistance.

Proposals for slum removal have floundered because the net consequence has been a change in the location of the slums elsewhere in the core; proposals for highway construction to renew the core areas economically have resulted on balance in more congestion and more outward movement. Recent analysis of mass transit systems suggests much the same net incentive toward outward spread. What would work to revitalize the core? Essentially little is known about the forces that could stay central city erosion. Much of what has been tried has not been successful to date. Some national policies such as urban renewal and interstate highway systems are now thought to have contributed to the creation of the urban crisis.

Some urge incentives toward metropolitan-wide governments. Removal of artifically small political boundaries within a single metropolitan area should facilitate revenue raising; however, the differences even within one taxing jurisdiction between those who pay the taxes and those who reap the benefits may continue to serve as a brake on public service levels. Disparities and inequalities could remain unchanged in a metropolitan government.

The real question remains how best to achieve the ends sought, and over what time period. If improved urban living is to be achieved, economic incentives for central city location to industry and individuals must be strong.

17 Financing Public Employment

MELVILLE J. ULMER

Any decision about how to finance public service employment must depend in some part at least, on what we expect its functions to be. So I'd like to discuss those functions before going on to the matter of financing.

First of all, I think one expected and desirable result of a public employment program is that it would get *additional* public services performed. In other words, the program would be intended to make a net contribution, by providing services that either are not available at all now, or are not being performed at the quantity or quality level considered desirable. Furthermore, the new or additional services would be expected to relate to the highest priorities among these inumerable public goods that are now so notably lacking. In fact, any other approach, one that ignored the priorities, would be wasteful, or as economists like to say, irrational, from society's point of view.

Second, I think that public service employment, as matters now stand, is coming to be recognized as a national moral obligation. Periodically, in this country, we courageously determine to fight inflation by creating unemployment, although not all of us enlist in the conflict with the same fervor. Those drafted in the war against inflation — that is, those thrown out of jobs — are largely, to the tune of about 80 percent, the unskilled and the semi-skilled, or the weakest among us, financially and psychologically. Hence, it may be said we owe them jobs in the public sector, when they can't get them elsewhere, along with the on-the-job training and further education that can and should be provided at public expense at the same time.

Thirdly, I have shown elsewhere that a public employment program can be used, along with certain other new tools, to achieve what is conventionally considered unattainable in this country — that is, full employment without inflation, or a close approach thereto. I obviously can't go into that plan here — it would take too long — but I believe that everyone can see that a public employment program could have some beneficial anticyclical uses, and that's all that's necessary for present purposes. Incidentally, I am not suggesting in this that I think public service employment should be turned on and off with the business cycle; I think it would be a desirable permanent institution, but it could still be expanded and contracted with changes in private sector employment levels.

I have cited three main objectives of public service employment, and should like to show that everyone of them requires that the federal government retain

341

central control over the program, including not only its overall dimensions, but also the specific character of the particular projects that comprise it.

In other words, the considerations I have outlined would rule out the revenue-sharing approach, in which state and local governments would be left free to use federal funds exactly as they wished, with no restrictions. I would not bother to mention this except that I have been told that revenue sharing has been seriously proposed as a method for organizing and financing public service employment. And so I want to show why that would frustrate or pervert the basic objectives of a public employment program.

Take the initial objective that I cited — that of making a *net* contribution, that is, providing new or additional public services. We all know, I believe, from various surveys taken in connection with the president's general revenue-sharing plan, that some states and cities would use such funds, if they got them, for reducing their own taxes. This has been amply documented, and apparently the dissipation of revenue-sharing funds in this way would occur on a very broad scale. Now what is to prevent essentially the same thing from happening in the present case? For example, public service employees, received on a federal tab, could be substituted for regular employees, clearing the way for a reduction in state and local taxes. This could be accomplished, with reasonable patience, without firing anyone — simply be filling vacancies as they occur among clerks, garbage collectors, building maintenance crews, and so on. More simply, the same objective might be achieved, conceivably, without substitution, merely by paying ordinary civil service workers with revenue-sharing funds, and saving a corresponding amount in state and local revenue. Now a reduction in taxes is not a bad thing, but if *that* were the purpose of this program it would be far better — fairer and simpler — to reduce the federal income tax, and never mind public employment. The point is that insofar as states and cities used their revenue shares in the way just described, we would get neither more public employment nor more public services.

Secondly, the revenue-sharing approach to public service employment would represent a retreat from federal responsibility for national priorities. As a practical matter, in this connection, I think we've got to recognize that the states and localities differ very widely not only in administrative skill and political integrity, but in the degree of responsibility they exhibit for social obligations — their social consciousness. Anyone should know this, it seems to me, by just looking around and reading the newspapers. But not everyone concedes it. Some have contended, for example, that education is horrible in some states because they are poor and can't afford any better, that the tax efforts of some states is small and ineffective because they are poor and can't do any better, or that welfare payments are brutally, negligibly small in some instances because these poor states can't afford any more. Now differences among states in income levels obviously account for *some* part of the differences we observe in expenditures for education, welfare, and in their tax efforts — but only in *smaller* part. That's the important point. The greater part of these differences, it turns out, is due to variations in those intangibles I mentioned, in their social consciousness, their political, administrative, and moral maturity. How do we know? Well, in two ways. First of all, you can see this easily in particular instances.

Florida and Wisconsin have almost exactly equal per capita personal incomes. But Wisconsin has one of the highest and most effective income taxes of all the states. Florida has no income tax. Wisconsin pays an average benefit of $185 monthly to its welfare families. Florida pays only half as much — $95. Wisconsin spends almost $900 per pupil on its primary and secondary school education. Florida spends only $700, or 25 percent less. Something other than income levels account for these differences. Secondly, one can derive the same conclusions more generally by systematic statistical analysis. Thus, in a multiple correlation study I found that income differences among the fifty states account for only one-third of the observed differences in the amounts they spend on education, per pupil. I found no correlation at all between the tax efforts made by states and their per capita income levels.

Now the lesson provided by all this for public employment, I hope, is clear. If the states differ so widely in those intangibles of morality, ethics, responsibility, and the rest, how can we logically suppose that all or even most public service employees would be put to socially effective use if the states were free to do with them as they wished? And yet revenue sharing rests on such faith, on a naive faith that somehow these free resources would be used conscientiously, that the lurid experiences of the past year in some revenue-sharing pilot studies will not be repeated, and that if we were to visit the homes of state officials around the country we would never, but never, find their lawns tended, their floors scrubbed, or their tables served by public service employees.

If you think that my last reference is a gratuitous exaggeration of the possibilities, let me remind you of what happened recently in Alabama to federal funds allocated to that state, with no strings attached other than they be used for law enforcement. Leading state officials, bureau chiefs, division heads, and so on sent their sons to college not only tuition-free but with salaries of $6,000 on the grounds that after they received their degrees they might consider careers in the police department. Some of you will recall that Mae West once said that, despite her reputation, she never yielded to temptation — except when she couldn't resist it. For reasons that Wilbur Mills has emphasized, revenue sharing provides a special temptation to the frivolous, or even dishonest, use of public funds, and there is nothing in experience that assures us that all the states and all the cities would successfully resist it.

Now I'd like to get back to two other aspects of a public employment program that require federal supervision. First, using public employment as a countercyclical device would involve very careful timing, and also strategic geographical placement of the various projects undertaken. I do not see how this would be possible at all without a central control. And without proper timing, the stabilizing efforts could easily become self-defeating, developing a Milton Friedman type ratchet effect in which our attempts to ameliorate business fluctuations only made them greater.

Another condition requiring federal control relates to the public service workers. Presumably they are to be the direct beneficiaries of the program. The first prerequisite here is that they be given work that is obviously useful. Any suggestion of boondoggling would be demoralizing, and incidentally would also spell an early demise for the entire program. In addition, I think a great opportunity would be lost if public service employment were not coupled with some kind of systematic on-the-job training, and provisions for further adult education. Providing these conditions — useful work and opportunities for self-improvement — I think would be more feasible under federal supervision than under the laissez faire system of revenue sharing.

One final point. Even if the states were all to behave in the most conscientious way conceivable, it is highly unlikely, in the absence of federal controls, that public service employees would be used in line with national priorities. More and more of the social and economic problems that confront us today transcend the economically meaningless borders of the forty-eight contiguous states. The cleansing of most rivers patently requires regional action, under federal guidance, since no single state or city could possibly do the job on its own. The substandard education provided in one area of the country inevitably poisons the rest of the nation. No barrier that we can erect will prevent polluted air from crossing state lines. So simply dispensing money, or free manpower, around the country, with no strings attached would be an expensively anachronistic gesture running counter to the major trend of modern economic history. What we need more than ever today is federal leadership.

A comprehensive textbook on manpower planning for the private sector in the United States is Thomas H. Patten, Jr., *Manpower Planning and the Development of Human Resources* (New York: John Wiley and Sons, 1971). Very little has been written on manpower planning for the public sector in the United States. Three experimental monographs, each reflective of work in progress, are: Sidney A. Fine and Wretha W. Wiley, *An Introduction to Functional Job Analysis* (Kalamazoo, Michigan: The W. E. Upjohn Institute for Employment Research, September 1971); Washington Center for Metropolitan Studies, *Manpower Needs Study for Maryland Local and State Governments* (Washington, D.C.: Washington Center for Metropolitan Studies, 1970); and Paul A. Roberts, et. al., *Manpower Planning for the Public Service* (Chicago: Public Personnel Association, 1971). A number of excellent monographs on public employment planning in Europe are available, particularly those published by the Organization for Economic Cooperation and Development. Cf., *Manpower Problems in the Service Sector*, 1967; *The Long Term Unemployed* (by Adrian Sinfield), 1968; and *Promoting the Placement of Older Workers*, 1967.

Quantitative information on public sector employment in the United States is almost as scarce as research on public sector manpower planning. For example, while the Bureau of the Census conducts a regular *Census of Governments* every five years – and the Bureau of Labor Statistics has conducted a series of *Municipal Wage Surveys* – neither agency has looked closely at public sector vacancy or turnover rates. In this regard, a path-breaking study is Jacob J. Rutstein, "Survey of Current Personnel Systems in State and Local Governments," *Good Government*, Spring 1971. This report on the National Service League's survey of 357 state and local jurisdictions in 1970 is summarized in Bennett Harrison, "State and Local Government Manpower Policies," *Industrial Relations*, February 1971. A recent and quite sophisticated econometric study of employment in state governments is Ronald Ehrenberg, *An Econometric Analysis of the Demand for State and Local Government Employees* (Lexington, Massachusetts: Heath-Lexington Books, 1972).

The debate over methods of financing state and local expenditures – all of which have implications for employment, both public and private – has been underway for many years. The most comprehensive presentation of the well-known Pechman-Heller revenue-sharing plan appears in Walter Heller, *New Dimensions of Political Economy* (New York: W. W. Norton, 1967). For a collection of papers on the subject, see the Subcommittee on Fiscal Policy, Joint Economic Committee, Congress of the United States, *Revenue Sharing and Its Alternatives; What Future for Federalism?*, Vol. 2, 90th Congress, 1st Session, Washington, D.C., 1967. Professor Ulmer's criticisms of revenue sharing, presented to the Upjohn Seminar, are elaborated in his article: "The Limitations of Revenue Sharing," *The Annals of the American Academy of Political and Social Science*, September 1971.

Part VI
Public Service Employment and the
Rural Sector

Introduction to Part VI

Originally, no seminar session had been planned on the problems of rural unemployment and underemployment. Staff members representing heavily rural constituencies — especially Ed Pena from the office of Senator Yarborough — were scathing in denouncing this lapse, and insistent that it be remedied.

They were absolutely right. At the very root of the urban job crisis is the wholesale migration continuing unabated since the end of World War II of workers from rural areas into the cities. Between the 1950 and the 1960 census, Mississippi lost 50 percent of her agricultural workforce. Preliminary returns from the 1970 census indicate that the flow of migrants has not stopped.

Meanwhile, the entry level manufacturing jobs that provided wages, self-respect, and hope for the future to generations of immigrants who arrived through Ellis Island, have moved to the suburbs or disappeared altogether. The post-war wave of newcomers to the city — arriving through the bus terminal rather than the dock — coming not from Southern Europe, but from our own exhausted hinterland and mechanized cotton fields — found a very different prospect than earlier hopefuls.

Professor Ray Marshall has studied the pattern of migration from the rural south into American cities. He reports that poor families in rural areas are much poorer than poor families in metropolitan areas. Rural poverty families average incomes of only $1,169 in contrast to $2,125 in metropolitan areas. In the rural areas one-half of all blacks are poor as contrasted with one-seventh of all whites. In the deep southern states, Mr. Marshall said, "Poverty in rural America runs to as much as 80 to 90 percent of the nonwhite population. More disturbing is the evidence we get that the income gap is widening between white and nonwhite in the rural South. It is fair to say that during the first half of the 60s black farmers in the South made no real progress at all." The crucial measure in a situation where most people work, underemployment, has increased greatly, according to Marshall. He states that in 1950 there were seven full-time jobs for every ten workers in the rural South and in 1959 there were less than five full-time jobs for every ten workers. In that nine year period about 2.3 million full-time jobs were eliminated from southern agriculture, about 14 percent of the southern agricultural work force. These figures are only the latest in a long trend. In 1940 in the United States 25 percent of the population was classified as "farmer." In 1969, the figure was 5 percent. There are now only 13 percent as many black farmers in the South as there were in 1950. There are only 30 percent as many white farmers as there were in 1950.

Who has left the South and what has happened to them after they have left? Marshall looked at black males and found that 80 percent of the black males that left between 1950 and 1969 had less than seven years of education; 52 percent less than four years. "In other words," Marshall stated, "a majority of all the black males who were displaced from the rural south during the 1950s and 1960s were functionally illiterate." The effect of the outmigration from rural areas has been disastrous. Despite their lack of education, the farmers who have left have been the better educated, so that migration has caused a decline in the productive population base.

Programs to provide migrant training, supportive services, and help in finding jobs, Marshall says, work well enough when the people chosen to migrate are the youngest, best educated, and most flexible of the rural workers. But encouraging the most talented people to move to the city leaves the rural areas in worse shape than ever. In any case, manpower training for people in rural areas has not received much financial support. Non-metropolitan areas have about 22 percent of the manpower funds. Attempts to establish urban growth centers in rural areas have lacked for sufficient federal funds and have been only marginally successful. We have "very few success stories anywhere in the world of what the regionalists call 'hot-house developments' in rural areas," Marshall said. The economic disadvantages of locating in rural areas are such that it is hard to attract any but marginal industries. Marshall is encouraged by the rural co-op movement, modest as its gains have proven to be.

We studied about 100 of those co-ops that had about 25,000 people attached to them. In some cases people were able to make four or five thousand dollars a year but there were not many of those. The average was somewhere in the neighborhood of two hundred or two hundred and fifty dollars increase per year. If you are only making $800 to $1,000, moving up $200 or $250 a year can be extremely meaningful.

Marshall attributed national inaction on the problems of rural poor to their powerlessness:

There is a very limited organizational basis for people to try to correct the problems of rural areas. Rural poor have very limited political power. They have very limited economic power and as a consequence of that, legislation like our agricultural legislation, which is supposed to be doing things for the small farmers and the poor farmers, has actually aggravated their condition rather than improving it. For instance, it is hard for me to think of legitimate economic grounds for [the fact that] agricultural workers [are excluded] from representation under the National Labor Relations Act, or [the fact that] agricultural workers [are excluded] from workmen's compensation.

Marshall stated that there is an obvious need for jobs in rural areas and that public service employment could play a meaningful role. Operation Mainstream and the Neighborhood Youth Corps are very successful programs in some rural areas of the South and Southwest. But what is most needed is "overall rural development policy in this country which would include job creation, both public and private, improvements in education, manpower, and antidiscrimination programs."

Juan Gutierrez, a former justice of the peace in Hidalgo County in the lower Rio Grande, painted for the Seminar a bleak picture of the employment situation facing Chicano workers in South Texas.[a] Gutierrez is now a senior associate of Interstate Research Associates, of Washington, D.C., and Edinburg, Texas. With Mexico just across the river and Mexicans earning the equivalent of 26 cents an hour for labor, he said, there is an endless supply of labor for whom work in Texas, even at wages very low by American standards, is extremely attractive. The steady flow of underpaid workers from Mexico into the South Texas employment pool kept wages for Chicanos low and unemployment ever high. The situation of the American city is in some ways analogous to that of South Texas. The industrialization of agriculture has forced rural Americans to the inner city in a steady flow for the last half century. And the pressure of new arrivals keeps wages low in the inner city. Gutierrez underlined Professor Marshall's points about steady out-migration and pointed out that the depressed wages earned in rural areas makes operation of nationally sponsored manpower programs often very difficult.

We felt we could use the National Alliance for Businessmen's program to really assist Chicanos and entrepreneurs in the area. However, we found that most of the businesses in that area could not afford to pay $1.60 an hour which you have to pay under the National Alliance of Business program. Why? Because the prevailing wage rate in the rural Southwest is $1.25 an hour to $1.45 an hour.

Public service employment, he said, would run into the same difficulty. According to Gutierrez, the rural towns in South Texas today — and throughout the Southwest — pay $1.25 for their sanitation department and $1.25 an hour for their water and sewage treatment operators.

So if you go into those communities and say you can have public service employment but you must pay $1.60 an hour, you are going to shake their whole structure, man! They won't touch you with a ten-foot pole.

To meet the unemployment problems in the rural Southwest, Gutierrez urged protecting the Chicanos by controlling the border. "You can talk about the whole nice good neighbor policy, but the fact remains and the fact is that the Chicanos in the Southwest are paying for that good neighbor policy," he said.

The discussion of Professor Marshall's and Mr. Gutierrez' remarks concentrated on the need for a national strategy for economic growth, manpower training and job supply if the chronic problems of rural areas are to be met. Such a program would include cooperatives, community economic development, the development of growth centers and the provision for more public service employment jobs. It is hard to establish a priority for the poor in rural public service employment because jobs on the public payroll are known as the best paying jobs, the steadiest jobs around. There is sharp competition among the

[a]Mr. Gutierrez gave an informal presentation to the Seminar, and hence there is no formal paper by him in this volume.

ablest for public jobs now. The fact is, whether it is at the minimum wage or below the minimum wage, by and large public employment in rural areas, more so than it is in city areas, is a high wage employment, because it is full-time employment, it is not seasonal. Agriculture workers do not work a total of 2,000 or even 1,000 hours a year. Public service employees have full-time work. Dr. Marshall pointed out that in northern New Mexico $3,000 a year is enough for a "middle-class standard of living. So it is difficult — in a situation where public service jobs are considered the best jobs available — to establish a federal program which will increase federal public service jobs and make it a priority that those jobs go to the unemployed. Public service jobs in many rural areas are very desirable. They are the jobs that politicians seek for their relatives."

The Seminar discussion raised the issue of public service employment in rural areas as part of a larger overall strategy. National public service employment legislation was first passed during the Depression in the 30s. But as Mr. Gutierrez said of rural areas, "we are in a depression all the time since 1930."

The problems and dilemmas of the rural areas are further spelled out in the chapter following Professor Marshall's paper, adapted from the 1971 *Manpower Report of the President.* That material provides us with the necessary background of trends concerning migration from rural areas; which types of groups are primarily invoved in this cityward process; the changing nature of employment patterns and opportunities for those who stay behind; and the impact of farm consolidation. A special section is devoted exclusively to the disadvantaged groups in our nation's rural areas, including the migratory workers. Equally important are the descriptions of the limited participation of rural workforces in our training and work-experience programs; and of programs designed to redevelop rural areas and regions.

18

Obstacles to a Public Employment Program in the Rural South

F. Ray Marshall

I have done a lot of thinking about public service employment, but I don't know if I know much about exactly what kinds of things can be done in rural areas. I know some of the things that seem to make a lot of sense, but it is, it seems to me, a fairly complicated problem.

What I would like to do is to first lay out the problem of rural America, as I see it, and to warn you that my perspective is Southern and, more particularly, my perspective is black. I have paid particular attention to the problems of black workers in the rural South.

I have recently paid more attention to the problems of Chicanos, but I am a long way from understanding that problem even as well as I do the problem of blacks, the problems of blacks in rural America. But I know something of the dimensions of the problem, and I would like to say something about that and then make a few comments about some of the kinds of proposals that have been made to deal with the problems of rural areas.

I am going to slide very quickly over the question of what is rural. But it is also indicative of the neglect of this area that the agencies in Washington themselves don't even agree about what they mean by a rural area. The Labor Department, the Census, and the U.S. Department of Agriculture, all use different definitions of "rural."

A study was recently made, for example, by the U.S. Department of Agriculture to show that non-farm employment grew faster in rural areas during the 1960s than it did in metropolitan areas. But it is not at all clear exactly what that means. It is not clear whether this non-farm employment was within the orbit of, say, a major metropolitan area, or whether it was really open country. And from the standpoint of policy, it makes a whole lot of difference whether you are talking about plants locating in open country or whether you are talking about plants locating in the orbit of a major metropolitan area.

Poverty in this country is concentrated very heavily in rural areas, by whatever definition anybody uses. And if you look at the latest figures, one-half of the poor live outside of metropolitan areas, but only one-third of the total population live outside of metropolitan areas. If you break it down further, in the whole United States, one-fifth of all people who live in rural areas are below the government's official poverty definition, as contrasted with one-tenth in cities, and one-fourteenth in metropolitan areas.

Not only are people in rural areas poor, and not only is more poverty concentrated in rural areas, but the rural poor are poorer than people elsewhere. The non-metropolitan poor family had an average income in 1969 of $1,923. In farm areas it was $1,169 – even less than that. And in metropolitan areas, $2,125.

Not only is there a heavy concentration of poverty in rural areas, but it is heavily concentrated in the South and among blacks. For the whole country, one-half of all blacks in rural areas are in the poverty category, as contrasted with one-seventh of all whites.

Sixty percent of all poor people who live outside metropolitan areas live in the South, and if you break it down further in the South, poverty takes a different dimension than it does in the rest of the country:

A much larger proportion of the poor people in the South work full-time than any other place in the country. One-third of all nonwhite men who are classified as poor work full time, as contrasted with one-seventh of all white men who are classified as poor. These figures conceal great diversity.

In the deep South states, poverty in rural areas is as much as 80 to 90 percent among nonwhites, according to the latest figures that we are able to get; it is 55 percent for whites.

More disturbing is the evidence that the income gap is widening between whites and nonwhites in the rural South. We use Social Security statistics, which are very useful in many ways, because they make it possible to follow identical individuals.

We found that from 1960 to 1965, the income of black farmers in the South increased by 6.5 percent, which was about the same as the increase in the cost of living. So it is fair to say that during the first half of the 60s, black farmers in the South made no real progress at all. White farmers, on the other hand, gained 40 percent during that same period, and they started with average income over twice that of the black farmers, so you don't have a base problem. We therefore are safe in concluding that the income gap widened absolutely and relatively during this period.

What obviously is happening is that in the South, particularly, as well as in the country as a whole, the farm population is declining at a fairly rapid rate. The displacement in the South has been very fast, and the displacement among blacks has been extremely fast. The ability of black people to survive in the rural South is obviously almost non-existent, as I will indicate with the numbers that we have accumulated.

We have put together an annual series from 1950 through 1969 by race, to try to see what is happening to the population.

In a bird's eye view, what is happening is that the blacks and whites are being displaced from agriculture, but blacks are being displaced at a much faster rate. It is important to note, however, that the *rural* population is not declining. The rural population stayed about constant during the 1960s, and that is because the rural non-farm population increased enough to offset the decline in the agricultural population. That means that even though you have had considerable out-migration from agriculture, the rural problem remains.

What seems to be happening to the people who leave the rural South, as much as we can follow them, is that among those who leave agriculture, a very large proportion are becoming rural *non*-farm simply by definition.

Underemployment has greatly increased. We found that in 1950, there were seven full-time jobs for every ten workers. In 1959, there were less than five full-time jobs for every ten workers. During that period about 2.3 million full-time jobs were eliminated from southern agriculture. That amounts to about 14 percent of the total Southern, non-agricultural work force right now — 14 percent of the total. What happened is that there are 30 percent as many white farmers in the South now as there were in 1950; there are 13 percent as many black. Now, obviously, what was going on during the 1960s was that a lot of people were leaving the South, a lot of people were leaving the rural areas, but a lot of people also couldn't leave and stayed where they were.

Another real problem, of course, is that if you trace these people into Southern urban labor markets, you find that the effect of their migration has been to widen the racial income gap within the many Southern labor markets — places like Memphis, Miami, and other places that we are studying, because blacks who are better educated and have labor force experience are moving out of those labor markets and are being replaced by people from rural areas who have less education.

The white pattern is the reverse. Many whites, who have the same characteristics as the blacks who are moving out, are moving into Southern labor markets, which means better educated whites are moving in and better educated blacks are moving out, and that causes the income gaps within those labor markets to widen.

Some indication of the extent of the adjustment problem for people who have been displaced can be found by looking at the education characteristics of the people who got displaced from agriculture. We have compared these characteristics with the educational requirements for the jobs that are opening up in the area. The conclusion that we come to is probably what you would expect, although the dimensions of the problem were greater than we expected. The conclusion is that very few of the blacks who are being displaced in the South can meet the educational requirements of the industry that is moving into the South.

We looked at black males, and we found that 80 percent of black males who left between 1950 and 1969 had less than seven years of education. We found that 52 percent had less than four years of education. In other words, it is fair to say that a majority of all of the black males who were displaced from Southern agriculture during the 1950s and 1960s, were functionally illiterate. This is an average. Fifty-two percent had less than four years education — and that means that an awful lot had zero.

We have learned to discount the raw educational figure by two years. So it means that a very large proportion of these people were actually second graders.

You might conclude that there has been a tremendous improvement in educational characteristics of population by 1970, and therefore people in rural areas ought to be a whole lot better off. The figures don't show that.

The figures show that what has happened is that migration has frequently hurt everybody involved in the migration process, that is, every area in the migration stream. These people, even though they had a very large proportion with only eight years of education, were still the best educated of the Southern rural labor force. That still meant that they moved into labor markets where they weren't prepared to compete for better jobs. At the same time there is also pretty good evidence that those blacks who move out of the rural South and into the urban areas of the non-South are no worse off than blacks of similar characteristics who are already there. Indeed, we are also finding that Southern migrants to northern cities are usually better off in economic terms than blacks with similar characteristics who were either born in those cities or who moved into that area from other Northern cities. There are probably demand and supply explanations that we could give for that. Blacks from the rural South probably are more willing to work for marginal jobs than blacks in Northern cities, and Northern employers probably prefer Southern migrants to Northern-born blacks for marginal jobs.

If you look at the figures nationwide now, 45 percent of the rural population twenty-five years of age and over has less than eight years of education.

The really important question is, what do you do about all of this? I think the picture that emerges is that poverty is very intense in rural areas generally, but particularly in the rural South. It is especially intense among black farmers and farm workers in the South.

Some people say that there are a variety of things that you can do to solve the problem. One answer is migration; that is, to depopulate the rural areas of the South, and that is the only long-run solution to the problem. It seems to me that this is very much of an oversimplified view. Partly, it is clear that the process of out-migration has been going on for a long, long time, and far from improving the situation in rural areas, it has aggravated it. And it has aggravated it because it has caused a decline in rural services in rural areas generally.

We could mention something about the mobility or relocation studies, the mobility experiments that the Labor Department has undertaken, but I won't go into those in detail. The idea that you take people from the rural areas, where they have low levels of productivity, and move them to areas where they can be more productive, is clearly a good one. Between 1965 and 1968 the Labor Department screened 40,000 people, and moved about 14,000 people. I think that the key to whether the mobility projects were successful or not depends on a number of things: (a) whether you gave supportive services of any kind, (b) whether there were jobs at the other end, and (c) if you were talking about a relatively young – thirty-five or less – population and usually if you combined the project with some basic education.

The conclusion that I draw from looking at all of those mobility projects is that although they are beneficial to some people, they aren't likely to solve the rural problem. They accentuate the "creaming" process. Moreover, once we have counted all of the costs, social cost as well as individual, the mobility projects appear as successful as they do if you count only those costs associated with *successful* moves and ignore those who returned, and the adverse effects of relocation on rural areas.

I think what you can say is that the mobility projects have affected the timing and direction of moves and have benefited those people who stayed in the demand areas.

There are, however, several defects with the suggestions that we establish programs to depopulate the rural areas.

1. There is a political defect, in the sense that it doesn't do you any good to recommend something to somebody who doesn't exist, or to tell political leaders that they ought to depopulate their districts. You are not likely to get very far with that one!
2. The second defect is that all the costs involved are not counted, and I think that that is an extremely important point. We don't count the cost to the area from which the people move, and the cost to the area to which the people move – that is, the receiving and the sending areas. Nor do they count the costs of the unsuccessful movers, many of whom return to their former homes.

Another strategy that has been recommended to solve the problem of rural areas is the growth center strategy. The basic idea here is that you ought not to congest the metropolitan areas, but you ought to select growth centers, which have different definitions, and you ought to direct the flow of people into those growth centers. My conclusion after studying the growth center for some time is that it is a good idea, but there are no success stories!

There is also the problem of size. That is, what do you mean by a "growth center"? I think that there is an awful lot of generalizing about rural America that is wrong. There are a lot of people who say, "well, all rural areas are declining, and the best thing you can do for the people is to get them out of there." I think that there are probably some growth centers of 10,000 population, although some of my colleagues disagree. They figure that you have got to have a place of at least 25,000 or 50,000, depending on the person who is doing the selecting. But if you are talking about places of that size, you go back to all of the problems involved with depopulation. It seems to me that the growth center strategy deserves careful consideration, but only after some study and demonstrations.

Another answer to what do you do about rural areas is that you industrialize them. That is, don't take the people out to the jobs, but bring the jobs to the people. This obviously is a very popular idea. Here again, however, there are very few success stories anywhere in the world of what the regionalists call "hot house developments" in rural areas, the basic conclusion being that the economic disadvantages of locating in rural areas are such that you are not likely to get many other marginal industries to locate there.

My answer to this is that marginal industries might be useful because there are a lot of people who are likely to work in marginal industries wherever they go; so I think that is is perfectly defensible to have a strategy to make it possible to attract marginal jobs to people who are likely to work in marginal jobs wherever they happen to be. And that is particularly likely to be true of the people left behind.

We studied about a hundred co-ops that had 25,000 people attached to them. The average age was about fifty-four. The average education was about four years. The average income was between $800 and $1,000 a year before they started. You aren't likely to make tool and die makers out of those fellows. And you are not likely to have any kind of growth center strategy that could help them.

In some cases, the real success stories, people were able to make $4,000 or $5,000 a year, and there weren't many of those. The average was somewhere in the neighborhood of $200 or $250 increase per year. Now, of course, I know that city audiences are likely to say "you really don't want us to work hard to get people $200 or $250 more a year." My answer is "yes." If you are only making $800 or $1,000, moving up $200 or $250 a year can be extremely meaningful in those areas.

The basic idea that seems to me to make sense is that if you are going to subsidize a firm to come in, you ought to be able to specify the characteristics of the work force it hires.

We are looking at some places in Mississippi and a lot of other places, where the people in those areas benefitted very little if at all from subsidization by the state for the location of that industry there. We are beginning to suspect very strongly that this might be the case, for example, with the big ship-building contract that Litton Industries got in Pascagoula. We need to see if many poor people in Mississippi really got jobs as a result of this activity.

They have even gone as far away as England to get their work force. But although this experience is currently being studied, so far it is hard for us to see where it has stimulated very much acticity in that area, and therein lies the chief defect, I think, of that plan. Let's say, if you are going to try to solve the problems of unemployment and underemployment in those areas by industrialization, then you frequently don't do very much by that industrialization unless you change the policy.

That is, if an industry comes in to rural areas, it is probably going to be subsidized, and if it is going to be subsidized, we ought to be able to specify something about the nature of the work force.

It doesn't do much good for industries to bring their work force with them from California, or to "cream" that local labor market and take people who might be better off working some other place. Simply because firms can come into rural areas and hire high school graduates, as they frequently do, does not mean that their impact on local unemployment and underemployment in that area will be significant.

The kind of thing that I am thinking about is that there are profitable activities in a lot of these rural areas that could be developed.

One fairly profitable activity involves the co-ops. These rural activities might not be the most profitable pursuits that can be made, but they are, nevertheless, profitable. Therefore they will be able to yield returns above their costs (and these costs could be incomes to many people in rural areas) to a community development organization, whereas a profit-making firm might avoid that place altogether.

Manpower Funds. Another area that I think a great deal of attention needs to be paid to is the manpower area. Manpower funds have not been spent very much in rural areas — nothing in proportion to their population. Non-metropolitan areas have about 22 percent of the population; they have received 6.9 percent of the manpower funds. They have a much larger percentage of the poverty population, as noted earlier.

There are a variety of reasons for this. I think that one of the most important ones is that rural areas lack people who are manpower experts. There are not many people to help write proposals and to be grantsmen in rural areas. The urban areas probably have a surplus of such types, but rural areas do not. The funds consequently go where the proposals are coming from.

Training Facilities and Job Opportunities. The other main problem, of course, is training facilities and job opportunities, once people get trained. I think that problem would be one of the main defects of the proposed Family Assistance Plan.

There are some things that are being tried that might prove useful. The Labor Department is now experimenting in rural areas, and Texas is one of the states in which they are experimenting, with what is called the "hitch-hike" system. The basic idea is to attract manpower experts to existing institutions, rather than to try and create a new manpower apparatus.

Education. Another area that obviously needs attention is education. It is obvious that the kind of situation which I depicted earlier aggravates the problems of the nation as well as those of the rural areas, and that the nation as well as rural America has a stake in equalizing the quantity and quality of education. We are not likely to do that until we break the dependence of local areas on property taxes as a means of financing the schools, and a new financial arrangement undoubtedly will have to be made.

Welfare. A fifth area that clearly is important, and one that we have done a great deal of work on, is welfare, in which we included health, housing, child care, and the like.

I will just emphasize one point. That is that Dr. Ray Wheeler has studied, as part of our O.E.O. project, the effects of early malnutrition and inadequate health care on the permanent physical and mental development of children. And the overpowering evidence was that these inadequacies cause permanent physical and mental damage for those children.

The real question that you ask, if you look at all of these things — and I think that one of the problems with the rural areas is that they are invisible, that people don't see them — is why doesn't something get done about it?

That leads me to the next problem, which I think is a very serious one. There is a very limited organizational base for people to try to correct the problems of rural areas. And certainly that is the case of the rural poor. They have very limited political power; they have very limited economic power. As a consequence, programs which are supposed to be doing things for the small farmers and the poor farmers have actually aggravted their conditions rather than improving them.

As you know quite well, rural people are excluded from most other protective social legislation. And the main reason for their exclusion is inadequate political power. It is hard for me to think of legitimate economic grounds for excluding agricultural workers, say, from representation in the National Labor Relations Act, or to exclude agricultural workers from workmen's compensation, or from a whole host of other social legislation. If anything, you can make a stronger case that they ought to be included.

The last question is, what role does public service employment play in all of this?

Perhaps we ought to start by defining what we mean by "public employment." Because that term covers a wide range of possibilities. And to some extent, our co-ops, which are federally subsidized, are public employment.

Public employment can mean regular public jobs, of which there are some fourteen million in the country. There is no problem, I take it, in expanding those jobs, because "regular" government jobs are expanding anyway. If you look at the government employment figures, you can see that the federal employment doesn't look that good, but the state and local government figures show considerable growth.

The conclusion I come away with is that so far we have only taken a very superficial look at public employment programs that have been working in the rural areas — things like the Neighborhood Youth Corps, Operation Mainstream, New Careers, the Public Service Careers idea, the Title Five O.E.O., which has been called "Happy Pappy" in Kentucky.

The conclusion I come to is that most of these people who are unemployed and underemployed in rural areas are not likely to be absorbed by the private sector, and if we are going to get full employment, it will have to be public employment to do it.

However, even though public employment is a very appealing idea, if you examine all of the problems, you will find that it is a very difficult one to implement.

If you look at the successful programs, it seems to me that they have had the following essential ingredients:

1. The successful programs worked with unemployed persons who had considerable work experience. That is, they either had worked as farmers — and Operation Mainstream fits that category — or as rural non-agricultural workers, like many of those put to work on New Deal Programs during the 1930s.
2. There was useful work to be done — and that work ordinarily was visible work. It seems to me that there is considerable work in this category.
3. They were straight work programs without other motives, even though sometimes the other motives were required by the legislation.

The less successful programs were those that:

1. combined work with other motives, like training, work experience, getting people off welfare, and a variety of other things;
2. were used purely as income maintenance programs, like some Neighborhood Youth Corps activities. In the Southwest, however, the Neighborhood Youth Program was a very successful program, and it is partly because of differences in the operation of the labor market;
3. made attempts to build career ladders.

I think that what you can say about the subsidies for private efforts to increase employment, which is another kind of public employment, is that the experience has been fairly mixed, and that it is hard to come to any definite conclusion about it.

Let me conclude with three observations:

First, I would emphasize that it is very difficult to generalize about rural areas because there are considerable differences.

Secondly, we need an overall rural development policy in this country which would include job creation, both public and private, improvements in education, manpower, and antidiscrimination programs. A great deal of legislation has been developed for urban areas in this country, but antidiscrimination programs in rural areas don't seem to be very effective, to put it mildly.

And finally I would say that public employment must be an important part of any overall rural development policy, but it should only be a *part*, because many things besides public employment also have to be done.

19

Rural Manpower Dilemmas

U. S. DEPARTMENT OF LABOR

Migration, Population, and Employment Trends

Only thirty years ago, nearly one out of every four people in this country lived on a farm. Today, the proportion is down to one out of twenty. Between 1940 and 1969, the farm population declined from 30.5 to 10.3 million. Within the last ten years alone, farm population has shrunk by more than one-third, and further declines are in prospect.

Residents of rural nonfarm areas now outnumber those on farms by four to one. (See figure 19.1). Their number has increased enough since 1960 to offset the decline in farm population. So, on balance, the rural population has remained at about the same overall level during this decade.[a]

This means, of course, that not merely farming areas but rural areas as a whole have a decidedly smaller proportion of the country's growing population than a few years back — that the trend toward urbanization of the population is proceeding rapidly. And even within rural areas, there is a pronounced shift away from farms in both population and employment. Many sections of rural America — especially near big cities and in the Northeastern and North Central states — are progressively losing their agrarian character and tending to merge with the urban economy.

Migration Trends

The outmigration of farm population, which has been going on for many years, reached a peak between 1940 and the early 1960s. In the 1940s and 1950s, net outmigration from farms averaged more than one million a year. This far exceeded the natural population growth resulting from the high birth rates in rural areas.

Adopted from *1971 Manpower Report of the President*, pp. 114-40.

[a]The terms "farm," "rural nonfarm," and "urban" are used in the census to describe places of residence. The "rural nonfarm" population includes residents of villages and small towns with populations of less than 2,500, as well as residents of the open country not living in places operated and classified as farms. In general, the urban population includes all residents of incorporated places with populations of 2,500 or more.

**Rural nonfarm population grows
and farm population declines . . .**

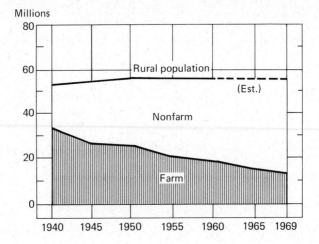

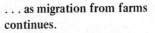

**. . . as migration from farms
continues.**

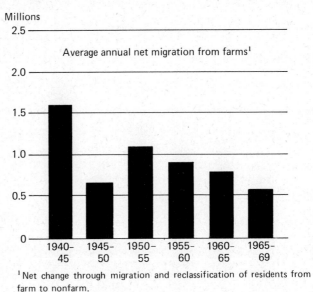

[1] Net change through migration and reclassification of residents from farm to nonfarm.

Figure 19–1. Source: Department of Labor, based on data from the Departments of Commerce and Agriculture.

In the mid-1960s, the volume of outmigration began to taper off. For the period 1965-69, the rate of net outmigration from farms, at 5.2 percent of the population, was not much different from the rate in the first half of the decade, 5.7 percent. However, with the steady reduction in the farm population, the actual number of outmigrants has declined and is expected to be still smaller in the 1970s. But the end of the movement off farms is not in sight, since continuing mechanization and consolidation of farms are anticipated.

This shift of population reflects a drop in manpower requirements in farming and also the attraction of better paying nonfarm jobs in cities and rural nonfarm areas. During World War II people left farms in droves for employment in industrial plants and for military service. In the 1950s and 1960s unprecedented technological progress in agriculture, industrial expansion into rural areas, and improvements in highways facilitated job mobility. But economic factors are not the only ones that motivate people to remain in or leave agriculture. Many farm youth are attracted to cities for higher education and for a change in social and cultural environment. On the other hand, there is a return flow of people to farms because of preference for farming as a way of life, as well as failure to make satisfactory adjustments in cities.

The total number of individuals involved in migration is much greater than net migration figures show. Between 1965 and 1969, when net annual off-farm migration averaged 582,000, some 858,000, people left farms and 275,000 returned (or moved to farms for the first time). Thus, the total number of individuals who shifted to and from farms annually may well have been over one million. Considering the age distribution of migrants, it is estimated that about 400,000 of these were members of the labor force, the rest being their dependents.

Off-farm migration takes place both to rural nonfarm areas and to cities, and simultaneously there are population shifts between rural nonfarm sections and cities. It is estimated that three-fourths of all farm-reared adults no longer live on farms. Many move back and forth during a trial-and-error period, testing the labor market in towns and cities before resettling on a permanent basis. The tendency of farm residents to work at nonfarm jobs and the corresponding employment of nonfarm residents in agriculture (discussed elsewhere in this chapter) often represent intermediate stages in the process of migration.

The outflow from rural areas to cities is not uniform throughout the nation. About half of the counties in the United States lost population between 1950 and 1960. The losses were heaviest in exclusively or primarily rural counties.[2] Relatively few urban and urban-oriented counties had population declines. Preliminary data from the 1970 census indicate a continuation of this pattern.

In the country as a whole, the majority of the people migrating from rural to urban areas have been white. Nevertheless, great numbers of Negroes have moved from southern rural areas to northern and western cities. Many social and economic factors have contributed to this migration pattern. One of the main reasons for this migration was the concentration of Negroes in cotton growing and the consequent heavy impact on them of the mechanization of cotton production during the last two decades. Ten years ago Negroes and other minority races constituted 16 percent of the population living on farms in the country as a whole; by 1969, they made up only 10 percent. Since birth rates are high among rural Negroes and since further technological changes in tobacco and other crops are impending, the potential for outmigration of Negroes continues to be large.

Another group which is in process of urbanization is the Mexican-American population of the Southwestern states. Originally, Mexican-Americans were for the most part agricultural workers, but the 1960 census showed that about 80 percent were located in urban areas. Sizable numbers of Mexican-Americans have moved from rural sections of Texas to California, while Mexicans from across the border have migrated to Texas. With relatively little education, language difficulties, and other adjustment problems, the Mexican-Americans in both cities and rural areas have high rates of unemployment and poverty.[3]

American Indians have so far shared to only a small extent in the rural-to-urban migration. About half of the 700,000 Indians in the population still live on reservations, while additional large numbers live in other rural sections. Though the reservations do not have enough economic resources to provide most Indians with an adequate living, many Indians are reluctant to give up their traditional way of life and have difficulty in adjusting to an urban environment. Government programs to assist the Indians, therefore, aim to develop more jobs on or within reach of the reservations, besides giving relocation assistance to those Indians wishing to move in hope of obtaining better employment opportunities in cities.[4]

Population Changes

The rural-to-urban migration — brought about basically by the decrease in employment opportunities in farming and, to a much lesser extent, in other extractive industries — has affected the rural population in ways that contribute to rural poverty and hamper the growth of nonfarm employment in many rural areas.

Since most migrants are young adults, they leave behind a population with an above-average proportion of older people. In 1969, less than one-fifth of the farm population were in the prime working age group of twenty-five to forty-four, compared with about one-fourth of the people in metropolitan areas. About 23 percent of the farm population were fifty-five years of age or over; the corresponding figure for metropolitan areas was about 18 percent.

Partly because of their youth, the people who migrate tend to be better educated than the adults who stay behind. The outmigration from rural areas has thus intensified the educational disadvantage of the rural population, especially of those living on farms. In 1970, nearly half (45 percent) of the farm residents aged twenty-five or over had only eight years of schooling or less.[b] In contrast, one-third of the people in rural nonfarm areas had as little as eight years of education, and the proportion was much lower still — about one-fourth — for those in metropolitan areas.

The educational deprivation was much greater for Negroes than whites (as further discussed later in this chapter). Three out of every four black farm residents aged twenty-five or over had only eight years of schooling or less — often much less — in 1970. Comparable statistics are not available for members of other minority groups, but the average number of years of school completed by Mexican-Americans in rural areas and Indians on reservations is probably even lower than the corresponding figure for rural blacks.

Both the age and the educational deficiencies of the adults now living on farms indicate the difficulties most of them would face in adjusting to urban jobs. These characteristics of the present farm population are also among the factors which hamper the development of industries requiring a relatively well-educated and skilled work force in many rural areas.

The decrease in population in many rural areas tends to reduce the number of potential customers for trade and service establishments. It also decreases the tax base which supports rural education, health, and other facilities, thus depriving such areas of the resources to attract new industries.

It is surprising to note that many rural residents already live within metropolitan areas or the surrounding counties. In 1960, 26 percent of the people classified as rural residents lived within the boundaries of SMSA counties, and 22 percent more were within a fifty mile radius of metropolitan areas.[5] In the Northeast, where the population is highly concentrated, nearly three-fourths of the rural residents lived in or near metropolitan areas. These proportions are probably higher today, though proof of this awaits the availability of data from the 1970 census.

Millions of people who live in the open country or in unincorporated suburban developments commute to jobs in cities. Large numbers of rural residents also commute to jobs in the outskirts of metropolitan areas, where there has recently been rapid industrial development and employment growth. And many others find nonfarm employment in smaller urban centers. With improved highways, commuting between rural and urban areas is becoming more and more common.

---

[b]These data for farm and rural nonfarm residents are for those outside metropolitan areas only.

Changing Employment Patterns

The drop in agricultural employment and the concurrent development of nonfarm industries in some rural areas are changing the industrial and occupational structure of rural America, although the transformation has not gone forward at the same pace in all rural counties. The picture that emerges is one of growing integration of rural and urban labor markets in many areas close to cities, and rather widespread deterioration of the employment situation in more remote rural sections that lack access to nonfarm employment.

Among people living on farms, the proportion engaged in off-farm work has been increasing. (See figure 19.2.) In April 1969, 44 percent of the employed labor force living on farms were reported to be working primarily at nonfarm jobs; the corresponding figure in April 1960 was 34 percent. On the other hand, a substantial proportion of the workers employed on farms in April 1969 were nonfarm residents — living in poor neighborhoods of cities and small towns, in city outskirts, or in the open country.

Farm Employment and Technology. The major cause of the decline in agricultural employment — from 7.9 million in 1947 to 3.5 million in 1970 — lies in the virtual revolution in farm production practices, which is still underway and which has been stimulated by research in publicly supported land-grant colleges. Between 1947 and 1970, farm output per man-hour rose more than 285 percent; nonfarm productivity advanced only 82 percent during that period. (See figure 19.3.)[c] The net result was a jump of over 35 percent in total farm output, while both farm employment and the number of farms decreased by more than half.

The harvesting of grains, cotton, sugar beets, and most other field crops is almost completely mechanized, and the manpower required for cultivation has been greatly reduced by the application of chemical as well as mechanical methods. But the country is now on the threshold of a new breakthrough involving fruit and vegetable and tobacco activities which may wipe out hundreds of thousands of seasonal farm jobs over the next five years. Current trends clearly foretell a smaller and more technically trained work force in these activities. Mechanization of operations provides an opportunity for upgrading part of the present work force to qualify for higher skilled jobs and more stable employment. However, some of the present work force may be forced to seek other occupations, as happened previously in the changeover to mechanical production methods in cotton and other crops. Steps need to be taken to aid in their readjustment through retraining and other programs.

---

[c]It is conservatively estimated that 10 million poor people were residents of "rural" as distinguished from "nonmetropolitan" areas in 1969. Persons living outside metropolitan areas include residents of small cities as well as rural areas. On the other hand, some rural sections are within the boundaries of metropolitan areas. Thus "nonmetropolitan" and "rural" are not synonymous.

**Farm work is done increasingly by
nonfarm residents . . .**

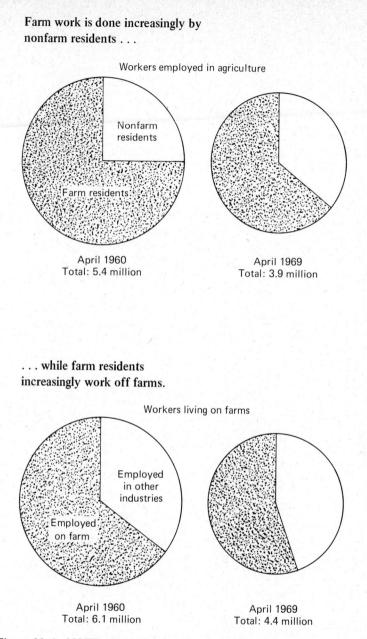

Workers employed in agriculture

Nonfarm
residents

Farm residents

April 1960
Total: 5.4 million

April 1969
Total: 3.9 million

**. . . while farm residents
increasingly work off farms.**

Workers living on farms

Employed
in other
industries

Employed
on farm

April 1960
Total: 6.1 million

April 1969
Total: 4.4 million

Figure 19-2. NOTE: Data from 1969 are used because 1970 figures
were not available at the time the graphic work was completed. Source:
Department of Labor, based on data from the Departments of Agriculture and Commerce.

**Farm employment has declined
sharply . . .**

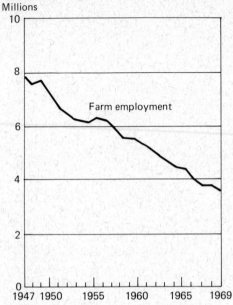

**. . . while output per man-hour
has risen dramatically on farms —
three times faster than in
nonfarm industries.**

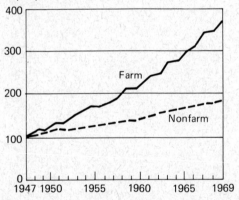

Figure 19-3. Source: Department of Labor.

Mechanization of fruit and vegetable production has been delayed by a combination of technical difficulties and cost considerations. Some products, such as sweet corn, peas for processing, and carrots, are now harvested almost wholly by mechanical methods, while others, such as fresh fruit for table use, are still far from mechanization. The future progress of mechanization will depend on the relative prices of fresh and processed fruit and vegetables, as well as on engineering innovations and other factors. Rapid mechanization and consequent sharp reductions in labor requirements are in prospect, for example, in the production of grapes, cherries, potatoes, lettuce, tomatoes, cucumbers, and beans. On the other hand, the mechanization of work on apples, pears, strawberries, and citrus fruit is expected to be more difficult. On balance, a loss of some 200,000 harvest jobs by 1975 is projected, as compared with the 1968 employment level.[6] States in which job losses will be greatest are California, Michigan, North Carolina, Oregon, and Texas.

An equally dramatic changeover is possible in the harvesting of flue-cured tobacco, which is highly concentrated in sections of the Southeast, centering in North Carolina. The technology now available, if fully adopted, would create serious human adjustment problems in a rural area where much of the available work is in the tobacco industry.[7] The use of mechanical harvesting equipment is being held back by technical problems and by the small size and scattered location of tobacco acreage (resulting from crop allotments under the price support program). On the other hand, the current uptrend in farm wage rates will add impetus to the introduction of the new technology and also to other developments in production methods which will tend to reduce labor requirements.

In tobacco, both hired workers and operators of small farms may be displaced. In fruit and vegetable production, most of the people affected will be seasonal farmworkers. However, the loss of their earnings will mean serious deprivation for many poor families who depend on this income to maintain even their present subsistence level of living.

Consolidation of Farms. Another factor which is reducing employment on farms is the trend toward consolidation of farms into larger units. This trend has been accelerated by increasing mechanization, since small farmers lack the capital to purchase expensive equipment and do not have enough acreage to use it efficiently. It has been encouraged also by changes in marketing and distribution practices which give large farms an increasing advantage.

Thus, the total number of farms dropped from 5.9 million in 1947 to 2.9 million in 1970, while the average number of acres per farm doubled (rising from 196 to 387 acres). In 1959, large farms with sales amounting to $20,000 or more per year represented 13 percent of all commercial farms and accounted for 52 percent of total sales of farm products; by 1969, 19 percent of all farms with 73 percent of total product sales were in this category.

As these figures imply, the number of small farms with less than 100 acres has declined precipitately (from 3.0 to 1.4 million) between 1950 and 1964, the latest year for which data are available. Among the farmers squeezed out were about 500,000 crop-share tenants in the South, largely from cotton plantations. Loss of farms for these tenant families often means not only cutting off cash income but also loss of housing and of the minimal security derived from having a plot of land.

It is expected that the number of farms will continue to decline for technological and economic reasons and also because the average age of farm operators is now over fifty. With the death or retirement of the large numbers of elderly men who are still holding on to small farms, many of these farms will probably be absorbed into larger units.

While contributing to the drop in farm employment, the growth of large-scale farms and the vertical integration of many farms into larger economic units that process and distribute farm products have definite advantages. In particular, large mechanized farms offer the possibility of more stable, better paid employment for a smaller, more skilled work force.

Trends in Nonfarm Employment. Another major change in the rural economic scene is the upswing in nonfarm employment. Between 1950 and 1960, the employment of rural residents in nonagricultural industries rose by over 20 percent, from 11 million to nearly 13.5 million. Gains were mainly in manufacturing, professional and related services, and wholesale and retail trade, in that order. Employment of rural residents in government, finance, insurance, and real estate, and the construction industry showed moderate advances. But these increases were not sufficient to offset the employment declines in agriculture and in other typically rural industries — forestry, fisheries, logging, sawmills, and mining. On balance, the rural work force had a net loss of more than 400,000 jobs between 1950 and 1960, creating great pressure for outmigration from rural areas.

This pressure has apparently eased since 1960, although definite conclusions on rural-urban employment changes during the past decade must await the availability of data from the 1970 census. Farm employment has continued to drop, but nonfarm job growth has accelerated outside metropolitan areas. In fact, nonfarm employment growth has been faster outside than within metropolitan areas in recent years, in relative though not in absolute numbers. Between 1962 and 1969, private nonfarm wage and salary employment increased by over 5 percent annually outside metropolitan areas, compared with only 4 percent within such areas.[8]

Some of the expansion in rural industries has been in the production and distribution of materials needed in agriculture. For example, certain types of cattle feed and fertilizers are now commonly purchased rather than produced on farms. Sorting, packing, and handling activities that were once done on farms have been transferred largely to off-farm sites.

Other factories attracted to rural areas have traditionally been in such low-wage, labor intensive industries as food processing, apparel, textiles, furniture, and wood products. These are still dominant in many rural areas, particularly in the South, but recently there has been an expansion in the manufacture of other consumer items and in electrical and nonelectrical machinery, aircraft components, and other industrial goods.[9]

The shift from farm to nonfarm employment is shown also by occupational data. (See table 19.1.) Of the male workers living outside metropolitan areas,

Table 19.1

Occupations of Employed Workers 16 Years and Over, by Sex and Residence in and Outside Metropolitan Areas, April 1960 and March 1969[1] (Percent Distribution)

Sex and Occupation Group	Metropolitan areas		Outside Metropolitan areas	
	April 1960	March 1969	April 1960	March 1969
Men				
Total: Number (millions)	27.8	31.5	15.1	16.5
Percent	100	100	100	100
Professional and managerial workers	25	31	18	23
Clerical and sales workers	17	14	10	9
Craftsmen	21	20	19	19
Operatives	21	20	21	22
Nonfarm laborers	7	6	8	8
Service workers	7	7	5	6
Farmers and farm laborers	2	1	20	14
Women				
Total: Number (millions)	1.42	19.0	6.7	9.6
Percent	100	100	100	100
Professional and managerial workers	18	19	18	18
Clerical and sales workers	44	45	32	31
Craftsmen, operatives, and laborers	18	15	19	20
Private household workers	7	5	10	7
All other service workers	13	15	17	19
Farmers and farm laborers	([2])	([2])	4	4

Source: Department of Commerce, Bureau of the Census.

Note: Detail may not add to totals because of rounding.

[1] Data for April 1960 are based on special tabulations from 63,000 households in a one-in-a-thousand sample of 1960 census data; data for March 1969 are based on approximately 53,000 households in the March 1969 Current Population Survey.

[2] Less than 0.5 percent.

only 14 percent were employed as farmers and farm laborers in 1969, compared with 20 percent in 1960. Their most significant occupational gain was in the proportion in professional and managerial work, which rose from 18 to 23 percent. For women workers, the most significant change in occupational distribution was a shift from private household to other service jobs. This occurred to about the same extent outside as inside metropolitan areas.

Disadvantaged Groups in Rural America

The growth of nonfarm employment in rural areas has not been sufficient to absorb workers displaced from agriculture plus the many rural youth entering the work force each year. This shortfall in jobs is a basic reason for the widespread underemployment and poverty in rural areas. Other contributory factors include the low incomes of operators of marginal farms, a decline in openings for farm tenants, and the traditionally low wages and intermittent employment of hired farmworkers. To these must be added barriers associated with racial discrimination, language handicaps, and inadequate education. Furthermore, though improved communication and transportation have made some rural areas less isolated than in the past, distance to urban labor markets is still a serious problem for most rural workers.

For all these reasons, the incidence of poverty is higher in rural areas than in cities.[10] (See figure 19.4.) In 1969, half of the nation's poor, some 12 million poor people, lived outside metropolitan areas, although little more than a third of the total population resided there.[d]

Poverty is not only more frequent but also more severe among rural than among urban families. The median income of poor families in metropolitan areas was $2,125 in 1969, compared with $1,973 for those living outside such areas. Poor farm families had an average income of only $1,669. Their income level was too far below that of the urban poor for the difference to be offset by the lower cost of living in the countryside.[e] And since rural families are typically

[d]It is conservatively estimated that 10 million poor people were residents of "rural" as distinguished from "nonmetropolitan" areas in 1969. Persons living outside metropolitan areas include residents of small cities as well as rural areas. On the other hand, some rural sections are within the boundaries of metropolitan areas. Thus "nonmetropolitan" and "rural" are not synonymous.

[e]The Census Bureau's poverty standard for farm families, based on a cost of living differential, is approximately 15 percent below that of nonfarm families. The threshold was $3,743 for nonfarm families of four compared with $3,195 for farm families in 1969.

**Black farm families
are hardest hit by poverty.**

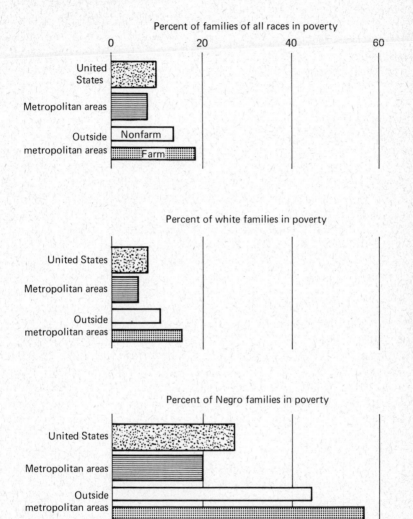

Figure 19-4. NOTE: Poverty status as of 1969. Source: Department of
Labor, based on data from the department of Commerce.

larger than urban families, the disparity in living standards is greater than appears from the difference in cash income.

The Rural Poor

The incidence of poverty is much higher among Negroes than whites in rural areas, as in the country generally. More than half of all Negroes living outside metropolitan areas had incomes below the poverty line in 1969, compared with only one out of every seven white people. In absolute numbers, however, there were, of course, more white than Negro poor (8.5 million compared with 3.4 million).

Every region of the country includes some rural poor, but the majority – 60 percent – of the poor outside metropolitan areas, including nearly all of the Negroes in this category, live in the South. Southern areas such as lower Appalachia, the Coastal Plains, the Ozarks, the Black Belt of the Old South, and the Mississippi Delta have long contained large numbers of rural poor. There are also many rural poor on the Indian reservations, as well as in the southwest border areas where Mexican-Americans are concentrated.

The families of many small farmers are among the rural poor. In 1969, some 349,000 families of farmers and farm managers – about one in five – were classified as poor.[f] Many farmers cling to marginal units because they lack alternatives or knowledge of other possibilities. Some are tied to their inadequate farms by a burden of debt; others by age, cost of moving, lack of education or preparation for urban jobs, uncertainties connected with urban life, or strong traditional attachment to the land. Others with potentially more productive farms lack the capital and "know-how" required to take advantage of modern farming methods.

The rural poor also include a great many hired farmworkers. In 1969, two out of every five families of farm laborers and foremen were reported to be below the poverty line.

Excluding very casual workers (those with less than twenty-five days of farmwork), 1.5 million persons worked as regular and seasonal farmhands in 1969. (See table 19.2.) They averaged 163 days of work and earnings of $1,886 from a combination of farm and nonfarm jobs during the year. However, close to half of them, including many women and school-age youth, were out of the work force most of the year, and little more than one-third reported that farm wagework was their chief activity. Men aged twenty-five to forty-four were the only group in which the average worker was employed

---

[f]The classification is based on the occupation in which the head of the family held his longest job.

Table 19.2
Annual Earnings and Number of Days Worked, for Persons With 25 or More
Days of Farm Wagework in 1969

Characteristic	Number of workers (thousands)	Average earnings, farm and nonfarm work	Average days worked		
			Total	Farmwork	Nonfarm work
Total	1,466	$1,886	163	131	32
White	1,125	2,054	167	132	35
Men	921	2,344	185	145	39
Women	204	748	88	73	14
Negro and other races	340	1,330	149	126	22
Men	237	1,624	173	150	22
Women	103	654	94	70	24
Migratory	172	1,937	152	113	39
Nonmigratory	1,294	1,879	165	133	31
Age of men workers:					
14 to 17 years	314	573	84	70	13
18 to 24 years	238	1,979	163	113	50
25 to 34 years	146	4,184	273	190	83
35 to 44 years	130	3,605	270	221	48
45 to 54 years	138	2,938	237	207	30
55 to 64 years	115	2,623	225	209	15
65 years and over	76	1,341	162	149	13

Source: The Hired Farm Working Force of 1969, Department of Agriculture, Agricultural
Economic Report No. 180, April 1970.
Note: Detail may not add to totals because of rounding.

substantially year round, with earnings large enough to lift a family of four
above the poverty line.

Additional evidence that lack of employment is a major problem for
farmworkers comes from the unemployment rates. In prosperous 1969, when
the national average rate of unemployment was only 3.5 percent, wage and
salary workers whose last job was in agriculture[g] had an unemployment rate of 6
percent, higher than that for workers in any other industry division.

---

[g]Includes farm wageworkers, workers in agricultural processing plants located in farm
areas, and a variety of agricultural support workers.

Still another indicator of the underutilization of rural manpower is provided by the statistics on involuntary part-time employment. In an average week of 1969, 4.8 percent of the rural farmworkers living outside of metropolitan areas were on part-time schedules for economic reasons (slack work, shortage of material, reduced orders, and so forth); the rate for workers in metropolitan areas was only 2.2 percent. Not only was the incidence of part-time work higher outside than within metropolitan areas, but the hours of work for those working part time for economic reasons were fewer (20.3 compared with 21.3 hours per week).

Migratory Farmworkers

From the standpoint of both working and living conditions, the most disadvantaged farmworkers are those who migrate from area to area, following the crops. For many years, the total number of migratory farmworkers in the country remained at about 400,000, but it had declined sharply to about 250,000 by the end of the last decade. The number of people who actually migrate is much higher than this, however, since nonworking family members often accompany the crews.

The migratory workers and their families may be away from their home base for several months out of the year. Their itinerary may span thousands of miles, many different employers, and a variety of crops. Jobs are intermittent, and slack periods with little or no earnings are common. In 1969, 172,000 migratory workers were employed more than twenty-five days at farm jobs. Their earnings averaged $1,937 for 152 days of farm and nonfarm work.

Migratory farmworkers travel out of economic necessity, not because of preference for nomadic life. Seasonal farm activities in the southern parts of Florida, Texas, and California, which are the home-base areas for the largest groups of migrants, do not provide sufficient employment and earnings. Workers depending on seasonal farm jobs must move with the crops in the hope of lengthening their periods of work and increasing their annual incomes. Migrants begin their annual trek northward in the early spring, following a cycle of activities in a number of crop areas. In California, they typically cultivate cotton and vegetables and then move into the harvest of a variety of spring vegetable and fruit crops. In other Western and North Central states, they find spring jobs in sugar beet cultivation and in the strawberry harvest. During the spring, migratory workers also are found in fruit and vegetable harvest activities in the Atlantic Coast states. Summer and fall are the most active seasons; migratory workers are relied on to supplement local labor in harvesting tomatoes, grapes, peaches, pears, melons, cherries, blueberries, cucumbers, apples, tobacco, and other crops.

The peak employment of migratory workers in areas reporting to the

Department of Labor usually occurs in August, with 197,000 employed in that month in 1970. Nearly three-fourths of these were interstate migrants. Virtually every state uses migratory workers at some time during the year, with the largest numbers in California, Michigan, Texas, and Florida. Other states with significant numbers of these workers were Ohio, Oregon, New York, Washington, and New Jersey.

Migratory workers' basic problem is, of course, irregularity of work, despite efforts by the public employment service to coordinate and regularize their employment. Harvest timetables may be upset by the vagaries of weather and crop failures. The number of workers needed may be overestimated, or the unexpected arrival of crews may upset prior plans and create labor surpluses in some areas while others are short of workers. And workers receive no pay for time spent in travel or waiting for work. In effect, some of the risks associated with the weather and other circumstances are shifted from employers to hired workers – to a much greater extent than in other industries where the labor supply is less flexible and workers are protected by collective bargaining agreements. Furthermore, housing and sanitary conditions are often unsatisfactory in the migrant workers' camps, and adequate health services and child care are generally lacking.

The majority of migratory farmworkers come from seriously disadvantaged groups. Many are Mexican-Americans or Negroes, whose employment problems are compounded by discrimination.

The average level of education is low. Since families are constantly on the move, the schooling of children is often interrrupted. Large numbers of migrant children who are in school are below the grade level normal for their age. Many drop out of school at an early age to help supplement family earnings and thus further handicap themselves in future efforts to enter more stable, better paid fields of work.

The difficulties faced by one of the largest group of migratory workers – the Mexican-Americans whose home base is in southern Texas – are illustrated by a recent study of the Lower Rio Grande Valley.[10] The typical household head in the families surveyed was over forty years of age, born in Texas, and employed in agriculture practically all his working life. He pieced together thirty-two weeks of employment in the course of a year, at a series of farm jobs in the valley and in other areas, for annual earnings of $1,813. (Female household heads earned only $1,007.) Most of the families are large, averaging six members, and wives and children were expected to work in the fields. The combined income of all family members averaged $3,350 during the year.

Training and Work-Experience Programs

People in rural areas are generally at a disadvantage in seeking occupational training, as well as other manpower services. Not merely the scattered population, but also the inadequacy of training facilities and the lack of local employment demand have hampered the development of federally assisted training and work-experience programs in rural areas, particularly those not close to cities.

Altogether, 250,000 people in rural counties were enrolled during fiscal 1970 in training and work-experience programs administered by the Department of Labor[h] – representing about one-fourth of total enrollments throughout the country. (See table 19.3.) This proportion was in line with these areas' share of the total population, but much below their share of the poverty population. About 40 percent of the nation's poor live in rural areas.

Table 19.3
Enrollees in Training and Work-Experience Programs Administered by the Department of Labor, by Urban and Rural Areas, Fiscal Year 1970[1] (Numbers in thousands)

Program	Total	Urban areas Number	Percent of total	Rural areas Number	Percent of total
Total	1,051.4	799.9	76	251.5	24
Manpower Development and Training Act:					
Institutional training	130.0	105.3	81	24.7	19
On-the-job training	91.0	73.7	81	17.3	19
Neighborhood Youth Corps:					
In school	74.4	43.2	58	31.2	42
Out of school	46.2	31.9	69	14.3	31
Summer	361.5	245.8	68	115.7	32
Operation Mainstream	12.5	4.1	33	8.4	67
Public Service Careers (New Careers)	3.6	3.2	89	.4	11
Concentrated Employment Program	110.1	98.0	89	12.1	11
JOBS (federally financed)	86.8	86.8	100		
Work Incentive Program	92.7	74.2	80	18.5	20
Job Corps	42.6	33.7	79	8.9	21

[1] Preliminary.

[h] The allocation of enrollees to urban and rural counties is based, in general, on place of residence at the time of application. Rural county residents are often enrolled in training in nearby urban counties.

It has been estimated that as many as 3 million poor rural residents may be in need of training and other services to upgrade their skills and increase their employability. However, manpower programs served only about 8 percent of this number in 1970, compared with over 10 percent of the much larger number of urban residents in need of such help.[11]

The limitations on manpower services to rural residents are even greater than is suggested by the overall data on enrollments. Five of eight enrollees in manpower training and work programs in 1970 were young people in the Neighborhood Youth Corps (NYC) – the majority of them in short-term summer work projects. In contrast, in urban areas only about three of eight enrollees were in the NYC. The opportunities for occupational training under the Manpower Development and Training Act (MDTA) and in other programs are limited in rural areas, and one major program – Job Opportunities in the Business Sector (JOBS) – has been operated only in metropolitan areas.

Though the Neighborhood Youth Corps has gone further in serving rural communities than any other manpower program, the NYC has had to overcome special difficulties including the lack of needed transportation and lack of functioning institutions to mount projects. Furthermore, since a large majority of the youth in the more remote rural areas are faced with the virtual certainty of migration, the projects need to provide occupational training rather than merely jobs as in some NYC projects. There is need for a wider range of fields than is now possible with limited training facilities in many areas. According to some observers, emphasis should also be given to training in social skills and adaptation to urban life.[12]

Some rural youth are also served by the Job Corps, which makes an effort to attract those who can benefit from comprehensive educational and training programs away from their homes. The centers designated as civilian conservation centers, located in rural settings, provide an especially favorable environment for young men from the country.

Institutional and on-the-job training programs conducted under the MDTA enrolled about 42,000 unemployed and underemployed persons in rural areas in 1970, about a fifth of the total number of first-time enrollments that year. Their training has covered a variety of occupations, oriented mostly toward nonagricultural industries. Relatively few have been trained for skilled jobs in mechanized farming operations. The possibilities in this latter area need to be explored fully, however, to aid in the readjustment of workers likely to be displaced by mechanization in the next few years, especially in fruit, vegetable, and tobacco activities. It is important that such training emphasize transferable skills so that workers can be prepared for both farm and nonfarm employment and that basic education be included along with skill training to help offset farmworkers' present educational handicaps.

Of special benefit to the unemployed and underemployed in rural areas is that provision of the act which authorizes training projects linked to economic development efforts in areas of chronic labor surplus. This small program is operated in places designated by the Department of Commerce as redevelopment areas under the Public Works and Economic Development Act, which are for the most part rural counties. During fiscal 1970, training opportunities in this program numbered about 14,000 in forty-five states. This figure included 1,700 training opportunities for Indians on reservations in Arizona and, to a lesser extent, in Idaho, Colorado, North and South Dakota, Utah, Montana, Wisconsin, Wyoming, and Oregon.

Operation Mainstream is another small program which is almost entirely rural. Its objective is to give unemployed workers meaningful work experience in projects that will, for example, enhance the beauty of rural areas, help to expand recreational and other community facilities, rehabilitate housing, and improve care for the elderly. The enrollees are typically displaced farmworkers or other older rural workers who lack formal training and nonfarm work experience, have little education, and are in effect "boxed in" in their rural areas. Work in the projects is often combined with basic education and counseling service. During fiscal 1970, some 8,400 adults in rural areas were newly enrolled in this program. Projects are sponsored by such organizations as the National Farmers' Union, the National Council of Senior Citizens, the National Retired Teachers Association, and the National Council on the Aging.

Concentrated Employment Programs (CEPs), designed to marshal the full range of manpower and supportive services in local areas with high rates of poverty and unemployment, also serve some rural people. Of the 82 CEPs in operation in late 1970, 13 were in rural poverty areas in as many States. Eastern Kentucky, for example, has a CEP which covers 22 counties and serves a population made up mainly of poor white families with agricultural and mining backgrounds. The Mississippi Delta program serves a poverty group consisting largely of blacks, most of them former farm laborers and sharecroppers displaced from cotton farms. Other examples are a CEP on the Navajo Indian reservation in Arizona and a program in northern Michigan that provides retraining and other aid to workers formerly employed in lumbering and iron mining. All these projects have made some progress in increasing the employability and employment of the widely different groups of poor workers whom they serve, but all have been hampered by the lack of job opportunities in the depressed areas where they are located, the expense of operating in rural areas, and difficulties of coordination with a multiplicity of independent political units and other agencies.

The Office of Economic Opportunity is funding a number of rural community action projects with the title Fuller Utilization of Rural Program Opportunities. These projects are designed to improve the economic conditions of the rural poor through a variety of approaches, including job development and aid to encourage new business enterprises, production and consumer cooperatives, housing development, and access to needed services such as health care, transportation, and personal credit.

A broader approach to coordination of manpower, educational, and economic development activities is the aim of the Concerted Services in Training and Education[13] with projects underway or planned in twenty rural areas in seventeen states by the end of fiscal year 1971. These projects are sponsored jointly by the Departments of Labor, Agriculture, and Health, Education, and Welfare. In each area a local coordinator works with community leaders and citizens groups, as well as representatives of federal, state, and local government agencies, to provide training, remedial education, and other services to disadvantaged workers and develop more employment opportunities.

Economic Development Programs

Programs aimed at redevelopment of the country's lagging areas and regions, rural as well as urban, have been underway since the early 1960s. The Appalachian Regional Development Act and the Public Works and Economic Development Act, both of 1965,[i] embody the concept of injection of public capital to stimiulate economic development and create jobs in depressed areas. These acts are significant in establishing the principle that the nation as a whole is concerned with attempting to halt the progressive deterioration of areas and regions characterized by declining industry and lack of opportunity and with setting up planning and administrative machinery to carry out redevelopment programs.

Since 1965, Congress has appropriated over $1.3 billion to carry out programs under the Appalachian Regional Development Act — about 60 percent for highways and the remainder for projects of other kinds, including health facilities and services, educational services, and economic development. There is a program of supplemental grants to communities that is of particular interest because of the leverage it provides in attracting additional funds into Appalachia. These grants enable communities to meet the matching requirements for federal grant-in-aid funds, which have been used to build a network of new health and education facilities, educational TV systems, libraries, airports, sewage treatment plants, and recreation and other facilities. A new feature is a program to assist public or nonprofit sponsors to build low-cost housing. Other provisions of the act support restoration of mining areas, land conservation, and water resources development.

Under the Appalachian program, sixty-three development districts have been formed as the basic local planning units. Within each district, growth areas have been identified as places where public investment in economic development

---

[i]The Public Works and Economic Development Act replaced the Area Redevelopment Act of 1961 and the Public Works Acceleration Act of 1962.

should be concentrated.

The Public Works and Economic Development Act provides aid to areas of substantial and persistent unemployment, low income, or declining population throughout the country. Areas of persistent unemployment are identified by the Department of Labor and designated as redevelopment areas by the Economic Development Administration (EDA) of the Department of Commerce when they have submitted and obtained approval of an overall economic development plan. Close to 1,000 areas are presently eligible for assistance; most of these are depressed rural counties with less than 25,000 residents. More than one-half of the designated areas are in low-income, high-unemployment sections in the southern tier of states stretching from West Virginia to Texas. Many others are in the Upper Great Lakes region, north and central California, Alaska, and Puerto Rico. There are also 107 redevelopment areas which are Indian reservations.

Federal aid to redevelopment areas may be in the form of public works loans and grants, business loans, or technical assistance and planning grants. The primary emphasis has been on loans and grants for public works and development facilities; over $900 million has been made available for such projects between fiscal years 1966 and 1970. Most of these have been for water, sewage, and waste treatment utilities and for industrial and commercial facilities, such as harbors, industrial parks, and airports. The remaining funds have been allocated for roads, health and education, and other public facilities and for tourism. Such improvements have an effect on the entire economy of the area and ultimately on employment opportunities, although this is indirect and difficult to measure.

A second type of assistance under the act consists of long-term, low-interest business loans to encourage private investment in lagging areas. Such loans cover part of the cost of purchasing land, buildings, and equipment for industrial and commercial enterprises, the balance being supplied by other lenders, and the firms themselves. Loans have been made to companies in many different industries, notably lumber and wood products; primary metals; food and kindred products; paper and allied products; textiles; stone, clay, and glass; and tourist services. Many of the loans were for enterprises in towns and cities close to rural areas.

To make possible broader economic development efforts, the act also provides for the establishment and financial support of multicounty economic development districts, containing at least two redevelopment areas and a growth center. The EDA has designated 103 multicounty economic development districts and 202 cities as growth centers. Most of the growth centers are not themselves redevelopment areas. However, they are all eligible for the full range of EDA assistance, on the theory that employment opportunities generated there will benefit the unemployed and underemployed in surrounding distressed areas.

The Public Works and Economic Development Act also authorized the

Secretary of Commerce to establish commissions somewhat similar to the Appalachian Regional Commission for five regions with pervasive problems of joblessness, underemployment, and poverty which overlap sections of several states. These are the Coastal Plains, Ozarks, Upper Great Lakes, Four Corners, and New England regional commissions. So far the work of these commissions has focused largely on identifying the causes of economic lags in their regions, formulating plans for economic and human resources development, and supplementing federal grant-in-aid programs.

Notes

1. Varden Fuller, *Rural Worker Adjustment to Urban Life* (Ann Arbor, Mich.: The Institute of Labor and Industrial Relations, the University of Michigan-Wayne State University, and the National Manpower Policy Task Force, under contract with the Department of Labor, Manpower Administration, February 1970).

2. Calvin L. Beale, "Rural Depopulation in the United States: Demographic Consequences of Agricultural Adjustments," paper presented at the annual meeting of the American Association for the Advancement of Science, Cleveland, December 1963.

3. Niles M. Hansen, *Rural Poverty and the Urban Crisis* (Bloomington, Ind.: Indiana University Press, 1970).

4. See chapter on New Developments in Manpower Programs in *1971 Manpower Report* and also *1970 Manpower Report*, pp. 103-106, for further discussions of the economic situation of American Indians and programs aimed at alleviating their problems.

5. Dale E. Hathaway, J. Allan Beegle, and W. Keith Bryant, *People of Rural America* (Washington: Department of Commerce, Bureau of the Census, 1968), 1960 Census Monograph, appendix tables A−1 and A−2. See also James S. Holt, Reuben W. Hecht, and Neil B. Gingrich, *Agricultural Labor in the Northeast States* (University Park, Pa.: Pennsylvania State University, under contract with the Department of Labor, Manpower Administration, August 1970).

6. See *Fruit and Vegetable Harvest Mechanization − Technological Implications* and *Fruit and Vegetable Harvest Mechanization − Manpower Implications,* ed. B.F. Cargill and G.E. Rossmiller (East Lansing: Michigan State University, 1969), Rural Manpower Center Reports Nos. 16 and 17. A third volume in this series, *Fruit and Vegetable Harvest Mechanization − Policy Implications,* is in process. See also J. Kamal Dow, *Historical Perspective of the Florida Citrus Industry and the Impact of Mechanical Harvesting on the Demand for Labor* (Gainsville: University of Florida, April 1970). These studies were made under contract with the Department of Labor, Manpower Administration.

7. *Potential Mechanization in the Flue-Cured Tobacco Industry with Emphasis on Human Resource Adjustment* (Washington: Department of Agriculture, Economic Research Service, 1969), Agricultural Economic Report No. 169 (report of a task group). See also Robert C. McElroy, "Manpower Implications of Trends in the Tobacco Industry," talk given at Association for Public Program Analysis Conference, Washington, D.C., June 1969.

8. Estimated by Department of Agriculture based on *County Business Patterns,* Department of Commerce, Bureau of the Census. These data are reported on the basis of place of work while data in the preceding paragraph from the *Census of Population* are based on the place of residence of workers.

9. Claude C. Haren, "Rural Industrial Growth in the 1960's," *American Journal of Agricultural Economics,* August 1970.

10. See *The People Left Behind* (1967) and *Rural Poverty in the United States* (1968), Reports of the President's National Advisory Commission on Rural Poverty.

11. See Leonard Lecht, *Poor Persons in the Labor Force: A Universe of Need* (Washington: National Planning Association, under contract with the Department of Labor, Manpower Administration, October 1970). This study defines the universe of need as the estimated number of poor persons at work or seeking work, including those employed all year at full-time or part-time jobs but earning low wages and those employed part of a year. Nearly 7.9 million persons in the 16-to-64 age group were in this category in 1966. In addition, about 1.6 million persons not in the labor force were potential candidates for manpower training. One-third of the people in the universe of need were in rural areas.

12. Guy H. Miles, William F. Henry, and Ronald N. Taylor, *Optimizing the Benefits of Neighborhood Youth Corps Projects for Rural Youth* (Minneapolis, Minn.: North Star Research and Development Institute, under contract with the Department of Labor, Manpower Administration, September 1969).

13. Guy Miles, W.F. Henry, and Ronald Taylor, *Optimizing the Benefits of Neighborhood Youth Corps Projects for Rural Youth* (Minneapolis: North Star Research and Development Institute, 1969).

The value of public service employment for rural families and communities can be gleaned from a reading of testimony before the Senate Subcommittee on Employment, Manpower, and Poverty *(Emergency Employment Act of 1971*, Hearings of February 8-24, 1971). See, for example, the testimony by Clifford Ingram, from Monterey, Tennessee, in which he provides statistical as well as anecdotal evidence of the unmet public needs in twelve rural counties, the numbers of applicants for potential public service positions, and the actual numbers of persons engaged in limited demonstration programs — including the types of activities engaged in. The materials also include his survey of industry and business in the area, along with public agencies, to determine how many extra persons could be employed if adequate funds were made available.

In addition to the information provided in the text, taken from the *1971 Manpower Report*, Ben Bagdikian's "The Black Immigrants" *(Saturday Evening Post*, July 15, 1967) is a sympathetic case study of a family from Mississippi, why they had to move to Springfield, Illinois, what they hoped for and what they found in their new urban destination.

The most systematic account of the "rural problem" (which is one of the roots of the "urban problem"), of course, is that of the President's National Advisory Commission on Rural Poverty, *The People Left Behind*, (Government Printing Office, 1967), especially chapters 3, 4, 10, and 14, dealing with economic development, manpower policies, and the role of government. Four years later, in 1971, the Economic Research Service of the Department of Agriculture updated this Presidential Commission report, at the request of the Senate Committee on Agriculture and Forestry, under the title of *The People Left Behind — Four Years Later* (Committee Print, November 30, 1971). Its 76 pages are organized by chapter title exactly as the original 1967 Commission Report, and provide some indication of the effectiveness of the implementation of the 1967 recommendations.

Also recommended are *Urban and Rural America: Policies for Future Growth* by the Advisory Commission on Intergovernmental Relations (Washington: GPO, 1968); and *Our Rural Problems in Their National Setting*, Proceedings of Third Annual Farm Policy Review Conference, Iowa State University, December 1962.

Part VII
Policy and Research Issues for the 1970s

Introduction to Part VII

The seventh and last session in the Upjohn Seminar Series on Public Service Employment was devoted to the development of a policy and research agenda. The session was held only one day after a Senate-House conference committee reported out the compromise Emergency Employment Act of 1971 (Congress subsequently passed the measure, and the President signed it on July 12, 1971).[a]

The chairman of the evening, Congressman William Steiger (R–Wisc.), therefore set the tone of the seminar by indicating one priority of his own: the careful evaluation and monitoring of the E.E.A. He urged that such an evaluation pay particular attention to the public and private sector work incentive effects generated by the new public service employment program, and that it contrast the impact of the E.E.A. with such previous programs as Operation Mainstream, the Neighborhood Youth Corps, and the New Careers program.

The first speaker, Michael Barth, began by distinguishing between three quite different "varieties" of public employment programs: public service employment, public works production, and work-conditioned income transfers ("more or less pure make-work"). The usefulness of the distinction was attested to by the great frequency with which the seminar participants returned to it throughout the evening.

The first of five research and policy priorities indicated by Barth concerned the potential labor supply response to the various types of public employment programs (including the public service jobs strategy embodied in the E.E.A.). *Who* would respond to the program(s), and to what mix of incentives? There are a number of target populations: the "experienced unemployed" (e.g., those dislocated by federal defense expenditure reductions), the long-term unemployed, "those who have become discouraged with the job search and have dropped out of the labor force so completely that they are not even included in the official statistics," and the working poor — "those employed at low-wage, dead-end jobs." The simultaneous existence of private sector vacancies with high unemployment suggests that workers are indeed selective in their decisions about which jobs they are prepared to take.[b] "Which designs tend to attract and retain

---

[a]The main provisions of the E.E.A. are summarized in Appendix A of Part II.

[b]Mr. Thomas Walsh of the U.S. Chamber of Commerce pointed out that, in Portland, Oregon, the owner of a trucking service ran an advertisement in a local newspaper for a $7-8,000 assistant managerial position. After four days, "he was a bit astonished that only nine persons responded to this ad," especially since "there were 80,000 unemployed people in the metropolitan area of Portland." Walsh asked the Seminar: "If a guy won't be an assistant manager for a trucking service, will he take a job as a dishwasher, garbage collector, or policeman?" Harrison replied that "there are waiting lines in every city in the country for jobs as garbage collectors, hospital paraprofessionals, policemen, and firemen." This may be

391

those who otherwise could not find work or would not seek work? How does job content relate to wage level in determining initial willingness of workers to enroll and their propensities to remain in the program or to quit?

One of the more obvious reasons why identification of the potential public employment labor force is so important is that the estimation of its particular skills and abilities, when compared with the technical requirements of the jobs themselves, will define the kinds of training programs needed. The "skill gap" is one (but by no means the only) variable whose values ultimately determine the "start-up" and "turn-down" costs of the employment program.

A second question concerns the extent to which the introduction of a federally-subsidized public employment program into a local labor market will affect the local wage structure. Harrison and Bluestone assume that a public service employment program paying non-poverty wages will create upward pressure on the indigenous low-wage industries; indeed, that is one of their reasons for advocating such a policy.[c] But this is actually an empirical question, which must be measured. If, as many economists believe, the supply curve of disadvantaged unskilled labor to most industries is highly elastic (at least up to some threshhold), then even a deliberate skewing of the demand for public employees toward the disadvantaged will probably *not* lead to a bidding up of wages for this group. In the left-hand diagram, a withdrawal of labor supply from the local market (reallocated to the public employment program) results in

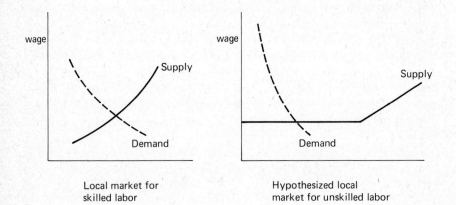

Local market for
skilled labor

Hypothesized local
market for unskilled labor

attributable not only to the salaries involved, but also to fringe benefits — including job tenure ("90 percent of all government employees in the country receive tenure after no more than a year of service," Harrison reminded the Seminar. "This is an enormously attractive benefit, not available to private sector workers"). These are some of the variables of concern to Barth.

[c]See chapters 2 and 5 in this volume.

a leftward shift of the supply curve, thereby increasing the bargaining power of the remaining workers and (as a result) the equilibrium wage. A reallocation of disadvantaged workers to the public employment program would also induce a leftward shift of the supply curve of this class of labor. If that curve has the shape shown in the right-hand diagram, however, a very large withdrawal would be required in order for wages to be bid up. The shapes of the relevant schedules and the magnitude of the public employment program relative to the size of the local labor market are among the variables of central concern to Barth.[d]

A third issue — this involving policy alone — concerns the "social effects" of a public employment program. "The participants could well become a stigmatized 'class'," as seems to have occurred in Sweden:

The economy appears to be dividing into a market which absorbs the attractive members of the labor force and an inferior world of socially-created work for the remainder.[1]

It would be tragic if a public employment program were simply to replace one form of labor market dualism with another. Prevention of such an occurrence will require the development of jobs whose *outputs* are of unquestioned social utility. Conversely, the risk of falling into the Swedish pattern is likely to be greatest with a work-conditioned, income-transfer program (such as that proposed by the Administration in connection with welfare reform).

Policy and research merge in Dr. Barth's fourth area for investigation. Enormous interregional differences in wage structures, civil service practices, and other "parameters" of any public employment program require that each individual local project be designed as flexibly as possible. Even so, there are likely to be certain problems created by local conditions which will require ingenuity and diplomacy to solve. Referring to Juan Gutierrez' remarks during the previous session of the Congressional Seminar (see Introduction to Part VI), Barth pointed out that "in regions such as South Texas, with large migratory flows (in this case involving foreign nationals), the public employment slots could well be fully subscribed by non-residents of the area."

The fifth and last item on Dr. Barth's proposed agenda concerns the need for program planners to familiarize themselves and to experiment with various key policy tradeoffs, particularly with respect to program budgeting. For any given slot cost, the amount to be allocated to wages must be traded off against the allocation to overhead. For a given project budget, there is a tradeoff between

---

[d]Another question raised at the Seminar was how sensitive workers would be — how much and how rapidly they would respond — to variations in the public/private wage differential resulting from competition for labor between the sectors.

cost per slot and the number of slots to be "created." With a given budget, a local "prime sponsor" (or "program agent," in the vernacular of the E.E.A.) can hire more workers only by reducing the rate of expenditure (salary plus overhead) for each. And for each slot, the planner can pay a higher wage only by reducing the investment in overhead (training, supportive services, etc.). This is an important decision; the wage is probably the single most important attraction of the program (particularly to the disadvantaged), while "the amount of overhead will determine in large part what the future productivity of the participant will be . . . if you decide to put some overhead into skill supervision, you may get more or higher quality current or future output; however, with a fixed budget, you are going to get less wages."

Barth concludes that "a combination of experiment, research and demonstration activities, some model building, very close monitoring and evaluation can provide many of the answers" to the question he has raised. A formidable agenda, indeed!

The second speaker of the evening was Edward Gramlich. He chose to concentrate his remarks on the issue of the so-called "inflation-unemployment tradeoff," and how public employment programs might be designed so as to minimize their inflationary impacts.

According to a widely-held theory of labor market operation, and given the "oligopolistic" (highly concentrated industrial) structure of the American economy, inflation and unemployment are substitutable for one another, and extremely difficult to reduce simultaneously. Thus, if we are "fighting inflation," one way of doing so is to deliberately sustain high unemployment.[e]

While "the Seminar series to this point has focused almost entirely on the unemployment side, a priority with which most of us would agree," we can't afford to neglect the problem of inflation, if only because most economists now believe that the *expectation* of continued inflation itself fuels inflation further, becoming a kind of self-fulfilling prophecy.[f]

From the perspective of this so-called "job search theory of inflation," Gramlich observed, "vacancy-creating" public service employment (PSE) programs would probably exacerbate inflationary pressures:

The reason is that we are augmenting the wage bargaining power of a certain group of workers. It is not clear how powerful these workers are presently, but to the extent that they have alternative possibilities of employment, they will be in general tougher in their wage negotiations with their employers. There may be more union pressure for wage increases. There may be less fear on the part of

---

[e]Several Seminar participants pointed out that it appears to be getting more difficult to "control" inflation in this way. The inflation-unemployment tradeoff is, in other words, worsening.

[f]Thus, students of inflation hoped that the wage-price "freeze" of 1971 would, if it accomplished nothing else, succeed in reducing popular expectations of continued inflation.

producers that goods will go unsold because there will now [after introduction of the PSE program] be higher local incomes and purchasing power. So, in general, we might expect the public employment program to make the inflationary problem worse.

One way of avoiding this result is to concentrate PSE subsidies "insofar as possible" on filling present public sector job vacancies, as opposed to creating new slots.[g] "If these job vacancies are real in the sense that employers are actually and actively trying to fill them, they will be bidding up the money wages and/or benefits, leading to a worse inflationary problem." To the extent that unemployed people can be placed in government jobs which were previously vacant (perhaps because of credentialism), then unemployment can be reduced without fueling inflation.[h]

Similarly, the more the PSE program can be "targeted" to the truly disadvantaged, the less the inflationary pressure created. Gramlich cited the results of research on the "dual labor market" theory which discovered a maldistribution of wage bargaining power in the economy. "People who belong to unions, who have the credentials, and who are skilled can exert upward pressure on wages. But the people in the secondary labor market who won't stay in jobs very long, and who have few resources on which to 'fall back', have little bargaining power." Thus, a PSE program which "creams" the labor force — whatever its political expediency — is more likely to contribute to wage-push inflation than a program which seriously attempts to fill existing vacancies with unskilled workers from the secondary labor market.[i]

Harvey Garn, Director of the Urban Development Processes Division of The Urban Institute, told the Seminar that the congressional authorization for the Emergency Employment Act itself was far too small to have much impact. An expenditure of $1 billion a year, assuming an (admittedly low) average slot cost of $5,000, would absorb only 200,000 workers. In March, 1971, unemployment in the 150 major labor market areas totalled 3.2 million. Thus the E.E.A. could

---

[g]According to the National Civil Service League's 1970 survey of nearly 400 state and local governments, average annual non-federal vacancies and public sector turnover together imply a labor-absorption capacity of nearly a million workers.

[h]It was pointed out that this analysis, which was originally developed to explain private sector "wage-push" inflation, may be less applicable to the public sector since short-term wages in the latter are generally fixed by local civil service administrative rules. Indeed, the inability of local government personnel directors to bid up their wage offers in the short run may well explain why public sector vacancy rates are so much higher than private sector rates.

[i]Harvey Garn of the Urban Institute expressed the opinion that, if Gramlich was correct, an explicitly "transitional" bill such as the E.E.A. probably has a built-in inflationary bias. "If a criterion for success is the rapidity with which a local project can move people *off* the subsidized rolls into non-subsidized employment, it seems reasonable to me to assume that what we will see is public employment for those people who are likely to be the easiest to transfer, rather than for those who most need the jobs."

absorb only 6 percent of the unemployed – an average of only 1,300 workers in each major urban area.[j] "It seems to me," said Dr. Garn,

that when, in fact, the largest growth industry in the United States between 1948 and 1968 was government, that we should recognize that some kind of statement is being made by the public that there is an increasing desire for the things which are produced by the government, or for which the government has responsibility.[k]

There is, suggested Garn, an additional way in which to achieve some of the ostensible goals of a PSE program. The point turns on an important distinction. The *supply* of public goods and services is, by definition and by economic logic,[2] the *responsibility* of the government. But that does not mean that government must actually *produce and deliver* all of these goods and services. Governments already contract private profit and non-profit companies and organizations to provide them with various products and services (see chapter 23 in this volume), but with the exception of defense production, this is seldom the result of deliberate, planned national policy. High-speed ground transportation, pollution control systems, and modular housing all have certain "public good" qualities. A comprehensive "public" employment program could generate private sector jobs by stimulating the production of these "quasi-public goods" through selective contracting.[1]

However, whether or not private companies are contracted to *produce* public goods and services, said Garn, it is the central government which must assume the responsibility for the administrative arrangements by which such a system is *managed*. This conflict between centralized and decentralized administration is a politically volatile issue. Garn's point is that these programs have multiple goals,

---

[j]However, as of April 1972, the Department of Labor estimated a "slot cost" of $7,200, which resulted in far less than 200,000 jobs and far below 6 percent of the unemployed.

[k]Congressman Steiger pointed out that the President's General Revenue Sharing legislation proposed to pass $5 billion on to state and local governments, most of which would undoubtedly go to the creation of public service employment, "without necessarily calling it that."

[l]The Seminar participants were generally enthusiastic about this suggestion. Harold Sheppard noted that, even in Sweden, many "public" services are provided by profit-making organizations. Austin Sullivan, administrative assistant to Congressman Carl Perkins (one of the sponsors of the House version of the E.E.A.), agreed that "we ought not to try to solve every public problem with a public employee." Couldn't we, for example, contract "a company like Boeing to produce something that is socially more useful than the Supersonic Transport plane? It seems to me that we ought to be thinking of ways in which the federal government can exploit the need for various public goods to maintain a strong economic institution like the Boeing company in the cities of Seattle and Everett, Washington, where Boeing employees have strong ties."

involving both the *efficiency* of public goods supply and *equity* in the distribution of the services (as well as in the jobs themselves). Garn himself is one of several economists who have contributed to a technical literature which shows that decentralized administration of programs with multiple goals tends to produce less than optimal results.[3] These observations lead him to the conclusion that "considerable concern should be given to designing evaluation and reporting systems, and to the design of a stated intent by the federal government to ensure that the funds are wisely spent."

While Dr. Garn had previously spoken about alternative "delivery systems," the fourth speaker of the evening, Geoffrey Faux, was concerned with one such alternative: the emerging network of community development corporations (CDCs) in the nation's ghettos.

Over the last five years we have witnessed the almost entirely spontaneous growth of a movement for "community economic development," involving community groups who have taken on the job of stimulating and directing economic development in their neighborhoods. An increasing number of these programs are being managed by CDCs: business corporations owned and operated by community residents for the purpose of achieving multiple social objectives, only one of which is the generation of profits. Most CDCs are engaged in planning, financing, and operating business and housing projects, various community services, shopping centers, and even light manufacturning plants. The concept has grown in response to a wide-spread discontent with the services and training orientation of the antipoverty program, and a feeling that, regardless of whatever success open housing and other "ghetto dispersal" programs might have, for a long time to come, the inner cities are going to be populated by large numbers of poor and mostly black people whose levels of living need to be raised now.[4]

The role of CDCs is predicated on the assumption that the ghetto is not now in a position to effectively absorb conventional capital investments. CDCs are intended to "nurture and organize the economy of the inner cities," to get the development process started. Ultimately, individual entrepreneurship and possibly even private "foreign" investment will become feasible. Until that time, however, only community-based collective approaches are likely to have much success.

CDCs operate on local savings, the income from a few relatively successful enterprises, and with equity capital made available by the O.E.O. Special Impact Program, the Model Cities Program of H.U.D., and the Ford Foundation. The Economic Opportunity Act amendments of 1971 institutionalized federal support for CDCs,[5] but at a very low level. Bills to create a community corporation development banking system have been introduced in every legislative session since 1968 without success.

In any case, said Faux, his experience suggests that CDCs could probably not effectively employ large amounts of investment capital at the present time. The reason is the very serious scarcity of skilled managers and technicians in the ghetto. And this is where the public service employment program enters. "For the next few years at least," Faux told the seminar, "the most important task in community development will be the development of the capacity of these organizations and their constituents to administer their own programs. This means training, technical aid of all kinds, and, then, a gradual increase in appropirations and investment capital." This skill deficit exists, to a great extent, because of the neglect of the federal government.[m]

The Public Service Employment program provides us with the opportunity of facilitating this development. The government should encourage prime sponsors to subcontract CDCs to provide outreach recruiting, placement, and training of public employees. In some cases, CDCs might be allowed to manage whole ghetto-based public service employment programs.[n] Such activities argued Faux, would help CDCs to develop their managerial and administrtive skills, and would improve their standing (or "legitimacy") in their respective communities.

Bennett Harrison, the fifth speaker, addressed his recommendations for policy and research to two separate groups: academic economists and congressmen. The first set of issues involves microeconomics; the second is largely macroeconomic in orientation.

The technical, microeconomic issue concerns public service production relationships. At the 1970 Meetings of the American Economic Association, Charles Schultze, former Director of the U.S. Bureau of the Budget, remarked that the estimation of what economists would call "public service production functions" may be the single most important area of applied economics in the next decade.[6] A production function is a set of mathematical "blueprints," a "recipe" for combining inputs in various ways in order to produce a certain output. Harrison told the Seminar that, while much theoretical and empirical

---

[m]Faux tells the story of a former government official in the antipoverty field who was asked by a new Assistant Secretary for advice. The former official told how, four years earlier, he had developed and tried to "sell" a "program of massive and intensive training of community people in managerial, entrepreneural, and technical skills. If, four years ago, we had entered on this program, today there would be no question about the capacity of people in the inner city to perform development tasks, and Model Cities and other programs would now be much more effective." The former official therefore recommended that the agency begin immediately to develop this technical capacity in its target population. The Assistant Secretary replied instantly: "Listen, don't tell me about four years from now. Maybe a year, maybe four months, but I am not going to be here four years from now!" In the words of Vietorisz and Harrison, "There is simply no mainstream tradition for economic planning in the United States."

[n]As finally written and signed into law, the E.E.A. prohibits all private, non-profit organizations from being prime sponsors. This eliminates most CDCs and Community Action Agencies.

work had been done on production functions for goods-producing industries, "we don't know nearly as much about the technology of producing services, especially public services such as health, education, welfare, sanitation, police and fire protection, and so forth." For example, when is a public service vacancy real and when is it not? How many men, working with what kinds of equipment, are needed to put out a fire?

The study of public service production relationships might usefully focus on four questions. The first and most important of these is: What are the various techniques – factor combinations and methods of application – by which a given public service can be produced and delivered? It is remarkable, said Harrison, that not even the most technically qualified participants in the seminar had ever raised this question, "an oversight which would be unforgivable and inexcusable in a discussion about employment generated by the production of physical goods. Undergraduates in the economics principles course are taught to ask such a question before they are taught almost anything else." The so-called Planning, Programing, and Budgeting System (PPBS) was introduced into general usage in the federal government – and its adoption by non-federal jurisdictions is advocated – on the grounds that it represents a methodology for estimating the social benefits and costs of public programs.[7] But PPBS analysts generally measure a program's output by the extra income (or tax revenue) it generates, or by income losses foregone (e.g., through crime prevention or strike settlement). These are nontechnological measures of the input-output relation, which tell us nothing about *how* the income is in fact generated, let alone how it could be generated by alternative means. PPBS analyses will show when a service is being inefficiently produced. But once we know that a public program is not cost-effective, what then? Because we do not know how the technology operates, we are forced to conduct a long and expensive heuristic search of alternative input combinations to see if we can stumble upon one which is cost effective. PPBS studies can provide useful information to public service technologists,[o] but they are not in themselves substitutes for technological models of public service production functions.

The second (and derived) question is: What are the alternative manpower requirements associated with the production of any particular level of service output, using a given production function? In terms of the diagram on the next page, how much labor is required to produce X units of service by "process" (method) 1? by process 2? by process 3? More importantly, what are the skill distributions of these derived manpower requirements? Harrison noted that "an enormous consulting industry has grown up over the last decade in connection with the federal government's manpower programs. This industry turns out endless quantities of alleged descriptions of training requirements. These exercises,

[o]Some examples of the application of PPBS techniques to the analysis of local government services are given in the Appendix.

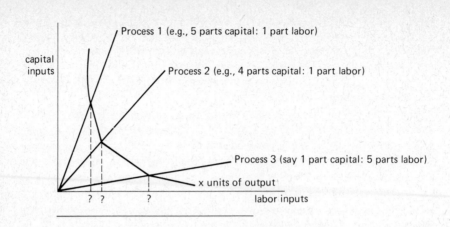

whatever their propaganda value, are technically rather meaningless unless they are related to estimates, projections or at least assumptions about output targets and the technology for "getting from here to there." It is the gap between the skills which are needed and the skills already possessed by a particular target population which defines the training requirements for that group. *This* is true manpower planning.

A third area for further investigation — one where PPBS has already made extremely useful headway — is the estimation of the costs associated with each alternative technique for producing and delivering a public good or service. Finally, Professor Harrison expressed an interest in

What are the alternative working conditions or environments which have to be created around each of these delivery methods? Here, I am concerned with work satisfaction as well as efficiency. All production takes place within some environment — work schedules, patterns of interaction among members of the work force, etc. These may seem to be somewhat peripheral to the central business of production, but these "peripheral" conditions may make all the difference between a program which workers will value, remain with, and be willing to train for, and a program which they wouldn't touch with the proverbial ten-foot pole.

The second major set of issues of concern to Professor Harrison — this time involving macroeconomic policy — had to do with the measurement of labor market activity.

I would paraphrase Charles Killingsworth's talk a month ago.[o] Obsession with

---

[o] See chapter 7 in this volume.

the conventional unemployment rate – the one which Walter Cronkite now reports faithfully along with the stock market reports – fooled us into believing that private economic growth was adequate to get us close to "full employment" in the 1960s when, in fact, that was not the case. And I would quote Willard Wirtz: "We do what we measure." The problem is that we are not measuring the right things.

Harrison proposed a series of statistical programs designed to help us understand not only how our labor markets are working, but also how various public programs such as PSE impact those markets.

The first and most obvious thing to do is to generate conventional unemployment rates for small areas on a regular basis. They should certainly be broken down by major industry category: construction, manufacturing, trade, services, and government. Once gathered – a task which will require new programs – these figures should be widely publicized.

Secondly, the government should undertake the development of job vacancy and turnover data, again by industry and area and on a regular basis. Only the most rudimentary statistics – principally for manufacturing – are now available.

Third, present BLS programs for periodically measuring *underemployment* – people who are involuntarily employed part time, people who are engaged in jobs whose skill requirements underutilie their own capabilities, and people who work (albeit full time) for poverty-level wages – should be expanded to permit reporting on a regular basis by area, industry, and demographic cohort (e.g., blacks, women, teenagers).

Finally, in response to the widespread demand for an official (and therefore unimpeachable) summary indicator of the efficiency with which our labor markets are operating, Harrison recommended the development of a new index of subemployment or underemployment, "modeled on although not necessarily identical to the index created by Wirtz in 1966." It is true, he pointed out, that the construction of an index number requires statisticians (or the policy makers for whom they work) to make value judgments in deciding how strongly to weigh the various components of the index. [p] This is an unavoidable consequence of the desire to *summarize* multifaceted phenomena. If that desire is genuine, then such judgments will have to be made. [q]

---

[p] "In fact," suggested Harrison, "one of the reasons why the social indicators movement hasn't proceeded as far or as fast as its heralds had predicted may well be because social scientists – and economists in particular – are so reluctant to make value judgments in their professional work."

[q] "In the 1966-67 subemployment index, the Labor Department decided – quite arbitrarily – that the person who drops out of the labor force to run numbers reflects just as serious a failure of the economy as does the person who isn't working because he can't find a job, even though he has been looking very hard for one. That is a particular value judgment. Perhaps Labor should change the weights, so that the dropout is considered only 'half' or a 'fourth' as serious a problem as that of the person who continues to search for work. In any case value judgments are always involved."

Harold Sheppard raised two broad research issues and a single question of policy.

The first of these issues – one raised earlier in the evening by Dr. Garn – concerns "the balance between private and public employment." What are the interdependencies between the two sectors? How fast must public employment grow in order to provide the private sector with sufficient infrastructure to facilitate *its* growth? How does the private sector, in turn, "feed" the public, through deliveries of goods and services? According to the *1971 Manpower Report of the President,* between 1962 and 1970, the number of private sector jobs attributable to the expansion of state and local government alone grew by 50 percent, while total employment in the country rose only 22 percent. The 1962-71 gap was even greater. Sheppard argues that we must make these facts more widely available, prepare them for more disaggregated areas and industries, and pulish them on a regular basis.[2]

Secondly, Sheppard commented on a point made earlier by Harrison, that outputs must be specified in some way before we can properly deduce manpower and training needs. "In my own writing," said Sheppard, "I have always tried to stress the central importance of the 'output side' of the public employment issue."

The problem, said Sheppard, is that well-defined markets do not exist for most public services. How, then, do we measure the demand for additional output? The "method" which we now use is to allow legislators to determine what the supply shall be (presumably in response to their perceptions of what the demand is – or should be), and to hope that policies with respect to public service supply will be judged by voters in the next election. Clearly, something more direct (and without such a delayed reaction) is needed, but what?

Finally, as a matter of policy, Sheppard urged government decision makers to integrate the public service supply question with more conventional matters of fiscal and monetary policy. If there is indeed a shortage of public services, then decision makers ought not to be indifferent between the stimulative fiscal policies of (a) tax cuts or (b) increased government expenditures. "I am," he told the Seminar, "concerned that we are still obsessed with the desire to

---

[1]At this point Mr. Faux amplified his earlier statement by suggestion that the shortage of public services in the urban ghetto and the need by community development corporations for administrative experience might be matched by a policy of hiring CDCs to perform (on contract) selected services in the ghetto, such as garbage collection and certain routine police functions. [Howard Hallman has made a similar suggestion with respect to C.A.A.'s and Model Cities agencies, which – he says – might be merged into one "multi-functional" community district with city contracts for the performance of such services as housing inspection, sanitation, street and alley maintenance, public education, and neighborhood aspects of police work. Howard W. Hallman, *Neighborhood Control of Public Programs: Community Corporations and Neighborhood Boards* (New York: Praeger Publishers, 1970).] Moreover, said Faux, ghetto enterprises might be encouraged to "export" some of their output to government purchasing agents, through "set-aside" and other special arrangements.

increase private affluence at the cost of what I call public poverty. And I think that, to the extent that we fail to deal with the issue of public poverty, even private affluence will suffer."

For fifteen years, John Kenneth Galbraith has been writing and speaking to the issue of the American system's propensity to starve itself of public services.[8] The standard argument for tax cuts as stimulative policy is "consumer sovereignty"; the consumer – not the government – should have the dollars to "look over the market" and choose what he or she wishes to purchase. Galbraith has taught us the folly of this argument. Consumers *have* no real choice between buying a car and buying a guaranteed hospital bed in case of illness. No terms of trade exist between a pair of shoes and additional police protection. Tax cuts in the name of consumer sovereignty will not solve the problem of public poverty – the continued shortage of public goods and services which are so instrumental in defining the quality of life in a post-industrial society.

The final discussant was Garth Mangum, Professor of Economics at the University of Utah and a member of the National Manpower Policy Task Force. Dr. Mangum was asked to "reflect" on the evening's proceedings, rather than to make an original statement of his own. He observed that consideration for the importance of the *output* of a public services program – the services them-selves – was a theme running through the entire evening, indeed through the entire Seminar series. Any yet, as Michael Barth had pointed out, the quality of the output and the efficiency of its production are rather beside the point if the program is in reality geared to what Barth very aptly termed "work-conditioned income transfers."

In Mangum's opinion, this was still how Congress and the White House perceived public service employment: as counter-cyclical make-work. "It is not a production-oriented program; it is a job-oriented program." All of the "PSE-like" programs of the 1960s – Neighborhood Youth Corps, Mainstream, New Careers, Public Service Careers – were fundamentally work-conditioned income transfer programs. They are easy to administer. And in the end, they come to nothing. Paradoxically, said Mangum, the very WPA, which so many opponents of PSE use as an example of the make-work nature of such a policy, probably had a more solid production orientation than anything which has been legislated since. During the Depression, local administrators (what we would now call "prime sponsors") had definite things which they wanted done.[8] Moreover, they cared very little about the "welfare" implications or impact of WPA. There was work to do, and – through WPA – a free labor force was being made available with which to do it.

"It would be a very surprising thing to me," Mangum told the Seminar, "if

---

[8]cf. Briscoe's survey of the WPA in chapter 4 of this volume.

jobs under the new bill turn out to be any more 'real' than their predecessors. What we are unfortunately talking about again is a work-conditioned transfer program which will almost certainly be administered as we have administered such programs in the past, without much concern for the output." Mangum predicted that the administration — "as had its predecessors" — would insist that the funds be spent as rapidly as possible. This kind of "quickie" hiring would certainly "get some badly needed income into the hands of some people who badly need income." But a straight income transfer program would also do that, and more efficiently. Moreover, as per the remarks offered to the seminar by Gramlich and Barth, to the extent that this administrative impatience prevents jurisdictions from recruiting the most seriously disadvantaged persons, it might well worsen the inflation-unemployment tradeoff.[t]

The final Upjohn seminar concluded on a pessimistic note, with comments by William Spring and Bennett Harrison. Spring urged economists and other social scientists to find the courage to "at least raise the question of what it would take in the American context to *have* a full employment economy," and to "devise an economic system for the United States which provides in fact what the very utopian Senate version of the Employment Act of 1946 promised: truly full employment." He expressed discouragement that so few continued to pursue these questions.

Harrison went even further. "We teach our students that full employment was in fact nearly achieved during the 1960s, and could be fully achieved if we were willing to accept severe inflation. Well, I don't think that it is very interesting or meaningful to reach 'full employment' any more. The presentations in these seminars lead me to doubt that 'full employment' is a goal of much value. I am more concerned with eliminating poverty than with eliminating unemployment, especially since it appears that the latter is no guarantee of the former."

I have a very strong feeling that we cannot achieve full economic maturity in the United States as its institutions are presently organized. It is unfortunate that so few in the economics profession are willing to consider the reorganization of the institutional structure of the society for the purpose of achieving true economic development. For surely that is the most important long-run "research" and policy issue of all.

---

[t]As of September 1971 it was clear that the administration was indeed emphasizing speed in its implementation of the Emergency Employment Act. "Getting the money out" was given the highest priority, and allocations totalling $600 million were made even before the Labor Department guidelines had been finalized. On August 12, the Secretary of Labor proudly told the press that: "We are moving as rapidly as we can so local and state governments will have the funds to put unemployed and underemployed people into worthwhile jobs and at the same time provide badly needed public services." (Department of Labor News Release, August 12, 1971.)

Notes

1. Beatrice Reubens, "A Foreign Experience: Swedish Active Manpower Policy," *New Generation*, Winter 1971, p. 31.

2. cf. Roland McKean, *Public Spending* (New York: McGraw-Hill, 1968), Chapter Five.

3. cf. Martin C. McGuire and Harvey A. Garn, "Problems in the Cooperative Allocation of Public Expenditures," *Quarterly Journal of Economics*, February 1969.

4. Cf. Geoffrey Faux, *CDC's: New Hope for the Inner City* (New York: The Twentieth Century Fund, 1971); William K. Tabb, *The Political Economy of the Black Ghetto* (New York: W.W. Norton, 1970); Thomas Vietorisz and Bennett Harrison, *The Economic Development of Harlem* (New York: Praeger Publishers, 1970); and Vietorisz and Harrison, "Ghetto Development, Community Corporations, and Public Policy," *Review of Black Political Economy*, Fall 1971. Faux emphasized that "the people in poverty neighborhoods sense that economic power is a prerequisite to the achievement of political power, and that both are essential for obtaining social equality."

5. *Economic Opportunity Amendments of 1971*, S. 2007, Title VII: Community Economic Development, Part A — Special Impact Program.

6. Charles L. Schultze, "The Reviewers Reviewed," *American Economic Review*, May 1971, p. 49.

7. cf. Harley H. Hinrichs and Graeme M. Taylor (eds.), *Program Budgeting and Benefit-Cost Analysis: Cases, Text, and Readings* (Pacific Palisades, California: Goodyear, 1969).

8. John Kenneth Galbraith, *The Affluent Society* (New York: Houghton-Mifflin, 1958).

20 Public Employment: Research Needs and Methods

Michael C. Barth

Public job creation as a tool in national manpower and welfare policy is receiving great attention, particularly in the Congress. Using as a precedent past experience with programs initiated since 1964 and the rather extensive public works and conservation projects of the 1930s,[1] recently enacted legislation (the Emergency Employment Act of 1971[2] and pending amendments to the Social Security Act (the Opportunities for Families Program)[3] authorize large-scale public employment programs to remedy present unemployment problems, the longer term needs of those in economically impacted urban and rural areas and the employment needs of welfare recipients. Even beyond current activities, it can be surmised that more is yet to come; that is, current job creation programs could be merely "a foot in the door," and may be followed by further expansion of this concept in pursuit of a guaranteed employment policy. The program and budgetary impacts of these moves could be enormous with the potential for jobs measured in millions and the needs for dollars in tens of billions.

Regardless of what the future may portend, subsidized public employment is no longer limited to a few, meagerly funded Economic Opportunity Act programs (e.g., Operation Mainstream, Neighborhood Youth Corps – Out of School, Public Service Careers). It is now a big business.

Despite rather extensive prior experience with job creation programs, it is clear that we know little about the operation of, or demand for such programs, or about their impact on the persons they serve or the communities in which they are located.

Thus the course of present policy and the likely direction of future policy regarding public employment (PE) require that a searching examination of the concept be undertaken. This chapter will note issues and questions which need to be examined and will suggest some of the methods which might be employed in this endeavor. Before turning to these tasks, however, it may be useful to note explicitly what we mean by public employment, and to enumerate some program types and program goals.

What Is Public Employment?

For the purposes of the present discussion it will suffice to define public employment as occuring when a unit of government remunerates a person for

407

performing a service or producing a good. Effective public demand for the good or service need not precede public employment. That is, in addition to its derived-demand employer role, government may directly demand labor in order to "produce," as it were, employment.

Within this broad definition we can stylize three broad categories of public employment which are relevant to the present policy discussion:

1. Public Service Employment generally refers to the provision of "soft" services; the terms "paraprofessional" and "aide" most readily identify jobs in this category.
2. Public Works includes light to heavy construction; since relatively high capital to labor and skilled labor to unskilled labor ratios are implied, overhead is likely to be a large component of total program cost.
3. Work-Conditioned Income Transfers require that labor be supplied before any dollar benefits accrue to an individual, or that recipients at least agree to take any jobs which are available. Certain projects in the Operation Mainstream and Neighborhood Youth Corps programs probably fall within this category, since they seem to be little more than a replacement for Public Assistance. The term "make-work" is popularly applied to this sort of public employment. Many observers, following Galbraith's arguments,[4] would hold that this third category need not exist at all, since there are so many real and unfilled public needs.

Now what are the goals or objectives of public employment? There seem to be many, not all of which are strictly consistent with each other. A nonexhaustive enumeration would include the following: (1) providing employment, per se; (2) producing publicly demanded or "needed" goods and services; (3) serving the needs of poverty amelioration; (4) providing a vehicle for civil service reform; (5) providing a means of fiscal relief to units of state and local government; and (6) serving as a counter-cyclical tool of aggregate economic policy.

Quite obviously there is a good deal of overlap among these goals. In fact, this overlap or interrelatedness highlights one of the more interesting aspects of public employment. In many instances public employment produces a joint product; that is, it satisfies more than one goal with but one "tool." The most commonly recognized example is that of providing needed services while simultaneously providing employment. On the other hand, as noted, not all of the goals are consistent. For example, a counter-cyclical or revenue-sharing motive for launching public employment is unlikely to define the most desirable sort of antipoverty program for the employable. Thus, the strict fulfillment of one goal may make the strict fulfillment of another impossible. In this case a policy tradeoff exists. One "good" program aspect can be had only at the price of *less* of another "good" or, perhaps, more of a "bad."

We shall not belabor the existence of both joint products and policy tradeoffs. What we must note is that they exist and complicate policy making as regards public employment. In particular, the existence of a range of program types and a number of program goals presents the policy maker with a broad spectrum of program designs, some point(s) on which must be chosen. In order to make the best possible (wisest?) policy choices, information on a number of program effects will be crucial. These program effects can be thought of as issues or questions surrounding public employment. We now turn to a brief consideration of some of these.

Issues and Questions Relating to Public Employment

The general range of issues and questions of an economic nature which surround public employment can be stated in many ways, from the very general and formal to the quite specific. Since we wish to identify researchable issues which will confront policy makers, we shall identify eight areas and note some specific questions within each.

Program Administration

Tasks must be defined, workers found, and the two matched. This is perhaps the most obvious and elementary issue in program administration. But who is the optimal supervisor? What is the best supervisor/worker ratio? How will this ratio differ among public employment models? Experience with programs such as the Neighborhood Youth Corps suggests that the role of supervisors is critical to program success. How is supervisor quality to be determined? Personnel and industrial relations systems will be necessary in non-civil service programs. How long will it take to set up workable systems? What is the most efficient delivery system? For example, should existing public employers be expanded, or should new "public employers" be formed? These are but a few of the thorny issues surrounding program administration. Surely projects can be initiated based on current knowledge, but problems are inevitable. And unless solutions to the problems are found before a national program is implemented, the entire concept of public employment could be discredited.

Program Cost

Program cost will depend upon wages and overhead, plus a relatively fixed amount for monitoring and evaluation. (Overhead is the non-wage component of cost, such as materials, supplies, and salaries of supervisory personnel.) Quite clearly overhead will differ dramatically between public works and public service employment, since the latter requires few non-labor inputs. In fact we know relatively little regarding the likely magnitude of overhead and its variation among program models. While there are of course relevant models from the construction industry to examine, we may not be able to generalize to the target population of a specific public employment program. For example, one program may require more supervision than is anticipated; another may necessitate unexpectedly large capital expenditures. Knowledge that enables more accurate predictions of these costs would seem crucial to rational budgeting, particularly for counter-cyclical programs.

With respect to the other dimension of program cost, wages, we note that determining a wage level and a wage structure are essential and critical to the program. Low wages will not increase the incomes of recipients greatly, but, within given budget constraints, they do expand the population that could be served. Also relatively high wages might attract nonpoor private sector workers, who may not be a target of the program but would be difficult to exclude. In addition to the wage level, a wage structure must be determined. Should such a structure mirror those in the private sector? How will program wages vary over time and across jurisdictions?

Response of Potential Supply Population

Presumably the existence of jobs will attract various sorts of persons. One of the most important things to be learned is the wage responsiveness of various groups: the short- and long-term unemployed; those who have become discouraged with the job search and dropped out of the labor force; those employed at low wage, dead-end jobs.

Knowing precisely what sorts of people will seek public employment program slots also is crucial to optimal program design. If the supply population does not possess basic verbal skills, for example, a minimal amount of training may be necessary before any actual public employment "output" can be expected.

Further, we need to know whether the desired target population can be reached. Will the program be such as to attract persons with a heretofore loose labor force attachment? If program design is to maximize the chances of fulfilling the program's goals we must know the answers to such questions as: Which designs tend to attract and retain those who otherwise could not find work or would not seek work? Is a mix of work and training superior to all of one or the other? How does job content relate to wage level in determining initial willingness of workers to enroll and their propensities to remain in the program or to quit. As will be seen below, the last question is crucial to determination of program-size variation.

Effect on Labor Market

Another wage-related issue is the effect of the program on the local labor market. Since public employment will presumably dip heavily into the pool of unemployed labor, the basic supply-demand relationship in the local labor market will be affected, but we don't know precisely how. Theory would predict that wages would be bid up, but if so, would the rise be significant? How will private sector employers react to wage pressure? They might substitute capital for labor, or they might raise wages to compete for the now scarcer labor. The possible effects of a large-scale public employment program on what has come to be called the "secondary labor market" could be striking (and, to many, desirable).[5] It thus is important to closely watch private sector wage levels in an area where a public employment program has been mounted. It is also important to know the sensitivity of workers to wage variations in the private sector. Are they likely to move back and forth in response to slight wage level variations?

Tasks to Be Performed

While much rhetoric suggests an unlimited supply of public service jobs, do they really exist other than on paper and in the guise of normal vacancies? Could a medium-sized city absorb enough new employees to make a dent in city unemployment? If it could, *would* it without the assurance of a permanent wage bill subsidy? In non-Public Service Employment models, what work would be done? Can the tasks be defined in sufficient quality and number so that the goals will be fulfilled?

Noneconomic Community Effects

The creation of a nontrivial number of jobs can be expected to have social as well as economic effects on an area. The participants could well become a stigmatized "class." That this is indeed a problem is attested to by Beatrice Reubens' description of Sweden's job creation dilemma:

There is a conflict between the ideal socially created job which is equal in status to a market job and the reality that the economy appears to be dividing into a market which absorbs the attractive members of the labor force and an inferior world of socially-created work for the remainder.[6]

The design of jobs that provided desired services for the community and produced self-respect as well as income for the worker would prevent such a "class" from forming. Reform of undesirable civil service practices such as race and sex discrimination and artificial credentialism would be an important consideration here. This aspect of job development would be one of the most significant and challenging aspects of public employment program design.

Variation in Program Size

As labor markets tighten we can expect some public employment participants to accept desirable private sector employment. This is of course not undesirable. But can the public employment program adjust to a variable workforce? If 200 men were at work on a project, for example, could 125 continue the same project if the labor market changed? How much flexibility is needed will depend on exit and entry rates. We know very little about how to design a program with sufficient flexibility; nor do we know what sort of start-up and turn-down times to expect.

Regional Variations

Frequently, there exist significant differences among localities with regard to prices, ethnic composition of the population, local mores, and institutions. Thus, for example, what might be a quite substantial wage in one area might be a relatively low "real" wage in a region with a high cost-of-living. Ought public employment to account for such differences? If so, how? (particularly given the paucity of local area data).

Local wage levels differ greatly. In some areas employees of local governments earn less than the minimum wage. Since no politically acceptable federal legislation is likely to specify sub-minimum wages, could the Public Service Employment model even exist in such cities?

In regions that experience large migratory flows the public employment slots could well be fully subscribed by non-residents of the area. In south Texas, for example, this would be a particularly serious problem (including the case of foreign nationals), while it might not exist in many other localities.

The force of these points is that the great regional diversity in this country would necessitate a good deal of regional variation in program design. Failure to account for the required design differences could lead what would be a good program model in one region to fail in another.

The preceding eight items are major examples of questions and issues surrounding public employment. This list is by no means preclusive; other problems could be considered. What is perhaps most striking is the interrelatedness of these issues. For example, high quality supervision will work to produce a better product — in terms of both participant and community — but will raise overhead and thus program cost. Low wages may insure reaching only the low-income population, but, by limiting the range of available skills, will limit the types of tasks which can be performed. If policy makers and program administrators are to make wise decisions when designing and running public employment programs they will need as much insight as possible into the qualitative nature and quantitative magnitude of the variables and responses identified in the preceding eight areas. The question we must now address is how to go about obtaining the needed information.

Research Methods

The techniques which could be used to obtain the information previously identified range from pure post hoc examinations of past programs to experimental research with new programs. Somewhere in the middle lie evaluations of ongoing and new programs, and standard theoretical-statistical research methods. Previous research has shown that beyond the provision of a large and significant number of "don'ts" the amount of information to be gained from examining past program experience is minimal.[7] Hence we shall concentrate on, in turn, evaluation, experimentation and demonstration activities, and standard research techniques. Our treatment of each research method will be general, but we shall give examples of instances in which a particular question is best (or only) answered by one particular research method.

Evaluation

. . . evaluation is research, the application of the scientific method to experience with public programs to learn what happens as a result of program activities. Evaluation includes the definition of program objectives, the development of measures of progress toward these objectives, the assessment of what difference public programs actually make, and the projection of what reasonably could be expected if the programs were continued or expanded.

The essence of evaluation is the comparison of both outcome — what happened that would not have happened in the absence of the program? — and relative effectiveness — what strategies or projects within programs work best?[8]

Thus evaluation examines existing programs. We may anticipate some of the discussion to follow by noting that in our characterization standard research would deal with hypothetical programs while experimentation would design the program in such a way as to be certain that desired information could be obtained.

Evaluation need not be purely post hoc. Indeed it is desirable that programs be designed with the data needs of evaluators in mind. Nevertheless, it is more often than not the case that congressional mandate and administrative guideline, to say nothing of the facts of life in the "real world," preclude this.

Wholey et al. distinguish four types of evaluation.[9] First, *program impact* evaluation seeks to guage the overall effectiveness of a national program in meeting its objectives. If a goal of public employment is to reduce unemployment, an impact evaluation should certainly be performed to see if the goal is met. It might be found, for example, that because of the cyclical sensitivity of the labor force,[10] the unemployment rate remained roughly the same in spite of the public employment program.

Second, *program strategy* evaluation assesses the relative effectiveness of different techniques used in a national program. Its goal is to measure the relative effectivenss of different strategies or methods used by projects in a national program. If we substitute "effects" for "effectiveness" many of the questions we seek to answer would fall within the purview of a program strategy evaluation. For example, if different projects which are sufficiently similar in other ways pay a different wage and elicit differential supply responses, we could conceivably detect a wage-supply relation.

Third, *project evaluation* assesses the effectiveness of individual projects.[a] Finally, *project rating* seeks to determine relative effectiveness of different local projects. It is the latter two types of evaluation which could shed the most light on the specific questions noted above. This is because in most instances we are concerned with how different projects would operate and with the different behavioral responses they would elicit.

We note that the language of evaluation stresses the term "effectiveness," while we are as concerned with effects. By closely observing local projects and the environments in which they operate answers to many of our questions as well as indices of effectiveness can be obtained. For example, close monitoring of local projects will provide information on overhead to total cost ratios across different types of projects. Simultaneously the degree of goal fulfillment (e.g., provision of jobs) can be determined.

The principal problem with employing evaluation of in-place programs as the tool to answer our questions is that it may not be able to relate effects to specific program components. Thus if something desirable "happens," and we wish to induce more of the same, we will not know which program component to augment. Such component-specific information is obviously quite important in decisions regarding program alteration. It is difficult to end social programs, but it is possible to redesign them.

Demonstration and Experimentation

In order to obtain estimates of program component-specific effects it may be necessary to design a set of programs in such a way as to be able to isolate statistically the component of interest. In the limit such an endeavor becomes a true social science experiment, such as the Office of Economic Opportunity — funded New Jersey Graduated Work Incentive Experiment.[11] We are under no

---

[a]A "project" is the local inplementation of a national "program."

illusions that the necessary degree of environmental control can be obtained when dealing with something so complex as a labor market so that a true "public employment experiment" could be launched.

However, it may be possible to simultaneously launch demonstration public employment projects in closely "matched" locations so that the effect of a few program components could be closely monitored. The crucial difference between this tack and evaluation as described above is that the "controlled demonstration" would carefully vary certain components so that we would be certain to have observations on variables of interest. Once the program and project design is specified, data collection and analysis for a demonstration would be virtually identical to that for an evaluation.

The key to the controlled demonstration is that the researcher works with the program manager in designing programs. Planners would try to hold constant (or anticipate the variation in) certain components, while letting others vary in observable (perhaps scalable) ranges. This may be the only possible way to gain insight into something so subtle as the question of how wage level and job content relate to program slot demand and to duration of stay in the program.

Given the inherent heterogeneity one observes both within and across labor markets, it is difficult to be terribly sanguine about the degree of precision of estimates one could expect from a controlled demonstration. But the potential benefit must be balanced against the real marginal cost of such a research method. The marginal cost would be relatively low since the public employment program would either be in operation under any circumstances (e.g., the Emergency Employment Act of 1971) or be putting people to work who would otherwise be idle. Thus only relatively small additions to cost (above those necessary for an evaluation) would be needed for the additional planning and data analysis necessitated by the controlled demonstration.

Standard Research Methods

By "standard research methods" we mean descriptive, theoretical, and/or statistical analyses of processes which we do not *directly* observe, as we would in the case of an evaluation or demonstration. This method is by far the least expensive research technique of the three discussed here since it does not entail extensive field surveys. It is also therefore limited in its usefulness.

A contribution which standard research methods can make to policy making in the public employment area is to specify the proverbial "ball park" for certain variables. For example, a range estimate of the demand for public employment slots can be obtained from a carefully specified and estimated econometric model. Such a model would account for the labor supply decisions of the measured and hidden unemployed and the presently employed as they related to a number of crucial variables. A list of these variables would include: wage rate;

job content; location of job; risk premium of worker (i.e., desire for stable job) local job vacancies.

If such a model predicted a great deal of variability in demand for program slots, then program managers might be forewarned to expect similar variation in available workers. Hence, one of the uses of standard research methods would be to suggest possible problem areas which might need close scrutiny in an evaluation. Similarly input-output techniques could be used to project future employment demand by sector so that public employment projects might be designed to fill labor bottlenecks or provide needed services. Such efforts might improve the "image" as well as the social value of public employment.

Conclusion

There is much to be learned regarding public employment. This chapter explicitly noted eight specific areas and many questions within each. We then considered alternative research techniques. Evaluations and controlled demonstrations were distinguished on the basis of the latter's being able to predetermine variation in program components of interest. Standard research methods can play an important role by setting, in advance of program implementation, the limits of certain variables as well as by identifying problem areas. We would urge that efforts in all three areas be undertaken. It does seem to follow from the discussion, however, that many of the information needs we identified can be satisfied best by close observation of variations in actual programs. That is, to get at the nitty-gritty issues involved with public employment a good deal of doing and watching will be necessary.

Notes

1. For a discussion of past programs and an annotated bibliography see Michael C. Barth and Frank H. Easterbrook, "Work Relief in the Depression, Europe, and the 'Manpower Decade': Some Implications for Programs of Public Employment," O.E.O. *Working Papers*, Series 3250, No. 1, Washington, D.C., November, 1970; and Frank H. Easterbrook, "Public Employment Programs: A Selected and Annotated Bibliography," O.E.O. *Working Papers*, Series 3250, No. 2, Washington, D.C., November, 1970, respectively.

2. Public Law-92-54, 92nd Congress, 1st Session, 85 Stat. 146.

3. United States House of Representatives, 92nd Congress, 1st Session, H.R. 1, Title XXI, Part A.

4. John Kenneth Galbraith, *The Affluent Society* (New York: Houghton-Mifflin, 1958).

5. For a discussion of the literature relevant to the secondary labor market

concept see David M. Gordon, *Economic Theories of Poverty and Under-employment* (Lexington, Mass.: Heath-Lexington Books, 1972); and Bennett Harrison, "Public Employment and the Theory of the Dual Economy," chapter 2 in this volume.

6. Beatrice Reubens, "A Foreign Experience: Swedish Active Manpower Policy," *New Generation*, Winter 1971, p. 31.

7. Barth and Easterbrook, "Work Relief in the Depression."

8. Joseph S. Wholey et al., *Federal Evaluation Policy,* The Urban Institute, 9-121-21, June 1970, p. 5.

9. Ibid. pp. 12-13. The following characterization draws heavily on this reference.

10. For a discussion of the literature on labor force-employment relations, see Jacob Mincer, "Labor-Force Participation and Unemployment: A Review of Recent Evidence," in Robert Aaron Gordon and Margaret Gordon, eds., *Prosperity and Unemployment* (New York: John Wiley & Sons, Inc., 1966).

11. For a description, see Harold Watts, "Graduated Work Incentives: An Experiment in Negative Taxation," *American Economic Review,* May 1969, pp. 463-72.

21 Public Service Employment and the Inflation Problem

EDWARD M. GRAMLICH

To this point the Upjohn Seminar Series has concentrated on unemployment. The seminars have examined the magnitude of unemployment, its composition among different social and demographic groups, and the extent to which we could reasonably expect to reduce it through public employment programs. But the exclusive focus on unemployment obscures what is really the fundamental labor market problem facing the United States today. It is not so much that we have much unemployment per se, but that we have a very poor tradeoff between inflation and unemployment. If our problem were only the number of unemployed workers, we could get them jobs by stimulating the economy, whether through public or private employment, in relatively short order. The missing element, which makes our labor market problem so much more intractable, is that presently we can not accomplish this stimulation without an unacceptable degree of inflation. Thus policy makers are prevented by their fear of inflation from eliminating the unemployment. In this chapter I will attempt to show why this is so and discuss ways in which public employment programs might improve the situation.

The cornerstone of any analysis of inflation and unemployment is the widely known Phillips Curve – the functional relationship between unemployment and the rate of inflation. This relationship is meant to explain the wage and price bargaining system in our economy. According to the logic of the Phillips Curve, when unemployment is high there will be slack in product and labor markets, firms will be reluctant to grant wage increases and unable to enforce price increases, and laborers will be less aggressive in pressing for wage increases because of their fear of unemployment. If, on the other hand, unemployment is low, product and labor markets will be tight, firms will need labor and be willing to grant generous wage increases, they will find it easier to pass along these wage increases in the form of price increases, and laborers will be more aggressive in their wage bargains when not haunted by the spectre of unemployment. The consequence is that when unemployment is high, the rate of inflation is low; and when unemployment is low, the rate of inflation is high. Since both unemployment and inflation are undesirable, the lesson of the Phillips Curve that you can only reduce one problem by creating another has sometimes been called the "cruel dilemma" for economic policy makers. Of late the dilemma has apparently become even more cruel for policy makers in the United States because we are now suffering what most people consider to be unacceptable amounts of both unemployment and inflation.

419

The existence of this tradeoff between inflation and unemployment has been questioned both by those with very short time horizons and by those with very long horizons. In the short run wages and prices respond slowly to economic conditions. Thus if labor markets have been tight over a period of time, it will take time before the wage increases unions demand and firms are willing to grant reflect any slackening in demand. It will take even more time for product prices to respond to changes in costs and demand conditions. This means that for short-run periods of up to, say, one or two years, there may be a rather loose relationship between unemployment and inflation. As in the past year, unemployment might rise from 4 to 6 percent without any visible reduction in the rate of inflation.

In the long run both laborers and firms become much more responsive to economic conditions. If we move from a regime of relative price stability to a regime of very strong demand for goods and labor, prices and wages will eventually begin to rise more rapidly. Once this initial inflation has taken hold, both unions and firms will *expect* it to continue and will build these expectations into their wage-price behavior. A union that previously was planning to ask for a 5 percent increase in wages will, when it expects prices to rise by 4 percent, ask for 9 percent. A firm that would be willing to grant a 5 percent wage increase in a world of stable prices will agree to the 9 percent boost. And then it will turn around and raise its own prices by 4 percent to stay even. The mere expectation of inflation thus insures its continuance.

It is apparent from the above example that once the inflation lasts long enough to create prevailing expectations of inflation, it becomes very difficult to control. Unions or firms which were planning to be timid will be forced to be more aggressive just to stay even in real terms. And in becoming more aggressive, they add to inflationary pressures and force others to become more aggressive. This adds pressure once again and forces still others to become more aggressive. In the very long run, when all firms and unions have had a chance to respond fully, this type of inflationary process will progress inevitably to uncontrollable hyper-inflation, such as was experienced in Europe between the world wars and is being experienced today in some underdeveloped countries. It is not a pleasant experience, and it is the reason many economists warn against overstimulating the economy. In their long-run view, there is no permanent tradeoff between unemployment and inflation because once we enter the range of excessive demand, we open ourselves to the danger of hyper-inflation which can only be stopped by retreating to higher unemployment rates. Rates of unemployment any lower than the so-called "natural rate" cannot be sustaineed.

One solution to this problem is, of course, outright controls on prices and wages. The government could step in to prevent unions and firms from gaining excessive increases in wages and prices, and thus allow the economy to achieve lower unemployment rates than it otherwise could. Although we still do not know enough about price-wage controls to know how effective they will be, it is clear that they are not without costs of their own. A small or large government bureaucracy must be established, there will be arbitrary enforcement and inequities, and over the long run price-wage controls will impede the market's ability to allocate resources. The controls will also be much more difficult to enforce the greater are the pent up inflationary forces. Thus even if we opt for price-wage controls, we should still not forget about the inflation-unemployment tradeoff. Measures to improve the tradeoff, or reduce the amount of inflation implied by any level of unemployment, are still in the national interest.

What has public employment to do with all of this? Very simply, the effect of public employment, like that of any other government expenditure, will be to move us along the Phillips Curve relationship to a regime of lower unemployment and higher inflation. Viewing the unemployment effect in isolation, this is undoubtedly a good thing: the country employs people who were otherwise idle, the people and their families benefit, and everybody else benefits for the output they produce. But, and this is the fly in the ointment, the move to higher levels of employment will set inflationary pressures in motion. The inflationary pressures may be small and controllable, yet if the public employment program is done on a large scale, they may very well not be. If we are not careful in guarding against these pressures, the program may not get us anywhere at all for it will only force an overall slowdown to stop the inflation it helped to create. Even if we try to control this inflation directly, the greater inflationary pressure will increase the difficulty of administering these controls, increase the bureaucratic inefficiencies and inequities, and increase the likelihood that the scheme of controls will eventually be abandoned. To put this another way, there is a direct tradeoff between the extent to which we minimize the inflationary forces implicit in our public employment program and the size of the program we can have. The more we minimize these inflationary force, whether we have outright controls or not, the larger the public employment program we can afford. Thus passionate advocates of public employment should be as much in favor of measures to reduce its inflationary pressure as are inveterate worriers about inflation.

There are three important ways in which public employment can actually reduce inflationary pressures while it stimulates employment. The first way is for public employment to concentrate on job vacancies in the public sector, vacancies which local governments are presently trying to fill and which are therefore adding to money wage inflation. There is a good deal of evidence, some of it presented in the Upjohn series, that problems such as racial discrimination, over-credentialism, lack of promotion opportunities, and poor placement procedures lead to a serious malfunctioning of the labor market for local government employment. On the one hand we have jobs which are vacant because there are no candidates with the required color or educational credentials to fill them; on the other hand we have people who would be qualified for and happy to fill these jobs being denied the opportunity because of the artificial job requirements. The artificially high job requirements aggravate this problem in another, more subtle, way. To the extent that a college education is required to perform a menial job, the overly educated person will sooner become bored with his job and quit, joining the ranks of the transitory unemployed while his job joins the list of transitory vacancies. If we could use public employment to attack these artificial impediments to the proper functioning of the local government labor markets, such as is done in, say, OEO's project Pacemaker, we could reduce unemployment by filling job vacancies which would have otherwise added to inflationary pressures, and thus reduce inflation while we are reducing unemployment.

A second important possibility is to look at the same consideration on the output side. Public service employment will produce output, and by gearing the program to certain bottleneck areas, the output can be used to reduce inflationary pressures. One obvious area is in health care, one of the most inflationary sectors in the whole economy since the mid Sixties. If some of the new public sector employees were used to increase the supply of health services, as nurses aides, laboratory workers, and so forth, possibly they could help stem the rise in medical care costs. Other bottleneck areas which might also be attacked include the provision of services for day care, transportation, and sanitation.

The third way in which the inflationary pressures of public employment could be minimized involves the type of labor benefitting from the program. Public employment could either be directed to temporarily unemployed middle-class workers suffering the effects of shifts in the economy's composition of output; or to more chronically unemployed lower income workers who are always either unemployed, underemployed, or temporarily employed in dead end jobs which they will soon be fired from or quit. If the public employment program should focus on middle-class workers, it would provide them temporary jobs while they looked for permanent jobs and, by virtue of this cushioning, make them more aggressive in their wage demands on their new job. If the program should focus on the lower-class workers, possibly because the public employment wage was set at a relatively low level, it would again provide temporary support for some workers who might be trying to locate private sector jobs, but it might also provide a vehicle which these low income workers could use to obtain permanent jobs with local governments. The effects of the program are favorable in either case, but probably much more favorable in the latter case. For not only does a program directed at low income workers generate a minimal increase in wage aggressiveness — these workers would not have much wage bargaining power even with a public employment program — but it also has a better chance of creating a permanent job match between local governments and workers they would not previously have considered hiring. Thus we should expect a program targeted to the low income workers who really need help not only to be more equitable, but also to be less inflationary.

The unifying theme of these remarks is that public service employment should be used to attack real labor market problems. To the extent that the program is not directed toward filling artificial public sector job vacancies, towards removing bottleneck areas on the output side, and supports middle-class workers who could get jobs regardless, public service employment is little different from any other government expenditure and would not materially improve the inflation-unemployment tradeoff. It would inevitably stimulate inflation as it reduced unemployment, and there would be a natural limit to the size of the program. But to the extent that the public employment program focuses on just the problems that have led to the Upjohn series in the first place, to the extent that it improves job matching for local governments, produces output presently in short supply, and is targeted toward lower income workers, it might have a much greater payoff. Not only will it reduce unemployment, but it will also reduce inflationary pressures and give room for a much more extensive program or for much greater aggregate demand stimulation of the economy.

22 Public Service Employment: Who Decides?

GEOFFREY FAUX

We have focused on public service employment as a device to absorb the unemployment that the workings of the private sector of the economy cannot. We have also discussed the need to make public service jobs themselves meaningful in improving the quality of life.

Underlying both of these issues — income distribution and the quality of life — is another question: Who decides? And what effect might public service employment have on the control of public resources in poor communities?

The issue of community control and participation in the War on Poverty has been discussed at such great length that one would think that it was the principle characteristic of that puny conflict. Writing on the basis of the first two years' experience with OEO and in the gloom of a personal political defeat, Dr. Moynihan said that community control didn't work. Dr. Robert Levine, who shares Moynihan's policy views if not his politics, says that community control was never really tried — and a good thing too!

Levine's perceptions of what happened in the War on Poverty are more accurate. For anyone who shared that experience, either as general or foot soldier, the notion that OEO was a master plan to subvert legitimate local authority was absurd. A few people certainly had this in mind, but few of their pet projects survived a call from the White House. Certainly after 1967 and the imposition of the Green Amendment, the vast majority of federal antipoverty bureaucrats fell in step with the "realpolitik" of the day. Radical chic might have flourished in the drawing rooms of New York, but it couldn't get past the front door in Washington.

There is no question but that many people in the ghettos and barrios of the nation were radicalized by the Poverty Program — but by its reality rather than its ideology. Saul Alinsky called the War on Poverty a "piece of political pornography," meaning I suppose that it aroused but could not satisfy. It is as good an analogy as I have seen. The Great Society sent out the message that there was a bright affluent future in America for anyone who worked hard to overcome his individual deficiencies. And so the poor took sixteen weeks of Labor Department training, enrolled their kids in Headstart, and sent their wives to the community action agency to learn how to shop.

But there weren't any jobs. And whatever the kids learned in the Headstart program was lost six months into the first grade. And despite the consumer programs the local supermarket still raised food prices the day that the welfare

425

checks were delivered. After seven years of this we policy makers are now prepared to admit something that the poor have always known; there are not enough jobs to go around. But we are not prepared to make more than a token act on the basis of that knowledge.

That is also something that the poor have learned, and that is why the issue of "who controls?" has become so important to them. For most of us, that issue is a bother, and the insistence of community leaders on that point only goes to prove that they can't be trusted to handle their own affairs. Why can't they stick to the issues like "housing" and "jobs"? What does it matter who controls as long as the job gets done?

But we professionals have had the control and still there is no housing and still there are no jobs and last year the number of poor people in the country rose by one million. Like it or not the issue of control will not go away. All our experience shows that it is inseparable from the so-called "substantive" issues of housing, jobs, services, etc.

As we all know, economists do not like to deal with the issue of control. It is intellectually messy and all the models are indeterminate. The preferred approach is to assume present patterns of control over resources and get down to the "substantive" questions of how to distribute whatever portion of society's resources have been left for the poor. Another solution is to take a flying leap over the problems and treat them as if power were irrelevant.

One example of the latter is the "development vs. dispersal" debate regarding policies toward the inner city. Whatever the deficiencies of the development strategy, the dispersal argument completely ignores the political realities of this society which will restrict a large proportion of the poor to the inner city for some time to come.

Considerations of power have and can be expected to dominate considerations of efficiency and, for the immediate future, development programs will be the central focus for expanded opportunity. They will also represent, for many, a necessary stage on the road to an integrated society. And the question of who controls that development is critical. The history of the urban renewal program is a good example of how a program based upon existing power conformations can become destructive to the process of growth and integration.

On the other end of the spectrum is a model that has been reproduced in a number of poor urban and rural areas over the past few years. It is the model of community-based economic development. Community-based economic development programs have grown rapidly over the last few years in poverty areas throughout the country. Despite the scarcity of funds and the resistence of policy makers and budget makers, demand for economic development has forced OEO, HUD, and others to expand dramatically their support for community development corporations, cooperatives, and similar organizations.

This growth is a natural evolution of the War on Poverty. It comes from two sources: (1) the failure of services and manpower training strategies — neither of which attempted to tamper with the job-creating mechanism of the private sector — to make more than a dent in the cycle of poverty, and (2) the clear evidence from the history of OEO that the poor, *because they are poor*, lack the political power to secure for themselves a decent share of the economic pie. In one sense, the war on poverty was a long verification of Michael Harrington's thesis that America is characterized by "socialism for the rich and free enterprise for the poor."

In its largest meaning, therefore, community economic development is an effort by the disadvantaged to pool their resources and take an active role in creating an economic platform for their assimilation into the broader economy and society.

All of this is quite in the American mainstream. The notion of social assimilation through the attainment of group power has precedents throughout the history of immigration to America. The precedents for the subsidization of business enterprises to achieve social goals begins with the Virginia Company in 1607, continues through the subsidization of railroads and the massive programs of land grants in the nineteenth century to some of the familiar examples in 1971. There is scarcely an industry in America today that is not subsidized by federal aid of one sort or another.

The most sophisticated model for development efforts in poor communities is the Community Development Corporation, of which there are probably more than a hundred operating in rural and urban areas.

Community Development Corporations are business corporations owned and operated by the people who live in an impoverished area. Since most have evolved out of local conditions and experiences, there is no one national prototype model. However, they all share the following distinguishing characteristics:

Economic Development. CDCs are engaged in all phases of economic development. They invest in, own, and operate businesses and housing projects.

Local Control. CDCs are controlled by residents of poverty areas.

Social Goals. The CDCs' ultimate purpose is to increase the economic well-being of the area they seek to serve.

CDCs have been started in both urban and rural areas, but thus far the longest experience has been gathered in urban programs. The Hough Development Corporation in Cleveland, the FIGHT Corporation in Rochester, the Restoration Corporation in Bedford-Stuyvesant, Progress Enterprises in Philadelphia are commonly recognized models. Shopping centers, light manufacturing corporations, retail stores, service businesses, housing programs and comprehensive development planning of all sorts are some of the activities in which CDCs are presently engaged.

The concept of the Community Development Corporation is relevant not only to the efforts to achieve economic advancement on the part of *minorities.* It addresses itself to the basic problem of economic development in all impoverished areas. By definition, these areas are generally unattractive places in which to invest. Therefore, approaches that rely *solely* on attracting private capital (e.g., by luring outside industry to the poverty area, by fostering minority entrepreneurs) can achieve development only by substantial subsidy of purely private economic goals. Furthermore, such approaches do not address themselves to the economic disorganization which is also a characteristic of impoverished areas.

Economic development which optimizes antipoverty and other social goals can be achieved only with the establishment of an organizing force which is accountable to local public control and direction. Not only does public accountability give greater priority to social goals, it allows social programs to be used in support of economic goals. High crime rates in cities and poor educational facilities in rural areas are often greater obstacles to economic development than wage rates and locational factors. Public accountability also encourages the combining of planning and implementation which is too often separated in economic development programing.

The organizing force for economic development must be able to put together the major elements necessary for effective programs. These include: (1) public investments; (2) private capital; (3) local decision making; (4) business organizations free from bureaucratic control.

The history of OEO programs, the Model Cities program, the Small Business Administration programs, the Economic Development Administration's programs and the hundreds of state and local programs aimed at economic development suggests that only through the leadership of a genuine community organization can these elements be put together. Despite inexperience and scarcity of talent, despite lack of training and the tendency to get bogged down in petty politics, only an organization with its roots in the community will have the will and the natural incentive to go through the long, hard process of economic development. The private sector lacks the incentive, and the bureaucracy lacks the competence.

This does not mean that Community Development Corporations can by themselves develop Hough or Watts or Bedford-Stuyvesant. The government, the outside investor, and the individual entrepreneur all have important roles to play. But it does mean that someone has to get it together:

a. to make those first high risk investments
b. to train managers
c. to secure land in the inner city
d. to generate the necessary political support
e. to plan and implement a comprehensive development program that will combine the capital, the land and the human resources.

The rest will follow:

a. outside investors will gain confidence in the area
b. banks will be more willing to make more loans
c. city services will improve as the city sees a potential expansion of its tax base.

In turn, new opportunities will be created and exploited and the process of economic development will become self-sustaining as it is in affluent areas. But with one difference. If the Community Development Corporation does its job, it will not only have catalyzed the economic development process, but through its ability to influence that process, it will have gained maximum benefits for the neighborhood residents.

Slowly but surely the need for such an economic development strategy is becoming apparent. Not only in urban ghettos, but also in many small towns and rural areas which in the next decade are likely to be the beneficiaries of programs aimed at alleviating the social and ecological pressures on major metropolitan areas. In the past year several bills have been introduced into both houses of Congress calling for domestic development banks to spur the flow of capital to poverty areas. And even a man as suspicious of new ideas as the current vice-president has been talking about the need for regional economic planning.

These proposals will not be implemented this year. But sooner or later a strong effort will be made to establish a national economic development policy. And to provide the new money to go with it. No matter what happens to revenue-sharing.

In one sense, it is fortunate for those concerned about the distribution of benefits between rich and poor that this policy is still a few years away. If a domestic development bank were created tomorrow, it is unlikely that many poor people would benefit. Most are simply not yet organized for it and are not yet experienced enough to use large chunks of development money effectively. The hustlers would end up with most of it — just as they have in the past.

And inner-city residents would be pushed out of the potentially valuable land they now live on and would be squeezed into other ghettos where the sores of poverty and racism would continue to fester.

So for better or worse we have time to prepare. Time to start some projects, have some successes, make some mistakes. But most of all, time to build a capacity among the people for running sensible development programs and operating viable businesses so that when the time comes to spend more funds on poverty programs, and it may come as soon as the spring of 1973, the people will be ready.

Because public service employment is such an important idea, one which will grow as it becomes clearer and clearer that the private sector does not generate sufficient jobs to provide everyone with work, it can be a useful and supportive force for community self-development. It can also undermine the process.

Public service employment can help accelerate the creation of strong self-development institutions if: (1) the decision making is located as close to the neighborhood level as possible, and (2) the program provides for the kinds of jobs that will give training in those professional and semi-professional skills needed to assist in the self-development process.

As we have seen, the question of control is critical. No one who is familiar with local politics of any kind can doubt that the most important immediate issue to people in the communities receiving public service employment funds will be its patronage dimension. Public service employment will mean patronage for someone. Economists cannot wash their hands of that fact. By compromising on that issue, the way the present bill apparently has compromised by excluding community action agencies (which are not neighborhood institutions, but closer to the neighborhoods than City Hall) as prime sponsors and including only mildly permissive language allowing community corporations to participate in the program, one in fact gives the new patronage and power to those who control City Hall and who will use it to suppress the growth of community organizations which are a potential threat. A bill like this is *not* neutral in its political impact.

The kinds of jobs available are also important. Concern that the public service jobs created will help attack the "quality of life" problems of the society as a whole is all well and good, but there needs to be at least as great an emphasis on the quality of life of those whom we are seeking to employ with this bill. The ghettos are desperately short of health technicians, housing specialists, child development workers and so on. The "New Careers" concept of creating opportunities for the poor to work on the problems that affect their lives should be a guiding force behind public service programs of any sort.

Since one of the questions before the panel concerns research needs, I should say something about that. I think that there are two broad areas that need more investigation. Both are at the micro level. One is a need for a greater understanding of the process of deterioration in the inner city. And I don't mean more surveys to tell us how lousy things are. What I mean is an analysis of the economic and political interactions that lead to this deterioration. What are the disincentives working against new investments? Of municipal corruption? Who profits from slums? Who profits from suburbanization? And how do these beneficiaries affect public policies and the distribution of resources at all levels of government?

The other area is that of identifying the manpower requirements for city rebuilding. What kinds of skills do we need? How are they developed? How much training is necessary and how much can be learned on the job? And how do we build a stability into funding domestic programs that will permit the conservation and full utilization of skills and experience?

I believe that the process of community-controlled development is essential for the resolution of the bitter racial and class divisions that rack this country.

America is not a melting pot. If you will pardon the metaphor, it is at best a mixing bowl of intermingled but distinct ingredients. For most of us, equality is a matter of being identified with one or more centers of power and privilege in a pluralistic society. Public service employment should be judged in large part on how it helps the poor gain some of that social and economic power most of us already enjoy.

Appendix

Private Sector Employment Generated by Government Purchases of Goods and Services

U.S. DEPARTMENT OF LABOR

Manpower requirements and the level of employment in this country are greatly influenced by government expenditures [see table A.1] . . . government agencies employed more than 16 million people in 1970 – 10.1 million in state and local governments, 3.2 million in the Armed Forces, and 2.9 million in federal civilian jobs (see table A.2). In addition, government spending for goods and services purchased from private industry generated more than 7 million jobs – 3.7 million attributable to federal spending and 3.6 million to state and local buying.[a] The total of over 23 million jobs thus created by "government purchases" (that is, compensation of government employees plus purchases from private industry) represented more than one-fourth of all U.S. employment, civilian and military, in 1970 (see figure A.1). [The interindustry distributions of the jobs generated by government purchases are shown in tables A.3 and A.4.]

This appendix comprises selections from chapter 5 of the 1971 *Manpower Report of the President*, U.S. Dept. of Labor, Manpower Administration.

---

[a]The estimates of private employment attributable to government purchases of goods and services are based on an interindustry employment table derived from an input-output table showing, for the base year, what each industry purchases from every other industry, as well as from itself, to produce its own output. The employment table relates the industry's employment to its output and shows the total domestic employment (wage and salary workers, self-employed, and unpaid family workers) attributable to $1 billion of delivery to final demand by each industry in the economy, including not only direct employment in the producing industry but indirect employment in all supporting industries. (For a detailed description of the input-output table and the employment table, see "Interindustry Employment Requirements," *Monthly Labor Review*, July 1965, pp. 841-850).

The resulting estimates of private employment generated by government purchases are subject to several limitations: (1) They reflect the employment required to produce all products made by the industry in the base year, and not necessarily the particular products purchased by governments; (2) they do not reflect the employment generated by the industry's workers when they spend their earnings on consumer goods; and (3) they exclude employment that would be required to replace the capital equipment consumed in production processes.

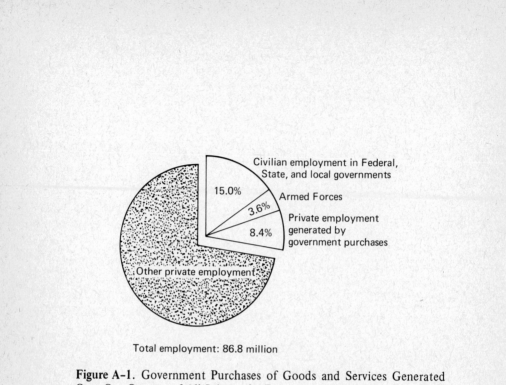

Total employment: 86.8 million

Figure A-1. Government Purchases of Goods and Services Generated Over One-Quarter of All Jobs in the Economy in 1970. Source; Department of Labor.

Table A.1
Government Purchases of Goods and Services, 1962-1970 (Billions of dollars)

Level of Government	Total[1]	Government purchases of goods and services[2]					Compensation of employees of government enterprises
		Total	Purchases from private industry	Compensation of general government personnel			
				Total	Civilian	Military	
Total							
1962	$123.1	$117.1	$62.5	$54.7	$43.2	$11.5	$6.0
1963	129.0	122.5	64.4	58.1	46.5	11.7	6.6
1964	135.7	128.7	65.7	63.0	50.4	12.6	7.0
1965	144.4	137.0	69.2	67.8	54.7	13.1	7.4
1966	164.9	156.8	80.2	76.6	60.8	15.8	8.1
1967	188.8	180.1	95.0	85.1	67.6	17.5	8.7
1968	210.0	200.2	105.3	94.9	75.6	19.3	9.8
1969	222.6	212.1	108.5	103.6	83.0	20.6	10.5
1970[3]	(4)	220.5	107.5	113.0	92.2	20.8	(4)
Federal Government							
1962	67.5	63.4	39.1	24.3	12.8	11.5	4.1
1963	68.7	64.2	39.0	25.3	13.6	11.7	4.4
1964	69.9	65.2	38.0	27.2	14.5	12.6	4.7
1965	71.9	66.9	38.4	28.5	15.3	13.1	5.0
1966	83.3	77.8	45.2	32.6	16.8	15.8	5.5
1967	96.6	90.7	54.8	35.9	18.4	17.5	5.9
1968	106.1	99.5	60.0	39.5	20.2	19.3	6.6
1969	108.4	101.3	59.2	42.1	21.5	20.6	7.1
1970[3]	(4)	99.7	55.0	44.7	23.9	20.8	(4)
Defense and Atomic Energy Programs							
1962	51.8	51.6	33.0	18.6	7.1	11.5	.3
1963	51.0	50.8	31.8	19.0	7.4	11.7	.3
1964	50.3	50.0	29.6	20.3	7.7	12.6	.3
1965	50.4	50.1	28.9	21.2	8.1	13.1	.3
1966	61.0	60.7	35.9	24.8	9.0	15.8	.3
1967	72.7	72.4	45.0	27.4	9.9	17.5	.3
1968	78.3	78.0	47.9	30.1	10.8	19.3	.3
1969	79.2	78.8	46.7	32.1	11.5	20.6	.4
1970[3]	(4)	76.6	43.7	32.9	12.1	20.8	(4)

Nondefense and Space
Programs

1962	15.6	11.8	6.1	5.7	5.7	3.8
1963	17.6	13.5	7.2	6.3	6.3	4.1
1964	19.6	15.2	8.4	6.8	6.8	4.4
1965	21.5	16.8	9.5	7.3	7.3	4.7
1966	22.3	17.1	9.3	7.8	7.8	5.2
1967	24.0	18.4	10.0	8.4	8.4	5.6
1968	27.8	21.5	12.1	9.4	9.4	6.3
1969	29.3	22.6	12.6	10.0	10.0	6.7
1970[3]	(4)	23.1	11.3	11.8	11.8	(4)

State and Local
Government

1962	55.7	53.7	23.3	30.4	30.4	1.9
1963	60.4	58.2	25.4	32.9	32.9	2.1
1964	65.8	63.5	27.7	35.9	35.9	2.3
1965	72.4	70.1	30.8	39.3	39.3	2.4
1966	81.6	79.0	35.0	44.0	44.0	2.6
1967	92.2	89.4	40.2	49.2	49.2	2.8
1968	103.9	100.7	45.3	55.4	55.4	3.2
1969	114.2	110.8	49.3	61.5	61.5	3.4
1970[3]	(4)	120.8	52.5	68.3	68.3	(4)

Source: Based on data from the Department of Commerce, Office of Business Economics.

[1] For comparability with data on government employment, compensation of government enterprise employees has been added to the total of government purchases of goods and services, as shown in the national income and product accounts. Capital expenditures by these enterprises are included in government purchases of goods and services. (Government enterprises include government-operated activities selling products and services to the public, such as the postal service, local water departments, and publicly owned power stations.)

[2] As defined in the national income and product accounts.

[3] Preliminary.

[4] Not available.

Table A.2
**Employment Resulting From Government Purchases of Goods and Services,
and Employment in Government Enterprises, 1962-1970**
(Millions of employees)

Level of Government	Total	Public and private employment resulting from government purchases of goods and services[1]					Employment in government enterprises[2]
		Total	Employment in private industry	General government personnel			
				Total	Civilian	Military	
Total							
1962	18.3	17.2	6.1	11.1	8.3	2.8	1.1
1963	18.8	17.7	6.4	11.3	8.6	2.7	1.1
1964	19.2	18.0	6.4	11.6	8.9	2.7	1.2
1965	19.3	18.1	6.1	12.0	9.3	2.7	1.2
1966	20.8	19.5	6.3	13.2	10.0	3.1	1.3
1967	23.0	21.7	7.8	13.9	10.5	3.4	1.3
1968	24.0	22.7	8.3	14.4	10.9	3.5	1.3
1969	24.1	22.7	7.9	14.8	11.3	3.5	1.4
1970[3]	23.5	22.1	7.3	14.8	11.6	3.2	1.4
Federal Government							
1962	9.0	8.4	3.7	4.6	1.8	2.8	.7
1963	9.1	8.4	3.9	4.5	1.8	2.8	.7
1964	8.9	8.2	3.7	4.5	1.8	2.7	.7
1965	8.9	8.1	3.5	4.6	1.8	2.7	.8
1966	9.6	8.7	3.6	5.1	2.0	3.1	.9
1967	10.9	10.0	4.5	5.5	2.1	3.4	.9
1968	11.2	10.3	4.7	5.6	2.1	3.5	.9
1969	10.7	9.8	4.2	5.6	2.1	3.5	.9
1970[3]	9.8	8.9	3.7	5.2	2.0	3.2	.9

Defense and Atomic
Energy Programs

Year							
1962	6.9	6.8	2.9	3.9	1.0	2.8	.1
1963	6.4	6.3	2.6	3.7	1.0	2.7	.1
1964	6.3	6.3	2.6	3.7	1.0	2.7	.1
1965	6.4	6.3	2.5	3.7	1.0	2.7	.1
1966	7.1	7.0	2.9	4.1	1.0	3.1	.1
1967	8.3	8.2	3.6	4.5	1.1	3.4	.1
1968	8.7	8.6	3.8	4.7	1.2	3.5	.1
1969	8.0	7.9	3.3	4.6	1.1	3.5	.1
1970[3]	7.1	7.0	2.8	4.2	1.0	3.2	.1

Nondefense and Space
Programs

Year						
1962	2.2	1.6	.8	.8	.8	.6
1963	2.7	2.1	1.3	.8	.8	.6
1964	2.5	1.9	1.1	.8	.8	.6
1965	2.6	1.9	1.0	.9	.9	.7
1966	2.6	1.8	.8	1.0	1.0	.8
1967	2.6	1.9	.9	1.0	1.0	.8
1968	2.6	1.8	.9	.9	.9	.8
1969	2.7	1.9	.9	1.0	1.0	.8
1970[3]	2.7	1.9	.9	1.0	1.0	.8

State and Local
Government

Year						
1962	9.3	8.9	2.4	6.5	6.5	.4
1963	9.6	9.2	2.5	6.7	6.7	.4
1964	10.1	9.7	2.7	7.0	7.0	.4
1965	10.5	10.0	2.6	7.4	7.4	.5
1966	11.2	10.7	2.7	8.0	8.0	.5
1967	12.2	11.7	3.3	8.4	8.4	.5
1968	12.9	12.4	3.6	8.8	8.8	.5
1969	13.4	12.9	3.7	9.2	9.2	.5
1970[3]	13.7	13.2	3.6	9.6	9.6	.5

Source: Based on data from the Department of Commerce, Office of Business Economics.

Note: Total government personnel, not shown separately, is the sum of general government personnel and employment in government enterprises.

[1] Derived from the national income and product accounts.

[2] Includes government-operated activities selling products and services to the public, such as the postal service, local water departments, and publicly owned power stations.

[3] Preliminary

Table A.3

Jobs Attributable to Federal Purchases of Goods and Services for Defense and Nondefense[1] by Major Sectors and Selected Industries, 1970[2]

Sector and industry	Thousands of jobs			Percent of all jobs in sector or industry		
	Total	Defense	Nondefense	Total	Defense	Nondefense
Total	8,922	7,013	1,909	10.3	8.1	2.2
Public sector	5,249	4,229	1,020	32.5	26.2	6.3
Federal Government	5,213	4,212	1,001	86.0	69.5	16.5
Civilian	2,053	1,052	1,001	70.8	36.3	34.5
General government	2,008	1,020	988	100.0	50.8	49.2
Government enterprises[3]	45	32	13	5.0	3.6	1.5
Military	3,160	3,160		100.0	100.0	
State and local government	36	17	19	.4	.2	.2
General government						
Government enterprises[3]	36	17	19	7.1	3.3	3.7
Private sector	3,673	2,784	889	5.2	3.9	1.3
Agriculture	41	65	−24	1.1	1.7	−.6
Mining	44	36	8	6.7	5.5	1.2
Nonferrous metal ores	9	8	1	14.5	12.3	2.2
Construction	202	111	91	4.9	2.7	2.2
Manufacturing	2,011	1,626	385	10.1	8.1	1.9
Ordnance and accessories	221	174	47	85.3	67.2	18.2
Primary iron and steel	74	58	16	8.0	6.2	1.7
Primary nonferrous metals	48	43	6	11.6	10.3	1.3
Metalworking machinery and equipment	33	26	7	9.5	7.5	2.0
Machine shop products	61	50	11	24.9	20.4	4.5
Electric industrial equipment and apparatus	61	49	12	14.0	11.2	2.8

Radio, television, and communication equipment	221	193	28	34.6	30.3	4.3
Electronic components and accessories	105	89	16	28.4	24.2	4.2
Aircraft and parts	425	367	58	59.4	51.3	8.1
Other transportation equipment	59	46	13	18.2	14.3	3.9
Scientific and controlling instruments	44	32	12	15.4	11.1	4.3
Services	1,375	946	429	3.3	2.2	1.0
Transportation and warehousing	251	214	37	8.8	7.5	1.3
Wholesale and retail trade	221	166	55	1.3	.9	.3
Hotels; personal and repair services, except auto	108	72	36	3.7	2.4	1.2
Business services, research and development	304	204	100	9.8	6.6	3.2
Medical and educational services and nonprofit organizations	290	137	153	4.6	2.2	2.4

Source: Estimates by Department of Labor, Bureau of Labor Statistics.

Note: Detail may not add to totals because of rounding.

[1] Defense includes the Department of Defense and the Atomic Energy Commission; nondefense includes all other functions of the federal government.

[2] Preliminary.

[3] Government enterprises are those agencies, with separate accounting records, that cover over half of their current operating cost by the sale of goods and services to the general public. To the extent that they rely on direct sales to the public, government enterprises function much like private industries and are treated as such in the gross national product accounts from which these estimates were derived. The employment of only 45,000 of the 892,000 employees of federal government enterprises can be attributed to federal purchases; the employment of the remaining workers – although they are undeniably public employees – depends on purchases by other final users. The Post Office Department, for example, sells its goods and services primarily to individuals and to businesses, which in turn sell primarily to consumers, so that ultimately personal consumption expenditures generate, directly and indirectly, most of the employment in the postal system.

Table A.4
Jobs Attributable to State and Local Government Purchases of Goods and Services for Major Functions, by Major Sectors and Selected Industries, 1970[1]

Sector and industry	Thousands of jobs			Percent of all jobs in sector or industry		
	Total[2]	Education	Health, welfare, and sanitation	Total[2]	Education	Health, welfare, and sanitation
Total	13,338	6,327	1,914	15.4	7.3	2.2
Public Sector	9,717	5,420	1,246	60.1	33.5	7.7
Federal Government	91	18	27	1.5	.3	.4
Civilian	91	18	27	3.1	.6	.9
General government						
Government enterprises[3]	91	18	27	10.2	2.0	3.0
Military						
State and local government	9,626	5,402	1,219	95.3	53.5	12.1
General government	9,591	5,386	1,214	100.0	56.2	12.7
Government enterprises[3]	35	16	5	6.8	3.1	.9
Private Sector	3,621	907	668	5.1	1.3	.9
Agriculture	85	19	35	2.3	.5	.9
Mining	62	22	9	9.4	3.3	1.4
Nonmetallic mining and quarrying	19	6	2	15.7	4.8	1.5
Construction	1,027	278	53	25.1	6.8	1.3

Manufacturing	1,200	372	226	6.0	1.9	1.1
Lumber and wood products	101	30	7	15.4	4.5	1.1
Furniture and fixtures	24	15	2	16.6	10.9	1.2
Printing and publishing	147	61	25	12.4	5.1	2.1
Paints and allied products	11	3	1	15.1	3.8	1.3
Stone and clay products	87	25	5	18.4	5.3	1.1
Primary iron and steel	83	25	7	8.9	2.6	.8
Heating, plumbing, and structural metal products	98	28	5	18.8	5.3	1.0
Services	1,247	216	345	3.0	.5	1.0
Transportation and warehousing	208	75	34	7.2	2.6	1.2
Wholesale and retail trade	264	46	52	1.5	.3	.3
Finance and insurance	122	35	20	3.9	1.1	.6
Business services, research and development	304	72	64	9.8	2.3	2.1
Medical and educational services and nonprofit organizations[4]	95	−9	91	1.5	−.1	1.4

Source: Estimates by Department of Labor, Bureau of Labor Statistics.

[1] Preliminary.

[2] Includes other functions not shown separately.

[3] See footnote 3, table A.3

[4] For the education function, sales to medical and educational services and nonprofit organizations exceed purchases from that industry group.

One of the principal areas for research identified by the Seminar was the study of the *technology* of producing public services, i.e., the realtionship between inputs and outputs. For several years, Harry P. Hatry has been in the forefront of those studying the characteristics of public service "production functions". Cf. his "Criteria for Evaluation in Planning State and Local Programs," in Harley H. Hinrichs and Graeme M. Taylor (eds.), *Program Budgeting and Benefit-Cost Analysis: Cases, Text, and Readings* (Pacific Palisades, California: Goodyear, 1969); Harry Hatry, Louis H. Blair, and Pasqual A. Don Vito, *Measuring the Effectiveness of Local Government Services: Solid Waste Collection* (Washington, D.C.: The Urban Institute, October, 1970); and Harry Hatry and Donald M. Fisk, *Improving Productivity and Productivity Measurements in Local Governments* (Washington, D.C.: The Urban Institute, June, 1971), prepared for the National Commission on Productivity. A good public finance and public economics text which also treats the technology and costs of producing local public services is Werner Z. Hirsch, *The Economics of State and Local Government* (New York: McGraw-Hill, 1970).

An important issue identified by the seminar concerns the distribution of public services themselves, by region and income class. One group of citizens whose consumption of public services appears to be clearly inadequate consists of the residents of the urban ghetto. Little academic research has been addressed thus far to this issue; two excellent journalistic discussions are Peter G. Brown, "The Issue of Comparable Levels of Public Services," *The Washington Post,* June 22, 1971, (p. A-12) on the shortage of public services in the Anacostia area of the District of Columbia. In his paper delivered to the seminar, Geoffrey Faux called for a role for community development corporations in the management of local employment programs. This proposal is given further consideration in Thomas Vietorisz and Bennett Harrison, *The Economic Development of Harlem* (New York: Praeger Publishers, 1970), chapter 6. In chapter 4 of the same monograph, the authors analyze the possibilities for creating jobs in the ghetto through the sale of goods and services to the federal government; ibid. pp. 116-25. An even larger potential market for the output of community enterprises is the panoply of state and local governments and nonprofit agencies physically located in central cities, frequently adjacent to or even within the ghetto itself.

The Seminar was especially concerned with the relationship between public employment programs and the inflation-unemployment "tradeoff." Work is now underway in the Department of Economics of the University of California at Berkeley on this and related issues. This research is expected to culminate in a series of reports to the Manpower Administration of the U.S. Department of Labor in late 1972 and early 1973.

Afterword

The Emergency Employment Act: A Further Case For Comprehensive Manpower Reform

CONGRESSMAN WILLIAM STEIGER

More than six months has elapsed since the final session of the Upjohn Institute's Seminar Series on Public Service Employment. In that time, information has begun to be developed on what was the prime concern of all the participants — successful implementation of the Emergency Employment Act which was to be signed into law by President Nixon on July 12, 1971.

The initial information, though limited, is encouraging. One of the best available sources of data is a study done by Robert Taggart, Executive Director of the National Manpower Policy Task Force, as part of a national study by the Ford Foundation. While the first report relates solely to the experience of the District of Columbia, it does indicate that the Public Employment Program has avoided many of the pitfalls some of us had initially feared. Taggart states:

On the whole, the District's experience with EEA suggests that, at least on a limited scale, public employment can be used effectively as a countercyclical strategy. Even on short notice, there are apparently a large number of public service jobs which can absorb the lesser skilled.

The report does, however, point out that one of the reasons for the effectiveness of the program was its manageable size. Had 1,000 or 1,500 jobs been created in the District instead of 500, the situation might have been different. Taggart also points out that the District has several advantages not present in other jurisdictions: (1) highly competent personnel recruited at federal pay scales: (2) effective administrative control through a central and extremely powerful budget office; (3) close coordination and access to the Manpower Administration; and (4) "because of the city's unique characteristics, decisions were not complicated or delayed by union opposition, political in-fighting, or allocational squabbles."

In fact, the degree of success has not been as great in other cities to judge by placement figures. As of December 10, 1971, only 90,000 out of a projected 130,000 jobs had been approved nationally, while 64,000 had been filled. In Washington, by comparison, all available funds had been allocated and almost all jobs filled. But Milwaukee, Boston, New York, Philadelphia, New Orleans, San Francisco, and most other large cities had filled less than two-thirds of their approved jobs by that time.

Given the time frame for implementation – a scant four months – and the number of placements demanded, I believe the effort can be termed at this time a relative success. Moreover, even that degree of relative success must be measured against the overall concerns of full employment that preoccupied the seminar participants.

Taggart puts the situation in fuller perspective with these words:

The Emergency Employment Act is trying to do too much with too little. The something for everyone approach of the legislation is totally unrealistic, and is bound to lead to frustrations from those expecting any particular accomplishment such as extensive civil service reform, job restructuring, upgrading of the underemployed or meaningful aid to any particular group such as engineers and scientists. That danger is that these frustrations will obscure the marginal but still important contributions which can be made under the program and which have been made in the District of Columbia.

Nevertheless, I believe the EEA experience may yet fully demonstrate local officials can – with adequate guidance and assistance – put into operation ambitious programs demanding flexibility, imagination, and coordinated effort. It proves cities and states can, on extremely short notice, determine their manpower needs and take action to fill them.

I see this situation in stark contrast to the one I described in introducing the Comprehensive Manpower Act on October 21 of 1970. Looking up from the local level, one is baffled by the incredible alphabet stew of programs, agencies and legislation. Each has its own slightly different entrance qualifications, training programs, supportive services, and objectives.

For the disadvantaged person with one dime in a phone booth, his chances are one in a hundred of finding the appropriate program, let alone receiving the services he needs.

I believe the Emergency Employment Act proves a person can now call the mayor's office and get the service he needs, that this experience will clearly establish the fundamental good sense of centralizing authority – and ultimate responsibility – for all manpower programs in a prime sponsor, one accountable to the people through the polls.

I think the time has again come when a case for a new manpower policy can be made. From rather modest beginnings almost ten years ago, the nation is now spending nearly three billion dollars a year on manpower services in efforts to prepare and place those persons unable to compete in today's sophisticated labor market. The rapid development of new manpower programs during this period has generally reflected a healthy period of innovation and progress in the manpower field. We have identified and to some extent explored the needs of many of the unemployed and underemployed. We have developed more effective educational and training programs to better prepare them for the competitive job market. We have attempted to provide a wider range of services for clients whose needs go beyond the mere matching of the person and the job. We have also made a great many mistakes. It is now clear to most everyone involved in this increasingly complex field of manpower that we are now at a stage where we can review the successes and the failures of the 1960s with the aim of comprehensive reform in order to better face the challenge of the 1970s.

It is a relatively easy matter to point out some of the shortcomings limiting the effectiveness of our efforts in this area: the fragmentation and duplication of programs and responsibilities, the lack of a working partnership among all levels of government involved, the lack of follow-up on persons trained, and the offering of training in skills for which no job exists. It is, of course, more challenging to develop systems that will overcome such problems.

The active federal manpower involvement began with the passage of the Manpower Development and Training Act of 1962 and the manpower provisions of the Economic Opportunity Act of 1964. By 1971, the following federal departments and agencies had programs dealing with the employment problems of the disadvantaged: Department of Agriculture, Civil Service Commission, Department of Commerce, Environmental Protection Agency, Department of Health, Education and Welfare, Department of Housing and Urban Development, Department of Interior, Department of Labor, and the Office of Economic Opportunity. Among the numerous programs administered are MDTA institutional training, MDTA on-the-job training, Neighborhood Youth Corps, New Careers, Public Service Careers, Operation Mainstream, JOBS, Opportunity Industrialization Centers, Concentrated Employment Programs Green Thumb, etc. The Labor Department alone is administering more than 10,000 separate grants and contracts with public and private organizations. With the passage and implementation of the Emergency Employment Act, the number has become substantially greater. The piecemeal legislative enactment of legislation in this area has caused a plethora of programs and service groups to be born. Each has its own particular focus and orientation, its own entrance criteria and qualifications, its own type of training program, and differing services. In the City of Chicago alone there are reportedly some forty-five separate agencies operating some 190 different programs costing the taxpayers some $92 million annually. I say "reportedly" because no one has been able to successfully catalogue all the federally funded manpower programs that exist in this one city.

In order to resolve the impossible administrative and delivery problems such a situation causes, flexible funding should be made available to units of government closest to the people in need of manpower services. The Comprehensive Manpower Act anticipates this can best be accomplished through consolidation of federal responsibility in the Secretary of Labor, and decategorization and phased decentralization of planning and program responsibility to the mayors, governors, and county executives. Decategorization could largely eliminate the unnecessary overlapping, confusion, and inefficiency of separate administration of each project. Not only would money be saved in the process, but funds would presumably go further and be more effective if services could be planned to meet the needs of individuals through lump sum allocations available to prime sponsors. Consolidation of responsibility at the federal level is crucial to the success of an overall effort. Not only is this necessary to establish accountability, but to minimize the amount of uncoordinated efforts such a large undertaking is bound to produce. In addition, during times of high unemployment and therefore increased dependence on manpower programs, additional money should be made available. Units of state and local government would use these funds to hire the unemployed to fulfill unmet public service needs in transition to permanent employment in the public and private sectors. Such a triggered funding process would thereby help to counteract periods of economic downturn as well as ease the effects such a downturn might have on the individuals affected.

Decentralization of planning and administrative responsibility locally is also necessary in order to insure that programs are properly tailored and responsive to local needs. At present, the organizations running manpower programs range from units of government to schools systems, community action agencies, private nonprofit agencies, as well as profit-making ones. In order to achieve the maximum coordination and results while maintaining sensitivity to local needs, the job of assigning priorities and allocating resources belongs to elected officials. Their one overriding qualification is the fact they must stand and run for election on the basis of the services they have provided to the people. Advisory councils made up of people knowledgeable about manpower affairs including representatives of clients, business, and labor would insure that the prime sponsor would have available to him the information necessary for sound policy decisions.

Manpower essentially is on the cutting edge of the "new federalism." As the federal government seeks to return to state and local officials the authority and resources necessary to deliver comprehensive manpower services, major planning efforts are needed. For this reason, phased decentralization of administration is the most appropriate vehicle for accomplishing the goal. Eligible prime sponsors would be funded to undertake a year of comprehensive planning to take a thorough look at the present programs operating in their areas. The programs would be evaluated as to their effectiveness and performance based on local needs. The prime sponsor would then submit a comprehensive plan of manpower services to the Department of Labor for approval and assume joint responsibility with the Department of Labor for the next two years. Following the two years of joint responsibility, the prime sponsor would thereafter no longer be required to submit plans to the secretary but would exchange plans for mutual approval with the governor or mayor as the case may be. The prime sponsor would be assisted in the development of policy and priorities by a Manpower Services Council to be appointed by him and to be representative of the local community with expertise in the manpower area.

I anticipate that many prime sponsors will allocate the funds to the manpower agencies on a performance contract basis in order that accountability and effective administration of the programs can be maximized. By centralizing the administration for all the programs, it is hoped that money presently being spent will be channelled into actual manpower services rather than being eaten up by the multiple costs of administration.

The need for manpower programs is clear. Unlike previous generations, disadvantaged persons in both rural and urban environments are no longer able to start at the bottom of the economic ladder and work up. The number of unskilled jobs has lessened. Increased technology and automation have largely replaced the need for unskilled labor. The trend is not only continuing but is accelerating. By 1980, only 5 percent of the jobs will be of a non-skilled variety.[a] This has been a key factor that has hindered any attempt to break the poverty cycle and skill training and the appropriate supportive services are thus essential in efforts aimed at economic independence for the poor.

For the unemployed person, a job represents the solution to many of his problems. Not only is it an escape from the grinding cycle of poverty, but with the self-esteem and financial independence it provides, he is thus better able to deal with his problems of housing, education, and health.

The Emergency Employment Act has demonstrated public service employment is an important ingredient in any comprehensive manpower program, especially in times of high unemployment. The act also demonstrates the feasibility of decentralization. Unfortunately, the example is not as well defined as we might like because of the conflicting purposes and ambiguous results of the act.

The legislation was vague, permitting all forms of public employment; and the implementation was so rapid that little time was left for administrative resolution. While it was clearly a counter-cyclical program in intent, there was little reason to believe it would be temporary in practice. While vital public service needs could be filled by hiring unemployed professionals or teachers, upgrading programs could also be established for the disadvantaged or work-relief for welfare recipients.

With the decentralization of decision making authority, all of these things have, in fact, occurred. In at least one state, the EEA has been used almost solely to employ welfare recipients. Some cities have hired nothing but firemen, policemen, and teachers, while others have employed the disadvantaged in paraprofessional positions. Many areas have operated under the assumption that they would eventually have to move EEA employees into regular positions, but many others ignored this directive and now demand permanent rather than temporary funding.

Thus, some will argue the experience of EEA is not likely to prove the effectiveness of public employment. Everyone will end up dissatisfied with the fact the program did not evolve in the way he anticipated. Until the underlying

---

[a]This is the opinion of the Congressman. The editors do not agree.

conceptual differences are identified and resolved, debate will continue ad infinitum over the effectiveness of public employment as a manpower strategy.

While the argument is well developed and probably accurate enough, I think it misses the central point. The effectiveness of the program can now be measured to some extent and debated on the local level, because the responsibility has been vested in one office, in one man: the mayor, city manager, county executive, etc.

Responsibility and authority have been fixed in one accountable office, and federal funds have not been used to generate more conflict among competing agencies, poverty representatives, ethnic minorities.

For once, the central issue that emerges in three well-phrased sentences from out of the countless pages of the Olympus Report, has been faced, if not mastered:

There is no place in the metropolitan manpower system, if it can be called that, where problems can be identified, objectives can be determined, resources can be marshalled, and any kind of comprehensive or integrated attack begun. Federal, state and local agencies and private manpower organizations respond to the presence of federal funds and within the limits of national directives.

There is no point at which the question can be asked and answered, "How can available resources, including those from the federal manpower programs, best be used in solution of this community's manpower programs?"[b]

To me, the problem isn't who asks the question, no matter how well or poorly it is phrased, but whether somehow one has the power to answer and make that answer stick.

The process, of course, will be lengthy, involved and acrimonious, but the possibility of altering basic urban dynamic movements is real.

In that context, and under the assumption that the ghettos, economic as well as racial and social, must be broken up, the delegation of manpower program responsibility to prime sponsors appears more feasible.

There will be trouble, of course. Officials of smaller communities can be expected to be unhappy with the designation of prime sponsorship to the largest community. But obviously officials of that community cannot expect to operate effectively without cooperation and assistance from the others.

Consequently, it can be assumed a great variety of mechanisms will be devised to share the power, i.e., councils, committees, consortiums, etc. But no matter what form is employed — and the variety can be no greater than the manpower program operations now under the present categorical system — responsibility will ultimately be rested in elected officials answerable at the polls.

---

[b]Olympus Research Corporation, *The Total Impact of Manpower Programs,* 1971, prepared for Manpower Administration, Department of Labor.

A politics of poverty can survive, but will not be entirely inner-directed, but rather capable of exercising leverage as a potent minority with the whole community.

Manpower programs will be an integral element in the overall distribution of education, housing and economic resources.

Of course, as the Olympus study points out, manpower people at the local level "will require the same decade of long trial and error experience as the federal staff." But it might be noted most of the federal staff has had, in fact, less than five years experience.

That observation simply underscores the service being done by the W.E. Upjohn Institute for Employment Research in sponsoring the Seminar on Public Service Employment. Now, in publishing the record, the Institute is making the experience and observations of the participants available to even larger audiences.

Sometime in the years to come, a reasonably definitive work on the manpower programs of the 1960s and 1970s may be produced. But now we still are in the midst of events, and capable, for the most part, only of supplying eyewitness, personal accounts. Some studies and analyses have been done but are much like battle histories compiled in the heat of conflict.

Nevertheless, like the seminar papers, they provide points of departure, possible hypotheses, debatable theories. Now, at least, we have some notion of what has been done, and, I believe, a guide to what can be done far more effectively in the future.

About the Contributors

Michael C. Barth is a staff economist at the U.S. Office of Economic Opportunity.

Ivar Berg is Professor of Sociology in the Graduate School of Business, Columbia University.

Charles L. Betsey is a staff economist at the U.S. Office of Economic Opportunity.

Barry Bluestone is Assistant Professor of Economics at Boston College.

Alden F. Briscoe is Manpower Coordinator for the City of Flint, Michigan, and was formerly a member of the staff of the Center for Governmental Studies.

Thomas F. Dernburg is Professor of Economics at Oberlin College.

Geoffrey Faux is on the staff of the Center for Community Economic Development in Cambridge, and was formerly the Director of the Special Impact Program in the U.S. Office of Economic Opportunity.

Sidney A. Fine is a member of the staff of the Washington office of The W.E. Upjohn Institute for Employment Research.

Edward M. Gramlich is Acting Director of the Policy Research Division of the U.S. Office of Economic Opportunity.

Bennett Harrison is Assistant Professor of Economics at the University of Maryland.

Charles C. Killingsworth is University Professor of Labor and Industrial Relations at Michigan State University.

F. Ray Marshall is Professor of Economics at the University of Texas in Austin, and Director of the University's Center for the Study of Human Resources.

Selma J. Mushkin is Director, Public Services Laboratory, Georgetown University.

The National Civil Service League is a nonprofit organization concerned with personnel management in the public sector under merit principles.

Gaylord Nelson is a Senator from Wisconsin, and Chairman of the Senate Subcommittee on Employment, Manpower, and Poverty.

Jacob J. Rutstein is on the staff of the National Civil Service League.

Harold L. Sheppard is a member of the staff of the Washington office of The W.E. Upjohn Institute for Employment Research.

William J. Spring is Director of the staff of the Senate Subcommittee on Employment, Manpower, and Poverty.

William A. Steiger is U.S. Congressman from the 6th District of Wisconsin, and a member of the House Education and Labor Committee.

Ben S. Stephansky is Associate Director of The W.E. Upjohn Institute for Employment Research.

Melville J. Ulmer is Professor of Economics at the University of Maryland, and a Contributing Editor to *The New Republic*.

Howard M. Wachtel is Assistant Professor of Economics at the American University.

E. Earl Wright is a member of the staff of the Kalamazoo office of The W.E. Upjohn Institute for Employment Research.

Index

achievement: as a class screen, 200
accountability: Faux, 429
administration: machinery, 12; WPA, 111
Advisory Committee on Allotments: WPA, 98
additional worker effects, 176
AFDC (Aid to Families with Dependent Children), 145; in Philadelphia, 56
aged: as a group, 16
agency: and WPA, 99
aggregate demand policies, 126
aggregate purchasing power, 11
aggregate unemployment: calculation controversy, 162; rate, 168
agriculture: and consolidation, 25; industrialization, 351; job projection, 24
aid: categorical program, 336
Alinsky, Saul, 425
Alioto, Mayor, 141
allocation of funds, 335; and Kalamazoo, 306
Anacostia, 443
antipollution: and public service needs, 37
Appalachia: grants-in-aid, 383; Regional Development Act, 1965, 383; and EEA, 152
armed forces personnel, 32
Arrington v. Mass. Bay Transport Authority, 271
Arrow, Kenneth: stability, 48; labor allocation, 43
assumptions: Sheppard, 3
automation, 449
AVCO Economic Systems, 251

barrier: administrative, 204; Civil Service exam, 199; Pacemaker, 269; in rural area, 374
Barth, Michael, 289; community effects, 409; progress cost, 409–412; regional variation, 412, 413; research methods, 413–416; service categories, 408
Bator, Francis: "market failure," 6
Becker, Gary: and discrimination, 42; human capital, 120
Bedford Stuyvesant, 145
behavioral attitudes: in Gintis, 49
Berg, Ivar, 199; credentialism, 214
Bergmann, Barbara, 43, 44, 59; crowding, 42
Betsey, Charles, 11
Bienstock, Herbert, 262
blacks: and employer attitude, 59; job distribution, 250; nationalism in Harrison, 63; outmigration, 365; rural poor, 274
Bluestone, Barry: budget, 65; core, 46; models and reality, 90; oversupply, 126; poverty line, 18; segmentation, 78; sexist designations, 69; structure of economy, 43; theory and reality, 117; upward pressure, 392
Boeing Corp.: and ground travel, 11; Sullivan, 396
"boondoggle," 279
Boston: Doeringer Study, 63
Bowen, William G., teenage workers, 175, 244
Bowles, S.: class discrimination, 70; socialization, 50, 62
Briscoe, Alden, 89
Brown, Claude, 45
Byrnes, James F., federal funds, 131
budgetary deficiency, 100
Bureau of the Census: March 1966 and March 1967, 61
Bureau of Employment Security, 210
Bureau of Labor Statistics, 44, 45; Minimum Urban Family Budget, 190; public sector employment, 74
Burke, J., 142
Burt, Samuel M., 28

Califano, J.: EEA, 136
California League of Cities, 337
CAMPS (Kalamazoo Cooperative Area Manpower Planning Committee), 307
capital equipment, 46
career: developers, 297; ladders in NCSL, 222
Carter v. Gallagher, 270
cash subsidies, 199
categorical programs: and veto, 138
community development corporation (CDC), 397; Faux, 427–431
central cities: and Harrison, 9
Central Park Zoo: and the WPA, 107
Central Ward: outreach, 256–257
Chicanos, 206, 351
Chinatown, S.F., 145
city: capital requirements, 337; core deterioration, 339; core-dominated, 328; fiscal needs, 327; and poverty, 21; satellite-dominated, 329; support criteria, 330–334
Civil Service, 66, 146
Civil Service Clerical Trainee Employment List, 257

455